15 YEARS OF THE UNESCO DIVERSITY OF CULTURAL EXPRESSIONS CONVENTION

This book queries, through the prism of the Convention for the Protection and Promotion of the Diversity of Cultural Expressions (the Convention), the ways in which the processes and substance of international law-making have shifted in response to new technologies and new actors. The essays, written by recognised experts in the field, engage deeply with the practice under the Convention. The four parts examine: the rise of new actors and their impact on the Convention's law-making and implementation; the specific implementation of Article 21; the role of cultural communities in promoting diversity of cultural expressions; and the effectiveness and coherence of the Convention. Scholars and practitioners in the field of international law of culture and international cultural cooperation will welcome this fascinating new book.

15 Years of the UNESCO Diversity of Cultural Expressions Convention

Actors, Processes and Impact

Edited by
Beatriz Barreiro Carril
Andrzej Jakubowski
and
Lucas Lixinski

•HART•
OXFORD • LONDON • NEW YORK • NEW DELHI • SYDNEY

HART PUBLISHING

Bloomsbury Publishing Plc

Kemp House, Chawley Park, Cumnor Hill, Oxford, OX2 9PH, UK

1385 Broadway, New York, NY 10018, USA

29 Earlsfort Terrace, Dublin 2, Ireland

HART PUBLISHING, the Hart/Stag logo, BLOOMSBURY and the Diana logo are trademarks of Bloomsbury Publishing Plc

First published in Great Britain 2023

A catalogue record for this book is available from the British Library.

A catalogue record for this book is available from the Library of Congress.

Library of Congress Control Number: 2022948147

ISBN: HB: 978-1-50996-144-3
ePDF: 978-1-50996-146-7
ePub: 978-1-50996-145-0

Typeset by Compuscript Ltd, Shannon

FOREWORD

I am delighted to see the publication of this volume on the occasion of the fifteenth anniversary of the (entry into force of the) 2005 Convention for the Protection and Promotion of the Diversity of Cultural Expressions (CDC, or the Convention).[1]

The Convention represents an important instrument for the protection of the living culture of individuals and communities. Although not a human rights instrument per se, it is important for my mandate as, by protecting the diversity of cultural expressions, it also indirectly protects the right of individuals and communities to take part in cultural life, and so express and develop their cultures, as well as having access to the creativity and cultural expressions of others. Indeed, recent work on the Convention has seen its further rapprochement with the human rights standards on cultural rights. The volume unveils how the Convention has gradually been moving towards a human rights framework, necessary for the implementation of the Convention in an effective and meaningful manner.

The gradual opening up of the Convention to more inclusive understandings of culture, both in terms of beneficiaries and in terms of content, relates directly to my priorities as the UN Special Rapporteur in the field of Cultural Rights and Cultural Diversity. I am glad to see the real effort to weaken the duality that exists in UNESCO instruments on recognising solely either the culture of the individual or the culture of the state. Advanced by General Comment 15 (2009) of the Committee on Economic, Social and Cultural Rights, it is rather agreed these days that the 'right to take part in cultural life' as recognised in Article 15 of the International Covenant on Economic, Social and Cultural Rights includes a collective element. Using the Convention to protect the rights of minorities and indigenous peoples to their living cultures is in my view a natural evolution of the Convention as a living instrument. Giving voice to the marginalised in ways that they will be able to protect their cultural expression and allow cultural diversity to be protected is important; and as the authors of this volume show, this is a process that has started within the Convention's remit. The right to decision-making in matters that affect one's cultural rights is an important element of the scope of cultural rights. I am glad to read of examples that push for these rights. The right to 'free, prior and informed consent' must also be upheld and not swallowed by the more generic (and weaker) right to participation and consultation. At the same

[1] (adopted 20 October 2005, entered into force 18 March 2007) 2440 UNTS 311.

time, I find the Convention's emphasis on artistic freedom of help in addressing current widespread violations in artistic freedom and in recognising its important contribution to civic space and democracy.

The application of the Convention to the current challenges to society and the emergence of cross-cultural themes are also very close to the priorities of my mandate. How culture intersects with trade, with the environment and with sustainable development are important questions that require further consideration and discussions. My 2022 report to the UN General Assembly is on Sustainable Development. The report argues that cultural rights have not yet been adequately considered in discussions on sustainable development, although their implementation can have transformative effects. Specifically, the report discusses how culture and cultural rights are rather absent from the work on Sustainable Development Goals. In this respect, my mandate is actively supporting the Culture 2030 campaign that will hopefully see culture as a free-standing goal in the post-2030 agenda. How the work of the Convention can be of support in this respect makes an interesting read.

This Convention has been the object of academic research before. However, while reading the volume, one can see how time and efforts by civil society, UNESCO and other interested parties have interpreted its provisions in a manner that addresses the real needs of the twenty-first century. It also demonstrates how much more the Convention has to offer. Both UNESCO and the UN benefit tremendously from volumes such as this one, that take stock of the state or art and reflect on the vision for the future.

Alexandra Xanthaki
United Nations Special Rapporteur in the field of
Cultural Rights and Cultural Diversity
Monemvasia, Greece
September 2022

ACKNOWLEDGEMENTS

In the early spring of 2020, we launched a call for papers addressing the societal operation the UNESCO Convention for the Protection and Promotion of the Diversity of Cultural Expressions (Convention) on the fifteenth anniversary of its adoption. The workshop, held in September 2020 within the framework of the activities of the Interest Group on International Law of Culture of the European Society of International Law, gathered a very large number of participants from all over the world. While this book stems from that joint endeavour, its scope and content go beyond that, opening into many new avenues and areas in which the Convention operates. Of course, our most sincere gratitude goes to the authors, who generously contributed with their individual chapters and expertise to this book. Each has committed to the richness and diversity of this collection. There are a number of other people to whom we owe a special debt of gratitude. For their invaluable advice and suggestions rendered during the workshop, we are very thankful to Yvonne Donders, Aliki Gkana, Moshe Hirsch, Laura-Maria Crăciunean-Tatu and Alexandra Xanthaki, to whom we are also immensely grateful for her most inspiring foreword to this book. We are all indebted to the staff at Hart Publishing-Bloomsbury Academic for their priceless assistance with the publication process. Our special thanks go to Chris Myers for his much-appreciated language revisions, to Compuscript Ltd for the most careful typesetting of this book and Sasha Jawed and Tom Adams for their stress-free guiding us through the entire process. We would also like to acknowledge the assistance rendered by Aleksandra Zych and Karolina Jerzyk. Without their meticulous edits, this book would not have become a reality. Last but not least, we would like to thank the European Society of International Law for its support to the work of the Interest Group on International Law of Culture since its inception.

The Editors

CONTENTS

NOTES ON CONTRIBUTORS

Beatriz Barreiro Carril is an Associate Professor of International Law at the Rey Juan Carlos University, Madrid. She is a member of the Observatory for Diversity and Cultural Rights (University of Freiburg) and one of the founders and co-convenors of the Interest Group of International Law of Culture (ESIL). She was a fellow at the Käte Hamburger Center 'Law as Culture' (University of Bonn). She writes on the links between international law and other social sciences, the humanities and the arts, and undertakes applied research with a particular focus on human rights, especially cultural rights. She collaborates in projects of the UNESCO Fund for Cultural Diversity. She has edited three books on topics of human rights and cultural diversity and is the author of *La diversidad cultural en el derecho internacional: La Convención de la UNESCO* (Iustel, 2011).

Laurence Cuny is a human rights lawyer and researcher specialising in cultural rights and artistic freedom. After working as a teaching assistant in international public law at the Geneva Graduate Institute, she worked as an independent consultant for civil society and international organisations. This included collaborations with the UN Special Rapporteur in the field of cultural rights for the reports on artistic freedom (2013), advertising (2014) and public spaces (2019). As a member of the UNESCO Expert Facility on the 2005 Convention she is the author of the report Freedom & Creativity: Defending Art, Defending Diversity (UNESCO, 2020). Other recent publications include Rights: International, regional and national legal frameworks for the protection of artistic freedom (Hildesheim Foundation, 2019), Relocating Artists at Risk in Latin America (ifa, 2021) and Protecting an atypical workforce: Why the law matters (IFACCA, 2022). She is a member of the UNESCO Chair on the Diversity of Cultural Expressions at the Faculty of Law of Université Laval in Quebec and an Associate Member of the Observatory of Diversity and Cultural Rights based in Fribourg, Switzerland.

Véronique Guèvremont is Professor at the Faculty of Law of Université Laval (Quebec, Canada). She holds the UNESCO Chair on the Diversity of Cultural Expressions and is co-responsible for the Arts, Media and Cultural Diversity axis of the International Observatory on the Societal Impacts of Artificial Intelligence and Digital Technologies (OBVIA). Graduated from the University of Paris 1 Panthéon-Sorbonne, she has been teaching international cultural law and international economic law since 2006. From 2003 to 2005, she was an associate expert with UNESCO's Division of Cultural Policies during the negotiation of the 2005 Convention. Her most recent researches and publications focus on cultural rights, the treatment of cultural goods and services in trade agreements, the preservation of the diversity of cultural expressions in the digital age and the cultural dimension of sustainable development. Since 2015, she has been part of the UNESCO Expert Facility on the 2005 Convention.

Andrzej Jakubowski, affiliated with the UNESCO Chair in Cultural Property Law at the University of Opole (Poland), has served as Chair of the ILA Committee on Participation in Global Cultural Heritage Governance and is a co-convenor of the Interest Group on the International Law of Culture (ESIL). He is deputy editor-in-chief of the *Santander Art and Culture Law Review*. Andrzej Jakubowski is also listed among mediators and conciliators of the UNESCO Intergovernmental Committee for Promoting the Return of Cultural Property to its Countries of Origin or its Restitution in Case of Illicit Appropriation (ICPRCP). He is the author or editor of numerous publications on the protection and governance of cultural heritage in both international and European law, including *State Succession in Cultural Property* (Oxford University Press, 2015) and *Cultural Rights as Collective Rights: An International Law Perspective* (Brill, 2016).

Lucas Lixinski is Professor at the Faculty of Law and Justice, UNSW Sydney. Alongside the other editors, he is one of the co-convenors of the ESIL Interest Group on the International Law of Culture, and Vice President (Conference) of the Association of Critical Heritage Studies. He is the author or editor of eight books. His latest monograph, *Legalised Identities: Cultural Heritage Law and the Shaping of Transitional Justice*, was published in 2021 by Cambridge University Press. His latest edited volume, *The 2003 UNESCO Intangible Heritage Convention: A Commentary* (co-edited with Janet Blake), was published by Oxford University Press in 2020, and received the American Society of International Law's certificate of merit for high technical craftsmanship and utility to lawyers and scholars in 2021.

Matina Magkou is a consultant, project manager and researcher in cultural and social impact programmes from Greece, currently based in Nice (France). She holds a PhD in Leisure and Human Development (University of Deusto, Bilbao, Spain). She is currently a postdoc researcher at the SIC.Lab of the University of Côte d'Azur on creative hubs, digital transformation and cultural policies. She has collaborated with European cultural networks such as EUNIC, ENCATC, In Situ, Eurozine and IETM, and has evaluated programmes of international cooperation for Goethe-Institut, Interarts and the German Commission of UNESCO (2015). Matina collaborates with Panteion University, the University of Hildesheim and the Open University of Catalunya, delivering lectures on cultural management, international cooperation and events. She is an alumna of the Global Cultural Leadership Programme of the Cultural Diplomacy Platform, board member of the Athens artistic collective UrbanDig Project and co-founder of ΚΟΛΛΕΚΤΙVΑ for Social Innovation and Culture.

Lily Martinet holds a Bachelor of Fine Arts from l'École Régionale des Beaux-Arts de Rennes, a law degree with a specialisation in international economic law and a PhD from the Sorbonne Law School. In 2014, she was admitted to the French bar. Her PhD dissertation focused on traditional cultural expressions in international law. From 2018 to 2021, she was a Senior Research Fellow at the Max Planck Institute Luxembourg for Procedural Law. She has worked on the implementation of the Convention for the safeguarding of the Intangible Cultural Heritage for the French Ministry of Culture, the French Center for Intangible Cultural Heritage, and the French National Commission for UNESCO. Her main research interests lie in international intellectual property, human rights and cultural heritage law.

Giacomo Mazzone has 40 years' experience in the information, sport and international relations sectors, trained as a journalist, and has a great deal of experience in international companies and organisations (RAI, Euronews, Eurosport, EBU). He has also worked for a range of traditional media (press, radio, general interest TV) as well as new media (all-news channels, Internet portals), and is an expert in European and international negotiations. Between 2014 and 2016 was member of the MAG Multi-stakeholder Advisory group, that advises UN Secretary General on Internet Governance matters, and within IGF he still is co-chair of the PNMA initiative and member of Strategy working group. Within UNESCO's Convention on the Protection and Promotion of the Diversity of Cultural Expressions (2005) he is Observer on behalf of the Eurovisioni association and was one of the experts elaborating its text (2004–05).

Ivana Otasevic is an Assistant Director and Coordinator of the UNESCO Chair on the Diversity of Cultural Expressions. She holds a doctorate in international law and is a lecturer at the Faculty of Law of Laval University. Since 2009 she has been interested in the relationship between the UNESCO Convention on the Protection and Promotion of the Diversity of Cultural Expressions (2005) and trade agreements, the cultural dimension of sustainable development and the legal status of the concept of cultural diversity in international law. In recent years, her research and publications have focused more specifically on cultural rights of migrants and minority groups, as well as the protection and promotion of their cultural expressions. She is an associate member of the CELAT Cultures – Arts – Societies Research Center.

Grischka Petri trained as a lawyer and holds doctorates in art history and law. He works at the Department of Intellectual Property Rights at FIZ Karlsruhe (Leibniz Institute for Information Infrastructure). He is a team member of the 'Legal Helpdesk' for NFDI4Culture, a consortium that forms part of the National Research Data Infrastructure, a project funded by the German Research Foundation (DFG). Grischka Petri teaches art history and art law at the universities of Bonn and Regensburg. He was a fellow at the Käte-Hamburger-Centre for Advanced Studies 'Law as Culture', Bonn.

Mónica Riaza de los Mozos is a doctoral candidate at the University of Girona (Spain). She is cultural manager at Cervantes Institute in Stockholm (Sweden) and researcher in cultural management-cultural cooperation and development at the University of Girona (Spain). In the last few years, she has combined her academic and professional interests in the promotion and development of culture with a particular attention to cultural diversity and intercultural dialogue. Previously, she was a project manager of plans and programmes focused on culture, youth and their relationship to education; technical consultant on culture and citizen participation; and director of a cultural centre in the city of Madrid. In the field of research, she was a researcher at the Centro di Studi sulla Cultura e L'Immagine di Roma (Italy), Universidad Nacional Autónoma de Mexico, National Heritage of Spain, Museo del Prado (Madrid, Spain) and Museo de América at the University of Complutense (Madrid, Spain).

Lilian Richieri Hanania is an attorney (Paris and São Paulo), PhD in international law (University Paris 1 – Panthéon-Sorbonne), accredited mediator (CNMA) and collaborative law practitioner. Graduating from the Law School of the University of São Paulo in 2001, she obtained a master's degree in international economic law in 2003 and a PhD in international law in 2007 at the University Paris 1. Her PhD thesis, publications and lectures address international economic law, international law on culture and sustainable development, with an emphasis on creative industries, new technologies and the 2005 UNESCO Convention on the Diversity of Cultural Expressions. Besides her activity as a consultant and lecturer in international law since 2003, she has worked in law firms in São Paulo, Paris and Houston (TX, USA), in a global technology firm and at the International Economic Affairs Division of the French MOFA. She founded her own law firm in 2017 (www.hananiaconsult.com).

Luanda Smith is a Mexican cultural manager. She holds a BA degree in plastic arts, and a postgraduate diploma in international cultural relations from OEI and Girona University. She has also studied cultural management and international relations studies at Guadalajara University and El Colegio de Veracruz, and is an alumna of the Global Cultural Leadership Programme of the Cultural Diplomacy Platform. She was a consultant for Veracruzana University, Veracruz Institute for Culture, UNESCO and UCCN in Mexico, the Embassy of Canada in Mexico, the Ministry of Cultures, Arts and Heritage of Chile and the Cultural Diplomacy Platform of the European Union. Luanda is the founder and executive director of Creatividad y Cultura Glocal AC, a Mexican NGO specialising in cultural and creative industries and public and private sector linkage with civil society within the framework of the 2005 UNESCO Convention's implementation in Latin America. In 2021 she was part of the coordinating group of the 3rd Civil Society Forum and was invited by Convention Secretariat as a reviewer of Chapter 4 (on civil society) of the 2022 Global Report – Re|Shaping Policies for Creativity.

Anna Steinkamp is an independent consultant for international cultural cooperation, specialising in strategies for networks of culture cooperation and impact-oriented project facilitation in the public sector. Currently, as the managing director of the German Association of the Independent Performing Arts, she is running a five-year programme for strengthening networks in the independent performing arts in Germany. From 2006 to 2016 and 2019 she worked for the German Commission for UNESCO within the Division of Culture. During that time she was co-founder and executive coordinator of the global U40 Network 'Cultural Diversity 2030' of young experts, led the task force of the 2015 World Heritage Committee session in Bonn and co-designed several projects and programmes of international cooperation in the field of cultural diversity. She holds master's degrees in public policy (Humboldt-Viadrina School of Governance, Berlin) and in cultural sciences (Europa Universität Viadrina, Frankfurt (Oder), Georg-August Universität Göttingen, Universidad de Xalapa, México, Universidad de Deusto, San Sebastián). See www.annasteinkamp.de.

Enzamaria Tramontana is Associate Professor of International Law at the Department of Law of the University of Palermo, where she teaches international law and the law of international organisations. After receiving her master's degree in law from the University of Palermo in 2006, she earned a PhD in international law at the University of Rome 'La Sapienza' in 2011 with a dissertation on 'Non-governmental Organisations and International Law'. Among her main research interests are: the participation of non-state actors to the dynamics of the international legal order; the international protection of the rights of indigenous peoples; and gender equality and non-discrimination.

Clémence Varin is a PhD candidate in international law at the Université Laval (Canada) and the Université de Rennes 1 (France). She holds a bachelor's degree in law and political science from the Institut Catholique de Paris (France) and a master's in international studies from the Institute for Advanced International Studies/HEI (Université Laval). From 2015 to 2017, she worked within the Secretariat of the 2005 UNESCO Convention on the Protection and Promotion of the Diversity of Cultural Expressions in Paris. Her doctoral research, funded by the Centre for International Governance Innovation (CIGI) and the Fonds de recherche du Québec – Société et culture (FRQSC), focuses on the impact of digital technologies on the diversity of cultural expressions, and the role of other forums in the implementation of the 2005 Convention in the digital environment. She is also a member of the UNESCO Chair on the Diversity of Cultural Expressions (Université Laval).

Actors, Processes and the Impact of 15 Years of the UNESCO Cultural Diversity Convention: An Introduction

BEATRIZ BARREIRO CARRIL, ANDRZEJ JAKUBOWSKI
AND LUCAS LIXINSKI

I. Introduction

This book queries, through the prism of the Convention for the Protection and the Promotion of the Diversity of Cultural Expressions (the Convention),[1] the ways in which the processes and substance of international law-making have shifted in response to new technologies and new actors. The treaty, adopted in 2005, has 152 parties, comprising 151 states and one regional organisation (the European Union). Its main objective is to reaffirm states' 'sovereign right to formulate and implement their cultural policies and to adopt measures to protect and promote the diversity of cultural expressions and to strengthen international cooperation to achieve [its purposes]' (Article 5), while recognising 'the distinctive nature of cultural … goods and services as vehicles of identity, values and meaning' (Article 1(g)). As the Convention enters its fifteenth year of operation, the moment is ripe for an original and trendsetting examination of its operation and influence on general international law. This volume starts filling this gap.

The contributors to this book engage deeply with the practice of multiple actors under the Convention, which has at once cemented, expanded and shifted three classic analytical prisms of international law: actors, processes and impact. All three are particularly relevant for the Convention in their own ways, and for several reasons.

First, it must be noted that the origin of this instrument goes back in part to the work of actors other than states, such as the coalitions for cultural diversity. In other words, this treaty, while relying on forms of interstate international law, has at its core a commitment to a much broader set of actors.

Second, the Convention may be credited as a paradigmatic case of 'new ways' of creation and implementation of international law. A paradigmatic example are

[1] (adopted 20 October 2005, entered into force 18 March 2007) 2440 UNTS 311.

states' 'obligations' to report on artistic freedom, a topic which had been excluded from the scope of the application of the Convention during its negotiation process and its final text.

Third, the Convention is a living instrument, whose articles are explained – and in a way developed – in the operational guidelines approved by the Conference of the Parties.[2] Some of these guidelines have been the object of lively and often difficult debates by states parties (this is the case of the 2017 'Operational Guidelines on the Implementation of the Convention in the Digital Environment').[3]

Fourth, regarding 'impact', the initial main goal in connection with the approval of the Convention was the protection of states' cultural sovereignty from possible threats emanating from other states, mainly through pressure actions to sign free trade agreements. Therefore, the Convention was intended to have an effect on international economic fora. However, due to the increasing digitalisation of nearly all aspects of life, something particularly relevant in pandemic and post-pandemic times, the Convention now reaches far more diverse spheres of international legal authority than those foreseen by its drafters. Beyond fora such as the World Trade Organization (WTO) and bilateral or multilateral free trade agreements outside this organisation, we also need to pay attention to other fora, including private institutions such as the Internet Corporation for Assigned Names and Numbers (ICANN).

What these challenges, transformations and expansions of the Convention show is a highly adaptable international legal regime, which challenges assumptions about the relatively static nature of international law and can therefore be a useful case study not only within, but also beyond the growing field of the international law of culture. It demonstrates evolving dynamics of international law, which, despite being constrained by the basic rules of international legal personality (a feature with significant substantive effects), can move away from the nation-state as the single unit of analysis for a treaty's effectiveness.

In the first years after its adoption – as well as during its negotiation – the Convention was the object of research by many international law scholars, who addressed classical issues at the heart of international law, such as conflict of norms, regime interaction and fragmentation.[4] This concern was particularly relevant since the Convention set up a 'cultural regime' for the international trade of

[2] UNESCO, Operational Guidelines to the Convention on the Protection and Promotion of the Diversity of Cultural Expressions [2009]. First approved in 2009; latest version available at https://en.unesco.org/creativity/sites/creativity/files/convention2005_operational_guidelines_en.pdf.

[3] See UNESCO, 'Operational Guidelines on the Implementation of the Convention in the Digital Environment' [2017] (UNESCO Docs CE/15/9.IGC/7, CE/15/9.IGC/INF.6a, and CE/15/9.IGC/INF.7), https://unesdoc.unesco.org/ark:/48223/pf0000378132.

[4] Professor Joost Pauwelyn brought this question to the attention of the American Society of International Law in 2005. J Pauwelyn, 'The UNESCO Convention on Cultural Diversity and the WTO: Diversity in International Law-Making?' (ASIL Insights, 2005), https://www.asil.org/insights/volume/9/issue/35/unesco-convention-cultural-diversity-and-wto-diversity-international-law.

cultural products, breaking away from the traditional practice that these matters be reserved to 'economic regimes' in which some cultural exceptions could be made in a very limited way. Further, international law scholars focused on the Convention to decipher its content and guide its practice. Doing so established the Convention as a rather enigmatic text. Ambiguities in the text in relation to specific purpose, scope of application and therefore rights and obligations of states parties meant that scholarly engagement with the treaty was and still remains vital to its implementation.

Moreover, the Convention today is increasingly the object of research in other social sciences, and international lawyers who continue to pay attention to the Convention do so most often through the prism of highly interdisciplinary projects.[5] International law analyses of the Convention now often require specific knowledge of issues such as new communication technologies. A significant shift can also be observed in relation to the Secretariat of the Convention – which supports its implementation – as well as the Committee. As we indicated above, these bodies have given relevance in their implementation work to topics like rights of artists, which were not a priority at the time the Convention entered into force. This shift is also an indicator of the need to rethink the role of international lawyers in relation to the Convention and the pertinence of a research agenda for the Convention, which is one of this volume's objectives.

This book contributes to the existing literature on the Convention by bringing up-to-date, law-centred commentary on the ways in which the treaty has evolved, alongside the different stakeholders and concepts that gravitate around this important instrument.[6] The book does not seek to be an extensive commentary,[7] nor to map out the origins of the treaty,[8] but rather aims to focus on the cutting edge of its current implementation, with an eye to the next 15 years of its operation.

The book is largely based on the proceedings of an online conference held under the umbrella of the European Society of International Law's Interest Group on International Law of Culture.[9] The book brings together contributions from

[5] See, eg LA Albornoz and MT García Leiva (eds), *Audio-visual Industries and Diversity Economics and Policies in the Digital Era* (London, Routledge, 2019) (written from the disciplinary perspective of communications).

[6] H Schneider and P van den Bossche (eds), *Protection of Cultural Diversity from a European and International Perspective* (Cambridge, Intersentia, 2008); L Richieri Hanania (ed), *Cultural Diversity in International Law. The Effectiveness of the UNESCO Convention on the Protection and Promotion of the Diversity of Cultural Expressions* (London, Routledge, 2014).

[7] See, eg M-F Labouz and M Wise (eds), *La diversité culturelle en question(s)* (Brussels, Bruylant, 2005). See also S von Schorlemer and P-T Stoll (eds), *The UNESCO Convention on the Protection and Promotion of the Diversity of Cultural Expressions* (Cham, Springer, 2012). Finally, we note that a new commentary is currently under preparation as part of the Oxford Commentaries on International Cultural Heritage Law, a series edited by AF Vrdoljak and F Francioni. The editors of the commentary to the 2005 Convention are Y Donders, A Strecker, and Beatriz Barreiro Carril.

[8] I Bernier and H Ruiz Fabri, *Evaluation of the Legal Feasibility of an International Instrument Governing Cultural Diversity* (Quebec, Bibliotheque nationale du Quebec, 2002) 50, www.unescodec.chaire.ulaval.ca/sites/unescodec.chaire.ulaval.ca/files/2002avril.pdf.

[9] Online Workshop, '15 Years of the Convention for the Protection and Promotion of the Diversity of Cultural Expressions and Lessons for New Ways of International Law-Making: Actors, Processes, Impact' (9 September 2020). The workshop was organised to sit with the overall theme of the 16th Annual ESIL Conference, 'Changes in International Lawmaking: Actors, Processes, Impact'.

that event that respond to the central analytical question posed above, alongside commissioned additional chapters to increase representativeness of contributors in terms of geographical spread, gender and career stage. Despite its European origins, therefore, this volume is structured to make a more global contribution to the field.

What follows discusses the main analytical threads in the volume, through the excellent chapters our contributors have written. In drawing these threads together, we seek to highlight major themes and connections across the volume.

II. The Volume's Running Threads

Part one, 'New Actors in the Legal Development and Implementation of the Convention', addresses the practice offered by the first 15 years of the Convention's life from the perspective of the 'new actors' that are becoming more and more relevant both in the 'law-making process' and in the implementation of the Convention. Taking into account the fact that the Convention's objectives and obligations are constantly developed through operational guidelines, and that civil society participation has been allowed in several ways within the organs of the Convention creating such guidelines, this part explores the concrete ways of such participation in order to assess its adequacy in relation to the objectives of the Convention. This part also points at possibilities for further refinement of the Convention's processes and rules (Enzamaria Tramontana).

We also look at the expansion of the roles of actors involved with the treaty. Namely, we examine the ongoing influence of civil society organisations beyond the drafting and in the implementation of the Convention. Of particular interest is the role of civil society within cultural cooperation (to development) frameworks under the Convention's relevant provisions (Articles 12–14), particularly in pandemic times (Anna Steinkamp and Matina Magko). Further, taking cultural diversity seriously also implies addressing the challenge of linguistic diversity. This part therefore addresses the challenges faced by civil society organisations willing to participate in the frameworks offered by the Convention to civil society organisations which are neither English- nor French speakers. In doing so, contributors query an important issue of linguistic hegemony that is familiar to international law, but dig deeper into one specific context that is more attuned to cultural diversity, in search of guidance to international law-making more generally (Luanda Smith).

Enzamaria Tramontana, in her chapter about civil society participation, shows how the Convention pluralises international law-making. She uses the Convention as a platform to ask questions about civil society participation in international law-making and implementation more broadly, querying the proper role of these entities, the justification for their participation, their accountability, and how to measure the quality and effectiveness of participation against what these entities bring to the international law table (technical expertise, operational efficiency, ability to bring new voices and opinions to the fore, and pluralisation of decision-making more broadly). Ultimately, she wonders whether and how civil society participation enhances the legitimacy of international legal processes. The Convention, she suggests, is a key battleground where a lot of these tensions play out and a successful example of the integration of civil society actors as central partners to contemporary international legal goals.

Anna Steinkamp and Matina Magkou take on the issue of civil society participation and focus on the perspective of specific networks of cultural cooperation. The Convention has helped catalyse major international cultural networks to pursue its implementation in varied economic sectors and social groups where otherwise the formality of international legal mechanisms would have a hard time gaining traction. Working as largely independent platforms leveraging tools for international cooperation, these networks also represent specific parts of the cultural sector to help them advocate for specific outcomes in the implementation of the treaty. Surveying a range of these networks, Steinkamp and Magkou show how capacity-building efforts can morph into self-sustaining advocacy that ultimately advances the goals of the Convention. Similarly, networks established to assist the negotiation of the treaty have morphed as the Convention itself has evolved. Steinkamp and Magkou suggest that these networks are an ideal way to keep the Convention relevant, and greatly multiply its impact.

Finally, this part concludes with Luanda Smith's examination of Latin American civil society's efforts to pluralise the treaty itself, and make it live up to its promise of diversifying cultural expressions also within its own operation. Drawing on the experience of introducing the Spanish language as a central language for the implementation of the treaty, Smith shows how the civil society organisations that drove this effort have grown the Convention's reach and impact beyond what UNESCO itself, or states parties, had been able to do. Linguistic diversity thus becomes a crucial means to localise the global, and to make international law more meaningful to those upon whom it bears.

Part two of this book, 'Impact of the Convention on Other Fora and Sectors of International Law', gives an account and assessment of the implementation of Article 21 of the Convention, which affirms the obligation of parties 'to promote the objectives and principles of [the] Convention in other international forums'. Chapters included in this part of the volume take into account the impasse at the WTO level, which motivates cultural diversity advocates and scholars to seek other fora. In this sense, part two examines bilateral or regional agreements such as the Comprehensive Economic and Trade Agreement,[10] the Comprehensive and Progressive Agreement for Trans-Pacific Partnership[11] and the

[10] (signed 30 October 2016; provisional application 21 September 2017) [2017] OJ L11/23.
[11] (signed 8 March, entered in force 30 December 2018) https://www.dfat.gov.au/sites/default/files/tpp-11-treaty-text.pdf.

Canada–United States–Mexico Agreement.[12] Doing so gives us the opportunity to assess the effectiveness of the Convention in implementing cultural policies in the digital environment, particularly in relation to e-commerce (Véronique Guèvremont and Ivana Otasevic). In fact, the 'Operational Guidelines on the Implementation of the Convention in the Digital Environment' underline the need for parties to promote the objectives and principles of the Convention in international fora other than UNESCO – as required by Article 21 of the treaty. This part also contributes to the state of the art in the field by shifting analytical focus to other fora that appear to be relevant for the purpose of the Convention in the near future. These include the International Telecommunication Union and the World Intellectual Property Organization, particularly in relation to artificial intelligence (Clémence Varin). Since actions taken in economic fora can have irreversible effects on cultural diversity, this part also analyses the relationships between the Convention and international economic law from a precautionary approach or 'logic', already implemented by WTO jurisprudence in areas such as health or the environment (Lilian Richieri Hanania). This approach can find a legal basis in Articles 8 and 17 of the Convention and their respective operational guidelines. Actions undertaken under this logic would likely require a dialogue between the Secretariats of the 2005 Convention and the 2003 UNESCO Convention for the Safeguarding of the Intangible Cultural Heritage,[13] therefore impacting other UNESCO treaties and regimes, and broadening the book's reach within international law of culture readers beyond the Convention's regime.

Véronique Guèvremont and Ivana Otasevic open this part of the book contextualising the central objective of the Convention (enhancing states' ability to support their own cultural industries) in relation to cultural exceptions present in myriad trade agreements around the world. They question the effectiveness of these exceptions in relation to e-commerce protections, particularly as much of the consumption of cultural products shifts to online platforms. They advocate for a new form of cultural clause that can embrace digital cultural products more effectively, thus keeping the Convention relevant in a shifting marketplace.

Clémence Varin, who works closely with Guèvremont and Otasevic at one of the world's major hubs for the study of the 2005 Convention, also pursues questions in relation to the treaty's effectiveness in the digital environment. Varin closely examines the relevant operational guidelines specific to the digital environment, offering novel insights for the implementation of this treaty. Specifically, Varin suggests examining the Convention's possibilities not just in trade fora, but also specific international institutions devoted to digital governance, including artificial intelligence, the regulation of algorithms and net neutrality debates. Varin

[12] (signed 30 November 2018 and 10 December 2019, in force 1 July 2020) https://ustr.gov/trade-agreements/free-trade-agreements/united-states-mexico-canada-agreement/agreement-between.

[13] (adopted 17 October 2003, entered into force 20 April 2006) 2368 UNTS 1.

reminds us that transnational, rather than public international, legal approaches can offer useful and agile tools to keep the Convention relevant, and have cultural diversity issues inform the agenda of a wider range of international standard-setting efforts. Since the implementation of the treaty cannot be limited to parties' territories, Varin forcefully argues, action is urgently needed beyond UNESCO to account for the transnational environment this treaty, wittingly or otherwise, is meant to regulate in favour of diversity objectives.

Lilian Richieri Hanania offers a pathway to better integrate fast-evolving technological environments so as to keep the Convention relevant. Specifically, Hanania calls for a precautionary approach to balance trade liberalisation ideals with cultural diversity protection imperatives. To the extent a precautionary approach already informs much of international trade law in other areas such as the environment, Hanania argues, the same logic can also be applied to culture and cultural diversity. She also maps the ways in which the precautionary approach already exists in other international regimes devoted to culture, so as to leverage the familiarity of the international law of culture with the idea. Therefore, if both trade law and the law of culture have successfully incorporated precautionary approaches in the implementation of their respective treaties, there is no logical reason why, at their juncture epitomised by the 2005 Convention, the same precautionary approach cannot be deployed to fulfil the treaty's mandate in relation to the diversity of cultural expressions.

Part three of the book focuses on 'Cultural Diversity (Still) Beyond the Convention? Communities, Private Actors and Law-Making'. The chapters in this part address the role of cultural communities in protecting and promoting the diversity of cultural expressions and the problems they face due to the monopolistic nature of private entities with regulatory capacity affecting the possibilities of cultural communities to promote their cultural expressions.

Until now, neither the Convention's organs nor parties have prioritised cultural communities, despite the latter being mentioned in both the Convention's text and its operational guidelines. In late 2020 there was a change in the Convention's Secretariat, which could shift implementation priorities. Danielle Cliche, who had been the Secretary for more than a decade, was succeeded at the end of 2020 by Toussaint Tiendrebeogo, from Burkina Faso. Time will tell how far this change will affect the Convention's priorities. For the moment, one of the calls, announced in March 2021, for contributions to the 'Policy Briefs' series published by UNESCO's Diversity of Cultural Expressions Entity on the topic of 'Diversity and Representation in Audio-visual Content' seems to point in the direction of a growing importance of 'empowering individuals and communities' as a way to allow 'diversity and representation' as 'powerful tools to fight systemic discrimination and strengthen fundamental human rights'.[14] The Secretary emphasises that need

[14] UNESCO, 'Extension of the Call for Expression of Interest: Policy Brief "Diversity and Representation in audiovisual content"' (16 March 2021), https://en.unesco.org/creativity/news/extension-call-expression-interest-policy-brief.

to address 'underrepresentation in audio-visual cultural contents including, but not limited to: television shows, films, theatre plays and video games, of marginalised communities due to factors such as race or ethnicity, gender, disability, migratory status and others'.[15]

The focus on representation is essential if the Convention wants to be effective in its goals and shift away from state-centrism. During the Convention's early years, the attention of its organs, and therefore the parties, was on the protection of states' (cultural) sovereignty in the context of asymmetrical free trade negotiations. Therefore, a 'states versus states' approach used to prevail. The objective stated in Article 1 of the Convention ('to protect … the diversity of cultural expressions'), in combination with Article 5 reaffirming the sovereign right of states 'to formulate and implement their cultural policies and to adopt measures to protect and promote the diversity of cultural expressions', was the main basis for states' actions: cultural expressions from one state needed to be protected from those of other states, particularly if the latter were especially dominant (Giacommo Mazzone).

If this approach was (and still is) necessary, it cannot by itself ensure real diversity, as cultural products of a state protected under Article 5 of the Convention from liberalisation measures are often not (sufficiently) culturally different from those of other states. There are in fact many audiovisual products that reproduce foreign ways of life. A complementary approach is needed, one that focuses on other objectives of the Convention that are still underexplored to ensure that national cultural products protected and promoted under the Convention are themselves diverse in the sense that the different cultural groups and communities within a country are represented.

Similarly, other objectives of the Convention could be better promoted. This is the case of Article 1(b) ('to create the conditions for cultures to flourish') or 1(e) ('to promote respect for the diversity of cultural expressions and raise awareness of its value at the local, national and international levels'). The international level is indeed essential for the (local) cultural communities. Given the increasing digitalisation of so many aspects of life, there are virtually no limits to these local communities interacting with others and sharing their cultural expressions around the world. Private institutions such as ICANN (Lily Martinet) or the Fédération Internationale de Football Association (FIFA) (Griscka Petri) indeed have an enormous capacity to affect cultural communities' expressions and ways of living.

The goal of this part of the book is to address these challenges, drawing conclusions on how the Convention can be further used to ensure that its Article 7.2 (which prompts states 'to recognize the important contribution of cultural communities and their central role in nurturing the diversity of cultural expressions') becomes a reality. In this way, this part of the volume contributes to fostering

[15] ibid.

the link between the Convention and the Right to Take Part in Cultural Life as developed in the 2009 'General Comment of the United Nations Committee on Economic, Social and Cultural Rights'.[16] This latter document places particular attention on communities, and can be a fruitful means to bridge the Convention across another key subfield of international law seldom associated with it: international human rights law.

In her chapter, Lily Martinet takes us through the history of community involvement in debates about linguistic and cultural diversity online, by examining debates around domain names. Martinet particularly uses the example of Catalonian domain names to work through the hurdles faced by communities in asserting their identities and presences in online fora. Her detailed examination of how domain names are attributed in this governance framework shows the difficulties faced by the Internet in living up to its promise of a pluralistic forum for cultural diversity, and how the struggle of the Catalonian community has helped reshape Internet governance practices, opening the door for an increasing number of linguistically diverse communities to use this pathway to assert their own distinctiveness and protect the economic interests vested in their cultural identities.

Also examining Internet platforms, alongside international sports associations, Griscka Petri further broadens the range of organisations with whose work the Convention intersects, and sees the Convention as playing a role to avoid and reduce monopolies in the cultural sector. Bringing the language of competition law to a discussion about cultural diversity underscores the different tactical pathways, as well as background norms, that can animate, elucidate or muddy the debate about the safeguarding and promotion of the diversity of cultural expressions. Petri shows that the Convention's organs would do well to pay more attention to other forms of expression of economic interests in the language of the law, instead of limiting themselves only to international trade law. Doing so opens wider pathways to query the activities of private actors, particularly as their size allows them to exert influence comparable to governments'. This influence, via transnational law mechanisms like self-regulation, allow for these actors to exert considerable law-making power, which is not always balanced by proper counterweights in favour of cultural communities. Petri calls for communities to be given greater legal relevance, so as to allow for the regulation of both Internet platforms and international sports associations as powerful actors in the diversity space.

In conversation with Andrzej Jakubowski, Giacommo Mazzone speaks to his personal experiences within organisations such as the European Broadcasting Union and within the Civil Society Forum linked to the Convention. These experiences become a platform from which to examine some relevant issues of this third part of the volume. This conversation starts from the parallel histories of

[16] UN Committee on Economic, Social and Cultural Rights (CESCR), 'General Comment No 21, Right of Everyone to Take Part in Cultural Life' (art 15, para 1a of the Covenant on Economic, Social and Cultural Rights, 2009, UN Doc E/C.12/GC/21).

the UNESCO Convention on Cultural Diversity and that of Internet governance, conducted mainly through the World Summits of the Information Society, and which now risks escaping sovereign state action. Mazzone reflects on the current state and challenges of cultural expressions channelled through the Internet from the point of view of sovereignty, human rights and communities.

Part four, 'Taking the Concept of Cultural Diversity Seriously: The Unavoidable Need of Connecting with Other Sectors of International Law and Other Disciplines', shifts attention to several issues which need to be addressed for the sake of the effectiveness of the Convention and its coherence. Neglecting these issues can jeopardise the Convention as a treaty that can compellingly and effectively contribute to a more culturally balanced interchange of cultural products. Already likened by some to a kind of Declaration – given the fact that many of its obligations are endeavour clauses – the Convention needs to address pressing inconsistencies to remain credible.

These inconsistencies include different understandings of cultural diversity used by parties and Convention organs, tactically deployed depending on the context. Specifically, trade negotiations tend to deploy different meanings of cultural diversity from those used in international cultural cooperation settings by the same states (particularly within the framework of the International Fund for Cultural Diversity). It is therefore illuminating and necessary to examine other international instruments – dealing with human rights, free trade or sustainable development – to ensure coherence between these other fields affecting cultural diversity and the development of the Convention.

Such is the object of this part of the book, which looks particularly at the relation between the Convention and the international legal frameworks on artistic freedom (Laurence Cuny), inclusive museums (Mónica Riaza) and cultural appropriation (Beatriz Barreiro Carril) as emerging foci of international regulatory action. Some of these issues, like that of artistic freedom, have already been approached by the organs of the Convention, contrary to what was anticipated when the Convention was adopted in 2005. All of them pose challenges for prosecuting the Convention's objectives and goals. This part also undertakes a dialogue with other social sciences beyond law, in line with what has been the approach at the origins of the Convention, when the role of social anthropologists like Arjun Appadurai was particularly relevant. Rescuing this dialogue makes an important contribution to new thinking about this treaty, and to the relationship between international law and other social sciences beyond international relations more broadly. The 15 years of the Convention's life offer relevant material for re-evaluating some of the conceptual basis of the Convention and guide its future implementation.

Focusing on artistic freedom as a cultural right, Laurence Cuny (part of the same team as Guèvremont, Otasevic and Varin) examines the link between human rights and the Convention. This link has been largely developed in the practice of the treaty, despite calls for issues such as artistic freedom not to be part of the Convention's framework during its drafting. The inclusion of this rights concern evidences the growing pervasiveness of the language of rights in international law, the importance of this language to open state-centric regimes to more actors and how the international law of culture itself is to a significant extent comprised of living instruments, much like international human rights law itself. Thinking of the Convention as a living instrument means the realisation that it can only be kept alive and relevant if its interpretation is adjusted to the changing circumstances of the societies in which it operates, and with whose cultures the treaty intersects. At the same time that Varin relies on the language of rights to get the concept of artistic freedom within the purview of the Convention, she notes that the definition takes a life of its own, bridging civil and political rights (freedom of expression) with cultural rights, in a display of the indivisibility of human rights that might not be as easily accomplished in a human rights forum. Cuny argues that this practice has contributed to our thinking about artistic freedom in international law more broadly, and has fed back into international human rights developments.

Shifting from artists to museums as institutions that hold art, Mónica Riaza uses the intercultural museum in Oslo, Norway to discuss the possibilities of dialogue and social inclusion in museums. The Convention, she argues, generates important momentum for museums to think of themselves as places of renewed social orientation. Museums can, and do, pursue objectives similar to the Convention in their pursuit of intercultural dialogue via the language of diversity, and more work connecting the two fields would be welcome.

Closing the volume, Beatriz Barreiro outlines the interdisciplinary possibilities of the law-centred debates in this volume. She does so through a case study of culture as a driver of development, and international economic law as a pathway to showcase cultural identity and distinctiveness. As globalisation offers increasingly stereotypical versions of culture for easy consumption, risks of cultural appropriation increase, and instruments like the Convention, in its alignment with international economic law, can offer regulatory possibilities to stem the tide. Barreiro contrasts anthropological and sociological readings of culture and diversity against international economic law's reductionism, to argue for greater reliance on human rights language as a pathway for more sophisticated and appropriate uses of diversity and culture in international legal discourse.

Taken together, the chapters in this volume showcase the radical potential of the Convention to not only live up to its promise in relation to protecting and promoting the diversity of cultural expressions, but also to help us reimagine what is possible in the language of international law. The contributors make calls for what is possible, what is bold and what is necessary, not only for the sake of cultural diversity, but for the future of international law-making and implementation as well. We hope you find these chapters enjoyable, challenging and stimulating, and that they help pave the way for the next 15 years of this Convention, and a much-needed recalibration of international law more broadly.

PART I

New Actors in the Legal Development and Implementation of the Convention

1

The Participation of Non-state Actors in the UNESCO Cultural Diversity Convention: Current Status and Proposals for Reform

ENZAMARIA TRAMONTANA*

I. Introduction

The 2005 Convention for the Protection and Promotion of the Diversity of Cultural Expressions (CDC, or the Convention)[1] is emblematic of the contemporary *ratione personae* pluralisation of international legal processes, because of the key role of non-state actors (NSAs) in its drafting, adoption and implementation.[2]

While significant scholarly attention, however, has so far been dedicated to the contribution of actors other than states to the Convention's negotiation and to its domestic implementation,[3] there has been comparatively little focus on their engagement in the work of the Convention's governing bodies: the Conference of Parties and the Intergovernmental Committee for the Protection and Promotion of the Diversity of Cultural Expressions (the Intergovernmental Committee).

On occasion of the fifteenth anniversary of the entry into force of the Convention, the present chapter tries to fill this gap by analysing the rules and mechanisms developed for 'accommodating' NSAs in the architecture of the Convention and assessing their space, voice and weight in the Convention's policy-deliberation and

* The Author is particularly grateful for comments and feedback from Beatriz Barreiro Carril, Andrzej Jakubowski and Lucas Lixinski, and wishes to thank Alexandra Xanthaki for her insightful suggestions on an earlier version of this chapter. Any errors remain the sole responsibility of the Author.

[1] (adopted 20 October 2005, entered into force 18 March 2007) 2440 UNTS 311.

[2] The growing pluralisation of the actors involved in international legal processes has been the object of an increasing scholarly attention over the last decade. For a general overview, see J d'Aspremont, 'Introduction: Non-state Actors in International Law: Oscillating between Concepts and Dynamics' in J d'Aspremont (ed), *Participants in the International Legal System – Multiple Perspectives on Non-state Actors in International Law* (Abingdon, Routledge, 2011) 1.

[3] See, *ex multis*, CM Merkel, 'Article 11. Participation of Civil Society' in S von Schorlemer and P-T Stoll (eds), *The UNESCO Convention on the Protection and Promotion of the Diversity of Cultural Expressions – Explanatory Notes* (Berlin, Springer, 2012) 307.

decision-making processes. This analysis is premised on the belief that policies and decisions made through appropriate participatory processes are likely to be more practical, equitable and ultimately effective.[4]

Furthermore, the chapter aims to get valuable insights from the practice of the Convention's bodies in order to discuss one of the most crucial issues concerning NSAs' participation in international governance: how to define, assess and promote the legitimacy of such participation.[5] In this regard, recent academic and political debates have brought to the fore different questions: what reasons justify the involvement of NSAs in policy-deliberation and decision-making processes? Under what conditions should they be rightfully entitled to have a place, alongside states, therein? And what exactly should their role be?[6]

Two main approaches have so far been adopted, both in scholarly and policy debates, to address these questions.[7] The first one – which can be defined as 'functionalist' – conceives the role of NSAs in terms of output legitimacy, that is, in terms of the results of international governance. It favours their inclusion in international decision-making based on the view that, by providing specialised expertise and promoting public understanding, they can increase the quality of decisions and facilitate their domestic implementation, and do this all for free.[8] It seeks to maximise the efficiency of international decision-making, but it is unconcerned

[4] This is especially true for the governance of cultural diversity, given its nature as a 'global public good', ie one of those common values and interests, like human rights, the environment or financial stability, to name just a few, that 'extend beyond the sovereign interests of states, and speak directly to populations'. See International Law Association – Committee on Participation in Global Cultural Heritage Governance, 'Interim Report: Participation in Cultural Heritage Governance at the Global Level' (Kyoto Conference, 2020) para 11 (ILA Interim Report).

[5] The term 'legitimacy' is notoriously used variably in the literature. In the present context, it refers to the justification of the exercise of power or influence, based on moral and other socially embedded values or beliefs. Since the turn of the millennium, the legitimacy of international law and governance has been discussed intensively. See, for all, R Wolfrum, 'Legitimacy in International Law from a Legal Perspective: Some Introductory Considerations' in R Wolfrum and V Roeben (eds), *Legitimacy in International Law* (Berlin, Springer, 2008) 1–24. More recently, see A Galán, 'The Shifting Boundaries of Legitimacy in International Law' (2018) 87 *Nordic Journal of International Law* 436.

[6] Authors from different disciplines have contributed to the debate. See A Vedder, 'Questioning the Legitimacy of Non-Governmental Organizations' in A Vedder (ed), *NGO Involvement in International Governance and Policy: Sources of Legitimacy* (Leiden, Martinus Nijhoff, 2007) 1, and references therein.

[7] Compare with P Willetts, 'The Cardoso Report on the UN and Civil Society: Functionalism, Global Corporatism, or Global Democracy?' (2006) 12 *Global Governance: A Review of Multilateralism and International Organizations* 305 (defining three normative arguments for the inclusion of NSAs in international governance: functionalism, neocorporatism and democratic pluralism); A Tancredi, 'L'ibridazione pubblico-privata di alcune organizzazioni internazionali' in M Vellano (ed), *Il futuro delle organizzazioni internazionali: prospettive giuridiche* (Naples, Editoriale Scientifica, 2015) 331–58 (outlining, as supplements or alternatives to the democratic rationale for NSAs' participation in international governance, a functionalist and a good governance-inspired frameworks).

[8] This approach is expressed, for instance, by the Organization of the American States (OAS). According to the 'Guidelines for Participation by Civil Society Organizations in OAS Activities' (15 December 1999), OEA/Ser.G CP/RES 759 (1217/99) corr 1, Introduction, the 'tradition of OAS cooperation with civil society organizations is based on the significant contributions these organizations can make to OAS work, since they can contribute knowledge and additional information to

about whether interests having a stake in decisions are unheard in, or marginalised voices are excluded from, the relevant processes.

The second approach – which can be defined as 'democratic' – emphasises instead the contribution of NSAs in terms of input legitimacy, that is, with reference to the procedures through which international decisions are made. In its original 'harder' version, which gained popularity at the beginning of the 1990s, it stresses the potential of NSAs, especially non-governmental organisations (NGOs), to reduce the democratic deficit of international decision-making processes by representing the views of world citizens therein.[9] In its 'softer' version, which originated, a decade later, from an increasingly widespread criticism against NGOs' representation and accountability,[10] it claims that NSAs' participation enhances the democratic character of international decision-making in the more limited sense of increasing their inclusiveness and pluralism, through the vocalisation of ideas and concerns that would otherwise risk being unheard therein.[11] It is in this version that the 'democratic' rationale is most widely accepted nowadays and will be used in this chapter.

The chapter is articulated as follows. Section II illustrates the CDC's legal framework for engagement with actors other than states. It shows that this

decision-making processes, raise new issues and concerns that will subsequently be addressed by the OAS, lend expert advice in their areas of expertise, and contribute to consensus-building in many spheres'.

[9] In this 'harder' version, the democratic rationale for civil society participation is particularly stressed, for instance, by the United Nations and the Council of Europe. The preamble of the ECOSOC Resolution 1996/31, setting the modalities to enter into consultative arrangements with non-governmental organisations (NGOs) pursuant to Art 71 of the UN Charter, provides that consultative arrangements are to be made 'to enable organizations that represent important elements of public opinion to express their views'. See ECOSOC Resolution 1996/31 (25 July 1996) Part II, para 20. In addition, the highest consultative status is given to NGOs 'whose membership, which should be considerable, is broadly representative of major segments of society in a large number of countries in different regions of the world' (para 22). Likewise, Resolution (2016)3 of the Council of Europe on the participatory status for international NGOs mentions 'the essential role of counterbalance played by NGOs in a pluralist democracy to intensify the active participation of all in conducting public affairs' as well as the conviction that 'initiatives, ideas and suggestions emanating from civil society can be considered as a true expression of persons living in the member States of the Council of Europe' (see Resolution CM/Resolution (2016)3 on Participatory status for international non-governmental organisations with the Council of Europe, 6 July 2016, Preamble).

[10] It has been observed that NGOs are self-appointed, since they lack a democratic mandate by global citizens; that they often do not have a democratic adopted constitution or internal democratic procedures; and that they are generally not accountable to the people on whose behalf they claim to speak. In short, it has been questioned how NGOs could foster democracy when they do not fulfil democratic requirements themselves. See, eg K Anderson and D Rieff, 'Global Civil Society': A Sceptical View' in H Anheier, M Glasius and M Kaldor (eds), *Global Civil Society 2004–2005* (London, Sage Publications, 2004) 29–30. In this perspective, it is often concluded that NGOs are primarily involved in international organisations to provide a certain form of window dressing. See, eg K Anderson, '"Accountability" as "Legitimacy": Global Governance, Global Civil Society and the United Nations' (2011) 36 *Brooklyn Journal of International Law* 841, 846.

[11] See, among others, A Peters, 'Dual Democracy' in J Klabbers, A Peters and G Ulfstein (eds), *The Constitutionalization of International Law* (New York, Oxford University Press, 2009) 316–17; I Rossi, *Legal Status of Non-Governmental Organizations in International Law* (Antwerp, Intersentia, 2010) 63–64.

framework expresses a 'functionalist' emphasis on NSAs' capacity to contribute to the adoption of higher quality decisions on the part of states and facilitate their implementation. Section III investigates the relationship between NSAs and the Convention's bodies. It argues that the existing 'functionalist-oriented' regulation has not only prevented basic stakeholders from having access to the Convention's processes, but has also created imbalances among participants, to the detriment of the Convention's very ambitions of promoting pluralism and cultural diversity. Section IV follows with some recommendations to enhance the Convention's governance by rendering it more inclusive. It is suggested that while the 'democratic' approach may be used to broaden the range of participants and to promote a more balanced representation among them, it is fundamentally flawed in that it does not challenge the privileged position of states in international governance, and consequently upholds a narrow understanding of NSAs' status therein. Therefore, this chapter proposes to include international human rights law as an additional means of framing NSAs' participation in the Convention, by looking at such participation as a way of realising the human right to take part in cultural life. The analysis shows that the proposed approach – which I will henceforth call the 'human rights-based approach' – may prompt an overcoming of the present state-centrism of international governance by converting NSAs' participation from a concession into a prerogative and, under certain circumstances, by requiring it to take place on an equal footing with that of states. Finally, Section V offers some concluding observations on how to advance a full understanding of the legitimate role of NSAs in international governance broadly. It is argued that, while seemingly competing, all three approaches to NSAs' participation – the 'functionalist', the 'democratic' and the 'human rights-based' – may, in practice, be variously combined to accommodate the different nature of the actors engaging in participation and of their expected contribution to international policy-deliberation and decision-making.

II. The Legal Framework for Non-state Actors' Involvement in the Convention

The CDC contains an express legal basis for the participation of actors other than states in its governance. Article 11 recognises 'the fundamental role of civil society in protecting and promoting the diversity of cultural expressions' and calls on states parties to 'encourage [its] active participation … in their efforts to achieve the objectives of [the] Convention'.[12]

[12] Art 11 CDC.

The potential contribution of NSAs (*rectius*, civil society) to the Convention's policy-deliberation and decision-making processes is explained in the Operational Guidelines to Article 11, adopted by the Conference of Parties at its second session, in 2009.[13] Further and more detailed regulation is set out in the Rules of Procedures of the Conference of Parties and of the Intergovernmental Committee respectively, which provide for a system of ad hoc accreditation whereby, upon request to the UNESCO's Director-General, civil society organisations (CSOs) that meet certain criteria may take part as observers to the sessions of the two governing bodies.[14]

The resulting framework expresses a strong strand of 'functionalism', with emphasis on the contribution of NSAs to the improvement of the output legitimacy of policy-deliberation and decision-making. This approach stems from all three key elements of the relevant regulation: the definition of who is allowed to participate; the procedure to access participatory status and privileges; and the nature and scope of participation. Each of these elements will be examined in turn.

A. Actors of Participation

While it is not the only UNESCO treaty expressively providing for collaboration with NSAs,[15] the CDC is unique in that, to identify these actors, it employs the notion of 'civil society'.

Recently come into use within international practice to replace the narrower reference to 'non-governmental organisations', 'civil society' is not a legal term of art, and every international organisation or treaty governing body that engages with it has its own definition.[16] There is, however, an increasingly accepted understanding that 'civil society' encompasses all those voluntary associations of individuals (outside the family and business) created to advance shared values and

[13] 'Operational Guidelines: Role and Participation of Civil Society', approved by the Conference of Parties at its second session (June 2009).

[14] See, respectively, Rule 2.3 of the Rules of Procedure of the Conference of Parties to the 2005 Convention, adopted by the Conference of Parties at its first session (2007), amended at its second session (2009) and at its seventh session (2019), and Rule 7.4 of the Rules of Procedure of the Intergovernmental Committee for the Protection and Promotion of the Diversity of Cultural Expressions, adopted by the Intergovernmental Committee for the Protection and Promotion of the Diversity of Cultural Expressions at its first session (2007) and approved by the Conference of Parties at its second session (2009). Rule 7.4 also provide the Committee with the opportunity to 'invite at any time public or private organizations or individuals to participate in its meeting for consultation on specific issues'.

[15] See Convention for the Safeguarding of the Intangible Cultural Heritage (ICHC) (Paris,17 October 2003, in force 20 April 2006) 2368 UNTS 3, Art 15: 'Within the framework of its safeguarding activities of the intangible cultural heritage, each State Party shall endeavour to ensure the widest possible participation of communities, groups and, where appropriate, individuals that create, maintain and transmit such heritage, and to involve them actively in its management.'

[16] For a general overview, see JA Scholte, 'Relations with Civil Society' in JK Cogan, I Hurd and I Johnstone (eds), *The Oxford Handbook of International Organizations* (Oxford, Oxford University Press, 2016) 712–29.

interests, including public benefit NGOs, trade unions and professional associations, faith groups and spiritual organisations, academia, research institutes and think tanks, and peasants' or indigenous peoples' organisations.[17] As such, it is a means for indirect, or mediated, rather than direct participation, which seems to respond to a 'functionalist' approach, as defined abroad, in one main aspect, that is, in favouring associations and other voluntary 'intermediary' entities over (and as stand-ins for) individuals and communities, with the result of reducing the costs without losing the added value of participation, by gathering and channelling the voices of relevant stakeholders and, thereby, keeping manageable the number of participants and translating their interests in the language being used in international public arenas.[18]

Quite significantly, only a limited subset of the wide-ranging universe that generally comes under 'civil society' is covered by the definition adopted for the purposes of the Convention, which refers to the sum of 'non-governmental organizations, non-profit organisations, professionals in the culture sector and associated sectors, groups that support the work of artists and cultural communities'.[19] As a result, participation before the Convention's Conference of Parties and Intergovernmental Committee tend to be restricted, once again in a clear functionalist perspective, to only those CSOs – such as organisations of artists and other creative professionals, organisations of cultural producers and distributors, arts agencies and advocacy groups – that are active in the field of culture; and that, because of their expertise and experience in this field, can strengthen the capacity of the two governing bodies to detect problems, and implement solutions, on matters of relevance to the Convention. Other, less specialised actors are in principle excluded from the Convention's policy-deliberation and decision-making processes, so as presumably to avoid time inefficiencies and streamline participation.[20]

[17] See, eg United Nations General Assembly, 'We the Peoples: Civil Society, the United Nations and Global Governance – Report of the Panel of Eminent Persons on United Nations-Civil Society Relations' (11 June 2004) UN Doc A/58/817, 13. At the regional level, the Council of Europe (COE) defines civil society as the 'ensemble of individuals and organised, less organised and informal groups through which they contribute to society or express their views and opinions', including 'professional and grassroots organisations, universities and research centres, religious and non-denominational organisations and human rights defenders'. See 'Guidelines for Civil Participation in Political Decision-Making' (CM (2017) 83 final, 27 September 2017). For the OAS, to take another example, 'civil society organization is understood to mean any national or international institution, organization, or entity made up of natural or juridical persons of a nongovernmental nature'. See 'Guidelines for the Participation of Civil Society Organizations in OAS Activities' (CP/RES 759 (1217/99) corr 1, 15 December 1999) para 2.

[18] On the contrary, the ICHC's approach of speaking of 'communities, groups, and individuals' can be interpreted as a choice for directed participation. For an in-depth analysis of this provision, see M Jacobs, 'Article 15: Participation of Communities, Groups, and Individuals – CGIs, not just "the Community"' in J Blake and L Lixinski (eds), *The 2003 UNESCO Intangible Heritage Convention: A Commentary* (New York, Oxford University Press, 2020) 273–89.

[19] 'Operational Guidelines' (n 13) para 3.

[20] The prevalent reliance on experts in the context of global cultural governance more generally is critically underlined by the ILA Interim Report (n 4) para 42.

B. Access to Participation

Civil society participation is subordinated to an accreditation procedure, conceived as a tool to control access to the Convention and make sure that only 'appropriate' actors get to participate in the activities of its governing bodies.

The criteria for accreditation require CSOs to: have interests and activities in one or more fields covered by the Convention; have a legal status in compliance with the established rules of the jurisdiction in the country of registration; and be representative of their respective field of activity or the respective social or professional groups they represent.[21] Requests for admission, to be submitted to the Director-General, should be signed by the official representative of the organisation concerned and should be accompanied by: a copy of its statutes or bylaws; a list of members or, in the case of non-membership entities, a list of board members; and a brief description of the organisation's recent activities, which illustrates their representativeness in the fields covered by the Convention.[22]

Both requirements that CSOs must have a substantial membership base in their fields of competence, and that they must demonstrate their representativeness in these fields, clearly express a functionalist approach to participation. The first is directed at ensuring that only those entities which have a functional contribution to make in terms of raising support among relevant stakeholders, and facilitating the effective implementation of the Convention's provisions, may claim observer status before its governing bodies. The second is aimed at restricting access to the Conference of Parties and the Intergovernmental Committee exclusively to those entities that have the potential of enriching policy-deliberation and decision-making processes, thanks to their established experience and expertise.

C. Nature and Scope of Participation

Finally, what is expected from accredited CSOs is to provide a functional contribution to the achievement of the Convention's objectives and the enhancement of its governing bodies' performance. Organisations entering into formal relationships with the Convention are looked at as strategic allies, which are required to engage in: increasing the visibility and furthering the understanding of the Convention's provisions at the local, national and international levels, by organising seminars and distributing information materials; contributing to the Convention's policy-deliberation and decision-making processes, by asking to be accredited to the meetings of the Conference of Parties and the Intergovernmental Committee or, otherwise, being invited by the latter to participate in its meetings for consultation

[21] 'Operational Guidelines' (n 13) Annex, Art 1.
[22] ibid.

on specific issues; advocating and driving the implementation of the Convention at the national level, by carrying out capacity-building activities in specific domains linked to the Convention; and contributing to the Convention's compliance monitoring, by participating in the preparation of quadrennial periodic reports by state parties.[23]

CSOs accredited to the Conference of Parties or the Intergovernmental Committee hold an 'observer' status, which only enables them to attend meetings, deliver oral statements with the consent of the chairperson and submit written contributions relevant to the meetings' agenda when authorised by the chair, to be circulated to all delegations by the Convention's Secretariat as information documents.[24] This limited status is aimed at maximising the advantages and minimising the shortcomings of the relationship with civil society; and to do so, in a clearly functionalist perspective, by taking advantage of the wealth of specialised knowledge offered by CSOs, without challenging the role of States as the only international decision-makers or risking overcrowded agendas, disrupted negotiations, or delayed deliberations.[25]

III. The Practice of Civil Society Participation to the Convention's Governance: A Critical Assessment

During the first years of the CDC, the participation of civil society in the meetings of the Conference of Parties and the Intergovernmental Committee was rather limited.[26] Civil society representatives increasingly expressed dissatisfaction with

[23] 'Operational Guidelines' (n 13) paras 6–7.

[24] Ibid para 9. The model for this status is provided by ECOSOC Resolution 1996/31, adopted pursuant to Art 71 of the UN Charter (see n 9 above). The Resolution distinguishes between a 'general consultative status', a 'special consultative status' and 'listing on the Roster'. NGOs enjoying 'general consultative status' are informed of the provisional agenda of the Council and they may propose to place items on it. Furthermore, they may sit as observers at public meetings, submit written statements that do not exceed 2000 words and make oral presentations during those meetings, subject to the approval of the Council. NGOs with 'special consultative status' are informed of the provisional agenda of the Council, may be observers at public meetings of the Council and submit written statements with a maximum of 500 words for circulation to the Members of the Council. They cannot propose items for the agenda of the Council, nor can they make oral statements at meetings of the Council. Finally, NGOs that fall into 'Roster' are informed of the provisional agenda of the Council, may only send representatives to public meetings which concern matters within their field of competence and may only submit written statements if they have been invited to do so (see ECOSOC Resolution 1996/31 on Consultative Relationship between the United Nations and Non-Governmental Organizations (25 July 1996) UN Doc E/RES/1996/31). Since the beginning of the 21st century, some major international organisations, including the COE, the OAS and the African Union (AU), have introduced enhanced forms of dialogue and interaction with civil society, using a language of 'participation' as opposed to 'consultation'. In no case, however, have CSOs been granted direct participation in decision making.

[25] Tancredi, 'L'ibridazione pubblico-privata', 333.

[26] See nn 27–36 below, and accompanying text.

their narrow participatory opportunities before the Convention's bodies and denounced the consequent lack of motivation in contributing to its governance.[27]

In response to this criticism, in 2017, the Conference of Parties and the Intergovernmental Committee introduced new patterns of interaction with CSOs that, without strengthening their legal status by adding new rights or privileges, have allowed them to be more actively involved in the Convention's processes. In particular, the practice of holding government–civil society consultations prior to officials meeting of the Convention's bodies, first introduced in 2008,[28] has been progressively streamlined and consolidated. CSOs have been invited to hold a two-day civil society forum before each Conference of Parties, where they are encouraged to exchange views and make suggestions to the Conference, and to attend a working meeting with the Convention Bureau before each session of the Intergovernmental Committee, where to discuss the Committee's agenda items and put forward ideas and proposals.[29]

This new practice has stimulated a growth in civil society participation.[30] Whereas only 7 CSOs participated in the first meeting of the Committee in 2007,[31] 49 organisations were present in 2017,[32] and 62 CSOs attended the meeting in 2018.[33] Similarly, participants to the Conference of Parties grew from 9 organisations in 2015[34] to 32 participants in 2017[35] and to 78 participants in 2019.[36]

[27] UNESCO, Intergovernmental Committee, 'Item 9 of the Provisional Agenda: Assessment of the Participation of Civil Society in Implementation of the Convention' (CE/15/9.IGC/9 of 16 October 2015) para 20.

[28] The first session was organised in June 2008 and was entitled 'The Role and Participation of Civil Society in the Implementation of the Convention for the Protection and Promotion of the Diversity of Cultural Expressions: An Exchange of Views between Civil Society and the Parties to the Convention'. The second session was organised in December 2011 and was devoted to 'Promoting Inclusive Governance of Culture: The Role of Civil Society in the Quadrennial Periodic Reports'. For summary reports, see www.unesco.org/new/en/culture/themes/cultural-diversity/periodicreports/exchange-sessions.

[29] The first Civil Society Forum on the Diversity of Cultural Expressions took place before the Sixth Session of the Conference of Parties, on 12 June 2017, at the UNESCO Headquarters in Paris. The second edition of the Civil Society Forum took place before the Seventh Session of the Conference of Parties, on 4 June 2019. For more information, see https://en.unesco.org/creativity/events/civil-society-forum.

[30] A Firmin, 'Engaging Civil Society in Cultural Governance' in UNESCO Global Report, *Re|shaping Cultural Policies: Advancing Creativity for Development* (Paris, UNESCO, 2017) 85, 93.

[31] Conference of Parties, First Ordinary Session (Paris, 18–20 June 2007, E/07/1.CP/CONF/209/9-INFO, 21 June 2007) 59–63.

[32] Intergovernmental Committee, Eleventh Ordinary Session (Paris, 12–15 December 2017, DCE/17/11.IGC/INF.2, 19 December 2017) 22–28.

[33] Intergovernmental Committee, Twelfth Ordinary Session (Paris, 11–14 December 2018, DCE/18/12.IGC/INF.2, 14 December 2018) 21–27.

[34] Conference of Parties, Fifth Ordinary Session (Paris, 10–12 June 2015, CE/15/5.CP/INF.2, 12 June 2015) 32–34.

[35] Conference of Parties, Sixth Ordinary Session (Paris, 12–15 June 2017, DCE/17/6.CP/INF.2, 15 June 2017) 20–21.

[36] Conference of Parties, Seventh Session (Paris, 4–7 June 2019, DCE/19/7.CP/INF.2, 7 June 2019) 22–28.

Nonetheless, a review of the list of participants to the meetings of the two governing bodies indicates that, by design or in their implementation, the Convention's functionalist-oriented participatory rules have not only limited the circle of actors involved in its policy-deliberation and decision-making processes, but have also fuelled great imbalances among them. On the one hand, the Convention's approach of allowing indirect, or mediated, rather than direct participation, and its narrow definition of what is meant by 'civil society', have essentially restricted participants to professional or advocacy organisations of the cultural sector, preventing other basic stakeholders, especially communities, including minorities and indigenous peoples, from finding a place in the Convention's processes.[37] On the other hand, the emphasis put on recognised standing and substantial membership base as accreditation criteria has worked to the disadvantage of the smallest and less resourced CSOs and thus, in general, of organisations based in the Global South.[38]

This poses two main problems. First, non-state participation through CSOs, while promoting efficiency, raises serious questions of representativity and accountability, insomuch as such organisations are frequently not effectively connected to, or responsive towards, the constituencies on whose behalf they claim to speak. This is particularly troublesome when, as in the case of the Convention, CSOs are the only participants in decision-making other than States and tend to coincide with functional interest groups, creating a risk of corporatism.[39]

Secondly, inequalities between Northern and Southern CSOs in participation in the Convention's processes run counter to the Convention's very aim of counterbalancing the levelling force of dominant societies and mitigating the cultural homogenisation effects of the processes of globalisation.[40] The prevalence of organisations headquartered in the Global North, whatever their good intentions, may cause an undue influence of Western interests, values and concerns over the

[37] The exclusion of local communities from international cultural governance more generally, and its consequences, are thoroughly discussed by L Lixinski, *International Heritage Law for Communities: Exclusion and Re-Imagination* (Oxford, Oxford University Press, 2019).

[38] See Intergovernmental Committee for the Protection and Promotion of the Diversity of Cultural Expressions, 'Reports of Civil Society Organisations on their Activities – Civil Society Report to the Intergovernmental Committee UNESCO 2005 Convention: An African Perspective' (DCE/17/11.IGC/ 6REV, 11 December 2017) Annex II, 37. The overrepresentation of Northern-based civil society organisations is a common phenomenon in the practice of international organisations. *Ex multis*, see C Focarelli, *International Law as a Social Construct: The Struggle for Global Justice* (Oxford, Oxford University Press, 2012) 195.

[39] I Bernier and H Ruiz Fabri, 'Aplicación y seguimiento de la Convención de la UNESCO sobre la protección y promoción de la diversidad de las expresiones culturales – Perspectivas de acción' (Gouvernement du Québec, Ministère de la Culture et des Communications, 2006) www.mcc.gouv.qc.ca.

[40] In this perspective, the Preamble observes that 'while the processes of globalization, which have been facilitated by the rapid development of information and communication technologies, afford unprecedented conditions for enhanced interaction between cultures, they also represent a challenge for cultural diversity, namely in view of risks of imbalances between rich and poor countries': Cultural Diversity Convention, Preamble, para 19. On this, see L Pineschi, 'Convenzione sulla diversità culturale e diritto internazionale dei diritti umani' in L Zagato (ed), *Le identità culturali nei recenti strumenti UNESCO – Un approccio nuovo alla costruzione della pace?* (Padua, Cedam, 2008) 164.

Convention's policy-deliberation and decision-making processes, contributing to the consolidation of stereotyped cultural models and the concomitant frustration of the value of cultural pluralism and diversity.[41]

Addressing these problems is necessary to ensure the role of civil society – envisaged by Article 11 – as a key partner in achieving the Convention's objectives: the protection of cultural expression diversity cannot be effective unless meaningful participatory processes are in place that promote pluralism by reproducing the rich diversity of civil society itself. In what follows, some proposals for reform are presented that, bringing together the 'democratic' approach with a 'human rights-based' approach, seek to overcome the shortcomings resulting from a strict implementation of the 'functionalist' approach to participation.

IV. Proposals for Enhanced Non-state Participation within the Convention

As introduced above, the 'democratic' approach, in its currently most widely accepted version, stresses NSAs' potential to make international decision-making processes more inclusive and plural by expressing ideas and concerns that would otherwise risk being unheard therein.[42] As such, it offers a framework for expanding the range of actors involved in the CDC's governance and encouraging a more balanced representation among them.

Being unconcerned about maximising the efficiency of decision making, the 'democratic' approach may encourage a widening of the notion of who can participate and a loosening of accreditation criteria. It can constitute the basis, on the one hand, to open up the Convention's processes to actors beyond 'intermediary' associations, providing direct avenues for individuals, groups and communities to take part in decision-making, and on the other hand, to modify accreditation criteria in order to ensure that not only those actors that 'add value' in terms of technical knowledge or expertise are engaged, but also those that, simply because of the interests or concerns that they represent or embody, may enrich policies and decisions.[43]

[41] This geographical imbalance also risks feeding the criticism of Western centrism that has been directed against the Convention's understanding of what cultural diversity is and what should be done for the purpose of its promotion and protection. For this argument, see, eg C De Beukelaer and M Pyykkönen, 'Introduction: UNESCO's 'Diversity Convention' – Ten Years on' in C De Beukelaer, M Pyykkönen and JP Singh (eds), *Globalization, Culture, and Development: The UNESCO Convention on Cultural Diversity* (London, Palgrave Macmillan, 2015) 9.

[42] See nn 9 and 10 above, and accompanying text.

[43] Obviously, this would imply the realisation of awareness-raising campaigns, especially at the grassroots level, and the provision of technical and financial support in favour of less-resourced actors, particularly those of the Global South. Opening up the CDC's doors to a greater number and diversity of participants may, in fact, be of limited effect if concrete efforts are not made to sensitise local stakeholders on the value of engaging in the Convention's processes and to enhance their capacity to access its governing bodies and contribute to their activities.

However, more widespread and varied participation does not amount to enhanced participation: despite being laudable in its main goals, the 'democratic' approach is fundamentally flawed in that it falls short of challenging the privileged position of states in international governance. Not dissimilarly from the 'functional' approach, it endorses a narrow understanding of participation, where states retain control over formal appointments and ultimate regulatory responsibility, while NSAs are only admitted to voice their different perspectives, without any possibility of engaging in negotiating or deliberating functions on an equal footing with governmental delegations.

This leads to the proposal of integrating the 'democratic' approach with a 'human rights-based' approach to participation, by looking at NSAs' involvement in the domain of international cultural governance as a way of realising the human right to take part in cultural life, as set out in several international instruments and the practice of relevant monitoring bodies.[44]

Over time, participation in cultural life has come to be interpreted as the opportunity for both individuals and groups not only to choose their own cultural identity and engage in their own cultural practices, but also to actively be involved in the design and implementation of policies and decisions on cultural matters of relevance to them, at both the domestic and the international level.[45] It is recognised as an integral part of, and a condition for the full enjoyment of, all cultural and other fundamental human rights.

Although the CDC is not a cultural rights instrument as such, several of its provisions invite the adoption of a human rights-based approach, by explicitly linking the protection of cultural diversity to the full realisation of human rights and fundamental freedoms.[46] In the Preamble, for example, it is stated that cultural

[44] The right of everyone to participate in cultural life is provided under Art 27 of the Universal Declaration of Human Rights (New York, 10 December 1948) UN Doc A/810 and Art 15(a) of the International Covenant of Economic, Social and Cultural Rights (New York, 19 December 1966, in force 3 January 1976, 993 UNTS 3), and is enshrined in many other international human rights law instruments, including the International Convention on the Elimination of All Forms of Racial Discrimination (New York, 21 December 1965, in force 4 January 1969, 660 UNTS 195); Convention on the Elimination of All Forms of Discrimination against Women (New York, 18 December 1979, in force 3 September 1981, 1249 UNTS 13); Convention on the Rights of the Child (New York, 20 November 1989, in force 2 September 1990, 1577 UNTS 3). For an overview, see L Pineschi, 'Cultural Diversity as a Human Right? General Comment No. 21 of the Committee on Economic, Social and Cultural Rights' in S Borelli and F Lenzerini (eds), *Cultural Heritage, Cultural Rights, Cultural Diversity: New Developments in International Law* (Leiden, Martinus Nijhoff, 2012) 44–47.

[45] See Committee on Economic, Social and Cultural Rights, 'General Comment No 21, Right of Everyone to Take Part in Cultural Life (Art 15 of the Covenant on Economic, Social and Cultural Rights)' (21 December 2009) UN Doc E/C.12/GC/21 para 15(a). Even though this, as well as other relevant documents, defines the right to participation with reference to domestic decision-making processes, it can be argued that this right may also apply, by extension, to international governance. Given the increasing shift of regulatory activities from the national to the international level, to argue the contrary would render the right meaningless. On this, see E Tramontana, 'Civil Society Participation in International Decision Making: Recent Developments and Future Perspectives in the Indigenous Rights Arena' (2012) 16 *International Journal of Human Rights* 173.

[46] For this, see YM Donders, 'Cultural Rights in the Convention on the Diversity of Cultural Expressions: Included or Ignored?' in T Kono and S Van Uytsel (eds), *The UNESCO Convention on the*

diversity is important for the full realisation of human rights, as proclaimed in the Cultural Diversity Declaration and other universal instruments, and that it can be sustained through the 'constant exchange between cultures' and 'the right of access of all people to a rich and diversified range of cultural expression from all over the world'. Article 2 recognises that 'cultural diversity can be protected and promoted only if human rights and fundamental freedoms … are guaranteed', and proclaims 'the equal dignity of and respect for all cultures, including the cultures of persons belonging to minorities and indigenous people'. Article 7 further pays special attention to the situation of minorities and indigenous peoples, recognising their fundamental right 'to create, disseminate and distribute their cultural goods and services, including their traditional cultural expression'.[47]

By prompting a consideration of individuals' and communities' rights that relate to participation, a human rights-based approach offers a stronger framework for advanced modalities of NSAs' involvement in the CDC. Two main features are worthy of note.

First, this approach leads to conceive non-state participation as a right of those affected by the decisions of the Convention's governing bodies, rather than as a concession by states. This implies the need to go beyond the system of accreditation, conceived of as a filter assessing a predefined set of admission conditions, to include more open ways of influencing policy-deliberation and decision-making processes.[48] Secondly, it brings to recognise varying degrees of access and involvement in the Convention's processes, based on the diverse interests that individuals and communities may have according to their

Diversity of Cultural Expressions: A Tale of Fragmentation in International Law (Cambridge, Intersentia, 2012) 165–82. See also Pineschi, 'Convenzione sulla diversità culturale', 166–67.

[47] For an analysis of these provisions, see A Meijknecht, 'The Convention on the Diversity of Cultural Expressions: What Is Its Added Value for Minorities and Indigenous Peoples?' in Kono and Van Uytsel, *The UNESCO Convention on the Diversity of Cultural Expressions*, 201. Participatory rights are crucial to guarantee the effective protection of the rights and interests of ethno-cultural groups. Accordingly, many international instruments such as the UN Declaration on the Rights of Persons Belonging to National or Ethnic, Religious and Linguistic Minorities, the Framework Convention on the Protection of National Minorities and the UN Declaration on the Rights of Indigenous Peoples expressly affirm the right of members of minorities and indigenous peoples to participate effectively in decisions affecting their interests. For an overview in the sphere of minority rights, see M Weller, 'Effective Participation of Minorities in Public Life' in M Weller (ed), *Universal Minority Rights: A Commentary on the Jurisprudence of International Courts and Treaty Bodies* (Oxford, Oxford University Press, 2007) 477; on indigenous rights, see M Barelli, 'Free, Prior, and Informed Consent in the UNDRIP: Articles 10, 19, 29(2), and 32(2)' in J Hohmann and M Weller (eds), *The UN Declaration on the Rights of Indigenous Peoples: A Commentary* (Oxford, Oxford University Press, 2018) 247.

[48] In this regard, an example of a good practice of participation at the international level (consisting in the calls for online submissions in response to given questionnaires) from all concerned stakeholders, including academics, experts and civil society organisations, is offered by the practice of the UN Special Rapporteur in the Field of Cultural Rights and other special procedures of the United Nations Human Rights Council. See, eg www.ohchr.org/EN/Issues/CulturalRights/Pages/ClimateChange.aspx. Another example, in the same field, is provided by the Special Rapporteurship on Economic, Social, Cultural, and Environmental Rights of the Inter-American Commission on Human Rights. See www.oas.org/en/iachr/jsForm/?File=/en/IACHR/r/DESCA/Cuestionarios.asp a. For more on this way of accessing cultural governance, see ILA Interim Report (n 4) paras 83–84.

relationship with the specific matters at stake. Consequently, giving a voice to all affected stakeholders may not be sufficient; rather, participation should entail substantive input in decision-making, including the requirement of free, prior and informed consent, at least when vulnerable cultural communities, particularly indigenous peoples, are affected.[49] Similarly, participation should take place through culturally appropriate procedures, according to the concerned community's traditional mechanisms of decision-making, and providing all the members of the community with the opportunity to engage without discrimination, individually or as collectives.[50]

V. Conclusions

Legitimacy has traditionally informed the debate about the place of NSAs in international governance and continues to do so. Once the reasons that justify the participation of NSAs have been identified, one can define which actors should be involved in international policy-deliberation and decision-making processes, what roles they should play and which requirements they should fulfil to be rightfully entitled to have a place therein. Two main approaches have so far been adopted, both in scholarly and policy debates, to address these questions: a 'functionalist' approach, that promotes NSAs' participation in decision-making based on the view that, by providing expertise and promoting public support, they can

[49] The normative framework of the right to free, prior and informed consent consists in a series of legal international instruments, including the United Nations Declaration on the Rights of Indigenous Peoples (UNDRIP), the International Labour Organization Convention 169 (ILO 169) and the Convention on Biological Diversity (CBD). See J Anaya, 'Report of the Special Rapporteur on the Rights of Indigenous Peoples' (6 July 2012) UN Doc A/HRC/21/47, para 49; 'Expert Mechanism on the Rights of Indigenous Peoples, Final Report of the Study on Indigenous Peoples and the Right to Participate in Decision-Making' (17 August 2011) UN Doc A/HRC/18/42, paras 63–69.

[50] These elements can be drawn from the practice of international human rights bodies, at both the universal and regional levels. The United Nations Special Rapporteur on the Rights of Indigenous Peoples and the Inter-American Court of Human Rights (IACtHR), for instance, have expressively indicated that consultation processes must respect the internal decision-making processes of the concerned communities and their organizations. See J Anaya, 'Report of the Special Rapporteur on the Situation of Human Rights and Fundamental Freedoms of Indigenous People' (5 October 2009) UN Doc A/HRC/12/34/Add.6, Annex A, para 31; 'Kichwa Indigenous People of Sarayaku v Ecuador (Merits, Reparations, Costs)', IACtHR Series C No 245 (27 June 2012) para 202. The Inter-American Commission on Human Rights (IACommHR), among others, has underlined the importance that *all* the members of the community are provided with an effective opportunity to participate. See IACHR, Report No 75/02 (Case 11.140, Mary and Carrie Dann (United States), 27 December 2002) para 140. Both the UN Expert Mechanism on the Rights of Indigenous Peoples and the IACommHR have particularly underscored the duty of states to guarantee the participation of indigenous women in both internal and external decision-making processes and institutions. See UN Expert Mechanism on the Rights of Indigenous Peoples, 'Final Study on Indigenous Peoples and the Right to Participate in Decision-Making' (26 May 2011) para 36; IACommHR, 'Indigenous Peoples, Afro-Descendent Communities, and Natural Resources: Human Rights Protection in the Context of Extraction, Exploitation, and Development Activities' (2015) OEA/Ser.L/V/II Doc 47/15, para 211.

increase the quality of decisions and facilitate their domestic implementation, and a 'democratic' approach, that, in today's more broadly accepted version, looks at the contribution of NSAs in terms of increased inclusiveness and pluralism of decision-making.

Looking at the practice of NSAs' involvement in the Convention's governing bodies, the foregoing analysis has revealed the shortcomings that may result from a strict implementation of the 'functionalist' approach to participatory governance. A review of the list of those attending the meetings of the Convention's bodies indicates that, by design or in their implementation, existing functionalist-oriented rules have worked to the detriment of the Convention's ambitions of promoting pluralism and fostering the diversity of cultural expressions.

It is argued here that these shortcomings may in part be remedied through a set of reforms inspired by the 'democratic' approach to participation. As a result, the Conventions' policy-deliberation and decision-making processes will be open not only to those actors that add value in terms of experience and expertise, but also to those entities that, because of the values or interests they embody, can enhance the pluralism of such processes through the vocalisation of ideas, opinions and concerns that would otherwise risk being unheard therein.

The 'democratic' approach is, however, flawed in that it does not challenge the centrality of states in international governance, and consequently upholds a narrow understanding of NSAs' status therein. Therefore, a proposal is made to include international human rights law as a complementary means of shaping non-state participation in the Convention, by looking at such participation as a way of realising the right to take part in cultural life, as set out in several international instruments and the practice of relevant monitoring bodies. This would imply, on the one hand, a shift from the current system of accreditation towards more unrestricted ways of accessing and influencing policy-deliberation and decision-making by all concerned stakeholders, and on the other hand, the recognition of varying degrees of access and involvement in the Convention's processes, including free, prior and informed consent, at least when vulnerable communities, particularly indigenous peoples, are affected.

While apparently competing, the three theoretical approaches to participation that have been taken into consideration here – the 'functionalist', the 'democratic' and the 'human rights-based' – are not mutually exclusive. In practice, they may be variously combined to design tailored participatory arrangements, according to the different characters of the international fora where participation takes place, the different nature of participants, and the different types of contribution that they seek (or are expected) to make to policy-deliberation and decision-making processes.

Indeed, the legitimacy of NSAs' involvement in international governance can be ascribed to the fact that they provide information and technical skills, to their aptitude for vocalising values, concerns and interests that would otherwise risk being neglected, or to their own right to take part in decision-making, as defined by international human rights law. Emphasis on experience and expertise does not necessarily run counter to democracy or human rights, provided that participants are not strictly selected according to these requirements. Increased pluralism and broader participatory rights do not necessarily put at risk the efficiency of decision-making processes, provided that effective devices are adopted to keep the number of participants manageable (by, for example, promoting coalition-building among stakeholders), to promote consensus-building and to prevent stalemates (by, for example, providing for the views of those who are most affected by a decision to prevail when everyone's consent is not reachable[51]).

It is only if understood and operationalised by integrating these three different approaches that NSAs' participation can promote the adoption of more practical, equitable, and ultimately effective decisions, both within and beyond the field of cultural governance.

[51] ILA Interim Report (n 4) para 73.

2

The 2005 UNESCO Convention as an Instrument for International Cooperation: The Example of Networks of Cultural Cooperation

ANNA STEINKAMP AND MATINA MAGKOU

I. Introduction

Cooperation is at the very heart of the UNESCO Convention on the Protection and Promotion of the Diversity of Cultural Expressions (CDC, or the Convention)[1] – not only when it comes to the Convention's values, objectives or content, but also regarding its genesis, its implementation and especially its operating architecture. Several articles of the Convention explicitly emphasise cooperation as key to reaching the Convention's objectives (Articles 12–15). Recognising the sovereign right of states to maintain, adopt and implement policies to protect and promote the diversity of cultural expression, both nationally and internationally, the CDC supports governments and civil society in finding policy solutions for emerging challenges. Cooperation is needed at various levels: among parties to the Convention (international level), within the parties' country cultural ecosystem (national level), and with private stakeholders and civil society. All these different cooperation levels are key for fulfilling the Convention's complex objectives.

At the civil society level, networks – by definition, one of the most cooperative organisational forms of our time – have been present and active from the very beginning of the CDC process. Besides the important role of international and regional networks during the genesis of the CDC, networks also play a key role in filling the Convention with life. Accordingly, this chapter advocates for a strong, competent and skilled civil society, as the protection and promotion of the diversity of cultural expressions regards not only state players, but also – among others – artists, consumers and cultural producers. Otherwise, the implementation of the

[1] (adopted 20 October 2005, entered into force 18 March 2007) 2440 UNTS 311.

Convention would remain at a governmental level only and the concept of liberty and freedom enshrined in the Preamble of the Convention would be just empty words.

As civil society players are often organised as networks, the present chapter will first examine the specificities of networks and their presence at the cultural cooperation level internationally. The second part of the chapter will focus – through a multiple case study approach[2] – on networks that have emerged around the globe due the Convention's existence. It will demonstrate how they become drivers of the Convention and of cultural cooperation themselves. The case studies presented are informed by the direct involvement and observation capacity of one of the authors in them, as well as additional desk research.

Finally, the last part discusses the accentuated role that cultural networks have acquired during and following the COVID-19 pandemic. The pandemic brought to the surface the vulnerability of the artistic and cultural sector, but also gave an opportunity for solidarity and joint action. Cultural networks functioned as amplifiers of the concerns of artists, cultural and creative workers, institutions and entities. As such, their own raison d'être and own importance on the international level became clearer than ever before. The last part of this chapter is informed by desk research-based observations made during the first lockdown period following the outburst of the health crisis (spring/summer 2020).[3]

Consequently, this text mainly contributes to the literature about networks, especially international cultural networks, and more precisely their contribution to informed and participatory systems of governance for culture as ideated in the Convention. It is argued that cultural networks should be further strengthened to play their role as advocates, actors of change and catalysts for cooperation. The CDC provides a legitimate framework to reflect on their role as civil society actors and on what is needed for them to thrive, where they meet challenges and what their limitations are.

II. Networks as Catalysts of Action and Change in International Cultural Cooperation

Networks are not a new phenomenon, but they are at the core of societal constitution. However, networks appear more apposite nowadays than ever. Social networks are considered to be one of the most appropriate organisational forms of the twenty-first century, given their flexible, adaptable, non-hierarchical and open character.[4] In a world of disorder and uncertainty, they offer the opportunity to

[2] See RE Stake, *Multiple Case Study Analysis* (New York, Guilford Press, 2013).

[3] See ch 10 of this book, by Laurence Cuny.

[4] See M Castells, *The Rise of the Network Society. The Information Age: Economy, Society, and Culture*, vol I, 2nd edn (Chichester, Wiley, 2010) xvii.

combine efforts, quickly connect people and knowledge, and provide orientation, although they often struggle to sustain continuity. This section examines the role of networks as catalysts of action and change in international cultural cooperation by first looking into the organisational side of networks and then into their role in international cooperation.

Social networks can be boundless groupings of people and relationships or can be a more concrete form of how people organise themselves to achieve common goals. In a world of disorder and uncertainty, social networks offer orientation and coherence.[5] Yúdice considers networks necessary in order to bring social and political change to societies where more traditional forms of organisation fail.[6] In their organisational appearance, networks have proved especially suitable for international collaboration and for the resolution of complex problems inter alia because their main resource is knowledge. Beyond institutional boundaries, networks are more flexible, adaptive, non-hierarchical, quicker at making decisions and thus more effective.[7] However, networks are often like a phoenix – they appear suddenly and they disappear just as quickly, sometimes without having had a significant impact. Their success and failure are both a result of their unique characteristics.

From an organisational perspective, social networks can be characterised as flexible, adaptable, with little hierarchy and most commonly without heavy institutional structures. Further, their organisational architecture strengthens the incubator function of networks when it comes to exchanging knowledge, services or goods. Social networks can be temporary, informal or adopt light structures similar to institutions, such as featuring a coordinating entity. They can be local or be of global scope. In addition, they can comprise only a few participating entities and/or people or as many as a thousand. They can be business networks, policy networks or cultural networks. Their raisons d'être might be diverse, but their common denominator lies in the fact that a common goal, shared objectives or shared values can be better achieved through cooperation among participants within the framework of the network, which can also bring further benefits to them. Social networks, whatever shape they take, are all forms of coordination of action.[8]

[5] See F Boos, A Exner and B Heitger, 'Soziale Netzwerke sind anders' (1992) 11 *Organisationsentwicklung* 54.

[6] See G Yúdice, 'Sistemas y redes culturales: ¿cómo y para qué?', speech presented during the international symposium 'Políticas culturales urbanas: Experiencias europeas y americanas', Bogotá, 5–9 May 2003, www.brasiluniaoeuropeia.ufrj.br/es/pdfs/sistemas_y_redes_culturales_como_y_para_que.pdf.

[7] See R Keast et al, 'Network Structures: Working Differently and Changing Expectations' (2004) 64 *Public Administration Review* 363.

[8] See KG Provan and P Kenis, 'Modes of Network Governance: Structure, Management, and Effectiveness' (2008) 18 *Journal of Public Administration Research and Theory* 229.

The increasing organisation in and around networks in the professional context, be it in the economic, political or cultural field, can be explained by the growing 'task complexity in conjunction with time pressures'[9] and the general acceleration of life. These facts make traditional organisational forms such as hierarchically structured institutions appear heavy and slow in decision-making.[10] Networks thus offer the opportunity of working together beyond traditional and especially geographical boundaries, and allow for quick transmission of relevant knowledge and information in resource- and cost-efficient synergies. Put another way, networks are especially practical when resources, eg people, are widely spread. Regarding the social aspects, networks provide their participants or members with orientation, affiliation and access to influence on matters they care about, while at the same time leaving enough space for their individual identity.[11]

The rapid increase of networks in the last two decades is a direct result of, as well as an answer to, globalisation. Globalisation is understood here as a 'container term' for various global phenomena, such as acceleration, climate change, social exclusion, poverty, technological progress, especially in the field of information and communication technologies (ICT), or political challenges, that can overwhelm the reach of national governments. Networks can navigate more easily in this globalised world because they are quicker, lighter, more flexible and more adaptive than traditional institutions. The latter are slowed down by their hierarchical structure, eg when it comes to decision-making. It is assumed that networks are generally the most suitable form of organisation and governance in the twenty-first century, especially for international cooperation.

International collaboration is one of the answers to the current demands of the societal, environmental, cultural, political and economic challenges facing us. The nation-state, as useful and meaningful as it was in the past and remains so in some areas to this day, can no longer handle these challenges alone, but must depend on the cooperation of new partners, such as civil society, the private sector or intergovernmental structures.[12] International cooperation and exchange are considered to be tools for innovation. Their innovative aspect is built upon diversity – diversity of people, perspectives, knowledge and resources.

International cooperation also takes shape in the so-called third sector, or civil society, non-governmental organisations, foundations, policy networks, etc. It mostly does not involve economic cooperation with clear monetary benefits, but is considered a tool and platform for exchange. International cooperation is especially about partnerships among state institutions and private and non-profit sectors across borders. Regardless of where and how it takes place, international

[9] See C Jones, WS Hesterly and SP Borgatti, 'A General Theory of Network Governance: Exchange Conditions and Social Mechanisms' (1997) 22 *The Academy of Management Review* 911, 921.

[10] See Boos, Exner, and Heitger, 'Soziale Netzwerke' (1992) 54.

[11] ibid 55–56.

[12] See Yúdice, 'Sistemas' (2003)l H Willke, *Smart Governance: Governing the Global Knowledge Society* (Frankfurt/Main, Campus Verlag, 2007) 8.

cooperation is about jointly achieving a common goal or interest. Ideally, international cooperation takes place on an equal footing between all of the partners involved. Hence, it can clearly be distinguished from development assistance.

International networks are therefore located in this context, together with a variety of other stakeholders. The interplay with other actors and the possible influence or impact on the environment of a specific network must be considered when talking about their role as catalysts and actors of change. Often networks are not as well equipped, in terms of human, financial and infrastructural resources, as other, bigger players of international cooperation. However, their benefit is that they are internationally present, through their members or participants, which allows access to information and knowledge resources at an international level.

Networks of cultural cooperation are actors that collaborate around the notion of culture. Culture here is understood in its broadest sense: it encompasses the arts, but also mentalities, lifestyles and 'value systems'.[13] Hence, at their core, networks of cultural cooperation spread knowledge to showcase and promote cultural diversity and often also to safeguard cultural heritage. This happens based on the assumption that cultural exchange enhances peace, solidarity and mutual understanding among different cultural groups and/or communities. Moreover, the recognition of culture and the promotion of culture contribute crucially to sustainable development – because of the richness of approaches, mental models and mindsets, solutions, processes, and knowledge and know-how possible in this world.

International cultural networks are also social change networks that 'undertake actions that have a (potential) impact in society by bringing people into an action-oriented framework. These actions could be directed to governments, the private sector or to the public at large.'[14] Brun et al argue that networks are especially convenient for artists, cultural experts and activists since 'the cultural field has been categorised for a while by its aversion against frontiers of all kind, the network channels this energy'.[15]

International networks of cultural cooperation can take various forms. They are constituted as informal working groups, forums, associations, federations or alliances, and often do not use the term 'network' in their name. Further, to distinguish networks from other kinds of organisational forms, networks do not feature hierarchical or heavily bureaucratic structures. They are dynamic, decentralised systems, yet have a coordinating node that acts as facilitator. Their origin is justified through the joint will to achieve one or various shared objectives. What is specific to networks of international cultural cooperation, however,

[13] See UNESCO, 'Mexico City Declaration on Cultural Policies' in *World Conference on Cultural Policies, Mexico City, 26 July–6 August 1982: Final Report* (Paris, UNESCO, 1982).

[14] See P van Paaschen, 'Cultural Networks – How to Assess?' in B Cvjetičanin (ed), *Networks: The Evolving Aspects of Culture in the 21st Century* (Zagreb, Institute for International Relations. Culturelink Network, 2011) 160.

[15] See J Brun, JB Tejero and P Canut Ledo, *Redes culturales: claves para sobrevivir en la globalización* (Madrid, Agencia Española de Cooperación Internacional para el Desarrollo, 2008) 83.

is that participating people and/or entities come from diverse countries and are aware of the importance of recognising and respecting their cultural differences and cultural diversity. Hence, it can be assumed that intercultural competence in networks of cultural cooperation is more widespread than in other kinds of networks,[16] and thus these networks are able to 'work in multiculturality' while at the same time working towards the objective of fostering intercultural communication and understanding.[17]

As already mentioned, networks of cultural cooperation are building upon diversity – diversity of members, diversity of cultures, diversity of approaches.[18] Consequently, and in accordance with their dynamic structure, they ensure their own potential for innovation.[19] Due to their international scope, these networks build their work internally and externally largely on ICT. Moreover, the quality of the relationships within the network and the external relationships of the network depend on the information and knowledge that 'circulates' among the involved parties, as well as their capacity to 'capture and redistribute' this information and knowledge.[20] Networks of cultural cooperation are all about knowledge and communication.

The above-described characteristics of networks, and especially of networks of cultural cooperation, shed light on the reasons why networks are catalysts of action: they bring together diverse kinds of people with different kinds of professional, personal and cultural backgrounds, which again create an ideal setting for collective action. As innovation and thinking out of the box are inherent to the arts and culture sector, this becomes especially real for networks in the field of cultural cooperation, and is another element that helps one to understand the role of networks as incubators.

This collective action often results in new impetus for international debates that ultimately might result in change. This makes the role of such networks even more interesting to explore in relation to the CDC, where cooperation and the respect and promotion of diversity are part of its DNA.

III. International Networks Around the CDC

Besides the close relationship of networks to the Convention as described above, the CDC has been a catalyst for the creation and work of some major international cultural networks. These networks were established thanks to the Convention, with the aim to implement it and/or spread its message into sectors, regions or communities that it had not yet reached.

[16] See Cvjetičanin, *Networks: The Evolving Aspects of Culture in the 21st Century*, 262.
[17] See Brun et al, *Redes culturales* (2008) 107.
[18] See van Paaschen, 'Cultural Networks' (2011) 160.
[19] See Brun et al, *Redes culturales* (2008) 51.
[20] ibid.

These networks play diverse roles in relation to the CDC. They are themselves platforms, tools and a result of international cooperation. At the same time, they represent different arts sectors, cultural associations or professional groups, and advocate their interests, thus they also become political stakeholders of the CDC. But especially, they play a crucial role in the cooperative architecture of the Convention.

Therefore, this part of the chapter presents some selected practices of these networks and their contribution to the implementation of the Convention at international level and on the ground – to make the role of networks more evident. The following three networks have been chosen as they were founded because of and/or thanks to the Convention: the International U40 Network 'Cultural Diversity 2030'; the International Federation of Coalitions for Cultural Diversity; and the Culture2030 Campaign. These three networks are of particular relevance and interest as their visions are very close to the Convention's values and ideas. Another reason is the personal component: one of the authors took active part in different stages of the life of these networks. Accordingly, the following analysis follows a participative observation approach to complement the desk research analysis.

A. International U40 Network 'Cultural Diversity 2030'

The International U40 Network 'Cultural Diversity 2030' (hereinafter U40 Network) idea was born with the ambition to give a voice to young experts (aged under 40) in the implementation of cultural policies and the promotion of the CDC. Initiated by the German Commission for UNESCO in 2007, the U40 Network has become an independent civil society network. It represents a concrete step towards the implementation of the Convention, by stimulating debates and ideas to better formulate cultural policies for cultural diversity around the world.

The network consists of young professionals from across the world involved in the field of cultural policies – experts, researchers, civil servants, cultural managers, graduate students, etc who believe in the power of cultural diversity. The network believes that members are stronger together and can make their voices heard through this civil society platform. Through awareness-raising activities, advocacy, knowledge and good practice exchange, the network aims to breathe life into the CDC. On top of the U40 Network, a series of U40 subgroups have been active in different parts of the world to better address local, national and regional issues and to foster regional cooperation in the cultural sector.

One of its main achievements, besides integrating young people into the debate around the Convention, is the first ever compilation of good practices on how to implement such a complex tool as the CDC in the arts and culture sector.[21]

[21] See A Sekhar and A Steinkamp (eds), *Mapping Cultural Diversity: Good Practices from Around the Globe. A Contribution to the Debate on the Implementation of the UNESCO Convention on the Protection and Promotion of the Diversity of Cultural Expressions* (Bonn, German Commission for UNESCO, 2010).

This publication was compiled by the young experts themselves and published in 2010. Received by the International Community during the December 2010 session of the Intergovernmental Committee of the Convention, it is a good example of how civil society networks, even loosely organised, can bring new impetus to the intergovernmental level.

Today, the U40 Network is active as an informal and self-organised network. Members are in touch as a group of like-minded people that became friends and colleagues for the sake of cultural diversity. As such, it is still interesting looking at some of its recent practices and initiatives to underline the impact of these organisations. One of these examples is the online seminar series on the CDC addressed at young, cultural, civil society actors in Latin America.[22] It was organised by one of the regional chapters, in cooperation with another international network.

A second example is an activity undertaken by the network in view of the global COVID-19 pandemic, which in early 2020 re-energised the network. This second example of what a network can achieve – even if only loosely organised – is the co-authoring of two articles[23] at the beginning of the pandemic: since late March 2020, the U40 Network has been regularly gathering online, discussing both the personal and professional implications of the global health crisis, as well as what some of the future implications for cultural diversity and related areas may be. The two articles gather views from network members on the early impact of the pandemic across several Asian, Latin American and European countries. The articles were shared publicly with wider audiences offering perspectives of professionals and practitioners – members of the network from all over the world. They are also evidence of how quick, non-bureaucratic, qualitative and well-informed data can be generated transnationally, trans-institutionally and trans-disciplinarily by civil society actors.

To conclude, the U40 Network remains a good example of how far a political instrument, such as the Convention, that stands for a certain set of objectives and values can become the binding element among a group of people spread over the whole globe. It demonstrates the convening but also cooperative power of the CDC.

B. International Federation of Coalitions for Cultural Diversity

The interconnectedness of global networks that have been mostly created during the negotiations process of the Convention is another aspect of this section. The

[22] See ch 3 of this book, by Launda Smith.

[23] See blog.transit.es/international-views-on-covid-19-and-cultural-diversity and blog.transit.es/cultural-diversity-civil-society-and-good-life-in-the-context-of-covi-19/?fbclid=IwAR2-MYgVOFCQxniTsemP4JzeQCJfwlCEaRwuCImkGU_2bzbSi4JdyoIqzec. See also ch 4 of this book, by Luanda Smith.

International Federation of Coalitions for Cultural Diversity (IFCCD), as a network of networks, is a relevant case when it comes to examining the role of networks as advocates, actors of change and catalysts for cooperation. Further, this example is interesting to make reference to, as IFCCD lost its primary cause – which was to facilitate cooperation and the development of common positions and actions to contribute to the 2005 Convention negotiations. Consequently, the network changed its mission as the Convention developed in order to first raise awareness about the need to adopt an international legal text on the diversity of cultural expressions, asking countries to ratify the instrument through targeted ratification campaigns, and further to monitor and accompany the implementation of the Convention from a civil society perspective. Thus, today, it is an enabler and coordinator of civil society efforts for the implementation of the UNESCO Convention and has evolved into 'a movement for the diversity of cultural expressions'.[24]

Today, it not only claims to be 'the voice of cultural professionals around the world',[25] but also provides relevant information digested from the international Convention level to those cultural professionals. This happens through its members, who bring together some 30 organisations representing creators, artists, independent producers, distributors, broadcasters and publishers in the book, film, television, music, live performance and visual arts sectors. Further, it actively contributes, together with other civil society networks, to the Civil Society Forum, which was established around the meetings of the organs of the Convention, including providing a joint civil society report that demonstrates how civil society directly contributes to the implementation of the CDC.[26]

To conclude, IFCCD is a good example of how networks can reinvent themselves when their cause or original purpose changes or dissolves and eventually become stronger through long-standing experience and visibility.

C. The Culture2030 Campaign

The third example of a culture cooperation network is the Culture2030 campaign. This initiative of networks is introduced to show why especially advocacy networks matter when it comes to linking different disciplines and communities, such as culture, cooperation and development – as does the CDC. It highlights how Article 13 'Integration of culture in sustainable development' can be put forward by civil society.

Culture2030 is the evolution of an initiative that was born when different cultural networks united in 2013 to launch a global campaign entitled #culture2015goal.

[24] See IFCCD, 'A Movement for the Diversity of Cultural Expressions' (2021) ficdc.org/wp-content/uploads/2021/10/Historique_FICDC_ENG_final.pdf.

[25] See ficdc.org/en.

[26] See UNESCO, 'Partnering with Civil Society' (2019) www.unesco.de/sites/default/files/2020-07/partnering_with_civil_society_2020.pdf.

Its aim at that time was to position culture as a pillar within the 2030 Agenda for Sustainable Development. The main rationale behind this mobilisation was that without culture explicitly being mentioned in the Sustainable Development Goals, it would not be possible for actors at different levels to elaborate policies and provide funds for initiatives, projects and actions that recognise culture as a driver and enabler of sustainable development. With the now ongoing implementation of the 2030 Agenda, the campaign remained active and evolved into #culture2030goal – aimed at achieving a stronger place for culture throughout the implementation of the Agenda, at incorporating culture as a distinct goal in the post-2030 development agenda and finally adopting a global agenda for culture.

The campaign advocates culture to be recognised when it comes to sustainable development, which is directly linked to the CDC. It is an example of networks joining forces and voices for a specific global cause – and also when external circumstances make it necessary: in 2020, the campaign released a 'Statement on Culture and the Covid-19 Pandemic'[27] to advocate for culture to be a part of the response to the global pandemic.

To conclude, the above-mentioned three networks serve as examples of how a policy document such as the CDC has served as an enabler of international cultural cooperation and a mobiliser of stakeholders globally. They highlight the multiplier effect of how a gathering of people and/or entities around a common goal, a shared narrative and a network structure – be it a loose or a more systematic one – can voice wider concerns and formulate the needs of the sector from an inclusive and diverse standpoint. This potential becomes even more important in times of crisis, such as the one provoked by the COVID-19 pandemic.

IV. Cultural Networks and the CDC in Times of Pandemic

This section expands on what have been the reactions of a number of cultural networks during the pandemic. In general, the COVID-19 health crisis put into question all activities in the field of arts and culture. And networks did not escape this. Hence, this section shares observations from cultural network activities to highlight their resilience especially developed during the first months of the COVID-19 pandemic. It should be noted that information included here refers only to the first wave of reactions until mid-2020, although further reactions and positions have been taken ever since.

Although the cultural sector has reacted all over the world in regard to the situation with COVID-19, the focus here is placed on reactions of European cultural networks for two main reasons: first, cultural networks in the European setting 'are

[27] See culture2030goal.net/?page_id=52.

far more institutionalized and count with greater access to funding'[28] than in other continents; and second, the EU has played an important role in the CDC as the protection and promotion of the diversity of cultural expressions is a key feature of the European construction itself and a legal competence is conferred on the EU when it comes to external relations.[29] The COVID-19 setting provides a framework to illustrate the importance of the Convention and the role that cultural networks can play in ensuring that its principles are taken into consideration, explicitly or implicitly, by relevant stakeholders when it comes to policymaking and action.

First of all, the complexity of the effects caused by COVID-19 on the arts and cultural sector required measurement. The need for exchanging, analysing and disseminating information on the diversity of cultural expressions has been recognised in Article 19 CDC. A first observation that can be drawn is that cultural networks were among the first organisations that took various initiatives in this direction, nurturing the work of international organisations and research institutions, as well as national, regional and local governments.

There were a considerable number of sectorial surveys in this respect. The Network of European Museum Organisations (NEMO),[30] the International Network for Contemporary Performing Arts (IETM),[31] the European Confederation of Conservator/Restorers,[32] the European Dancehouse Network,[33] the European Music Council,[34] Circostrada[35] and the Creative Hubs Network[36] are just some examples of organisations that launched surveys among their membership to learn about their concerns during this specific period of time.

The sectors that were most heavily impacted by the crisis, such as live performance and museums, were among those that mobilised the most in this direction. This rush in data collection to capture the collateral effects of the pandemic as it unfolded reveals the sectors' need to self-assess, self-measure and adapt in such unpredictable times. It also shows the willingness to take evidence-based actions, the connectedness and the willingness to talk to each other.[37]

However, the scientific quality of those surveys is open to question, and they can be considered a missed opportunity to use homogeneous data collection mechanisms across several sectors in order to have comparable results. Nevertheless, the surveys still reveal and once more confirm the role that cultural networks can play

[28] See M Delfin, 'The Promise of Cultural Networks in Latin America: Towards a Research Framework for the Study of Region-Specific Cultural Network Ecosystems' (2012) 21 *Cultural Trends* 239, 239.

[29] See V Bohnenblust, 'The EU's Representation at the UNESCO and the 2005 Convention on the Protection and Promotion of the Diversity of Cultural Expressions' (2017) ssrn.com/abstract=3033204.

[30] See www.ne-mo.org.

[31] See www.ietm.org/en.

[32] See www.ecco-eu.org.

[33] See www.ednetwork.eu.

[34] See www.emc-imc.org.

[35] See www.circostrada.org/en.

[36] See creativehubs.net.

[37] F Imperiale et al, 'Cultural and Creative Industries in Pandemic Times: Preliminary Understandings' (2021) *Economia, Aziende e Sviluppo* (special issue) 5.

in engaging actors in different geographical localities and initiating such a wide engagement. Information gathering was key during this period to achieve a better understanding of what was happening – and was also the only way of staying in touch and active.

More importantly, during the first months of the global health crisis, cultural networks in Europe acted as amplifiers of the concerns and claims of the cultural sector and its professionals. Culture Action Europe (CAE),[38] the network by definition working on advocacy for arts and culture on the European level, issued a joint paper together with the European Cultural Foundation[39] at the beginning of May 2020. The main points it addressed included the need to find solutions to help multi-stakeholder partnerships maintain their solidarity and to match public and private resources to further each solution's impact – very much in line with Articles 14 and 15 of the UNESCO Convention, which underlined the need to find such a balance within future EU programmes, such as Horizon Europe 2021–2027. More specifically, in the paper there was a direct plea to include cultural and creative industries in the economic, social and environmental recovery plans within the Multiannual Financial Framework 2021–2027, in particular earmarking 7% of the Recovery Fund for culture.

The above-mentioned network IETM also engaged in advocacy, focusing on both short- and long-term claims for the performing arts sector. Its main concern was to guarantee a continuous income for those working in the sector. A further concern included maintaining the sector's sustainability through specific and clear social distancing measures for venues and public performance spaces in order to sustain the creation and distribution of artistic work. IETM also underlined the need to reconsider the way performing arts collaborate and engage with audiences and introduce new, sustainable and environmentally friendly models. Furthermore, in the early days of the outbreak, the social partners in the field of live performance[40] call upon governments to adopt emergency measures that may adequately support the sustainability of the live performance sector in that unique situation, protecting the safety, but equally the livelihood, regardless of their contractual status, of the cultural workers who rely on these shows and events to earn a living. These efforts bring to mind Article 8 of the Convention on measures to protect cultural expressions on special situations.

Another element that is interesting is the effort invested in imagining the 'new normal'. NEMO, for example, by publishing its preliminary results, which reported on a digital momentum for museums who are expanding their online services, live content, podcasts, virtual tours, etc, highlighted several situations where museums were coping with the pandemic and what kind of future investments in the sector

[38] See cultureactioneurope.org.

[39] Culture Action Europe and European Cultural Foundation, 'The Future of Culture and Creative Sectors in Post-COVID-19 Europe' (2020) cultureactioneurope.org/files/2020/05/CAE-ECFstatement Post-COVID-19Europe.pdf.

[40] IAEA and Pearle, 'Covid19: State of Emergency in the Live Performance Sector!' (2020) ec.europa.eu/social/BlobServlet?mode=dsw&docId=12004&langId=en.

should be put into place. The European Institutes of Culture network[41] reflected on how hybrid, new and inclusive ways could be used to adapt cultural relations to the digital realm.

Finally, it should be underlined that the COVID-19 pandemic has also given a unique opportunity for cooperation between networks themselves. For example, under the coordination of CAE, in March 2020, cultural networks addressed a letter to the European Commission on the effect of COVID-19, underlying the challenges imposed by COVID-19 on the implementation of Creative Europe projects and making a number of proposals on how to cope with the consequences of COVID-19 in the cultural and creative industries. Also, the European Network on Cultural Management and Policy initiated a think-tank bringing various networks together to exchange ideas and to work together towards finding solutions for the new environment.

V. The Future Role of Culture Networks

Considering its content, all this advocacy work is itself in the spirit of the CDC. The examples presented highlight the crucial role of civil society actors in speaking out loud where and when 'it hurts', and thus giving crucial hints to the political class to set up adequate support mechanisms. Even if the Convention is not explicitly mentioned in the statements, its principles are reflected in them. Most importantly, they address Member States and other institutional stakeholders that are party to the CDC, committed to fulfilling what is described in the Convention.

As UNESCO's guide to ResiliArt for Mondiacult mentions, the COVID-19 crisis had an alarming effect on the creative economy, but 'what hides in plain sight is the threat against cultural diversity'.[42] This also explains how UNESCO has been active in putting forward the need to support artists and ensure access to culture for all through the global ResiliArt movement. ResiliArt started as a series of virtual discussions, even beyond the first months after the health crisis, that gathered together cultural industry professionals to focus on the impact of COVID-19 on the creative economy. Today, it has evolved into a permanent participatory consultative mechanism involving civil society, which is invited to participate actively in the preparation of the UNESCO World Conference on Cultural Policies and Sustainable Development (Mondiacult, Mexico City 2022).

Some initial reflections on the above-mentioned reactions of some cultural networks point to a shared understanding that the COVID-19 outbreak was a unique moment for cultural networks. On this line, two main observations lead to the following conclusions.

[41] See eunic.eu.

[42] See UNESCO, 'Your Guide to ResiliArt for Mondiacult' (2022) en.unesco.org/sites/default/files/resiliart_x_mondiacult_en.pdf.

First, investing in the capacity of cultural networks for self-organisation and self-reflection: established and less established cultural networks organised themselves to share their concerns and their hesitations on how to move forward, but also their determination to imagine the day after and to start working towards it. Loose and informal cultural networks became more active. More established networks were exposed to processes using (more) participatory mechanisms, of going back to listening to the needs of their members and creating spaces for exchange, of solidarity, of advocacy action and of joining forces. There is a continuous need for connection and an effort to reinvent ways of doing without considering a physical meeting as a prerequisite, something that international cultural networks know well already.

Second, the importance of the advocacy capacity of networks: at a time when solutions needed to be reached on the political level, the voices of the sector asking to place arts and culture at the heart of the recovery mechanisms at international, EU and national level and to adapt current and future funding programmes to this new scenario were heard widely beyond the cultural sector. All networks shared the fear that if no concrete, reasonable, evidence-based and sector (and subsector) specific actions and measures are taken, this might weaken the entire cultural ecosystem. This becomes even more important in a setting which, as Karima Bennoune, UN Special Rapporteur in the field of cultural rights, mentioned, requires a pan-normative approach which takes into consideration the indivisibility and interdependence of all human rights, including cultural rights.[43] Therefore, further action is needed to guarantee that cultural networks have the means and tools to fulfil their role as stakeholders of the CDC.

Although this chapter focuses on the role of networks with regard to the Convention, a systematic capturing of the networks' direct influences in cultural policy design is still missing. Further research should look at the direct links between cultural networks and policy-making using a results-based approach in the long-term post-COVID-19 period, considering how far the CDC provides a conceptual framework for action.

VI. Conclusion

Cultural networks – whether formal or informal – have been evolving into decisive actors in cultural management, policy and cooperation, contributing to the creation of communities of practice and an emancipated civil society. The CDC has been a catalyst especially for cultural networks at the international level – where

[43] See Karima Bennoune, UN Special Rapporteur in the Field of Cultural Rights, 'Cultural Rights in the Face of the COVID-19 Crisis', speech given at the International Congress of the Cultural and Creative Industries, Mexico, October 2020, www.ohchr.org/Documents/Issues/CulturalRights/Activities/Cultural_creative_industries_congress.docx.

joint action was needed, starting with the CDC's negotiation process and continuing even today, contributing to and monitoring the implementation process. These networks interfere at various levels of the CDC's implementation – as observatories, cooperation partners, initiators etc – and their role is important for various key articles of the Convention (Articles 9 and 11–15).

Rooted in common goals and values, they provide opportunities for interaction and contact among their members, and contribute to the creation of communities of practice. Especially in the European arena, cultural networks, with their 'non-hierarchical, dynamic, unpredictable, somehow anarchic and democratic nature', have contributed to an exceptional space of bottom-up cultural cooperation.[44] The COVID-19 crisis provoked a number of discussions at different levels and did not leave cultural networks indifferent. It is still a period of resetting that will leave a mark on the way cultural networks will be governed, on what they will do and how they will do it. Right now, we can only observe these processes, as the long-term consequences are yet to be revealed. The CDC can also serve as a lighthouse to the work of networks and networks can amplify the CDC, as the Convention gives orientation and structure, eg through statutory meetings, international standard setting or topics and research of global interest, as the latest presented 2022 Global Report, *Re|Shaping Policies for Creativity*,[45] does. At the same time, networks are a connection to and reflection of the cultural scene, and what matters or is at stake, eg at grassroots level, voicing the needs and aspirations of a sector, especially in times of crisis.

[44] See MA DeVlieg, 'Thoughts on European Cultural Networks, 1992–2016' (18 March 2016) 1, https://cultureactioneurope.org/download/?filename=/files/2016/02/MA-to-cultural-networks-CAE-03-2016-10225165.pdf.

[45] See UNESCO, *Re|shaping Policies for Creativity: Addressing Culture as a Global Public Good* (Paris, UNESCO, 2022).

3

Promoting the Objectives and Principles of the 2005 UNESCO Convention Among Latin American Civil Society: Challenges for Spanish Speakers. A Case Approach

LUANDA SMITH

I. Introduction: Linguistic Diversity, Cultural Diversity and the UNESCO CDC

> If you talk to a man in a language he understands, that goes to his head. If you talk to him in his language, that goes to his heart.
>
> Nelson Mandela[1]

The core function of language is to express identity. However, efficient communication is needed to achieve consensus in an interconnected and globalised reality, particularly in the multilateral arena. In the words of Judith Munat,

> those who wish to navigate in international waters must have at least a basic command of English. It is the language of air traffic control, of the worldwide web, of computer technology, of diplomacy, and much more. While some of us may question the legitimacy of that primacy and stubbornly insist that our own national idiom is to be protected from the infiltration of insidious foreign terminology, we are nonetheless forced to succumb to this dominance and learn English – unless we choose to be accompanied by a costly personal interpreter when we venture into foreign environments.[2]

In 2019, at the 74th session of the United Nations (UN) General Assembly, 2021 was declared the International Year of Creative Economy for Sustainable Development.[3]

[1] After C Bwenge, 'Orality and Advertisement: Swahili Proverbs in Mobile Phone Service Ads in Tanzania' in A Akinyemi and T Falola (eds), *The Palgrave Handbook of African Oral Traditions and Folklore* (Cham, Palgrave Macmillan, 2021) 850.

[2] J Munat, 'English as a Vehicular Language: A Case of Globalization or Linguistic Imperialism?' in AK Isaacs (ed), *Languages and Identities in Historical Perspective* (Pisa, Università di Pisa, 2005).

[3] unctad.org/es/node/27659.

In this context, and in sight of the undeniable impact of the pandemic caused by SARS-CoV-2 on the cultural sector, the inequities lived by cultural professionals worldwide became more visible. Moreover, the main concerns addressed in the 1980 Recommendation concerning the Status of the Artist are still to be solved. Governments still have to address the impact of fair trade, cultural industries in the digital environment, the diversity of cultural content, algorithms and artificial intelligence, as well as recognising that cultural and creative professionals and artists, particularly in Latin America, were struggling to defend their economic, social and cultural rights long before the health crisis struck in 2020. But to carry out governance mechanisms for civil society (CS) and professionals in the creative and cultural sector to achieve the United Nations' Sustainable Development Goals 2030 (SDGs), all stakeholders have the right to have information or any capacity building needed in their own language.

The Preamble of the UNESCO Convention on the Protection and Promotion of the Diversity of Cultural Expressions (CDC)[4] recalls that 'linguistic diversity is a fundamental element of cultural diversity', and reaffirms 'the fundamental role that education plays in the protection and promotion of cultural expressions'.[5] But CS participation in the mechanisms of the CDC is limited by the working languages, English and French. From attending statutory meetings of the governing bodies or CS Forums to writing CS activities reports and from using the CS format for national quadrennial periodic reports (QPR) or applying to the International Fund for Cultural Diversity (IFCD), there is a lack of capacity building, particularly in the Spanish language, to help one to fully understand the principles and objectives of the CDC to support and reinforce the creative and cultural ecosystems at a local level.

When we talk about the diversity of cultural expressions, we cannot ignore linguistic diversity. Language is one of the primary and most essential components of identity and, therefore, diversity worldwide. The inherent characteristics in each language, endowed and nourished by the symbols, stories, knowledge and emotions of each society, foster understanding of other languages, of other peoples, themselves becoming forms of cultural cooperation and promoters of the culture of peace that has existed throughout history. In the case of the Spanish language, of the 21 countries in three continents that have it as their official language, 19 are from the American continent.[6] In addition to language, Argentina, Bolivia, Chile, Colombia, Costa Rica, Cuba, Ecuador, El Salvador, Guatemala, Honduras, Mexico, Nicaragua, Panama, Uruguay, Peru, Puerto Rico, Dominican Republic, Uruguay and Venezuela all share as a characteristic an enormous diversity of cultural expressions within their territories, with their own logics and stakeholders. This chapter seeks to address linguistic diversity from the experience of the Creatividad

[4] (adopted 20 October 2005, entered into force 18 March 2007) 2440 UNTS 311.
[5] 14th recital, Preamble.
[6] oei.int/oficinas/secretaria-general/lenguas-en-numeros/espanol-y-portugues-en-el-mundo.

y Cultura Glocal AC (CyCGlocal) Mexican Civil Society Organization, as an observer of the governing bodies since 2021, with regard to how networking and capacity-building mechanisms for Spanish speakers in Latin America are needed to make their voices and proposals heard on the international stage to strengthen regional representation within the framework of the good governance and implementation of the CDC.

II. Civil Society Participation in the Implementation of the CDC

Civil society (CS) is as diverse as languages in the world. Artists and cultural professionals deal with specific needs, depending on the region, and struggle with different obstacles and challenges at the local level. However, no matter the differences, the cultural sector worldwide also has a watchdog role that ideally should lead to monitoring the impact of public policies, and being actively involved in policy-making through problem-solving and solution-building processes. Therefore, civil society organisations (CSOs), as stakeholders, should be prepared to link with other local, national and international CSOs, different levels of government at and multilateral agencies.

In this regard, the innovative inclusion of Article 11 of the CDC, on participation of CS, acknowledges the fundamental role of CS in protecting and promoting the diversity of cultural expressions, and that state parties should encourage CS's active participation therein. This obligation is reflected in the categories of participants in the statutory meetings of the governing bodies: member states of the Intergovernmental Committee for the Protection and Promotion of the Diversity of Cultural Expressions (Committee); parties to the Convention that are not members of the Committee; state members of UNESCO that are not parties to the Convention; intergovernmental organisations; and non-governmental organisations. In this last category can be included CSOs.

Even before the CDC was adopted, CSOs, particularly coalitions of cultural professionals, worked together to raise their voices and brought their insights to achieving policies that fully addressed the diversity of cultural content in trade agreements. One relevant example of this is the International Liaison Committee of Coalitions for Cultural Diversity (ILC), created in 2003 at the Coalitions for Cultural Diversity's initiative to facilitate cooperation and the development of common positions and actions. In particular, the ILC encouraged the elaboration of the CDC by coordinating the participation of CS representatives and professionals from the cultural sector in international negotiation sessions.[7] After the CDC's

[7] International Federation of Coalitions for Cultural Diversity (IFCCD) ficdc.org/en/about/#a1.

ratification in September 2007, the ILC became the International Federation of Coalitions for Cultural Diversity (IFCCD). Since then, the IFCCD has coordinated CS efforts for the implementation of the CDC and to represent its voice on the two governing bodies, the Conference of Parties (COP)[8] and the Intergovernmental Committee (IGC).[9]

The process for the formalisation of CS participation as observers in the CDC's statutory meetings started in the second session of the COP in 2009, in which the operational guidelines on the role and participation of civil society were approved. These guidelines defined civil society as 'non-governmental organizations, non-profit organizations, professionals in the culture sector and associated sectors, groups that support the work of artists and cultural communities'.[10] Also, the guidelines state that CS plays an 'essential role in the implementation of the Convention' by bringing their concerns to public authorities, monitoring policies and serving as 'value-guardian and innovator', while contributing to transparency and accountability in governance.[11]

One interesting issue to add is that, despite the fact that the definition of CS does not consider the private sector, it was already represented, as micro-, small- and medium-sized cultural and creative enterprises are often members of coalitions through sectoral associations.

A. Working Languages and Representation at Statutory Meetings

The criteria and steps provided for CS participation in statutory meetings of the CDC's governing bodies[12] state that attending CSOs must have interests and activities in one or more of the fields covered by the Convention; must have a legal status in compliance with the established rules of the jurisdiction in the country of registration; and must be representative of their respective field of activity, or of the respective social or professional groups they represent. This standard has great

[8] 'The *Conference of Parties* is the plenary decision-making body and meets every two years. The Conference of Parties includes all signatory Parties and makes key management, operational and strategic decisions' (en.unesco.org/creativity/governance/governing-bodies).

[9] 'The *Intergovernmental Committee* works under the authority of the Conference of Parties to promote and implement the Convention. Twenty-four Parties from all regions of the world, elected for a four-year term by the Conference of Parties, meet on an annual basis to ensure that the implementation of the Convention remains relevant in a constantly evolving world. On the request of the Conference of Parties, the Intergovernmental Committee can also develop and revise Operational Guidelines' (en.unesco.org/creativity/governance/governing-bodies.).

[10] 2 CP, Annex to Resolution 2.CP 7: Article 11 of the Convention. Operational Guidelines. Role and Participation of Civil Society (17 June 2009) UNESCO Doc CE/09/2.CP/210/Res.

[11] ibid.

[12] en.unesco.org/creativity/criteria-steps-civil-society-participation-sessions-conventions-governing-bodies.

relevance for and great impact on the participation of CS from different regions due to the diverse levels of challenges faced by a multiplicity of stakeholders, political contexts and capacity-building access. Added to these internal challenges, and following the same working lines as the UN Secretariat, the resolution from the second CDC COP in 2009 regarding the use of the working languages for the IGC was put in place:

> **Rule 40 Working languages**
>
> 40.1 The working languages of the Committee shall be English and French. Every effort shall be made, including through extra-budgetary funding, to facilitate the use of the other official languages of the United Nations as working languages.
>
> 40.2 Statements made at a meeting of the Committee in one of the working languages shall be interpreted into the other language.
>
> 40.3 Speakers may, however, speak in any other language, provided they make their own arrangements for interpretation of their statements into one of the working languages.
>
> 40.4 The documents of the Committee shall be issued simultaneously in English and French.[13]

This decision, of course, came with significant challenges for non-English or French native speakers. Even though both chosen working languages are widely used across the world, it limits the international advocacy of local and national CSOs despite their work at the national level. So far, the list of observers to the IGC and COP shows a low rate of Latin America CSOs participants. Concerned by this, CSO observers to the statutory meetings, including the IFCCD, CyCGlocal and the Chilean Coalition for Cultural Diversity, had identified that this low rate could be related to the working languages, but could also be due a lack of awareness of the CDC itself and its positive impact at the national level, and an absence of the financial resources needed to attend presential meetings at UNESCO headquarters. Despite the difficulties due to COVID-19 pandemic mobility restrictions, one positive side was that statutory meetings and the CS Forum had to be held online during 2021, allowing CSOs with no travel funds to participate, which was an excellent opportunity to open spaces to more CSOs worldwide. However, there is still no official decision on a hybrid format (presential–online) for statutory meetings in the upcoming years. Actually, in 2022, a registration process was started for a presential IGC, but it had to be changed to the online format again.

These phenomena affect the representation and regional knowledge sharing not only of Latin American CSOs, but also of stakeholders from other regions of the world with languages not considered as working languages or UN official ones, despite multilingualism being recognised as a core value of the organisation, which furthermore led to the appointment of a Coordinator for Multilingualism on

[13] 2 CP, Annex to Resolution 2.CP 6: Rules of Procedure of the Intergovernmental Committee for the Protection and Promotion of the Diversity of Cultural Expressions (17 June 2009) UNESCO Doc CE/09/2.CP/210/Res.

3 September 2019,[14] endorsed by the General Assembly in its Resolution 71/328[15] on multilingualism.

But what mechanisms have been put in place to raise awareness of the CDC principles and objectives in the local languages? Is there governmental support for CS participation, even those CSOs tied to anti-censorship advocacy? How can CS engagement in the implementation of the CDC be increased at the local, national and regional levels, and how can CS engage directly in the work of the Convention's governing bodies?

B. The Civil Society Forum: A Global Approach to Local Needs

In 2016, at its tenth session, IGC invited parties to the Convention, the Secretariat and CSOs to continue developing mechanisms to strengthen the participation of CS in the implementation of the Convention, notably through the organisation of a biennial forum (Decision 10.IGC 6).[16] The vision for this biennial event was to provide an interactive framework with an adaptable agenda to enable coordination amongst CS actors active in the fields covered by the CDC. The overarching goal was to give CS representatives a platform to share their experiences and discuss their common concerns, and to provide them with an opportunity to make proposals to the COP on issues or problems that they consider to be priorities and that they would like to see reflected in the work of the CDC's governing bodies. The CS Forum is held one day before the COP, so the recommendations gathered can be presented to the parties. The first edition of the CS Forum took place on 12 June 2017, the second on 3 June 2019 and the third on 31 May 2021. This last one was held online for the first time due to the sanitary restrictions caused by the COVID-19 pandemic, with 16 CSOs[17] working virtually in coordination with the CDC Secretariat, defining the coordination processes, concept note and activities, which included two plenary sessions and four breakout sessions.[18] As stated

[14] www.un.org/sg/en/multilingualism/index.shtml.

[15] UN General Assembly Resolution 71/328: Multilingualism (adopted on 11 September 2017) UN Doc A/RES/71/328.

[16] 10 IGC, Report on the Involvement of Civil Society in the Implementation of the Convention (10 November 2016) UNESCO Doc DCE/16/10.IGC/6.

[17] CSOs that volunteered to support the organisation of the third Civil Society Forum: AC Eurovisioni, Arterial Network, Coalición chilena por la diversidad cultural, Coalition française pour la diversité culturelle, Coalition malienne pour la diversité culturelle, Coligação portuguesa para la diversidade cultural, Contact Base, CyCGlocal, Cultural contra conflict, Culture et développement, Culture Funding Watch, International Federation of Coalitions for Cultural Diversity (IFCCD), International Council for Film, Television and Audiovisual Communication (ICFT), International Federation of Library Associations and Institutions (IFLA), International Music Council (IMC), International Theatre Institute (ITI).

[18] UNESCO, 'Third Civil Society Forum' (2021) en.unesco.org/creativity/sites/creativity/files/civil-society_forum_2021_en.pdf.

during the fourteenth IGC in February 2021, the coordination came from civil society representatives of CSO observers who volunteered to support the preparation of the Forum (Decision 14.IGC 15).[19] During the coordination meeting among the CSOs' coordination group and CDC Secretariat, the language barrier was addressed by representatives from the Arabic region and CyCGlocal. As a result, and after analysing available resources, interpretation into Spanish and Arabic was provided for the plenary session of the third CS Forum. However, this facility was not intended to be permanent. As stated by the CDC Secretariat, given the category of the event, the official working languages are English and French, but the interpretation facility into other languages can be renewed if funds are made available.

The recommendations elaborated by the CSOs to inform the future work plan of the IGC for 2022–23 addressed four topics: (i) culture and sustainable development; (ii) sustainable ecosystems in the cultural and creative sectors; (iii) CS participation in the monitoring and implementation of the CDC, as well as in the work of its governing bodies; and (iv) digital environment, rights and trade. The main findings related to CS participation produced recommendations such as:

To parties: to support the implementation of the CDC and CS participation at local and regional levels, notably by developing permanent programmes for information, training and networking platforms to support more structuring processes among CSOs and with parties; and to evaluate the possibility of creating a label for the support and recognition of projects at the local level that are aimed at the implementation of the CDC.

To parties and to the Secretariat: to recognise that CS has limited resources to make activity reports and to organise CS Forums (this needs to be taken into account especially since there is no formal feedback mechanism); to involve CS in research and analysis, including the chapter on civil society in the Global Report, based on calls for manifestations of interest; to give increased attention to the work of minorities and indigenous peoples in the implementation of the CDC, including by indigenous peoples' organisations, and explore links between the UN Declaration of the Rights of indigenous peoples; and to make available a database of CSOs that are observers to governing bodies, participating in their country's QPR, or IFCD beneficiaries, among others, so that they can communicate better and develop synergies.

To the IGC: to involve CS in the still important effort to be made to secure a broader ratification of the Convention; and to consider a proposed feasibility study on a new cooperation mechanism with micro-, small- and medium-sized cultural and creative enterprises (Decision 14.IGC 16),[20] and the proposed new partnerships

[19] 14 IGC, Decision 14.IGC 15: Collaboration with Civil Society to Implement the Convention (5 February 2021) UNESCO Doc DCE/21/14.IGC/Dec.

[20] 15 IGC, Feasibility Study on the Creation of a Regular Consultation Mechanism with Micro, Small and Medium-sized Cultural and Creative Enterprises Involved in the Implementation of the 2005 Convention on the Protection and Promotion of the Diversity of Cultural Expressions (7 February 2022) UNESCO Doc DCE/22/15.IGC/INF.9 REV.

with cultural institutions reflecting the fact that these segments are already represented in CSOs that participate in the work of the Convention's governing bodies. If necessary, parties could consider reviewing or clarifying the definition of civil society in the Operational Guidelines related to Article 11 to avoid confusion and to take into account evolutions since the adoption of the CDC.

One recommendation to UNESCO was to create opportunities for CS to contribute to the planning and implementation of the World Conference on Cultural Policies and Sustainable Development – MONDIACULT 2022, with the Mexican government as the host again 40 years after the first Mondiacult World Conference on Cultural Policies was held in Mexico City in 1982.[21] In order to open a space to cultural and creative stakeholders to share their experiences and perspectives on how to improve cultural policies in line with the SDGs, and in the context of the recovery process from the COVID-19 pandemic, the ResiliArt x Mondiacult dialogues were implemented, following the methodology of the ResiliArt movement. Another direct result of the recommendations of the third CS Forum was the invitation from the CDC Secretariat to the CSO observers of the governing bodies to participate as reviewers of Chapter 4 (on civil society) of the 2022 Global Report, *Re|Shaping Policies for Creativity*. Representatives from IFCCD, Eurovisioni, Cultura Contra Conflict, Culture Concepts and Culture and Development participated in the peer-review process, coordinated by CyCGlocal. They can be found as the CDC Civil Society Global Coordination Group in the section External Reviewers of the Global Report Team.[22]

C. The Glocal Normal: English and French as Working Languages for CS Reports, QPR and IFCD Applications

The mechanisms to reinforce CS participation in the implementation of the CDC are mostly focused on formats and surveys that lead to the gathering of information based on indicators and statistics in order to facilitate public policymaking. The Policy Monitoring Platform and the UNESCO Culture for Development Indicators platform (CDIS) already gathered relevant information, and the inclusion in 2019 of the CS electronic form developed by the CDC Secretariat for the QPR (Resolution 7.CP 12)[23] gave the opportunity for CSOs' work to be seen. However, all the forms must be filled in in English, and in the case of the

[21] articles.unesco.org/en/articles/unesco-mondiacult-2022-countries-latin-america-and-caribbean-advocate-paradigm-shift.

[22] UNESCO, *Re|shaping Policies for Creativity: Addressing Culture as a Global Public Good* (Paris, UNESCO, 2022).

[23] 14 IGC, Item 11 of the Provisional Agenda: Collaboration with Civil Society to Implement the Convention and the Conclusions of the Third Civil Society Forum (11 January 2022) UNESCO Doc DCE/22/15.IGC/11.

CS activity reports, a French version is also needed. For CS participation in QPR, the governance processes vary in each country, and is strictly linked to countries' capacities to mobilise CS. One example of CS mobilisation for QPR was given with the publication of *Re|Shaping Policies for Creativity* in 2022, regarding the process that Uganda set up with the objective of assuring all their voices were heard. During the launch, the Ugandan representative answered a question from the audience and expressed that a significant amount of resources had been put in place to achieve the goal. In the case of the third QPR of the Mexican government (2020), CyCGlocal coordinated the consultation carried out with CSOs without financial support.[24]

Assuring CS participation and regional representation in international forums also requires a significant amount of resources, including for capacity building and effective promotion to reach different levels of stakeholders at the local level and to raise their awareness of the importance of being active in the participatory mechanisms of the CDC, such as CS activity reports.[25] Even though this mechanism gives visibility to the actions of CSOs, in 2022 only two reports were received: one from IFCCD and the other from CyCGlocal.[26] This is particularly relevant due to the progression in the number of reports received, with a total of 70 CSOs participating in 2017, with this figure decreasing to 40 in 2019. This situation was addressed during the preparatory meeting with the Bureau of Civil Society prior to the fifteenth IGC, and the main concern from CS was the absence of feedback and communication with the parties regarding these reports. What is this information needed for? Are the time and resources that CSOs invest in producing such reports on a voluntary basis worth it?

Regarding financial resource allocation and its impact on regional representation, another point of concern for CSO observers at the fifteenth IGC was the estimated costs should a regular consultation mechanism be established with micro-, small- and medium-sized cultural and creative enterprises as a result of the feasibility study, commissioned by UNESCO, of the European Creative Business Network (ECBN) and the cultural consultancy 3Walks, carried out from October to December 2021.[27] The proposal was based on the result of the study and established three scenarios for the operativity of the new mechanism for a two-year period.[28] Even though this study, presented in February 2022, was a preliminary

[24] es.unesco.org/creativity/governance/periodic-reports/submission/5539.

[25] 14 IGC, Decision 14.IGC 15 (5 February 2021) UNESCO Doc DCE/21/14.IGC/Dec.

[26] 15 IGC, Civil Society Activity Reports (5 February 2022) UNESCO Doc DCE/22/15.IGC/INF.11b.

[27] 15 IGC, Feasibility Study (7 February 2022) UNESCO Doc DCE/22/15.IGC/INF.9 REV.

[28] Scenario 1: establishment of a forum of micro-, small- and medium-sized cultural and creative enterprises to be held online every two years, before the sessions of the Conference of Parties and in parallel with the Civil Society Forum. Estimated cost: 201,000 USD. Scenario 2: setting up of thematic focus groups on issues on which the Committee might wish to consult micro-, small- and medium-sized cultural and creative enterprises. The focus groups, which would abide by the principle of equitable geographical representation. Estimated cost: 168,200 USD. Scenario 3: geographical focus groups with cross-cutting themes. Estimated cost: 168,200 USD.

analysis, it was based on only a very small number of participating organisations, with poor regional representation. Only 34 persons answered the survey, but from Africa and the Arab states there were only two from each region, and no representatives from Asia and the Pacific, Latin America and the Caribbean answered the survey. The representation for the interview part of the study was proportionally better, but the basis was low, with only 19 enterprises or CSOs, with only two from the Latin American region, both from Chile. In addition, the study was conducted only in English and French, and none of the CSO observers to the governing bodies from Latin America were invited to participate. This reflects not only a language barrier problem, but also misrepresentation of regional voices, perspectives, good practices and knowledge.

As an observer to the governing bodies, CyCGlocal suggested avoiding duplication and reinforcing existing mechanisms like the CS Forum with a wide regional perspective that can also include regional forums. During the presentation session of the feasibility study, parties were also reminded of Article 23.7 CDC, which stipulates that the Committee, in accordance with its Rules of Procedure, 'may invite at any time public or private organisations or individuals to participate in its meetings for consultation on specific issues'. A common agreement among CSOs was that, if necessary, instead of creating a new mechanism, parties could consider reviewing or clarifying the definition of civil society in the Operational Guidelines to Article 11 to avoid confusion and to take into account evolutions since the adoption of the Convention. After looking at the estimated costs of setting up a new mechanism (around 200,000 USD), CSOs active in the work of the governing bodies agreed during their preparatory meetings that this amount of financial investment would help improve and optimise the work in the context of the current voluntary mechanisms of CS participation, and would reach more CSOs from all continents to ensure better regional representation.[29] CyCGlocal also strongly recommended at both the fourteenth and fifteenth IGC meetings that CSOs should be included in the work of the governing bodies when technical, assistance or professional expertise from other regions was needed, in addition to the voluntary work already put in place. As a result of the joint dialogue among the CSOs and parties, Decision 15.IGC 9[30] was made and UNESCO launched a survey across its networks to identify concrete proposals to facilitate the consultation processes of micro-, small- and medium-sized cultural and creative enterprises within the framework of existing mechanisms, the results of which will be presented to the IGC at its sixteenth session in February 2023.[31]

Regarding applications to the IFCD, during the third CS Forum in 2021 it was noted that not only are there language barriers: the lack of clarity around the scoring criteria for the selection of projects at the national level phase, and also the low

[29] ficdc.org/wp-content/uploads/2022/02/interventions-ficdc-v7.pdf.
[30] 15 IGC, Decisions (15 February 2022) UNESCO Doc DCE/22/15.IGC/Dec.
[31] en.unesco.org/creativity/news/unesco-consulting-its-networks-facilitate-consultation.

level of knowledge and visibility of the financed projects, raised concerns from CSOs that invest a significant amount of resources into presenting a proposal for funding and not having feedback when an application is rejected. For example, in 2020, from 34 applications of CSOs in Mexico, 32 failed in the first accreditation hurdle, with a score of 0.[32] It is necessary to clarify to participants whether or not their projects fulfil administrative criteria, including addressing national priorities, or whether the CSOs need capacity-building programmes to better prepare their proposals. In addition, financial resources for the IFCD diminished. In 2020, from 1027 applications, only six were selected for funding. Despite the growing number of parties contributing financially to the fund, the amount reached in 2020 was roughly 600,000 USD, the third lowest since the fund's creation. One of the difficulties in financing the IFCD is likely to be the degree of uncertainty about the real impact of the financial investment.

Consideration could be given to reinforce permanent programmes to support more structuring processes between CSOs at the country level, in particular by developing information and training platforms on the Convention and networking spaces in national languages, not only the working languages of the CDC. This strategy could be supported by national commissions, UNESCO's regional and national offices and other partners, particularly from CS. Also, several lines of support could be developed under the IFCD, including support for the efforts of CSOs that already promote the CDC in the field, and support for south/south mobility for the development of cooperation projects. National governments can establish support programmes for organisations wishing to submit a project to the IFCD to provide more information about the IFCD itself and the selection process, and to enable organisations to submit a project in their national language.

III. Capacity Building for Community Building: A Case Approach

A. About the U40 Network, Cultural Diversity 2030

The participation and roles of civil society from the perspective of the implementation of the CDC is defined in the Operational Guidelines. The roles include capacity building by raising the visibility of the CDC by organising seminars, workshops and forums at every level; developing and publishing information tools

[32] http://en.unesco.org/creativity/ifcd/apply/results?field_fund_type_value_selective=All&field_ifcd_pp_applicant_type_tid=896&field_ifdc_pp_contact_country_target_id[]=1199&field_ifcd_pp_document_status_value_1=All&field_ifcd_pp_submission_date_value_1[value][year]=2020&field_project_title_ifcd_value.

to facilitate understanding of the CDC; and disseminating information to stakeholders through national media, websites and newsletters.

It is interesting to note that awareness of the CDC's objectives and importance varies from region to region. Even though cultural and creative industries, the status of artists and the economic, social and collective rights of artists, creative and cultural professional workers are at the core of the multilateral dialogue in the context of Mondiacult 2022, there are still gaps on how the CDC is understood by all stakeholders.

To tackle CDC awareness, in 2007 the German Commission for UNESCO (GCU) started a programme offering young professionals under 40 years old (U40) a platform to participate in the debate on cultural diversity and the implementation of the CDC at the local level.[33] This process was initiated as a capacity-building programme in the context of the international conference 'Cultural Diversity – Europe's Wealth' (April 2007, Essen, Germany) as part of the German European Union Council presidency. Seventeen young Europeans participated in the programme over an eight-month period.

The next stage (2008–10) of the U40 process aimed to involve excellent researchers, academics, professionals, future decision-makers and communicators from all over the world. The U40-World Forum (June 2009, Paris) was at the heart of this phase. In cooperation with the IFCCD and over 30 partners from all over the world, this phase widened the regional scope of the programme to include all world regions. Held on the occasion of the second COP (15–16 June 2009), the Forum included the participation of U40 Fellows. It marked the transition from a programme to an international network, called U40 Network, Cultural Diversity 2030 (U40Net).

The network was formed by professionals from across the world involved in the field of cultural policies – experts, researchers, civil servants, cultural managers, graduate students, etc. Through awareness-raising activities, advocacy, knowledge and good practice exchange, they gave life to the 2005 UNESCO Convention. On top of U40Net, a series of U40 subgroups started in different parts of the world to better address local, national and regional issues and to foster regional cooperation in the cultural sector.

When the global network reached more regional representation, Red U40 Mexico was funded as a result of 'Aplicación de la Convención: cada agente tiene un papel que desempeñar', a project presented by the Toluca town hall to the IFCD and financed from 2011 to 2012.[34] The project implementation included the organisation of the U40 Inter-America Meeting for Cultural Diversity, consisting of a series of four conferences open to the public and three workshops aimed at discussing the implementation of the Convention at the local, national, regional

[33] All the information regarding U40 Network, cultural diversity 2030 in the next three paragraphs was taken from the official website: u40net.org/who-we-are/about-us.

[34] es.unesco.org/creativity/ifcd/projects/aplicacion-de-convencion-de-2005-cada-agente.

and international levels. Cultural professionals from Mexico City, State of Mexico, Jalisco, Michoacan, Tamaulipas, Coahuila, Queretaro and Veracruz joined the Mexican network in 2011. This new national network aimed to strengthen ties and facilitate content and capacity building for Spanish speakers in Mexico to address the challenges and opportunities of implementing the CDC at national and local level. Representatives from IFCCD participated during this Inter-America Meeting, and kept in touch with coordination staff in Toluca Town Hall in order to facilitate content and support.

Even though the GCU's coordination and financial support of U40Net ended in 2014, it is still active as an informal and self-organised network, and its members develop projects and activities related to the implementation of the CDC. In 2015, members of Red U40 Mexico (which works with artists, creators, independent producers, distributors, broadcasters and publishers in the book, film, television, music, performing and visual arts sectors, cultural professionals from the public and private sectors and civil society organisations), started an internal election process that aimed to formalise its coordination structure and CyCGlocal was selected as the CSO coordinator of the national network.

B. About Creatividad y Cultura Glocal AC

Creatividad y Cultura Glocal AC (CyCGlocal) is a Mexican not-for-profit CSO based in Xalapa, city member of the UNESCO Creative Cities Network (UCCN). Since its foundation in 2014, CyCGlocal has been an associate member of the IFCD. It promotes the principles and good practices of the CDC (as stated in its bylaws) among creative and cultural professionals and networks in Latin America and the Caribbean. By designing and operating international cultural cooperation projects, CyCGlocal's goal is to raise awareness of the positive impact of the implementation of the CDC at the local level on the sustainable urban development and cultural value chain. One of the achievements as the new coordinator of Red U40 Mexico was the invitation of the Ministry of Culture of the Federal Government in 2019 to participate in the third QPR of Mexico. It was the first time the CS electronic format was used for QPR in the country. Of the measures and initiatives submitted, 80% were considered relevant and included in the national report in 2020.[35]

CyCGlocal also works to ensure the implementation of the CDC by designing and operating capacity-building programmes in the Spanish language to eradicate language barriers that lead to inequities in access to information. It is active in the work of the governing bodies and, through its networking and online programmes and activities, encourages the participation of more Latin American and Caribbean CSOs in the work of the governing bodies. As an example of its

[35] es.unesco.org/creativity/governance/periodic-reports/submission/5539.

engagement on the implementation of the CDC at the regional level, CyCGlocal was part of the volunteer group of CSOs that worked on the design and coordination of the third CS Forum in 2021, in which it co-moderated the working session '3. Participation of civil society in the implementation of the Convention'. In February 2022, it designed and operated five ResiliArt x Mondiacult events, three in coordination with the UNESCO Field Office in Mexico, which included panellists and participants from the Ministries of Culture from Argentina, Chile and Peru, UCCN Mexican focal points, the CDC Secretariat and International CSO observers to the governing bodies.

C. IFCCD, CyCGlocal, U40Net and the Construction of a Capacity-Building Programme for Latin American Spanish Speakers

During the initial impact of COVID-19, U40Net restarted communications with the aim of designing a capacity-building and mobilisation project called 'Choices for Future: Young Cultural Diversity Professionals Addressing Current & Future Challenges for the Cultural Value Chain in Times of Digitization and Crisis'[36] in order to present it in response to the IFCD call in 2020. It was decided that CyCGlocal should be the applicant and coordinator of the project. Supported by 14 national and international organisations and public cultural institutions (Freemuse; German Commission for UNESCO; UNESCO Chair of Cultural Diversity; Istanbul Bilgi University; African Cultural Policy Network; Selo PPGCOM/UFMG; Asia-Europe Foundation; Circular; Universidad Nacional de Colombia Sede Manizales; corporación cívica de Caldas; Inizjamed Malta; IFCCD; Museo Regional de Guanajuato; and Racines), the project focused on capacity building in English, aimed at strengthening collaborative ties between young professionals in the cultural sector in Mexico, Brazil, Colombia, Turkey and Morocco. Due the relevance of the proposal, the IFCCD support was also accompanied by a specific request

> to call on the U40 network to develop a training programme in Latin America from autumn 2020. Largely inspired by the issues and themes identified, this programme will be offered to IFCCD members in Chile, Paraguay, Argentina and Mexico, but also to non-members of the Federation in the countries of the region.[37]

Even with the IFCCD's wide vision and high level of commitment, and with the diversity of the cultural actors in the region, the project did not pass the IFCD's Mexican national selection phase. Despite the disappointment of this, the seed of

[36] es.unesco.org/creativity/ifcd/apply/results/4012.
[37] en.unesco.org/creativity/sites/creativity/files/lettre_appui_ficdc_u40_2020.pdf.

inspiration led the network to create a programme in Spanish to raise awareness of the importance of the implementation of the CDC in the Latin American context. The Spanish online training programme called 'Convención de la UNESCO de 2005 sobre la Diversidad de las Expresiones Culturales: Una herramienta para el sector cultural latinoamericano'[38] arose from the rejected 'Choices for Future' project. In this regard, one of the main challenges, besides delivering content in the local language, was to raise awareness and understanding of the importance of the implementation of the CDC at the regional level. It was not a matter of 'having the text in Spanish' (or another language besides the working languages of UNESCO in the case of other regions of the world); it was about talking about the life of the CDC in Latin America.

To address not only the language barriers but also how to better understand the implementation of the CDC, the IFCCD commissioned CyCGlocal to coordinate with U40Net in the design and delivery of an online training programme in Spanish focused on Latin American contexts. The capacity-building programme was financed by the IFCCD and the GCU, former founders and coordinators of U40Net. The GCU also supported the nomination of the 'Choices for Future' project. In the words of Christine M Merkel,

> The 15th anniversary of the Convention seems to us to be an excellent opportunity to celebrate artistic creation in all its forms, in Mexico and across the globe. We are confident that this project will foster new collaborations among young professionals and experts from around the world and will contribute to increased South-South-North dialogue on the diversity of cultural expressions. We strongly support the goal to make the voices of the next generations heard in the context of implementing the 2005 UNESCO Convention and welcome a renewal of the U40 Network.[39]

This innovative programme, the first of its kind in the region and in the Spanish language, benefited cultural professionals from 13 Latin American countries, allowing them not only to deliver content about the Convention, but also to connect with more than 200 new agents in the region and to start new CSO collaboration networks, which resulted in stakeholders on the ground reflecting on the reality of the cultural sector.

This training programme adds to the goals of the IFCCD to strengthen existing coalitions and to encourage the creation of new coalitions or support the reconstruction of those that are no longer active. Considering the needs that have become visible and have intensified since the COVID-19 pandemic, the development of this programme is aimed at facilitating training processes and identifying cultural actors in the region to promote networking, making the IFCCD, its lines of work and its mission visible.

[38] In English, 'UNESCO Convention 2005 for the Diversity of Cultural Expressions: A Tool for the Latin American Cultural Sector'.

[39] GCU Head, Division of Culture, Communication Memory of the World, Bonn, 10 June 2020.

Another challenge of the programme was to mobilise cultural networks in Latin America. Even though one aim was to reinforce Chilean and Paraguayan Coalitions for Cultural Diversity, it was not just about supporting existing members of the IFCCD. It also wanted to reach people, cultural rights defenders,[40] who were already doing the work of the 2005 UNESCO Convention but maybe were not aware of it.

It was also about giving tools and opportunities to expand networks at the national and regional levels. Further, it sought to increase the visibility and reach of the IFCCD in the Latin American region, so the selection process of candidates took this objective into account. The recipients were professionals from the public, private or civil society sector, who were already working in the cultural sector or wished to work in it and wanted to participate in the issues promoted by the IFCCD. To do so, it was necessary to know the profile of the registered participants to enable networking and facilitate the organisation of further programmes and events.

The capacity-building programme took place in November 2020. There were eight sessions in total, two sessions per week. The sessions lasted two hours, with an hour and a half of presentation of topics and half an hour for the questions of the participants. For each session, there were up to two experts and a moderator, who was in charge of following up the questions of the participants and selecting those that were discussed during the half hour of questions. All the content of the programme can be found at the official CyCGlocal website[41] and at the official IFCCD platform created for the project.[42]

The pedagogical objective was for the participant to identify the impact of the CDC on their local reality, and the potential actions that would be carried out for its implementation, including joining or forming a network/coalition. For this purpose, each session had a key question that sought to trigger in the participant interest in designing and implementing proposals within the framework of their regional reality. All the sessions, designed and delivered by guest experts and specialists from U40Net,[43] addressed a variety of topics on the CDC for beginners, with a regional approach methodology. Included were essential concepts (diversity of cultural expressions, and different approaches to cultural policies); culture and sustainable development; cultural rights (international agreements, human rights, gender equality, indigenous peoples); history; content; recent developments and challenges; the living arts and the cultural and creative industries; culture and free trade agreements (cultural exception clauses/reservations, preferential treatment,

[40] www.ohchr.org/en/special-procedures/sr-cultural-rights/cultural-rights-defenders.

[41] www.cycglocal.org.

[42] formacion2020.ficdc.org.

[43] Jordi Baltà, Beatriz Barreiro, Jordi Pascual, M Trinidad García Leiva (Spain); Lilian Hanania (Brazil/France); Sandra Velásquez (Colombia); Julio Vega, Mauricio Delfin (Peru); Rostam Neuwirth (Austria-Macau); Octavio Kulesz (Argentina); Anna Steinkamp (Germany); Luanda Smith, Sandra Villarreal (Mexico).

digital trade, intellectual property, most-favoured-nation); cultural diversity in the digital environment (opportunities, adaptation of laws, artificial intelligence); CS and the CDC (the experience of national coalitions and other networks); and challenges and choices for the future in Latin America in the context of a global crisis.

D. From Global to Local: Achievements from the Programme: To Leave No One Behind

The wide reach of the online programme allowed 250 cultural professionals from the public sector and CS from Argentina, Bolivia, Brazil, Chile, Colombia, Costa Rica, Cuba, Ecuador, Mexico, Panama, Paraguay, Peru and Uruguay to participate. Even staff from the regional UNESCO office in La Havana benefited from the programme. The networking project concluded with an online seminar on 21 May 2021 (Diversity of Cultural Expressions Day) exclusive for the participants, IFCCD members and allies of CyCGlocal in Latin America, such as UNESCO Mexico, the Ministry of Culture of Peru and the Canadian Embassy in Mexico. This provided an opportunity to discuss various issues, ranging from public policies before and during the pandemic to social, economic and cultural rights of artists, cultural and creative professionals, and challenges posed by digital and web giants, on the basis of a shared knowledge and understanding of the CDC.

Findings from the programme included, from the participants' perspective: the need to have support from parties for the construction and permanence of cooperation networks with CSOs, based on the recognition of Spanish as an important language in the region; the need to have permanent training spaces delivered by experts from CS that address the importance of the CDC and its implementation at the local level; and the need to establish permanent contact with UNESCO's national and regional commissions to address local needs, build consensus and enable projects that strengthen the participation of CS in international forums. The delivering of the programme in the Spanish language certainly allowed community building through shared cultural values that should produce strategies and methodologies for conventions to implement.

Since our capacity-building programme was designed and put into operation, its impact had been reflected in a number of countries. CS participants from Bolivia are working towards building a coalition, and those in Argentina want to reactivate theirs. Regarding participants from the public sector, public servants from the Ministry of Culture, Arts and Heritage in Chile coordinated an international seminar inspired by our programme, and hired part of our panel of experts to present the topics on the Convention. The Government of Chile, in the context of its constitutional process, aimed at enshrining human rights and strengthening democratic participation,[44] now has one of the most complete platforms for

[44] www.ohchr.org/en/stories/2022/06/chiles-constitutional-process-historic-opportunity-enshrine-human-rights.

sharing information in Spanish on the CDC.[45] Also, special recognition should be given to the cultural rights defender Mané Nett, President of the Chilean Coalition for Cultural Diversity and Vice President of IFCCD for the Americas, a great promoter of the use of Spanish as a working language of the CDC and a supporter of our capacity-building programme in her country. Her recent loss, in February 2022, has reinforced our commitment to the importance of the implementation of the CDC at the local level in our region.

As a Latin American CSO, CyCGlocal sees this moment as an opportunity to address not only language barriers, but also representation issues. There is an urgent need of knowledge sharing and use of professional expertise from our region, in order to facilitate valuable information for international reports and studies aimed at analysing global realities. Particularly in the context of the UNESCO World Conference on Cultural Policies and Sustainable Development – MONDIACULT 2022, hosted once again in Mexico, 40 years after the first one in 1982, it is also important to highlight that the use of online formats had helped communication and work in the cultural sector during the pandemic period, making it a mechanism for inclusiveness that needs to be taken into account for the upcoming work of the governing bodies. By considering hybrid formats, it may allow the participation of individuals with limited or no mobility, and individuals without resources for mobility. The monitoring framework of the CDC includes SDG 10 'reduction of inequalities' in the mobility section, but not in the governance section. Its inclusion in relation to the participation of CSOs in the work of the governing bodies can be an asset for the good governance of the CDC.

As an additional remark on the importance of the use of the Spanish language in the UN System and the still important work to be done regarding working languages, establishing communications with the Grupo de Amigos del Español de las Naciones Unidas (GAE),[46] a working group created in 2013 with representatives of the 20 Spanish-speaking countries of the UN,[47] can be a good starting point for allocating resources to and support of the vital endeavour of protecting linguistic diversity in the implementation of CDC, and strengthening its good governance for Spanish speakers.

[45] diversidadcultural.cultura.gob.cl.

[46] news.un.org/es/story/2013/10/1283821.

[47] Argentina, Bolivia, Chile, Colombia, Costa Rica, Cuba, Ecuador, El Salvador, Spain, Guatemala, Equatorial Guinea, Honduras, Mexico, Nicaragua, Panama, Paraguay, Peru, Dominican Republic, Uruguay and Venezuela. From its formal establishment, the GAE was empowered to coordinate and carry out activities to promote the use and dissemination of Spanish in the work of the UN.

PART II

Impact of the Convention in Other Fora and Sectors of International Law

4

Protecting and Promoting the Diversity of Cultural Expressions in the Context of Digital Trade: Make the Cultural Exception Great Again!

VÉRONIQUE GUÈVREMONT AND IVANA OTASEVIC

I. Introduction

The UNESCO Convention on the Protection and Promotion of the Diversity of Cultural Expressions (hereinafter CDC or the Convention)[1] was born out of an awareness within the international society during the 1990s of the impact of free trade rules on the regulatory power of states. The failure of the cultural exception at the World Trade Organization (WTO), caused by the strong opposition of the USA to any kind of specific treatment accorded to culture under the General Agreement on Trade in Services (GATS),[2] as well as their victory against Canada in the Periodicals case,[3] prompted states to turn to UNESCO in order to develop a legal instrument that would allow them to protect and promote the diversity of cultural expressions.[4]

[1] (adopted 20 October 2005, entered into force 18 March 2007) 2440 UNTS 311.

[2] For an analysis of the treatment of cultural goods and services in the WTO agreements, see in particular I Bernier, 'Trade and Culture' in PFJ Macrory, AE Appleton and MG Plummer (eds), *The World Trade Organization: Legal, Economic and Political Analysis* (Boston, Springer, 2005) 2331–77.

[3] WTO, 'Canada – Certain Measures Concerning Periodicals' Panel Report (14 March 1997) WTO Doc WT/DS31/R; Appellate Body Report (30 July 1997) WTO Doc WT/DS31/AB/R.

[4] The relationship between the CDC and trade agreements was one of the most debated issues during the negotiations of the Convention that took place from 2003 to 2005. On this point, see I Bernier, 'Les négociation de la convention de l'UNESCO sur la protection et la promotion de la diversité des expressions culturelles' (2005) 43 *Annuaire Canadien de Droit International* 3. See also M Burri, 'The Protection and Promotion of Cultural Diversity at the International Level' (2009) 10 *NCCR Trade Regulation Working Paper*; M Hahn, 'A Clash of Cultures? The UNESCO Diversity Convention and International Trade Law' (2006) 9 *Journal of International Economic Law* 515; A Vlassis, 'La mise en œuvre de la Convention sur la diversité des expressions culturelles: portée et enjeux de l'interface entre commerce et culture' (2011) 42 *Études internationales* 493; T Voon, 'UNESCO and the WTO: A Clash of Cultures?' (2006) 55 *International & Comparative Law Quarterly* 635.

At the bilateral and regional level, many states have succeeded in incorporating into their trade agreements various clauses – cultural exceptions, exemptions or reservations – that recognise the specific nature of cultural goods and services and preserve their sovereign right to intervene in this sector,[5] in accordance with Article 5 of the CDC.[6] Given the impasse in the multilateral trade negotiations at the WTO since the launch of the Doha round in 2001, this approach gave rise to the 'practice' of the cultural exception, which for a long time seemed sufficient to allow states to adopt and implement policies of their choice in the cultural sector.

As we celebrate the fifteenth anniversary of the entry into force of the Convention, however, it appears that states now fear a progressive limitation of their ability to support their cultural products in the digital environment. In recent years, the increased presence of commitments on digital trade[7] in free trade agreements has raised questions about the effectiveness of clauses they have previously developed to preserve their sovereign right to intervene in the cultural sector. The concern of several states is now to extend the protection offered by these clauses in order to preserve their right to implement cultural policies in the digital environment, including through measures promoting national and local cultural content on digital platforms.

The general objective pursued by parties to the CDC is to 'protect and promote the diversity of cultural expressions [and] to reaffirm their sovereign right' to do so.[8] The CDC also aims 'to give recognition to the distinctive nature of cultural activities, goods and services as vehicles of identity, values and meaning',[9] which justifies that these goods and services can be treated differently in trade agreements. In addition, the 'Operational Guidelines on the Implementation of the Convention in the Digital Environment' adopted in 2017 confirm that these objectives can be pursued online,[10] so as to promote a 'balance in the flow of cultural goods and services in the digital environment'.[11] These Guidelines also encourage parties to consider

> introducing cultural clauses in international bilateral, regional or multilateral agreements, namely provisions that take into account the dual nature of cultural goods and services … with particular attention to the status of e-commerce that shall recognize the specificity of cultural goods and services.[12]

[5] See V Guèvremont and I Otasevic, *Culture in Treaties and Agreements: Implementing the CDC in Bilateral and Regional Trade Agreements* (Paris, UNESCO, 2017) 24.

[6] Under Art 5 – General rule regarding rights and obligations, parties to the CDC reaffirm 'their sovereign right to formulate and implement their cultural policies and adopt measures to protect and promote the diversity of cultural expressions and to strengthen international cooperation to achieve the purposes of this Convention'.

[7] The terms 'electronic commerce' and 'digital trade' are used interchangeably in this chapter, depending on the terminology used in the agreements being described. Although some authors consider that the two terms do not have the same meaning, a reading of the trade agreements presented in this chapter does not support such conclusion.

[8] See Art 1(a) and (h) of the CDC.

[9] See Art 1(g) of the CDC.

[10] UNESCO, *Operational Guidelines on the Implementation of the Convention in the Digital Environment* (Paris, UNESCO, 2017) para 8.4.

[11] See para 8.6 of the Guidelines.

[12] See para 19.4 of the Guidelines.

However, the specificities of digital commerce and the new types of commitments regarding data flow create uncertainty as to which clauses should be included to preserve the power of intervention of states.

Taking into account these Guidelines and the commitment of the parties to promote the objectives and principles of the CDC in other forums,[13] this chapter reflects on cultural clauses that parties may use to preserve their right to intervene to protect and promote the diversity of cultural expressions in the digital environment. After identifying some trends and new challenges surrounding the implementation of cultural policies aimed at promoting local content online in a free trade context (section II), it takes a critical look at the scope of the cultural exemption integrated into almost every trade agreement signed by Canada, the first state to negotiate such a clause as early as 1988,[14] a clause that has not evolved since then (section III). Finally, this chapter looks at other cultural clauses that states have used in their most recent trade agreements to recognise the specific nature of digital cultural content (section IV). The purpose of this chapter is to highlight the fact that no cultural clause negotiated to date offers full protection of the sovereign right of the state to intervene through cultural policies applicable to the digital environment, which may reflect the need for parties to the CDC to renew their approaches in order to achieve the objectives of this treaty.

II. Promoting Local Content Online: Trends and New Challenges in a Free Trade Context

In recent years, several parties to the CDC have adopted national policies to protect and promote the diversity of cultural expressions in the digital environment. A well-known example is the new EU Audiovisual Media Services Directive,[15] which commits EU Member States to ensure a requirement of at least a 30 per cent share of European works in the catalogues of providers of on-demand audiovisual media services, as well as a prominence of these works.[16] All EU Member States had to transpose these obligations into national legislation by September 2020.

Several other parties have adopted or could adopt similar measures in the near future. Mexico has introduced a bill that imposes a 30 per cent share of Mexican works in the catalogues of providers of on-demand audiovisual media services.[17]

[13] See Art 21 of the CDC.

[14] See Canada–US Free Trade Agreement (signed 2 January 1988, entered into force 1 January 1989) Art 2005, www.international.gc.ca/trade-commerce/assets/pdfs/agreements-accords/cusfta-e.pdf.

[15] See Directive 2018/1808 of the European Parliament and of the Council of 14 November 2018 amending Directive 2010/13/EU on the coordination of certain provisions laid down by law, regulation or administrative action in Member States concerning the provision of audiovisual media services (Audiovisual Media Services Directive), in view of changing market realities [2018] OJ L303/69.

[16] ibid Art 13 §1.

[17] Bnamericas, 'Mexico Set to Oblige Online Platforms to Stream 30% Local Content' (26 March 2020) www.bnamericas.com/en/news/mexico-set-to-oblige-online-platforms-to-stream-30-local-content.

Colombia adopted a decree to oblige these service providers to include a section of national content easily accessible by users of their platforms, which implies a high visibility.[18] In a White Paper published in October 2020, South Africa announced its plan to impose local content quotas on streaming services.[19] In Australia, the 'Media Reform Green Paper' published in November 2020 also contains recommendations to impose local content requirement on digital platforms that target local audience.[20]

Canada is currently looking in the same direction. The Yale Report on Canada's communications future[21] (January 2020) contains several recommendations that relate to Canadian content online. The experts recommend, in particular, that the Canadian Radio-television and Telecommunications Commission (CRTC) impose discoverability[22] obligations on all audio or audiovisual entertainment media content, in order 'to ensure … that Canadian content has sufficient visibility and is easy to find on the services that Canadians use'. These obligations could include catalogue or exhibition requirements, prominence requirements, obligations to offer Canadian media content choices and transparency requirements, such as that companies be transparent with the CRTC regarding how their algorithms operate, including audit requirements.[23] A bill – introduced in November 2020, dropped due to federal election in 2021, then reintroduced in January 2022 – to amend the Broadcasting Act could allow the CRTC to impose on broadcasters, including on digital platforms, 'the proportion of programs to be broadcast that shall be Canadian programs and the proportion of time that shall be devoted to the broadcasting of Canadian Programs'.[24]

The policies and measures mentioned above reflect the objectives and principles of the CDC and its 'Operational Guidelines on the Implementation of the Convention in the Digital Environment'. As stated in paragraph 16 of these

[18] Ministerio de Tecnologías de la Informacion y las Comunicaciones, 'Contenidos colombianos contarán con una sección propia en las plataformas digitales de video por demanda que operan en el país' (22 May 2020) www.mintic.gov.co/portal/inicio/Sala-de-Prensa/Noticias/144889:Contenidos-colombianos-contaran-con-una-seccion-propia-en-las-plataformas-digitales-de-video-por-demanda-que-operan-en-el-pais.

[19] South African Government, Department of Communications and Digital Technologies, *Draft White Paper on Audio and Audiovisual Content Services Policy Framework: A New Vision for South Africa 2020* (9 October 2020) www.gov.za/sites/default/files/gcis_document/202010/43797gon1081.pdf.

[20] Australian Government, *Media Reform Green Paper. Modernizing Television Regulation in Australia* (November 2020) 30, www.infrastructure.gov.au/sites/default/files/documents/media-reform-greenpaper-december2020_0.pdf.

[21] J Yale et al, *Canada's Communications Future: Time to Act: Broadcasting and Telecommunications Legislative Review: Final Report* (January 2020) www.ic.gc.ca/eic/site/110.nsf/eng/00012.html.

[22] Discoverability refers to the capacity to easily discover an item, whether it be an application or a piece of content. See Canada Media Fund, *Discoverability: Toward a Common Frame of Reference*, Part 1 (2016) 10, www.cmf-fmc.ca/now-next/research-reports/discoverability-toward-a-common-frame-of-reference/.

[23] ibid 148, Recommendation 63.

[24] House of Commons of Canada, Bill C-10 (2020) Art 9.1(1)(a); House of Commons of Canada, Bill C-11 (2022) Art 9.1(1)(a).

Guidelines, 'Parties shall aim to support and provide opportunities for works to be distributed in the digital environment', and relevant measures could aim to

> encourage the diversity of digital media, including the multiplicity of digital distributors or cultural goods and services and digital actors (online platforms, Internet service providers (ISP), search engines, social networks), while also ensuring visibility and discoverability of national and local cultural content.[25]

The Open Roadmap adopted in 2018 to assist parties to the CDC suggests clear expected results and concrete actions in this regard, including the implementation of 'regulations, policies and measures to ensure discoverability of local and diverse cultural content, fair remuneration for creators, [and] greater transparency in the use of algorithms'.[26]

However, in order to be able to implement such measures in a context of free trade, states may have to incorporate in their trade agreements cultural clauses whose scope extends to commitments related to digital commerce. This becomes crucial when an agreement contains a chapter setting out binding commitments on digital commerce, including a commitment to non-discriminatory treatment of digital products.

Several trade agreements concluded over the past 20 years include such a commitment, stating, for instance, that

> [n]o Party shall accord less favourable treatment to digital products created, produced, published, contracted for, commissioned or first made available on commercial terms in the territory of another Party, or to digital products of which the author, performer, producer, developer or owner is a person of another Party, than it accords to other like digital products.[27]

Considering that a digital product is often defined as 'a computer programme, text, video, image, sound recording or other product that is digitally encoded, produced for commercial sale or distribution, and that can be transmitted electronically',[28] this commitment to non-discriminatory treatment clearly extends to cultural goods and services distributed or disseminated online. National regulations on media and audiovisual services that contain local content requirements could be deemed incompatible with this type of undertaking.

Other electronic commerce commitments found in trade agreements may also be relevant when it comes to the implementation and monitoring of cultural policies in the digital environment. This is the case of the provisions that could restrict the access to data related to cultural content in the digital environment, an access

[25] Para 16.1 of the Guidelines.

[26] UNESCO, *Open Roadmap for the Implementation of the 2005 Convention in the Digital Environment* (2018).

[27] See, eg the Comprehensive and Progressive Agreement for Trans-Pacific Partnership (signed 8 March 2018, entered into force 30 December 2018) Art 14.4, www.dfat.gov.au/sites/default/files/tpp-11-treaty-text.pdf.

[28] ibid Art 14.1.

that states may have to maintain in order to achieve and monitor public policy objectives. In this regard, states must be vigilant when they undertake commitments relating to the free flow of data, access to source codes or data localisation. The monitoring of cultural policies that promote local content online, for instance, may require the states to access data collected by a platform, a right that could possibly be restricted in a free trade context.

For those reasons, the recognition of the dual nature of cultural goods and services, and the preservation of the sovereign right of states to adopt and implement policies to protect and promote the diversity of cultural expressions, require the integration of appropriate cultural clauses whose scope extend to the digital environment. In this regard, the fact that the Canadian cultural exemption has not evolved since 1988 may raise some concerns.

III. Uncertainties Surrounding the Canadian Cultural Exemption Model in the Digital Age

For decades, Canada has used a general cultural exemption to preserve its cultural sovereignty in a free trade context.[29] In some of its most recent trade agreements, Canada has changed its approach and favoured the incorporation of several clauses in selected chapters. With respect to the agreements that contain commitments on electronic commerce, it is far from clear that the cultural exemption or the other cultural clauses used in the past will allow for the implementation of measures promoting Canadian content in the digital environment. Legal uncertainty arises from the scope of Canada's current commitments in the area of electronic commerce in at least three agreements: the Comprehensive Economic and Trade Agreement[30] (CETA) (a), the Comprehensive and Progressive Agreement for Trans-Pacific Partnership[31] (CPTPP) (b) and the Canada–United States–Mexico Agreement[32] (CUSMA) (c).

A. The Comprehensive Economic and Trade Agreement

The CETA, concluded between Canada and the European Union and its Member States, has been innovative in several ways. One reason is that it is the first trade

[29] The Canadian cultural exemption is a clause that has the effect of excluding certain categories of cultural goods and services produced by cultural industries from the scope of a trade agreement. This exemption is referred to as 'general' since it applies to all chapters of a trade agreement.

[30] (adopted 30 October 2016, entered into force 21 September 2017) [2017] OJ L11/23.

[31] (signed 8 March 2018, entered into force 30 December 2018) www.dfat.gov.au/sites/default/files/tpp-11-treaty-text.pdf.

[32] (signed 30 November 2018 and 10 December 2019, entered into force 1 July 2020) ustr.gov/trade-agreements/ free-trade-agreements/united-states-mexico-canada-agreement/agreement-between.

agreement concluded by Canada that contains an explicit reference to the objectives of the CDC, affirming the right of states to preserve, develop and implement their cultural policies.[33] Considering the interpretative value of the Preamble, this reference could potentially be taken into account in the context of a dispute settlement involving the implementation of cultural policies. Another reason is that the CETA is the first trade agreement to demonstrate a change in the Canadian approach, which has abandoned its general cultural exemption in favour of a plurality of exemptions incorporated into certain chapters only. The relevant chapters are the ones on subsidies, services, investment, domestic regulation and government procurement. At least two chapters relevant to cultural sectors are excluded from this list.[34] The first one is the chapter on 'National Treatment and Market Access for Goods',[35] which means that certain cultural policies, particularly in the book and publishing sectors, fall outside the scope of the cultural exemptions.[36] The second one is the chapter on 'Electronic Commerce',[37] which merits further comment.

Chapter 16 of the CETA, on electronic commerce, contains only seven articles, most of which encourage cooperation, dialogue and transparency. One exception is Article 16.3, which prohibits parties from applying customs duties on deliveries transmitted by electronic means. In addition, the chapter contains a clause that could be described as evolutionary. Indeed, under Article 16.2 of the CETA, 'The Parties recognise that electronic commerce increases economic growth and trade opportunities in many sectors and confirm the applicability of the WTO rules to electronic commerce'. The new rules that are being negotiated under the auspices of the WTO could therefore bind Canada and the EU not only within the framework of the multilateral trade system, but also within the framework of their commitments within the CETA. Given that the CETA's e-commerce chapter does not contain a cultural exemption, such a development could have an impact on Canada's cultural industries.

The foregoing analysis of bilateral and regional agreements and the approaches favoured by some parties to the Convention provide some indication of the proposals being made at the WTO in the context of negotiations on trade-related aspects of electronic commerce. The EU and its Member States, for instance, have expressed their willingness to 'maintain the possibility to define and implement cultural and

[33] CETA, Preamble, para 7: 'Affirming their commitments as parties to the UNESCO *Convention on the Protection and Promotion of the Diversity of Cultural Expressions*, done at Paris on 20 October 2005, and recognising that states have the right to preserve, develop and implement their cultural policies, to support their cultural industries for the purpose of strengthening the diversity of cultural expressions, and to preserve their cultural identity, including through the use of regulatory measures and financial support'.

[34] CETA, respectively cc 7, 8, 9, 12 and 19.

[35] CETA, c 2.

[36] On this point, see V Guèvremont (ed), *Le renouvellement de l'exception culturelle à l'ère du numérique* (Montreal, RIJDEC, 2015).

[37] CETA, c 16.

audio-visual policies for the purposes of preserving their cultural diversity, including by not taking commitments on audio-visual services'.[38] However, the communications submitted by other parties to the Convention, including Canada, do not contain specific remarks relating to the cultural sector.[39] The available documents attest to a low level of mobilisation of parties to the Convention around its objectives and principles, which should find some resonance in the proposals aimed at guiding the negotiations on electronic commerce at the WTO.

This situation could create a favourable context for the emergence of binding commitments in the area of electronic commerce, as advocated in particular by the USA. While this is desirable for the expansion of electronic commerce generally, certain commitments may limit the right of states to adopt cultural policies applicable to the digital environment. As stated in its recent communication, the USA supports a strict application of the non-discrimination principle to 'digital products like apps, songs, books, games, and videos'.[40] This position is not surprising, since the USA has always refused to recognise the specific nature of cultural products in WTO agreements.[41]

The recognition of the dual nature of cultural goods and services would be difficult to reconcile with a strict application of this principle in the cultural sector. Considering the fact that the CETA does not provide for any cultural exemptions in its chapter on electronic commerce, the conclusion of the WTO negotiations in this domain could open the door to the challenge of certain cultural policies applicable to the digital environment, unless Canada and the EU refrain from doing so in light of their commitment to the CDC.

B. Comprehensive and Progressive Agreement for Trans-Pacific Partnership

The CPTPP is the second agreement that marked a shift in Canada's approach to preserving its cultural sovereignty in the context of a free trade agreement. In this case, Canada opted for a plurality of cultural reservations[42] of varying scope

[38] WTO, 'Joint Statement on Electronic Commerce: EU Proposal for WTO Disciplines and Commitments Relating to Electronic Commerce – Communication from the European Union' (26 April 2019) WTO Doc INF/ECOM/22, para 3; WTO, 'Joint Statement on Electronic Commerce; Communication from the European Union: EU Proposal for WTO Disciplines and Commitments Relating to Electronic Commerce: Revision of Disciplines Relating to Telecommunications Services' (15 October 2019) WTO Doc INF/ECOM/43, para 4.

[39] It should be noted that the communications submitted by several WTO members have not been made public.

[40] WTO, 'Joint Statement on Electronic Commerce Initiative: Communication from the United States' (25 March 2019) WTO Doc INF/ECOM/5, para 3.1.

[41] I Bernier, 'Cultural Goods and Services in International Trade Law' in D Browne (ed), *The Culture/Trade Quandary. Canada's Policy Options* (Ottawa, Centre for Trade Policy and Law, 1997) 108, 110.

[42] In trade agreements based on 'negative lists' of commitments – which means all goods and services fall into the scope of the agreement unless otherwise specified – parties may formulate 'reservations' to preserve their power to adopt and implement cultural policies of their choosing. Reservations may

incorporated in a limited number of chapters. The chapter on electronic commerce does not exclude the cultural sector from its scope, but the commitment to non-discriminatory treatment for digital products does not apply to broadcasting.[43] For the purposes of this chapter, 'digital product means a computer program, text, video, image, sound recording or other product that is digitally encoded, produced for commercial sale or distribution, and that can be transmitted electronically'.[44] This means that all other commitments therefore apply to several cultural products, including film, video and music available online.

More specifically, the chapter on electronic commerce 'appl[ies] to measures adopted or maintained by a Party that affect trade by electronic means'.[45] However, the definition of the scope of this chapter must be read in conjunction with any other relevant provisions in the CPTPP. This means that

> measures affecting the supply of a service delivered or performed electronically are subject to the obligations contained in the relevant provisions of Chapter 9 (Investment) [and] Chapter 10 (Cross-Border Trade in Services) … including any exceptions or non-conforming measures set out in this Agreement that are applicable to those obligations.[46]

Nevertheless, uncertainties remain as to how these non-conforming 'services' or 'investment' provisions, exceptions and measures relate to the rules of the chapter on electronic commerce.

A difficulty arises from the distinction between commitments related to *a text, video, image or sound recording digitally encoded* on the one side and a *cultural service* delivered electronically on the other side. Only the latter are covered by the chapters on investment and services and their applicable exceptions. Thus, the definition of a digital product could be a source of confusion in determining the rules applicable to the transmission of a cultural content. Multiple issues seem difficult to resolve. For example, while 'book' is covered by the rules of chapter 2, on national treatment and market access for goods, a 'digital book' could also qualify as a 'digital product' and therefore be subject to the rules of chapter 14, on

exclude certain cultural goods or services from the scope of certain rules. They may also be intended to maintain certain existing policies, or to preserve a state's right to adopt new policies when it deems appropriate. For more details, see V Guèvremont and I Bernier, *Guide to the Negotiation of Cultural Clauses in Trade Agreements* (2020) 12, www.unescodec.chaire.ulaval.ca/sites/unescodec.chaire.ulaval.ca/files/guide_-_10_fevrier_2021_-_eng_-_final_0.pdf.

[43] CPTPP, Art 14.4.4.

[44] ibid Art 14.1.

[45] ibid Art 14.2.2.

[46] ibid Art 14.2.4. This article is particularly relevant for Canada, since Annexes I and II, on cross border trade in services and investment non-conforming measures, contain several reservations in the cultural sector. It should be recalled that these reservations must be read in accordance with the side letter agreements signed by Canada with each party to the CPTPP. According to these letter agreements, 'Canada may adopt or maintain discriminatory requirements on service suppliers or investors to make financial contributions for Canadian content development and may adopt or maintain measures that restrict access to online foreign audio-visual content'. See, eg www.international.gc.ca/trade-commerce/trade-agreements-accords-commerciaux/agr-acc/cptpp-ptpgp/text-texte/sl_la-australia_australie.aspx?lang=eng#1.

electronic commerce. Two legal regimes could coexist and regulate trade in products that qualify as 'books'. The situation is even more complex in the case of 'film', which is a 'good', but whose production, distribution and exhibition qualify as a 'service', and which, under the CPTPP, could also fall into the category of 'digital products' if it takes the form of a 'digitally encoded product'.

The undefined articulation between the chapters on goods, services, investment and electronic commerce creates a situation of legal insecurity not only for states, but also for actors working in the cultural industries sector. Considering the fact that the chapter on electronic commerce does not provide for any reservations applicable specifically to digital products, the parties' right to adopt and implement policies aimed at preserving the diversity of cultural expressions and promoting local content in the digital environment appears to be reduced. Canada's commitments under the CPTPP could therefore be interpreted in a way that limits its power to support Canadian content online.

These commitments include non-discriminatory treatment of digital products, cross-border transfer of information by electronic means, location of computing facilities and source code.[47] It has to be underlined, however, that the parties to the CPTPP have succeeded in preserving a flexibility that could benefit the monitoring of some cultural policies in the future. With regard to the commitments related to the transfer of data and location of computing facilities, they have agreed that nothing shall prevent a party from adopting or maintaining measures inconsistent with these commitments 'to achieve a legitimate public policy objective'. Two conditions must be respected: the measure should not be 'applied in a manner which would constitute a means of arbitrary or unjustifiable discrimination or a disguised restriction on trade', nor should it 'impose restrictions [on transfers of information, or the use or location of computing facilities] greater than are required to achieve the objective'.[48] With regard to the commitment on source code, they have agreed that nothing shall preclude 'a Party from requiring the modification of source code of software necessary for that software to comply with laws or regulations which are not inconsistent with this Agreement'.[49] It will be interesting to see the policy space such exceptions will give to Canada and other state parties in the field of culture.

C. Canada–United States–Mexico Agreement

The CUSMA, concluded on 1 October 2018, replaces the North American Free Trade Agreement (NAFTA) of 1992. Under the new agreement, Canada has succeeded in maintaining the cultural exemption that already existed in the 1992

[47] CPTPP, Arts 14.4, 14.11, 14.13 and 14.17.
[48] ibid Arts 14.11.1 and 14.13.3.
[49] ibid Art 14.17.3.

NAFTA, and previously in the 1988 Canada–United States Free Trade Agreement. The exemption covers all chapters of the CUSMA, including the new chapter on digital trade.[50]

This chapter contains 18 provisions applicable to digital products[51] with varying levels of constraint. Several commitments encourage the parties to cooperate to achieve various objectives related to trade by electronic means, such as electronic signatures, consumer protection, paperless trading, limitation of unsolicited commercial electronic communications and cybersecurity.[52] Binding commitments include the non-application of tariffs to digital products and the non-discriminatory treatment of these products.[53] However, the latter commitment does not apply 'to a subsidy or grant provided by a Party, including a government-supported loan, guarantee, or insurance'.[54] This is an important exclusion for the cultural sector, as subsidies and other forms of government support are tools frequently used in Canadian cultural policies. Nevertheless, the scope of this commitment to non-discriminatory treatment of digital products remains broad and could, for instance, prohibit a party from imposing a percentage of local content in the catalogues of audiovisual media services providers.

CUSMA also contains important provisions related to data. Article 19.11 requires the parties not to prohibit or restrict the cross-border transfer of such information, but, just as in the CPTPP, it 'does not prevent a Party from adopting or maintaining a measure inconsistent with [this commitment] that is necessary to achieve a legitimate public policy objective'.[55] Article 19.12, on location of computing facilities, states that 'no Party shall require a covered person to use or locate computing facilities in that Party's territory as a condition for conducting business

[50] This should not lead to the conclusion that Canada has no commitment in the cultural sector. There are clauses in other CUSMA chapters that explicitly limit Canada's regulatory authority in the cultural sector. An example of such limitation is found in ch 15 on cross-border trade in services, and more specifically in Annex 15-D, on programming services. Under this annex, Canada commits to 'rescind Broadcasting Regulatory Policy CRTC 2016-334 and Broadcasting Order CRTC 2016-335', which deals with simultaneous substitution of signals when retransmitting certain programmes in Canada. See CRTC, 'Broadcasting Regulatory Policy CRTC 2016-334 and Broadcasting Order CRTC 2016-335', 2016-37 (19 August 2016) www.crtc.gc.ca/eng/archive/2016/2016-334.htm. To the extent that this policy falls within the jurisdiction of the Canadian Radio–Television and Telecommunications Commission, it appears that the commitment in Annex 15-D directly interferes with Canada's regulatory authority in the cultural field. On this point, see M Geist, 'The Full "Culture Exception" That Isn't: Why Canada Caved on Independent Cultural Policy in the USMCA' (11 October 2018) www.michaelgeist.ca/2018/10/usmcaculture/.

[51] According to Art 19.1, 'digital product means a computer program, text, video, image, sound recording, or other product that is digitally encoded, produced for commercial sale or distribution, and that can be transmitted electronically. For greater certainty, digital product does not include a digitized representation of a financial instrument, including money'.

[52] CUSMA, Arts 19.6, 19.7, 19.9, 19.13 and 19.15. See also Art 19.14 on Cooperation.

[53] ibid Arts 19.3 and 19.4.

[54] ibid Art 19.4.2.

[55] Again, two conditions must be respected. According to Art 19.11.2, such restrictive measure '(a) is not applied in a manner which would constitute a means of arbitrary or unjustifiable discrimination or a disguised restriction on trade; and (b) does not impose restrictions on transfers of information greater than are necessary to achieve the objective'.

in that territory'. In this case, and contrary to the CPTPP, no flexibility is allowed to pursue legitimate public policy objectives. Finally, it is prohibited for a party to

> require the transfer of, or access to, a source code of software owned by a person of another Party, or to an algorithm expressed in that source code, as a condition for the import, distribution, sale or use of that software, or of products containing that software, in its territory.[56]

An exception that may be relevant to the cultural sector is nevertheless provided for, since this

> Article does not preclude a regulatory body or judicial authority of a Party from requiring a person of another Party to preserve and make available the source code of software, or an algorithm expressed in that source code, to the regulatory body for a specific investigation, inspection, examination, enforcement action, or judicial proceeding, subject to safeguards against unauthorised disclosure.

Such access to a source code or algorithm – which are widely used by platforms to recommend certain cultural content to their subscribers[57] – may be something that a government may want to preserve to monitor policies that require a platform to ensure prominence of local content, for instance.

Unlike the CETA and the CPTPP, however, the CUSMA contains a general cultural exemption applicable to all chapters. The relevant clause states that 'This Agreement does not apply to a measure adopted or maintained by Canada with respect to a cultural industry'.[58] But the protection offered by this exemption to Canadian cultural industries can only be truly assessed if the retaliation clause provided for in the same article is also taken into account. According to this clause, 'Notwithstanding any other provision of this Agreement, a Party may take a measure of equivalent commercial effect in response to an action by another Party that would have been inconsistent with this Agreement but for paragraph 2 or 3'.[59] Such a clause could, for example, be used by the USA to sanction Canada when one of its cultural policies is inconsistent with CUSMA commitments and can only be maintained through the protection afforded by the cultural exemption. In other words, the use of the 'shield' provided by the cultural exemption clause could have a significant economic impact on Canada.[60]

This scenario also deserves to be nuanced in light of the differences of interpretation that could otherwise arise regarding the actual scope of the cultural exemption clause and its applicability to digital products. Indeed, according to some plausible interpretations, the CUSMA could directly limit Canada's right to

[56] CUSMA, Art 19.16.1.

[57] See R Hunt and F McKelvey, 'Algorithmic Regulation in Media and Cultural Policy: A Framework to Evaluate Barriers to Accountability' (2019) 9 *Journal of Information Policy* 307, 308.

[58] CUSMA, Art 32.6.2.

[59] ibid Art 32.6.4.

[60] It is worth noting that the retaliation clause was already present in the 1992 NAFTA, and was therefore renewed in the CUSMA, despite Canada's ratification of the CDC.

adopt certain cultural policies for the digital environment. This could be a consequence of the words used to define cultural industries and thus the scope of the cultural exemption.

It should be recalled that the cultural exemption covers 'cultural industries', which are defined by an exhaustive list of cultural goods and services: books, magazines, periodicals, newspapers, film or video recordings, audio or video music recordings, music compositions and radiocommunications.[61] In the field of publishing and music compositions, the definition refers to products that are 'in print or machine readable form'. For other cultural industries, the definition includes references to specific types of technologies, such as cable or satellite broadcasting. This vocabulary differs significantly from the words used to define a digital product, ie 'computer program, text, video, image, sound recording, or other product that is digitally encoded'. As a result, the wording of the cultural exemption could in practice have the effect of limiting the scope of this clause to certain chapters of the CUSMA, excluding the chapter on electronic commerce.

In the event of a dispute between the parties to the CUSMA, the choice of words could be decisive in the interpretation of the cultural exemption. According to the Vienna Convention on the Law of Treaties, 'A treaty shall be interpreted in good faith in accordance with the ordinary meaning to be given to the terms of the treaty in their context and in the light of its object and purpose'.[62] In the case of the CUSMA, not only does the ordinary meaning of the words used in the definition of cultural industries and digital products differ, but the object and purpose of the agreement supports a restrictive interpretation of the cultural exemption clause since the main purpose of the treaty is trade liberalisation. In addition, unlike the CETA, the Preamble of the CUSMA does not contain any statement recognising the right of states 'to maintain, establish and implement their cultural policies'.[63]

This analysis reminds us that, since the conclusion of the first free trade agreement with the USA in 1988, Canada has maintained a cultural exemption based on the same definition of 'cultural industries'. However, digital technologies have transformed this sector and given rise to the emergence of new players. In the event of a dispute, Canada could rely on the principle of evolutionary interpretation to update its definition of cultural industries and rely on the cultural exemption to preserve its right to adopt and implement cultural policies applicable in the digital environment. This path, however, creates an insecurity for the actors of the cultural sector. Moreover, if the cultural exemption is used to implement a cultural policy applicable to digital technology, the retaliation clause could give rise to sanction. It must therefore be concluded that the legal insecurity does not disappear completely, even if one accepts the idea of an evolutionary interpretation of the cultural exemption.

[61] CUSMA, Art 32.6.1.
[62] (adopted 23 May 1969, entered into force 27 January 1980) 1155 UNTS 331, Art 31.1.
[63] Above n 26.

IV. Other Approaches Favoured by States to Preserve their Right to Implement Cultural Policies in the Digital Environment

In recent years, states have adopted different approaches in order to exclude digital cultural goods and services from the scope of their free trade agreements. The cultural clauses used by states, which differ in scope, protect to varying degrees their power of intervention in the cultural sector and their ability to promote a diversity of cultural expressions in the digital environment. Some have made reservations that explicitly apply to the digital environment in their annexes to the chapters on trade in services and investment (a). Others, like the European Union and its Member States (b) and New Zealand (c), have gone further, using a cultural clause to explicitly limit the scope of their commitment regarding electronic commerce. Despite this progress, however, it appears, that none of these clauses fully preserve the sovereign right of the parties to the CDC to implement all measures that may be necessary to protect the diversity of cultural expressions in the digital environment.

A. Cultural Reservations Applicable to Digital Products

The liberalisation of trade in services and investment can be done on the basis of two different approaches: the positive list or the negative list of commitments. The first one is chosen by states to institute progressive liberalisation. In this case, the parties draw up schedules of specific commitments, with or without limitation. With respect to cultural concerns, this method has the advantage of allowing states to select the services they wish to liberalise. In other words, a state may simply decide to refrain from making commitments on cultural services. This approach thus enables the state to preserve its power to intervene in the cultural sector. A riskier option for states is to include cultural services in their schedules, but to modulate their commitments on these services. In this case, cultural clauses, in the form of 'limitations', can be drafted in such a way as to preserve the right of states to maintain certain types of policies. The schedules of commitments can also be drafted in such a way that liberalisation of cultural services is limited to certain modes of supply or specific types of services.

The second approach is chosen by states wishing to carry out rapid liberalisation. With this method, all sectors are covered by liberalisation. In order to preserve its power to adopt and implement its cultural policies, a state therefore needs to formulate appropriate reservations. Reservations may exclude identified cultural services from the scope of certain rules. They may also seek to maintain certain existing policies, or to preserve the right of a state to adopt new policies when it deems it appropriate. In other words, every policy and measure, cultural or non-cultural, that may affect free trade in the cultural sector must be subject to one or more reservations to that effect.[64] Hence, the negative list approach necessarily entails some risks, especially since certain reservations may not have anticipated the evolution of trade and the transformation of cultural industries increasingly oriented towards e-commerce. A few states have, however, managed to formulate cultural reservations whose wording contains an explicit reference to digital technologies. This is the case of Australia and Chile.

In recent years, Australia has formulated some reservations of its trade agreements that relate to digital cultural services. An example of this is found in the CPTPP, where Australia

> reserves the right to adopt or maintain any measure with respect to: (a) Transmission quotas for local content on free-to-air commercial television broadcasting services; (b) Non-discriminatory expenditure requirements for Australian production on subscription television broadcasting services; (c) Transmission quotas for local content on free-to-air radio broadcasting services; (d) Other audio-visual services transmitted electronically, in order to make Australian audio-visual content reasonably available to Australian consumers.[65]

This reservation applies to several obligations applicable to broadcasting and audiovisual services found in the chapters on services and investment, namely national treatment (Articles 9.4 and 10.3), most-favoured-nation treatment (Articles 9.5 and 10.4), performance requirements (Article 9.10), market access (Article 10.5) and local presence (Article 10.6).[66] A wide range of cultural policies could fall into the scope on this reservation, including policies aimed at promoting Australian content online.

In other agreements, Australia has used a different wording for its reservations.[67] For instance, it 'reserves the right to adopt or maintain any measure with respect to: (a) the creative arts [footnote 11], cultural heritage [footnote 12] and other cultural industries, including audiovisual services, entertainment services and libraries, archives, museums and other cultural services'.[68] This reservation applies to the same obligations as those mentioned above, in addition to the obligation relating to senior management and board of directors.[69] Footnote 11 defines *creative arts* as

> the performing arts, including theatre, dance and music, visual arts and craft, literature, film, television, video, radio, creative online content, indigenous traditional practice and contemporary cultural expression, and digital interactive media and hybrid art works which uses new technologies to transcend discrete art form divisions.[70]

[64] See Guèvremont and Otasevic, *Culture in Treaties* (2017) 24.

[65] See CPTPP, Annex II – Australia.

[66] A similar reservation can be found in the Peru-Australia Free Trade Agreement (signed 12 February 2018, entered into force 11 February 2020) Annex II – Australia, www.dfat.gov.au/trade/agreements/in-force/pafta/full-text/Pages/fta-text-and-associated-documents.

[67] See, eg Annex II of the Australia–Hong Kong Free Trade Agreement (signed 26 March 2019, entered into force 17 January 2020) www.dfat.gov.au/trade/agreements/in-force/a-hkfta/a-hkfta-text/Pages/default.

[68] ibid.

[69] ibid. The relevant obligations are contained in Arts 7.3, 7.4, 7.5, 7.6, 12.4, 12.5, 12.6 and 12.7.

[70] ibid Annex II.

This reservation thus covers several cultural goods, services and activities, including digital cultural products. Moreover, the definition of creative arts overlaps with the definition of a digital product included in the chapter on electronic commerce, which 'means a computer program, text, video, image, sound recording or other product that is digitally encoded, produced for commercial sale or distribution, and that can be transmitted electronically'.[71] Therefore, the application of the cultural reservation to digital products covered by the e-commerce commitments is more explicit.

In the case of Chile, some of its recent trade agreements contain a clause that

> reserves the right to adopt or maintain any measure granting differential treatment to countries within the framework of any existing or future bilateral or multilateral international agreement with regard to arts and cultural industries, such as cooperation agreements in the audiovisual field.[72]

For the purposes of this reservation, the expression 'arts and cultural industries' has been defined as including 'a) books, magazines, periodicals, or newspapers in printed or electronic form … e) visual arts, artistic photography and new media; g) media or multimedia services'.[73]

The agreement between Chile and Argentina[74] is particularly interesting, since it contains cultural reservations which explicitly refer to digital technologies. Argentina, for instance, has included in the chapter on investment a reservation on cultural industries that are broadly defined. As mentioned in the agreement, 'cultural industries' includes, among others:

> (a) the publication, distribution or sale of printed *or electronic* books, magazines, periodicals or newspapers …; (b) the production, distribution, sale or exhibition of motion picture recordings *in any of their existing formats*; (c) the production, distribution, sale or exhibition of music recordings in *any of their existing formats*; … and (e) radio communications in which the transmissions are intended to be received directly by the general public, as well as all activities related to radio, television, cable *and Internet transmission*, artistic photography and new media[75] (emphasis added).

[71] ibid Art 13.1.

[72] Chile has formulated this reservation in most of its free trade agreements recently adopted in Annex II, under the sub-sector 'Arts and cultural industries'.

[73] This reservation can be found in the CPTPP and in the Chile–Brazil Bilateral Trade Agreement (signed 22 November 2018, entered into force 25 January 2022) www.sice.oas.org/TPD/BRA_CHL/FTA_CHL_BRA_s.pdf.

[74] Argentina–Chile Free Trade Agreement (signed 2 November 2017, entered into force 1 May 2019) www.sice.oas.org/Trade/ARG_CHL/ARG_CHL_FTA_s.pdf.

[75] ibid Annex 8.11, para 7. The official version of the agreement is in Spanish: '"industrias culturales" incluye, entre otras: (a) la publicación, distribución o venta de libros, revistas, publicaciones periódicas o diarios impresos o electrónicos …; (b) la producción, distribución, venta o exhibición de grabaciones de películas en cualquiera de sus formatos existentes; (c) la producción, distribución, venta o exhibición de grabaciones de música en cualquiera de sus formatos existentes; … y (e) las radiocomunicaciones en las cuales las transmisiones tengan por objeto ser recibidas directamente por el público general, así como todas las actividades relacionadas con la radio, televisión, transmisión por cable y por Internet, fotografía artística y nuevos medios'.

This reservation protects Argentina's right to adopt and implement measures inconsistent with national treatment and most-favoured-nation treatment. The statement that cultural services are covered regardless of their format, including the digital format, preserves Argentina's power of intervention in the digital environment, which gives the reservation a broad scope that covers the commitments related to electronic commerce. In a certain way, such a reservation creates a bridge with Article 11.2.3 of chapter 11, on electronic commerce, which states that this chapter is subject to the provisions, exceptions or non-conforming measures set out in other chapters or annexes of this or other relevant treaties concluded between the parties.

The choice of words is therefore crucial to ensure that a cultural reservation also covers measures relating to digital cultural products, such as policies to promote local content or other cultural policies applicable in the digital environment. Nevertheless, for greater legal certainty, parties should consider including such reservations or similar cultural clauses directly in the provisions contained in the chapter dedicated to electronic commerce.

B. Exclusion of the Audiovisual Sector from e-Commerce Commitments

In most of its trade agreements, the EU has excluded the audiovisual sector from the scope of its commitments related to cross-border services and investment. In its first agreements that included a chapter on electronic commerce, the EU kept the same approach, without paying much attention to the impact of commitments related to digital products on the cultural sector. One example of such approach is the CETA mentioned above.[76] In its latest agreements, however, the EU has adopted a new strategy aiming to exclude the audiovisual sector from its electronic commerce commitments. Several agreements illustrate this trend, notably those concluded with Mexico, Japan, Tunisia, Singapore and the MERCOSUR countries.[77]

For example, chapter 8 of the EU–Japan Economic Partnership Agreement on Trade in services, investment liberalisation and electronic commerce begins with the reaffirmation of the right of parties to adopt regulatory measures within their territories to achieve 'legitimate policy objectives, such as the … promotion

[76] Above n 27.

[77] See EU–Mexico Agreement (in negotiation) announced on 21 April 2018 (the text of this agreement is not the final version as trade negotiations are still ongoing between the EU and Mexico); EU–Japan Economic Partnership Agreement (signed 17 July 2018, entered into force 1 February 2019) policy.trade.ec.europa.eu/eu-trade-relationships-country-and-region/countries-and-regions/japan/eu-japan-agreement/eu-japan-agreement-chapter-chapter_en; Deep and Comprehensive Free Trade Area (DCFTA) between the EU and Tunisia (signed 26 April 2016, not in force); Free Trade Agreement between European Union and the Republic of Singapore (signed 19 October 2018, not in force); EU–Mercosur Trade Agreement (signed 28 June 2019, not in force).

and protection of cultural diversity',[78] which implicitly refers to the objectives and principles of the CDC. Then, section B, on investment liberalisation, section C, on cross-border trade in services, and section F, on electronic commerce, each contain a specific provision that seeks to exclude the audiovisual sector from their scope. In section C, subsidies are also excluded, while in section F, the exclusion also covers broadcasting.[79] Another point of interest in section F is the clause on the free flow of data. Rather than making an immediate commitment, the parties preferred to agree on a future reassessment of the situation. Hence, Article 8.81 states that 'the Parties shall reassess within three years of the date of entry into force of this Agreement the need for inclusion of provisions on the free flow of data into this Agreement'.

The EU–Japan Economic Partnership Agreement and similar texts negotiated with Mexico, Tunisia, Singapore and MERCOSUR are the first agreements that contain binding commitments specifically applicable to electronic commerce, while explicitly excluding the audiovisual sector from their scope. There is no doubt that these exclusions were specifically requested by the Europeans. In doing so, the EU has extended to e-commerce a long-standing approach applied to trade in services and investment. In addition, the EU has ensured that it will be able to implement measures applied on this territory to promote European cultural content in the digital environment, such as the Audiovisual Media Services Directive revised in 2018, which provides for a requirement of at least a 30 per cent share of European works in the catalogues of providers of on-demand audiovisual media services, as well as a requirement of prominence for these works.[80] It should be emphasised, however, that by excluding only the audiovisual sector, the European Union is giving up its power to intervene with respect to other digital cultural products. The scope of its cultural exception is therefore more limited than the clause used by Canada, or the cultural exception used by New Zealand in some recent agreements (see section IVC below).

In addition, it is worth noting that there remains one important element for the implementation of the CDC in the digital environment that does not seem to have been addressed in trade agreements, either by the EU or by any other party: the implementation of Article 16.[81] This article requires parties to 'facilitate cultural

[78] EU–Japan Economic Partnership Agreement, Art 8.1.2.

[79] The relevant provisions are: EU–Japan Economic Partnership Agreement, c 8, s B, Art 8.6.2c); s C, Art 8.14.2d) and e); s F, Art 8.70.5. For similar examples, see V Guèvremont et al, *Comments Presented by the UNESCO Chair on the Diversity of Cultural Expressions as Part of the Consultations in Anticipation of Possible Negotiations on Electronic Commerce at the World Trade Organization (WTO) to the Directorate of Trade Policy on Services (TMS)* (Global Affairs Canada, 25 April 2019) 8.

[80] Above n 10.

[81] Between 2008 and 2012, the EU concluded three trade or economic partnership agreements to which a protocol on cultural cooperation implementing Art 16 of the CDC was annexed. These agreements are the Economic Partnership Agreement between the CARIFORUM States, of the one part, and the European Community and its Member States, of the other part (signed 15 October 2008, entered into force 1 November 2008) [2008] OJ L289/3; the Free Trade Agreement between the European Union and its Member States, of the one part, and the Republic of Korea, of the other part (signed 6 October 2010, entered into force 1 July 2011) [2011] OJ L127/1; and the Agreement establishing an Association between the European Union and its Member States, on the one hand, and Central

exchanges with developing countries by granting … preferential treatment to artists and other cultural professionals and practitioners, as well as cultural goods and services from developing countries'. Such commitment must now be implemented in the context of digital trade.[82]

Between 2008 and 2012, the EU had developed an inspiring model for the implementation of Article 16, using a Protocol on Cultural Cooperation (PCC) to grant preferential treatment to its trade partners.[83] Since then, however, it seems to have abandoned the PCC approach and the implementation of Article 16 in the digital environment does not appear to have been the subject of new provisions in trade agreements. It could be assumed nevertheless that the exclusion of the audiovisual sector from the EU's commitments in this area will enable it to give preference to works from developing countries. However, it would be desirable for such treatment to be formally enshrined in a trade agreement or in a new model of cultural cooperation protocol annexed to it.

C. General Cultural Exception in the Chapter on Electronic Commerce

Another approach to the treatment of cultural goods and services in the digital environment is the inclusion in a trade agreement of a general cultural exception that explicitly applies to digital products. New Zealand has used this approach for

America, on the other (signed 29 June 2012, entered into force 1 August 2013) [2012] OJ L346/3. This approach was later abandoned. On this point, see A Vlassis, 'European Union and Online Platforms in Global Audiovisual Politics and Economy: Once Upon a Time in America?' [2020] *The International Communication Gazette* 1, 10. Although some clauses of the three protocols previously concluded by the EU may be applicable to the digital environment, to date, no trade agreement includes a preferential treatment clause specifically applicable to the digital trade.

[82] See Art 18 of the Guidelines, which states that: 'Parties shall aim to introduce preferential treatment provisions to facilitate more balanced flows of cultural goods and services from developing countries in the digital environment, pursuant to Article 16 of the Convention. Parties may: 18.1 improve the distribution of cultural goods and services in the digital environment produced by artists and cultural professionals, enterprises and independent organizations from developing countries, including through artistic and cultural collaboration, co-production and co-distribution agreements; 18.2 take into account the provisions of international trade agreements they have concluded and will conclude, and their respective mechanisms with a view to offering preferential treatment in favour of cultural goods and services from developing countries in the digital environment.'

[83] A scientific study, carried out in 2017, examined 59 regional and bilateral trade agreements concluded between states of all continents after the adoption of the CDC. Its main objective was to analyse the implementation of Arts 16 and 21 of the CDC and, therefore, to examine the treatment granted to cultural goods and services and to artists and cultural professionals of the parties within regional and bilateral trade agreements. See Guèvremont and Otasevic, *Culture in Treaties* (2017). The study shows that the most innovative model agreement is that developed by the EU to which a PCC is annexed. This model was used in the following agreements: EU–CARIFORUM, EU–Republic of Korea, EU–Central America. Three aspects of these PCCs are particularly relevant for trade: (i) the temporary entry and stay of artists and other cultural professionals; (ii) the negotiation of new co-production agreements; and (iii) a preferential access for co-produced audiovisual works through the attribution of the 'European works' status (only in the PCCs annexed to the EU–Republic of Korea and EU–CARIFORUM agreements). See ibid 43–45.

over a decade to preserve its right to adopt and implement measures relating to a broad category of cultural goods and services.[84] Two elements should be noted: first, this clause is incorporated into the chapter on general exceptions and therefore applies to all chapters contained in these agreements, including the chapter on electronic commerce where relevant; second, the scope of this exception is defined so as to cover digital products.

For example, in the Free Trade Agreement between New Zealand and the Republic of Korea, chapter 20, on general provisions and exceptions, states in Article 20.1.3 that

> [f]or the purposes of this Agreement, subject to the requirement that such measures are not applied in a manner which would constitute a means of arbitrary or unjustifiable discrimination between the Parties where like conditions prevail, or a disguised restriction on trade in goods or services and investment, nothing in this Agreement shall be construed to prevent the adoption or enforcement by a Party of measures necessary to protect national works or specific sites of historical or archaeological value, or to support creative arts [Footnote 1] of national value which is customarily practiced.

In the footnote, *creative arts* is defined as including

> the performing arts – including theatre, dance and music – visual arts and craft, literature, film and video, language arts, *creative online content*, indigenous traditional practice and contemporary cultural expression, and *digital interactive media and hybrid art work*, including those that use *new technologies* to transcend discrete art form divisions. The term encompasses those activities involved in the presentation, execution and interpretation of the arts; and the study and technical development of these art forms and activities (emphasis added).

The scope of this cultural exception is broad and covers digital cultural products. It provides New Zealand with a policy space to intervene and regulate the cultural sector in the digital environment and to push its local content online if it deems it

[84] Pacific Agreement on Closer Economic Relations (PACER) Plus (signed 14 June 2017, entered into force 13 December 2020) www.dfat.gov.au/trade/agreements/in-force/pacer/documents; Free Trade Agreement between New Zealand and the Republic of Korea (signed 23 March 2015, entered into force 20 December 2015) www.mfat.govt.nz/assets/Trade-agreements/Korea-NZ-FTA/NZ-Korea-FTA-consolidated-text.pdf; Agreement between New Zealand and the Separate Customs Territory of Taiwan, Penghu, Kinmen, and Matsu on Economic Cooperation (signed 10 October 2013, entered into force 1 December 2013) www.treaties.mfat.govt.nz/search/details/t/3795/c_1; New Zealand–Hong Kong, China Closer Economic Partnership Agreement (signed 29 March 2010, entered into force 1 January 2011) www.mfat.govt.nz/assets/Trade-agreements/Hong-Kong-China-CEP/NZ-HK-CEP.pdf; New Zealand–Malaysia Free Trade Agreement (signed 26 September 2009, entered into force 1 August 2010) www.mfat.govt.nz/assets/Trade-agreements/Malaysia-NZ-FTA/mnzfta-guide-to-fta.pdf; Agreement establishing the ASEAN–Australia–New Zealand Free Trade Area (AANZFTA) (signed 27 February 2009, entered into force 1 January 2010) www.dfat.gov.au/trade/agreements/in-force/aanzfta/official-documents/Pages/agreement-establishing-the-asean-australia-new-zealand-free-trade-area-aanzfta; Free Trade Agreement between the Government of the People's Republic of China and the Government of New Zealand (signed 7 April 2008, entered into force 10 January 2008) www.mfat.govt.nz/en/trade/free-trade-agreements/free-trade-agreements-in-force/nz-china-free-trade-agreement/new-zealand-china-fta-resources/.

necessary. It would be interesting, however, to see how this exception will be interpreted in the context of a dispute regarding a measure relating to a digital cultural product. The exception contains a passage that recalls the 'chapeau' of Article XX of the General Agreement on Tariffs and Trade (GATT) 1994 (or Article XIV of the GATS 1995).[85] The WTO jurisprudence demonstrates that conditions set out in this 'chapeau' can be particularly difficult to fulfil by states wishing to maintain the measure otherwise inconsistent with their trade commitments.[86]

Additionally, it is worth noting that in 2020 Chile, New Zealand and Singapore signed the Digital Economy Partnership Agreement (DEPA),[87] which is a trade agreement exclusively dedicated to electronic commerce. It is part of a new generation of agreement entirely dedicated to electronic commerce.[88] The DEPA gives interesting indications as to commitments that could emerge from the ongoing negotiations on electronic commerce within the WTO.

With regard to culture, a first element to underline is that the Preamble of this agreement underlines the importance of promoting diversity and cultural identity.[89] A second relevant element is the presence of provisions relating to

[85] It should be recalled that for a measure to be adopted under Art XX of the GATT 1994, it must not only fall under at least one of the general exceptions listed, but also be consistent with the 'chapeau' of Art XX. See WTO, 'Brazil – Measures Affecting Imports of Retreaded Tyres', Appellate Body Report (3 December 2007) WTO Doc WT/DS332/AB/R, para 139; WTO, 'United States – Measures Affecting the Cross-Border Supply of Gambling and Betting Services', Appellate Body Report (7 April 2005) WTO Doc WT/DS285/AB/R, paras 306–07; WTO, 'China – Measures Affecting Trading Rights and Distribution Services for Certain Publications and Audiovisual Entertainment Products', Panel Report (12 August 2009) WTO Doc WT/DS363/R, para 7.746.

[86] Compliance with the requirements of the 'chapeau' of Art XX of the GATT 1994 is the evidence of good faith. With respect to the requirement of good faith, the fundamental element is found in the purpose and object, which is to avoid the abuse or the illegitimate use of the exceptions to the substantive rules provided for in Art XX. As such, for a measure to pass the good faith test in the practice of the WTO Dispute Settlement Body, it must not arbitrarily or unjustifiably discriminate between countries where the same conditions exist, and it may not be applied in such a way as to constitute a disguised restriction on international trade. The Appellate Body in United States-Gasoline (Appellate Body Report) stated that 'this is necessarily a more onerous task than that which consisted in showing that an exception … is applicable to the measure at issue'. See WTO, 'United States – Standards for Reformulated and Conventional Gasoline', Appellate Body Report (26 April 1996) WTO Doc WT/DS2/AB/R, 23.

[87] (signed 12 June 2020, entered into force 7 January 2021) www.mfat.govt.nz/assets/Trade-agreements/DEPA/DEPA-Signing-Text-11-June-2020-GMT-v3.pdf.

[88] Two other agreements dedicated to digital commerce have been signed to date: the Australia–Singapore Digital Economy Agreement (signed 20 March 2020, entered into force 8 December 2020) www.dfat.gov.au/sites/default/files/australia-singapore-digital-economy-agreement.pdf (which mainly replaces the provisions of the chapters on Electronic Commerce and Financial Services of the Singapore–Australia Free Trade Agreement concluded in 2003); and the Agreement between the United States of America and Japan Concerning Digital Trade (signed 7 October 2019, entered into force 1 January 2020) ustr.gov/sites/default/files/files/agreements/japan/Agreement_between_the_United_States_and_Japan_concerning_Digital_Trade.pdf.

[89] In para 13 of the Preamble, the parties 'Reaffirm the importance of promoting corporate social responsibility, cultural identity and diversity, environmental protection and conservation, gender equality, Indigenous rights, labour rights, inclusive trade, sustainable development and traditional knowledge, as well as the importance of preserving their right to regulate in the public interest'.

the cross-border transfer of information by electronic means and the location of computing facilities allowing parties to adopt or maintain measures inconsistent with their commitments 'to achieve a legitimate public policy objective'.[90] This flexibility could benefit the implementation and monitoring of policies aimed at protecting and promoting the diversity of cultural expressions. Given that such policies are currently under development in many parties to the CDC, it may be desirable that similar flexibility be provided with respect to all e-commerce commitments.

Finally, a third element to highlight is the incorporation of the general cultural exception mentioned above,[91] which again covers a wide range of digital cultural products and could protect the right of the parties to implement cultural policies in the digital environment. This exception clearly indicates the openness of the parties to take into account the specific nature of *creative arts of national value*, which is consistent with the objectives and principles of the CDC and its Guidelines. As mentioned earlier, however, there is uncertainty as to how this exception could be interpreted in the context of a dispute.[92]

V. Conclusion

In recent years, bilateral and regional trade agreements have reflected the willingness of the parties to the CDC to extend the recognition of the specific nature of cultural goods and services to the digital environment. This trend reflects important political and legislative changes that are taking place within the territory of states in the field of cultural policies to extend their scope to activities that take place online. The adaptation of the legislative framework in the specific areas of audiovisual and broadcasting demonstrates, among other things, the states' concerns about the homogenisation of cultural offerings on the Internet and their desire to continue to promote local content to their own audiences.

The developments presented above concerning cultural clauses applicable to digital trade are coherent with the willingness of parties to the CDC to implement this instrument in the digital environment. Several states seem to be aware of the effects on their cultural sector of binding commitments applicable to electronic

[90] DEPA, Arts 4.3 and 4.4. Certain conditions must be respected, namely that the measures are 'not applied in a manner which would constitute a means of arbitrary or unjustifiable discrimination or a disguised restriction on trade; [and do] not impose restrictions on transfers of information greater than are required to achieve the objective'.

[91] ibid Art 15.1.4.

[92] This problematic was raised in discussions during the public seminar 'Taking into Account the Specific Nature of Culture When Negotiating and Implementing E-commerce Commitments: Why? How?', organised by the UNESCO Chair on the Diversity of Cultural Expressions (Laval University, 31 January 2020) www.unescodec.chaire.ulaval.ca/fr/activites/seminaire-culture-et-commerce-electronique.

commerce. However, several examples have shown that there is still room for improvement, as none of the cultural clauses negotiated to date seem to have the potential to apply to all digital cultural products.

Moreover, not all parties to the Convention show the same level of awareness of this matter. The impetus to integrate cultural clauses applicable to the digital environment seems to come exclusively from developed countries, and more specifically from those that were already pushing for a recognition of the dual nature of cultural goods and services in their previous trade agreements. One of the next challenges for developing countries will be to secure their right to implement cultural policies in the digital environment, without giving up all the benefits that can be derived from the growth of digital trade. Another challenge will be for them to formulate clear demands in order to benefit from Article 16 and obtain preferential treatment for their cultural goods and services in the digital environment.

Finally, for all parties to the CDC, the outcome of the WTO negotiations on electronic commerce will be crucial. The ongoing negotiation in this area offers them an unprecedented occasion to unite and promote the objectives and principles of the Convention in this trade forum, in conformity with their commitments.[93] Resistance from the USA is predictable. After all, the USA was the first to promote binding commitments on electronic commerce in its bilateral trade agreements, and its positions expressed at the WTO in the context of the negotiations on electronic commerce reflect a strong determination to expand such commitments to the multilateral system.[94] Nevertheless, if parties agree to show political will, they will be able to build on their experience and practice developed in recent years to achieve their objectives. This will involve suggesting innovative cultural clauses applicable to electronic commerce that will preserve their policy space in the field of culture, in order to ensure consistency with their commitments under the CDC, and *Make the Cultural Exception Great Again*.

[93] CDC, Art 21.

[94] On this point, see I Bernier, *The Recent Free Trade Agreements of the United States as Illustration of Their New Strategy Regarding the Audiovisual Sector* (Quebec, Ministry of Culture and Communications, 2004).

5

Promoting the Objectives and Principles of the 2005 UNESCO Convention in the Digital Environment: New Forums to Consider?

CLÉMENCE VARIN

I. Introduction

On 18 March 2007, the Convention on the Protection and Promotion of the Diversity of Cultural Expressions (hereinafter CDC or the Convention)[1] entered into force, marking on the international scale the wish of a group of states to preserve their power to intervene in the cultural sector at a time when cultural policies were particularly vulnerable to trade rules. For 15 years now, parties have been for the most part progressing toward the treaty's objectives, despite many challenges.[2] The growing use of digital technologies and their possible negative effect on the diversity of cultural expressions is one of those challenges, and has prompted parties to reaffirm their commitment to protect and promote the diversity of cultural expressions in this environment. In June 2017, they approved the 'Operational Guidelines for the Implementation of the Convention in the Digital Environment' (hereinafter Digital Guidelines).[3] Among the many actions put forward, the Digital Guidelines underline the need for parties to promote the objectives and principles of the Convention in international forums other than UNESCO – as required by Article 21 of this treaty. However, the digital environment may require some adaptations in that respect at a time when the landscape of international law is changing.

[1] (adopted 20 October 2005, entered into force 18 March 2007) 2440 UNTS 311.

[2] C Varin and V Guèvremont, 'La *Convention sur la diversité des expressions culturelles* quinze ans après: une mise en œuvre effective d'un instrument juridique faiblement contraignant' (2019) 32.2-2 *Revue québécoise de droit international* 1.

[3] 'Guidelines on the Implementation of the Convention in the Digital Environment' in UNESCO, *Basic Texts of the 2005 Convention on the Protection and Promotion of the Diversity of Cultural Expressions* (Paris, UNESCO, 2019) 87–95.

These past few years, a variety of forums have been addressing digital issues and trying to reach a consensus on a set of rules to better address some challenges raised by digital technologies and their use in all spheres of society. The Organisation for Economic Co-operation and Development (OECD), for example, has been working towards establishing common rules for the taxation of the digital economy, while other forums attempt to regulate other aspects of Internet governance or emerging technologies such as artificial intelligence (AI). These forums are very diverse, in terms of both the actors they bring together (states, civil society, private entities, etc) and their nature (formal organisations, informal meeting, etc), but they contribute to building a consensus on certain issues.

The protection and promotion of the diversity of cultural expressions in the digital environment depends on decisions taken within those forums, and questions whether parties should promote some of the objectives and principles of the Convention within these forums from the moment they might be at stake. This chapter suggests that parties should adapt their strategies to the digital environment and consider a wider diversity of forums, as long as their actions could have an impact on the CDC objectives and principles. Parties already have a broad interpretation of the term 'international forum' in Article 21; however, the implementation of the Convention in the digital environment might require further broadening the kinds of forum in which to promote the treaty. After briefly presenting the raison d'être and content of Article 21 CDC (section II), this chapter will focus more specifically on the importance of considering other types of forum to ensure that the objectives and principles of the Convention apply within the digital environment (section III).

II. Promoting the Objectives and Principles of the Convention in Other Forums: A Crucial Provision

Commitments made by parties under the Convention may affect others they have taken, or are likely to take, in other sectors.[4] Because of this, parties are committed under Article 21 to promote the CDC objectives and principles in other forums. Before entering into an in-depth analysis of Article 21 (B), a quick diversion is necessary to explain its origins and what was intended by the drafters (A). This section aims to show that Article 21 is still very much relevant today within the

[4] Cultural policies put in place to protect and promote the diversity of cultural expressions may, for example, 'impact on free trade, interfere with foreign investment, foster respect for fundamental rights, support the achievement of sustainable development, influence international cooperation, interact with rules regarding the media and telecommunications, or impinge upon the digital'. V Guèvremont, 'The Convention in Other International Forums: A Crucial Commitment' in D Cliche (ed), *Re|Shaping Cultural Policies. Advancing Creativity for Development* (Paris, UNESCO, 2017) 161.

new reality of the digital environment and, more broadly, its implementation is crucial to achieving the objectives of the Convention in this environment.

A. Chapter V of the Convention: Managing the Relationship between the Convention and Other Instruments

Article 21 CDC, on international consultation and coordination, contains two kinds of interrelated obligations.[5] The first sentence commands parties to the Convention to 'promote the objectives and principles of this Convention in other international forums', while the second determines that they shall, 'For this purpose, consult each other, as appropriate, bearing in mind these objectives and principles'.[6] Originally drafted as Article 13 and situated in the section on the rights and obligations relating to international cooperation, Article 21 was moved to chapter V, on the relationship between the Convention and other instruments during the negotiations of the Convention.[7] By placing Article 21 in this section, negotiators appear to have wanted to 'enshrine specific procedures aimed at specifically addressing the situation dealt with in Chapter V and the preceding Article 20 – namely, the potentially conflicting relationship between the [Convention] and other instruments'.[8] Article 21 should thus always be read with Article 20, devoted to the relationship to other treaties, with mutual supportiveness, complementarity and non-subordination in mind.[9] Article 20 can be seen as an 'interpretative provision' aimed at clarifying the relationship between the Convention and other instruments, while Article 21 is an 'operational provision' aimed at encouraging and supporting 'the taking into account of the objectives and principles of the Convention in other international forums'.[10] Indeed, insofar as some actions taken by parties on the international scale could go against the objectives and principles contained in the Convention, both Articles recall the principle of good faith in international law.[11]

[5] PT Stoll, 'Article 21. International Consultation and Coordination' in S von Schorlemer and PT Stoll (eds), *The UNESCO Convention on the Protection and Promotion of the Diversity of Cultural Expressions. Explanatory Notes* (Berlin, Springer, 2012) 549.

[6] The text of Art 21 is the following: 'Parties undertake to promote the objectives and principles of this Convention in other international forums. For this purpose, Parties shall consult each other, as appropriate, bearing in mind these objectives and principles.'

[7] Stoll, 'Article 21. International Consultation and Coordination', 545.

[8] Art 21 thus adds a 'procedural dimension' to Art 20, which Stoll refers to as the 'Conflict Clause' of the Convention. ibid 546–50.

[9] For a detailed analysis of these articles, see I Bernier, 'The Relationship between the UNESCO Convention on the Protection and Promotion of the Diversity of Cultural Expressions and Other International Instruments: The Emergence of a New Balance in the Interface between Commerce and Culture' (Quebec, Chronique, Ministère de la Culture et des Communications, 2009).

[10] ibid 21.

[11] ibid 3–16.

Chapter V sparked the most debate during the drafting of the treaty and was adopted at the very end of the negotiation.[12] Indeed, two contradictory visions prevailed at the time. On the one hand, some countries wanted the future Convention to expressly stipulate that 'trade commitments would take precedence over the cultural commitments of the Parties in the Convention'.[13] On the other hand, and for a vast majority of countries, because 'cultural goods and services could not be considered exclusively as merchandise or consumer goods because they convey identities, values, and meanings', it was important that culture have 'a legitimate place next to the other concerns of the WTO'.[14] A consensus was reached with the current wording, which clearly establishes 'the absence of any relation of subordination between [the Convention] and other international agreements'.[15]

Chapter V therefore ensures the coherence between the commitments taken by parties with respect to the Convention. Articles 20 and 21 CDC are both considered 'crucial for managing the interactions and overlaps between … other instruments and the Convention',[16] in the sense that the other articles of the Convention 'can only have their full effect within [their] boundaries'.[17] They draw the limits between the 'obligations and rights deriving from the [treaty] and those deriving from other international agreements'[18] by recognising the possibility that some actions taken by parties outside of UNESCO could go against the objectives and principles of the CDC.[19] In those particular circumstances of conflict, parties are required to promote them. Article 21 is thus one of the most important CDC provisions, as the 'failure to implement [it] could jeopardize the achievement of the fundamental purposes of the Convention'.[20] Indeed, it refers to the Convention as a whole, its *objectives* and its *principles*, which means that a poor implementation of it might result in parties engaging in other agreements interfering directly with the commitments they took with regard to the protection and promotion of the diversity of cultural expressions. A closer look at the provision is now necessary to understand what is expected of parties when they implement this provision.

[12] ibid 1.

[13] ibid.

[14] ibid. For more details on the reasons that led to the adoption of the Convention, see I Bernier and H Ruiz Fabri, 'Évaluation de la faisabilité juridique d'un instrument international sur la diversité culturelle' (Quebec, Groupe franco-québécois sur la diversité culturelle, Gouvernement du Québec, Ministère de la Culture, 2002); I Bernier, 'Trade and Culture' in PFJ Macrory, AE Appleton and MG Plummer (eds), *The World Trade Organization: Legal, Economic and Political Analysis* (Boston, MA, Spinger, 2005).

[15] Bernier, 'The Relationship between the UNESCO Convention on the Protection and Promotion of the Diversity of Cultural Expressions and Other International Instruments', 1.

[16] V Guèvremont, 'Promoting the Convention in International Forums' in D Cliche (ed), *Re/Shaping Cultural Policies. A Decade Promoting the Diversity of Cultural Expressions for Development* (Paris, UNESCO, 2015) 137.

[17] RJ Neuwirth, 'The Convention on the Diversity of Cultural Expressions. A Critical Analysis of the Provisions' in T Kono and S Van Uytsel (eds), *The UNESCO Convention on the Diversity of Cultural Expressions. A Tale of Fragmentation in International Law* (Cambridge, Intersentia, 2012) 63.

[18] ibid.

[19] Bernier, 'The Relationship between the UNESCO Convention on the Protection and Promotion of the Diversity of Cultural Expressions and Other International Instruments', 16.

[20] Guèvremont, 'The Convention in Other International Forums', 161.

B. The Flexibility Offered by the Terms in Article 21

A first reading of Article 21 reveals the use of 'broad terms', such as 'promote the objectives and principles' and 'other international forums'.[21] This can offer a lot of flexibility to parties for its implementation, while at the same time being blurry and ambiguous.[22] Parties to the Convention did not deem it necessary to elaborate operational guidelines for its implementation, as is often the case for other articles of the CDC.[23] This decision might be explained by the tensions that surrounded the adoption of Articles 20 and 21, but it is nevertheless regrettable as it could have clarified the scope of Article 21.[24]

The first sentence of Article 21 – 'Parties undertake to promote the objectives and principles of this Convention in other international forums' – is 'unique in calling on Parties to actively promote the outreach of the Convention in other fora'.[25] It refers to Articles 1 and 2 CDC,[26] while also invoking 'any other part of the Convention closely linked to them'.[27] It is a commitment of means that allows parties to choose how they will promote the objectives and principles of the Convention in other international forums.[28] The elaboration of an 'illustrative list of relevant forums', as is the case in other international instruments, as well as examples of acts of 'promotion', could facilitate the implementation of this provision by parties,[29] but no such elaboration has been (officially) foreseen by the parties.

[21] Stoll, 'Article 21. International Consultation and Coordination', 546.

[22] Bernier, 'The Relationship between the UNESCO Convention on the Protection and Promotion of the Diversity of Cultural Expressions and Other International Instruments', 1.

[23] Art 21 was not identified as needy of operational guidelines by the Conference of Parties in 2007. However, for several years now, civil society organisations have been advocating for the adoption of guidelines to promote the Convention in other fora, especially in the context of digital trade agreements. See IFCCD, 'Intervention de la FICDC à la 15e réunion du CIG, février 2022' (International Federation of Coalitions for Cultural Diversity, February 2022) www.ficdc.org/wp-content/uploads/2022/02/interventions-ficdc-v7.pdf.

[24] Bernier, 'The Relationship between the UNESCO Convention on the Protection and Promotion of the Diversity of Cultural Expressions and Other International Instruments', 18.

[25] Stoll, 'Article 21. International Consultation and Coordination', 545.

[26] Art 1 recalls the objectives of the Convention and Art 2 its eight guiding principles.

[27] Stoll, 'Article 21. International Consultation and Coordination', 548.

[28] Bernier, 'The Relationship between the UNESCO Convention on the Protection and Promotion of the Diversity of Cultural Expressions and Other International Instruments', 16.

[29] This could be done in operational guidelines. Bernier gives two examples of international instruments using the term 'international forum' that provide such a list, namely the 2008 Canada–Colombia Free Trade Agreement and a decision rendered by the International Tropical Timber Organization. In the first case, Art 504.2(g), on the functions of the Committee on Sanitary and Phytosanitary Measures, considers, among others, the Committees of the Codex Alimentarius Commission, the World Organization for Animal Health and other international and regional forums on food safety, human, animal and plant health as relevant multilateral and international forums. The second example is even more explicit as it provides a long list of relevant international and regional organisations and forums, such as the World Bank, the United Nations Framework Convention on Climate Change (UNFCCC) and the Asia Pacific Economic Cooperation (APEC). See ibid 16–18.

For various authors, the term 'promotion' should be understood broadly as covering a 'wide range of activities', including 'any activity of agenda-setting, or submission of written or oral statements contributing to the discussion'.[30] The same can be said of the term 'international forums', which should be interpreted broadly in the CDC context.[31] It could encompass international governmental organisations, including their organs, commissions and special committees, and international non-governmental organisations, at the multilateral, regional or bilateral level.[32] It could also include 'bodies and processes with an informal or preliminary nature', such as the G7.[33] Events or bodies 'instituted by non-States actors, insofar as they aim at contributing to discussion and consensus-building and decision-making at an international level', could also be taken into consideration.[34] Thus, any 'public spaces for discussion',[35] as long as they are relevant to the 'field of application of the Convention', should be considered for the promotion of the objectives and principles of the treaty.[36] This broad definition is also the one adopted – to a certain extent – by the parties to the Convention, as we shall see in section III of this chapter.

The second sentence of Article 21 calls for parties '*to consult* each other, as appropriate, bearing in mind these objectives and principles' (emphasis added), and adds 'a duty to consult'[37] to this provision.[38] No detail is given on what is expected of parties, apart from that the Intergovernmental Committee shall 'establish procedures and other mechanisms for consultation' aimed at promoting the CDC objectives and principles in other international forums.[39] The wording does not seem to mean that a consensus must be reached during this consultation, nor does it indicate a specific order in which consultations should be done, such as 'prior to any act of promotion'.[40] It seems clear, however, that a coordinated promotion of the objectives and principles of the Convention by parties in

[30] For Stoll, this promotion 'must be seen in the context of the working procedures, rules and objectives of the other international forums in question … It is questionable whether any technical or financial effort is also included'. See Stoll, 'Article 21. International Consultation and Coordination', 548.

[31] ibid. For Bernier, 'International documents that use the expression make reference to international organizations of all types, but also to international conferences and meetings where states discuss matters of common concern'. See Bernier, 'The Relationship between the UNESCO Convention on the Protection and Promotion of the Diversity of Cultural Expressions and Other International Instruments', 18.

[32] ibid 18; Stoll, 'Article 21. International Consultation and Coordination'.

[33] Stoll, 'Article 21. International Consultation and Coordination', 547.

[34] ibid 548.

[35] Bernier, 'The Relationship between the UNESCO Convention on the Protection and Promotion of the Diversity of Cultural Expressions and Other International Instruments', 18.

[36] ibid. See also Stoll, 'Article 21. International Consultation and Coordination.

[37] Stoll, 'Article 21. International Consultation and Coordination', 549.

[38] For Bernier, this promotion could be done 'on an individual basis without consulting each [Parties] or, where circumstances allow, as a group after consulting amongst themselves'. Bernier analyses both possibilities. See Bernier, 'The Relationship between the UNESCO Convention on the Protection and Promotion of the Diversity of Cultural Expressions and Other International Instruments', 16.

[39] Art 23.6(e) of the Convention.

[40] Stoll, 'Article 21. International Consultation and Coordination', 550.

a specific forum would have a greater impact and maximise the chances that they will be taken into account in the works of such forums. This important aspect will, however, not be the subject of this chapter, which will mainly focus on the first sentence of the Article.

Thus, when ratifying the Convention, parties are committed to promoting the objectives and principles of this treaty in other forums when necessary. Failure to implement this provision could be harmful to the commitments they took with regard to the Convention, as some obligations taken in other forums could prevent them from protecting and promoting the diversity of cultural expressions on their territory.[41] The use of broad terms in Article 21, even if it appears to be problematic at first, offers a lot of flexibility to parties to implement the provision. It will also prove to be particularly useful for the implementation of the Convention in the digital environment and in the changing landscape of international law, as section III will show.

III. The Implementation of Article 21 in the Digital Environment

Various authors agree on the importance of the implementation of Article 21 for the achievement of the objectives of the CDC.[42] Since its adoption, some parties have been active on this matter, promoting the objectives and principles of the Convention in a variety of forums (A). However, the challenges raised by the digital environment show the relevance of the Article even more (B), but also the need for the Convention's promotion in other kinds of forum (C). The background and definitions provided in section II of this chapter show that the way Article 21 was drafted gives parties plenty of room to do so.

A. The Promotion of the Convention's Objectives and Principles in Other Forums

In 2011, the Secretariat of the Convention was requested for the first time by the Conference of Parties 'to present, in relation to Article 21, a compendium of cases wherein the Convention is invoked or utilized in other international fora'.[43]

[41] Some commitments made in free trade agreements, for example, could prevent states from putting in place policies and measures, such as subsidies, for their cultural sector without facing sanctions. On this matter, see V Guèvremont and I Otasevic, *Culture in Treaties and Agreements: Implementing the 2005 Convention in Bilateral and Regional Trade Agreements* (Paris, UNESCO, 2017).

[42] See, among others, Guèvremont, 'Promoting the Convention in International Forums', 147; Bernier, 'The Relationship between the UNESCO Convention on the Protection and Promotion of the Diversity of Cultural Expressions and Other International Instruments'.

[43] Resolution 3.CP 11, para 5. UNESCO, 'Resolution', Conference of Parties to the Convention on the Protection and Promotion of the Diversity of Cultural Expressions, Third Ordinary Session (Paris, UNESCO Headquarters, 14–15 June 2011, CE/11/3.CP/209/Res, 16 June 2011) 6.

The outcome of these consultations showed that parties had a broad definition of the notion of 'international forum', and had already implemented this provision 'worldwide in multilateral and regional forum administered by international governmental and non-governmental organizations, both within and outside the cultural sphere'.[44] International organisations, regional economic organisations, regional intergovernmental organisations, government institutes and networks operating on an international or regional level, as well as international non-governmental organisations were listed as relevant forums for the implementation of Article 21.[45]

Around 250 texts from dozens of international, regional or bilateral organisations have been listed as referring explicitly to the 2005 Convention.[46] The promotion of the objectives and principles of the Convention has taken various forms, such as explicit references to the Convention in the context of declarations adopted during meetings and summits. In bilateral and regional trade agreements, parties have chosen, for example, to incorporate references to the treaty, adopt cultural protocols, include cultural exemptions, use positives lists of specific commitments and/or formulate some reservations. These techniques aimed, among other things, at recognising the specific nature of cultural activities, goods and services, and preserving the rights of parties to intervene in the cultural sector to protect and promote the diversity of cultural expressions on their territory (Article 1(g) and (h) CDC).[47]

However, if the origins of Articles 20 and 21 remind us of the conflict between trade and culture from which the Convention was born, the promotion of the objectives and principles of this treaty is not limited solely to the trade area. Organisations that 'have competencies in the field of culture or related areas', as well as forums in which 'culture is not a priority action area', are also pertinent.[48] The General Assembly of the United Nations has adopted resolutions in the

[44] Surveys were sent to the parties in 2011, 2012 and 2014. UNESCO, 'Item 11 of the Provisional Agenda: Preferential Treatment and International Consultation and Coordination: Report on the Implementation and Impact of Articles 16 and 21 of the Convention', Intergovernmental Committee for the Protection and Promotion of the Diversity of Cultural Expressions, Eighth Ordinary Session (Paris, UNESCO Headquarters, 9–11 December 2014, CE/14/8.IGC/11, 21 October 2014) 13.

[45] Examples of forums listed by parties include: other institutions of the United Nations, the WTO or the World Intellectual Property Organization (WIPO); regional economic organisations such as the Association of Southeast Asian Nations (ASEAN), the European Union, Mercosur; regional intergovernmental organisations such as the Organisation for Economic Cooperation and Development (OECD), the Organisation international de la Francophonie (OIF); networks operating on an international or regional level such as the International Network on Cultural Policy (INCP), the Educational and Cultural Council of Central America (CECC); and international non-governmental organisations such as the International Federation of Musicians (IFM), International Federation of Coalitions for Cultural Diversity (IFCCD). See ibid 13.

[46] For more details, see Guèvremont, 'Promoting the Convention in International Forums'; Guèvremont, 'The Convention in Other International Forums'.

[47] Guèvremont, 'Promoting the Convention in International Forums', 139. For an analysis of the implementation of Art 21 in the trade sphere, and more specifically bilateral and regional agreements, see ch 4 of this book, by V Guèvremont and I Otasevic.

[48] Guèvremont, 'Promoting the Convention in International Forums', 144–45.

field of culture and sustainable development mentioning the Convention.[49] The Organisation internationale de la Francophonie (OIF) has also been very active in the promotion of the Convention by referring to it in declarations and resolutions, but also by asking its members to ratify the Convention only a few months after its adoption in 2005.[50] The European Union, a party to the CDC as well as a forum in itself, is another example of a forum actively promoting the objectives and principles of the Convention in its documents but also in the trade agreements it adopts.

These few examples not only show the resonance of the Convention's objectives and principles in forums other than UNESCO, but also reflect 'the coherence of the Parties in the various forums in which they are active[, as well as] the constructive dialogue between organizations whose fields of competence are complementary', such as UNESCO and the OIF.[51] The references to the CDC take different forms, from a simple mention of the Convention in the preamble of a resolution to more specific references to its objectives and principles for a precise purpose. This is evidence that parties recognise the impact of other types of instruments on their commitments toward the Convention, and that they are able to use the treaty when appropriate to protect the diversity of cultural expressions on their territory. It is also a sign that parties use the Convention as a lever for other causes.[52]

However, the promotion of the objectives and principles of the Convention in other forums remains a challenge, mainly because 'policies and measures in and for the cultural sector alone are not the only ones that impact upon [the] objectives' of the treaty.[53] The implementation of the treaty in the digital environment adds another layer of complexity and might require from parties promotion of the CDC in forums they might not have thought about or even been involved in with respect to the implementation of the Convention. The mere fact that their actions may have an impact on the diversity of cultural expressions should be sufficient for parties to engage in these forums.

[49] ibid.

[50] For example, the Resolution on the UNESCO Convention on the Protection and Promotion of the Diversity of Cultural Expressions and the Dakar Declaration adopted in Dakar in 2014. See Organisation internationale de la Francophonie, 'Rapport général de la CMF siégeant comme instance du Sommet', Conférence ministérielle de la Francophonie, 21e Session, Antananarivo, 22–23 November 2005, www.francophonie.org/sites/default/files/2019-10/rap_cmf_21_23112005.pdf.

[51] Guèvremont, 'The Convention in Other International Forums', 157. For more details on the implementation of Art 21, see Guèvremont, 'Promoting the Convention in International Forums'; see also the working documents: UNESCO, 'Item 11 of the Provisional Agenda' (CE/14/8.IGC/11); UNESCO, 'Item 11 of the Provisional Agenda: Preferential Treatment and International Consultation and Coordination: Report on the Implementation and Impact of Articles 16 and 21 of the Convention', Conference of Parties to the Convention on the Protection and Promotion of the Diversity of Cultural Expressions, Fifth Ordinary Session (Paris, UNESCO Headquarters, 10–12 June 2015, CE/15/5.CP/11, 23 April 2015).

[52] A nuance must be made here. It should not be ignored that the promotion of the objectives and principles of the Convention is uneven among the parties to the Convention, and even within the international commitments made by the same state. This may raise questions in some cases as to the achievement of the objectives of the treaty.

[53] Guèvremont, 'Promoting the Convention in International Forums', 145.

B. The Challenges Raised by Digital Technologies for the Diversity of Cultural Expressions

Parties to the Convention started raising concerns about the impact of digital technologies on the protection and promotion of the diversity of cultural expressions in 2012. Although the CDC is technologically neutral, meaning it applies 'whatever the means and technologies used',[54] the growing challenges posed by digital technologies led the parties to the elaboration of 'Operational Guidelines on the Implementation of the Convention in the Digital Environment' (Digital Guidelines). Approved by acclamation in June 2017, these guidelines are aimed at 'provid[ing] a strategic framework for understanding, interpreting and implementing the Convention … in a digital environment'.[55] They provide guidance for 'Parties in their efforts to meet the challenges and seize the opportunities offered by the digital environment', where digital technologies have had (and still have) a growing impact on the entire cultural value chain, the exchange of cultural goods and services, as well as the mobility of artists.[56] By adopting these guidelines, parties show their commitment to continue protecting and promoting the diversity of cultural expressions in this environment, 'where cultural goods and services are created, produced, distributed, disseminated, consumed and/or stored electronically'.[57] In 2019, these guidelines were complemented by an 'Open Roadmap for the Implementation of the Operational Guidelines to Promote the Diversity of Cultural Expressions in the Digital Environment' illustrated by good practices to better equip parties to implement the treaty.

Unlike most operational guidelines of the Convention, the Digital Guidelines apply to the Convention as a whole, and thus to Article 21, which is expressly mentioned. They stress parties should act both at the national level – by adapting their policies and measures to the challenges raised by digital technologies – and at the international level. This latter level of action can be directly linked to Article 21.[58] The obligations arising from this article are, for example, clearly mentioned in paragraph 19 of the Guidelines, which encourages parties to promote, among others, the

> complementarity and coherency among the various legal instruments addressing the diversity of cultural expressions in the digital environment; [as well as] transparency in bilateral, regional or multilateral negotiations having an impact on cultural goods and services in the digital environment.

[54] See Art 4.1 of the Convention.

[55] See para 1 of the Digital Guidelines.

[56] See para 7. UNESCO, 'Item 13 of the Provisional Agenda: Roadmap for the Implementation of the Guidelines to Promote the Diversity of Cultural Expressions in the Digital Environment', Conference of Parties to the Convention on the Protection and Promotion of the Diversity of Cultural Expressions, Seventh Session (Paris, UNESCO Headquarters, 4–7 June 2019, DCE/19/7.CP/13, 2 May 2019) 3.

[57] See para 1 of the Digital Guidelines.

[58] As well as international solidarity and cooperation, for instance.

This paragraph mentions specifically the introduction of cultural clauses in international bilateral, regional or multilateral agreements, as well as the 'incorporation of explicit references to the Convention and [the Digital Guidelines] in trade and investment agreements, as well as provisions that enable their implementation'.[59] It is unfortunate that the Digital Guidelines only explicitly mention Article 21 in the section dealing with rebalancing the flow of cultural goods and services. However, other parts of the guidelines could be linked to the implementation of Article 21, such as those referring to intellectual property or telecommunications, which support the argument that parties might need to get involved in a greater diversity of forums with regard to the promotion of the objectives and principles of the Convention in the digital environment.

C. The Specificity of the Digital Environment and the Need to Promote the Convention in a Greater Diversity of Forums

In a context where many international forums are tackling the regulation of digital activities and technologies, parties should remain careful not to make any decision that could go against the objectives and principles of the Convention. The use of digital technologies in everyday life implies the renegotiation of various instruments, and in some cases the elaboration of new rules in almost every sector, such as trade agreements – as already mentioned. The specificity of the digital environment – supposedly 'without frontiers' – means that it can be difficult for states to regulate this environment on their own. Some actions need to be taken at the international level to adapt existing regulations to the specificities of the digital environment, and to ensure some basic rights are respected. In this context, the digital environment is 'potentially conducive to more coordinated efforts'[60] by parties when implementing Article 21.[61]

The promotion of the objectives and principles of the Convention in trade forums,[62] as well as in the forums already cited, undoubtedly remains crucial for the implementation of the treaty in the digital environment, especially as initiatives related to the digital environment might take place within them.[63]

[59] See paras 19.4 and 19.5 of the Digital Guidelines.

[60] Guèvremont, 'The Convention in Other International Forums', 157.

[61] Varin and Guèvremont, 'La *Convention sur la diversité des expressions culturelles* quinze ans après', 27.

[62] Trade agreements including electronic-commerce chapters, for example, are being negotiated and imply special attention of parties to the Convention regarding the preservation of their capacity to intervene in the cultural sector, or the specificity of cultural goods and services. Negotiations are also ongoing at the WTO on e-commerce; see ch 4 of this book, by V Guèvremont and I Otasevic.

[63] The work carried out by some of these forums with regard to digital themes keep mentioning the 2005 Convention. For example, it is mentioned in para 61 of the European Audiovisual Media Services Directive. See Directive (EU) 2018/1808 of the European Parliament and of the Council of 14 November 2018 amending Directive 2010/13/EU on the coordination of certain provisions laid down by law, regulation or administrative action in Member States concerning the provision of audiovisual media services (Audiovisual Media Services Directive) in view of changing market realities [2018] OJ L 303/69.

However, a wider range of forums could also be considered because of the digital environment itself and could be identified based on their mandate and/or competences. The International Telecommunication Union (ITU) has already been identified as relevant for its competences in Internet-related public policies, fair access to technologies and the digital divide, as has the World Intellectual Property Organization (WIPO).[64] Even though intellectual property does not fall within the scope of the Convention, it is recognised as an important element for the diversity of cultural expressions, especially as cultural goods and services covered by the treaty carry copyright. The Preamble of the Convention recognises the 'importance of intellectual property rights in sustaining those involved in cultural creativity',[65] and certain objectives and principles of the treaty echo it. WIPO was also consulted during the negotiations of the Convention. Today, fair remuneration of artists is a pressing issue in the digital environment, especially on digital platforms, and is often referred to during statutory meetings or events organised by the Secretariat of the Convention.[66] The numerous mentions of this aspect, as well as the importance of its respect and protection in the Convention's Digital Guidelines, show the prominence it has taken today.[67] Regional organisations also play a role in the regulation of the digital environment and should not be overlooked. At the regional level, the Convention has, for example, been used by the Council of Europe as a 'cornerstone' when it 'comes to discussing the digital challenge, and ways to ensure full participation in and access to digital culture'.[68]

Forums whose decisions could have a positive or negative impact on the protection and promotion of the diversity of cultural expressions in the digital environment could also be relevant for the promotion of the Convention's objectives and principles. This could include 'international negotiation forums whose work could have an impact on the evolution of the digital environment'.[69] The ITU has already been mentioned, but any discussions linked to the technical aspects of the Internet,[70] the regulation of this environment and of certain technologies

[64] Guèvremont, 'The Convention in Other International Forums', 157.

[65] See para 17 of the Preamble of the Convention.

[66] The 1980 Recommendation concerning the Status of the Artist is also relevant today on this matter. This aspect was already present at the time of the adoption of the Convention but has become even more pressing today with the advent of digital technologies. Thus, 'by recognizing the central role of artists in the creation and production of a diversity of cultural expressions, the Convention provides a new normative framework for the implementation and monitoring of the Recommendation'. See UNESCO, '1980 Recommendation concerning the Status of the Artist' (2021), en.unesco.org/creativity/governance/status-artist.

[67] See in particular paras 14.6, 16.6 and 27.3 of the Digital Guidelines.

[68] The Recommendation of the Committee of Ministers to member states on the Internet of citizens (10 February 2016) calls for 'full respect for the 2005 UNESCO Convention on the Protection and Promotion of the Diversity of Cultural Expressions'. See Guèvremont, 'The Convention in Other International Forums', 157.

[69] V Guèvremont, 'Preliminary Reflection on the Implementation of the Convention on the Protection and Promotion of the Diversity of Cultural Expressions in the Digital Age', Conference of Parties to the Convention on the Protection and Promotion of the Diversity of Cultural Expressions, Fourth Session (Paris, UNESCO, 2013) 26.

[70] Net neutrality is important, for example, for the *discoverability* of cultural contents in the digital environment, and for access to a diversity of contents.

are particularly pertinent here. For example, the OECD, and more specifically the OECD/G20 Base Erosion and Profit Shifting Project,[71] should interest parties as it may impact their capacity to put in place specific policies and measures they already implement in the analogical world, such as taxes aimed at supporting the cultural sector. Indeed, some digital companies are not always subject to the same taxes as national companies offering the same services, mostly because they are not physically present on the territory of the country they do business in. The international consensus reached on the question of 'business presence' and 'activities without physical presence'[72] could enable parties to the Convention to tax revenues from digital cultural platforms operating on their territory, such as Netflix or Spotify. Some of the incomes generated could then be transferred into funds to support national cultural creation and production, for example; something states are not always able to do with the current regulation.[73] These discussions are broader than the cultural sector, but might directly impact cultural industries in the digital environment, and inspire the elaboration of their own policies and measures on their territory. In this case, the issue for parties is not to promote specific objectives and principles of the Convention per se, but to keep in mind the commitments they made with regard to the treaty and ensure they will be able to continue protecting and promoting the diversity of cultural expressions.[74] In this situation, it takes the form of preserving their right to put in place taxes for audiovisual companies, for example, operating on their territory, regardless of whether they are digital or analogical. In other cases, it could be to ensure individuals can participate in cultural life or have access to a diversity of contents of their choice, for example. Thus, such forums, even if they are at first sight sometimes far removed from cultural issues, should be considered for their possible impact on the diversity of cultural expressions, and might require actions from parties if necessary.

[71] This project aimed at addressing challenges arising from the digitalisation of the economy in the taxation area and, among others, ensuring fairness and equity in tax systems (see Action 1). See OECD, 'Action 1. Tax Challenges Arising from Digitalisation', www.oecd.org/tax/beps/beps-actions/action1/.

[72] Nowadays, companies can access their consumers without having to be physically present on the territory thanks to the Internet. The digitalisation and globalisation of the economy have 'challenged fundamental features of the international income tax system, such as the traditional notions of permanent establishment', impacting the ability of states to tax these foreign companies and creating inequalities between them and companies based in the country. This situation has highlighted the need for an extensive multilateral tax cooperation, and prompted the OECD to work on updating the international tax system and ensuring 'the allocation of taxing rights with respect to business profits is no longer exclusively circumscribed by reference to physical presence'. OECD, *Tax Challenges Arising from Digitalisation – Report on Pillar One Blueprint: Inclusive Framework on BEPS*, OECD/G20 Base Erosion and Profit Shifting Project (Paris, OECD Publishing, 2020) 10.

[73] V Guèvremont, C Varin and I Richer, 'Les nouveaux modes d'intervention de l'État visant à protéger et à promouvoir la diversité des expressions culturelles sur les plateformes numériques' in A Bensamoun and F Labarthe (eds), *Culture & Numérique: Rencontre franco-québécoise* (Le Kremlin-Bicêtre, Presses universitaires de Sceaux, Édition Mare & Martin, 2020) 179. See also C Varin, 'La vulnérabilité des engagements pris par les États pour protéger et promouvoir la diversité des expressions culturelles dans l'environnement numérique: quelle(s) stratégie(s) pour les Parties à la Convention de 2005 ?' (2020) 25 *Lex Electronica* 99.

[74] On this matter, see also I Bernier, 'The Convention on the Protection and the Promotion of the Diversity of Cultural Expressions. A Cultural Analysis' in Kono and Van Uytsel, *The UNESCO Convention on the Diversity of Cultural Expressions*, 122.

Nevertheless, the digital environment has its own specificities that might require adaptation from parties to the Convention when implementing Article 21. These past few years have seen the emergence of new global Internet governance forums as digital technologies have had a 'profound impact on governance forms overall [which] now increasingly depart from the conventional notion of law and shift toward more complex, heterogeneous, and uncoordinated mechanisms'.[75] Protecting and promoting the diversity of cultural expressions in the digital era has never been as much of a challenge.[76] Parties therefore need to 'consider all layers of the so-called "communications model", as regulatory choices, such as for instance with regard to technical standard-setting define access conditions for content and thus have repercussions for the freedom of speech and broader cultural processes'.[77] In that respect, a broad interpretation of 'international forum' in which to promote the Convention offers large room for manoeuvre for parties to consider these new kinds of forum.

As already discussed, as long as they are relevant 'with respect to the objectives and field of application of the Convention',[78] no forum should be overlooked by parties. The regulation of certain technologies, such as AI, has been a particularly fruitful field for multi-stakeholders' approach frameworks, bringing together private companies and civil society, including academics and engineers, to elaborate ethical frameworks for AI. However, the impact of such technologies on the diversity of cultural expressions[79] (and on the society as a whole) is far too important for parties not to be involved in them. These forums may therefore be interesting to consider by parties for their consensus-building capacity on specific matters[80] and be seen as possible stepping stones for the elaboration of more binding instruments. The earlier in those discussions that cultural considerations feature, the greater the chance they will be taken into consideration in the final document, or at least will be more difficult to erase. Parties should

[75] M Burri, 'Global Cultural Law and Policy and the Internet: A Tale of Parallel Worlds' (2016) 1 *Arts and International Affairs* 156.

[76] For Burri, 'The Internet and the underlying processes of digitization and convergence have definitely extended the scope of cultural governance in the past three decades and these extensions have become critical for the achievement of the fundamental cultural policy objectives'. See ibid 155.

[77] Burri details in her article the three layers of the 'communications model' established by the information technology literature, namely: '(i) physical layer consisting of the network plus the hardware attached as the fundament for information flows; (ii) logical layer consisting of software, applications, and protocols that as a whole enable connectivity and the performance of communication tasks; and (iii) content layer, where the actual human-readable messages are placed'. See ibid 155–56.

[78] Bernier, 'The Relationship between the UNESCO Convention on the Protection and Promotion of the Diversity of Cultural Expressions and Other International Instruments', 18.

[79] Various studies have been made on the impact of digital technologies on the diversity of cultural expressions. See in particular O Kulesz, 'Culture, Platforms and Machines: The Impact of Artificial Intelligence on the Diversity of Cultural Expressions', Intergovernmental Committee for the Protection and Promotion of the Diversity of Cultural Expressions, Twelfth Session (Paris, UNESCO, 2018); O Kulesz and T Dutoit, 'L'intelligence artificielle dans l'art et les industries culturelles et créatives. Panorama des technologies, expertises et bonnes pratiques dans l'espace francophone' (Paris, Organisation internationale de la Francophonie, 2020).

[80] Stoll refers to this aspect. Stoll, 'Article 21. International Consultation and Coordination', 548.

therefore seize this opportunity to include some objectives and principles of the Convention to maximise the chances these technologies will serve the diversity of cultural expressions. With regard to AI, most of the numerous ethical frameworks that have emerged in the past few years lack a 'cultural perspective'.[81] Only a few make references to 'cultural diversity',[82] which is far from sufficient, considering the growing use of this technology in the cultural sector and the challenges it poses to the diversity of cultural expressions. Moreover, most of these instruments originate from private foundations or large platforms, which present the risk of focusing on their own concerns. Instead, these declarations on AI should 'include concrete proposals, many of which have already been outlined by multilateral organizations', such as the objectives and principles of the Convention and the Digital Guidelines, and not be limited to abstract recommendations.[83] However, the recent adoption in 2021 of the Recommendation on the Ethics of Artificial Intelligence by UNESCO's member states is a first step in that direction. Indeed, the Recommendation includes many references to culture, cultural diversity and the diversity of cultural expressions, as well as a policy area dedicated exclusively to culture.[84]

Neither the nature (whether it is formal, informal, etc) nor the composition of a forum (ie only composed of states or, on the contrary, multi-stakeholder) should be seen as an obstacle by parties to the Convention. On the contrary, as long as it is relevant to the scope of the treaty, these forums should be seen as opportunities to promote the objectives and principles of the Convention, as well as formidable platforms to disseminate them. The Multi-Stakeholder Working Group on Diversity of Content Online launched by Canada is an interesting example as it includes representatives from governments, the private sectors and civil society.[85] In June 2021, the Working Group released 'Guiding Principles on Diversity of Content Online', aimed at guiding 'actions and measures that foster greater exposure to diverse cultural content, information and news online',[86] which should help

[81] Kulesz, 'Culture, Platforms and Machines', 12.

[82] It is the case, for example, of the Global Initiative on Ethics of Autonomous and Intelligent Systems and the Asilomar Principles. See ibid.

[83] ibid 13.

[84] This Recommendation was adopted during the 41st Session of UNESCO's General Conference. Recommendation on the ethics of Artificial Intelligence (Paris, 24 November 2021).

[85] Namely: Australia, Canada, Finland, France, Germany, Deezer, Google, Netflix, Vubble, Article19, Coalition française pour la diversité culturelle, International Federation of Coalitions for Cultural Diversity, Society of Authors, Composers and Publishers of Music, European Audiovisual Observatory. See Government of Canada, 'Canada Releases Guiding Principles on Diversity of Content Online' (30 June 2021).

[86] These guiding principles cover four themes deemed essential for the promotion of a diversity of content online: (i) creation, access and discoverability of diverse content online; (ii) fair remuneration and economic viability of content creators; (iii) promotion of diverse, pluralistic sources of news and information, as well as resilience against disinformation and misinformation; and (iv) transparency of the impacts of algorithmic treatments of online content. It should be noted, however, that the group has a broad definition of diversity of content online that is not limited to cultural contents but also includes information and news. Government of Canada, 'Guiding Principles on Diversity of Content Online' (June 2021) www.canada.ca/en/canadian-heritage/services/diversity-content-digital-age/guiding-principles.html.

promote the objectives and principles of the Convention on a larger scale. This forum also provides, to some extent, a consultation platform for five parties to the Convention, which is another important element contained in Article 21.

Thus, parties should find ways to turn to the advantage of the diversity of cultural expressions the 'interactions and overlaps resulting from the work of numerous organizations', or at least ensure they are not 'harmful to it'.[87] The engagement of parties within those forums can influence their decisions and prevent negative effects on the diversity of cultural expressions. That the CDC can influence debate is 'evidence of the implementation of Article 21 of the Convention'.[88] Civil society could play an important role in identifying these forums,[89] and promote the objectives and principles of the CDC alongside parties to the treaty.[90] Although Article 21 is specifically addressed to parties, civil society could play a part in identifying such forums and involve parties, when necessary, through a closer partnership. Besides, the Digital Guidelines mention numerous times the need for a multi-stakeholder approach to the implementation of the Convention in the digital environment.

IV. Conclusion

In the context of a changing landscape, where many instruments are being put in place or renegotiated to regulate the extensive use of new technologies in all sectors, the implementation of Article 21 is more than ever important for the future of the Convention. Greater efforts have to be made by parties to ensure the objectives and principles of the Convention last in the digital environment, which might imply being involved in forums sometimes far from the cultural areas. However, such a broad interpretation of a relevant 'international forum' comes with a set of difficulties and entails the risk of parties becoming involved in too many forums without it actually benefiting the implementation of the CDC. Finding criteria to identify these relevant forums at a time when international law-making processes and actors are multiplying can be complicated. It requires a very good understanding of the complexity of digital technologies and their possible impacts on the diversity of cultural expressions, but also of the outreach of instruments developed in such a context of regulation.

[87] Guèvremont, 'Promoting the Convention in International Forums', 145.

[88] UNESCO, 'Item 11 of the Provisional Agenda' (CE/14/8.IGC/11) 18.

[89] Civil Society plays an important role in the implementation of the Convention. See Art 11 of the Convention.

[90] Para 25.4 of the Digital Guidelines recognises that 'partnering with civil society organizations is essential in the digital environment [as it contributes] to monitoring the evolution of the digital world'. It may, for example, take the form of: 'collaboration between civil society representatives, including artists and cultural professionals, academics, researchers and experts, to provide input for reflection within other international organizations and to directly or indirectly focus on issues relating to the diversity of cultural expressions in a digital environment'.

Consultation and coordination of parties, as also requested by Article 21, is more than ever important in that regard to ensure effective promotion of the objectives and principles of the Convention in a space that is sometimes hostile to its values. In the coming years, the treaty's Intergovernmental Committee may have to play an important role in establishing clear procedures and mechanisms for this consultation. Over the past 15 years, much progress has been made that attests to the effectiveness of the Convention.[91] Nevertheless, the next few years will be pivotal. Parties must seize the opportunity offered by the regulation of the digital environment to promote the diversity of cultural expressions, and thus ensure societies of tomorrow can benefit from this richness.

[91] See Varin and Guèvremont, 'La *Convention sur la diversité des expressions culturelles* quinze ans après'.

6

Vulnerable Cultural Expressions in the Trade and Culture Debate: A Precautionary Approach to Culture in Times of Crisis

LILIAN RICHIERI HANANIA

I. Introduction

In international trade law, an adversarial relationship has often been identified between trade liberalisation and cultural policies which pursue cultural diversity. Indeed, trade liberalisation commitments undertaken by states when negotiating international trade or economic agreements, which are based on non-discrimination obligations, may limit cultural diversity when they reduce the capacity of states to adopt cultural policies favouring national cultural works or works originating from certain countries.[1] Trade liberalisation can thus be seen, under such specific circumstances, if not as a danger, at least as a source of significant challenges for cultural policies and, consequently, also as an obstacle for more balanced exchanges of cultural goods and services.

On the other hand, there can be no cultural diversity without cultural exchanges. While cultural diversity requires efforts to preserve existing cultures, it is by nature dynamic and cannot exist without interculturality, which refers to the 'existence and equitable interaction of diverse cultures and the possibility of generating shared cultural expressions through dialogue and mutual respect' (Article 4.8 of the 2005 UNESCO Convention on the Protection and Promotion of the Diversity of Cultural Expressions,[2] hereinafter CDC).

As envisaged by the CDC, such exchanges must, therefore, be balanced and equitable, ie they must ideally allow all cultures to be represented in the market of

[1] For a detailed analysis of this topic, see L Richieri Hanania, *Diversité culturelle et droit international du commerce* (Paris, La Documentation française, 2009) 83–250.

[2] (adopted 20 October 2005, entered into force 18 March 2007) 2440 UNTS 311.

cultural goods and services and, as such, be practically accessible and consumed. The lack of diversity of cultural goods and services on both the supply and demand sides can indeed gradually lead to the disappearance of certain cultural expressions conveyed by cultural goods and services, to the benefit of a minority of successful works that are not representative of the richness of cultures of our planet. The lower visibility of certain cultural expressions may in certain cases, therefore, imply a significant level of vulnerability. Cultural policies which comply with the principles and objectives of the CDC and favour national works or works from certain partner countries in order to promote a more equitable and diversified market of cultural goods and services aim at ensuring greater balance. They become all the more important when confronted with an evolving market, already constantly shaken by technological changes, and also particularly exposed during economic crises, such as the recent economic and health crisis caused by COVID-19. Although legitimate and sometimes fundamental to a cultural sector, such discriminative responses by states may sometimes create trade restrictions and be challenged from a trade liberalisation perspective.

The purpose of the present chapter is to examine to what extent we may (or should) have recourse to a precautionary approach when balancing trade interests and cultural diversity concerns in favour of vulnerable cultural expressions, and on what legal basis. In fact, the precautionary approach has been protected in international law through Principle 15 of the 1992 United Nations Rio Declaration on Environment and Development,[3] which states that 'Where there are threats of serious or irreversible damage, lack of full scientific certainty shall not be used as a reason for postponing cost-effective measures to prevent environmental degradation'. In practical terms, this approach implies that a response is needed in situations in which: (i) a potential risk of damage exists; (ii) the damage is serious and irreversible; (iii) the risk may not be entirely demonstrated or measured; and (iv) the consequences of such damage may not be completely determined because of a lack of scientific data.

In a nutshell, in international trade law, notably at the World Trade Organization (WTO),[4] such an approach has manifested as a 'precautionary logic' or 'caution' applied in health and environment-related cases. In such cases, the right of each WTO member to define its level of protection was recognised, and the judge conducted an analysis of the risks involved based on the available scientific data, which gave a fundamental role to experts. Such precautionary logic was applied precisely when a complete risk assessment was impossible. Based on

[3] United Nations, 'Rio Declaration on Environment and Development' in *Report of the United Nations Conference on Environment and Development* [1992] A/CONF.151/26 (Vol I) Annex I.

[4] For further details, see L Richieri Hanania, 'Le principe de précaution et son application dans l'OMC' in H Ruiz Fabri and L Gradoni (eds), *La circulation des concepts en droit international de l'environnement: entre fragmentation et mondialisation* (Paris, Société de législation comparée, 2009) 555–75.

such information, and in order to check if the challenged measures were adequate and acceptable according to WTO law, the WTO judge applied a necessity and proportionality test, in which the following elements were considered: the importance of the protected value (the more fundamental the value is for a society, the more a measure adopted to protect it is considered acceptable); the effects and the effectiveness of the measure (how it contributes to the objective pursued); and the degree of trade restrictiveness of the measure (is there another less restrictive measure allowing the WTO member to reach the same objectives and the desired level of protection?). A necessity presumption (in certain cases, the presumption of non-trade restrictiveness of a measure) may be applied if the measure is based on international standards.

While such precautionary logic does not clearly stem from the WTO agreements in the case of culture and has not yet been applied in practice to cultural concerns in the framework of international trade agreements, the above-mentioned elements considered by a trade judge and the reasoning of caution applied could likely be transposed to the cultural field and provide for a new and supplementary avenue for greater promotion of cultural diversity concerns, notably with respect to vulnerable cultural expressions. The following sections analyse such a path, by examining how a precautionary approach may influence the legal treatment of vulnerable cultural expressions, and through what mechanisms. It briefly analyses the application of such an approach to the articulation between cultural concerns and international trade law (section II), in order to inquire into how international treaties in the field of culture may legitimise and reinforce such an approach (section III).

II. The Precautionary Approach Applied to the Linkage between Trade and Culture

A precautionary approach, or at least some sort of prudence or caution, can be identified towards certain cultural sectors in the position of several states when establishing market liberalisation commitments during international trade negotiations. Such caution appears clearly in the use of cultural exception techniques in international economic or trade agreements. By means of these techniques, certain cultural sectors, or certain cultural policy measures applicable to specific cultural sectors, are excluded from the liberalisation commitments of a negotiating state. This allows the latter to maintain its cultural policy flexibility vis-à-vis its trading partners to the extent of these exceptions.

For example, in the trade agreements negotiated with the USA, trading partners may introduce, through so-called 'negative lists', reservations to the market opening commitments adopted in these agreements. A similar strategy may be observed within the WTO, where several members, including the European Union (EU), have not included the audiovisual services sector in their schedules of commitments to the General Agreement on Trade in Services (GATS).[5] Since trade liberalisation commitments in the GATS are limited to what is explicitly listed in each WTO member's schedule of commitments, if a WTO member wishes to exclude a sector from its commitments, all that member needs to do is not to indicate that specific sector in its schedule. Finally, in some bilateral and regional trade agreements, the introduction of general exceptions to the agreement or to specific chapters (cultural exceptions strictly speaking) has made it possible to exclude certain cultural sectors with respect to which a state wishes to adopt cultural policies. This is, for instance, the approach taken by the EU and Canada in their bilateral or regional trade negotiations. For example, the EU traditionally drafts a cultural exception for audiovisual services in its international economic and trade agreements in order to maintain the widest possible scope for EU member states to pursue cultural policy in this sector.[6] Canada expresses the same caution with respect to trade liberalisation regarding its cultural industries[7] more generally.

From the perspective of the recognition of a certain specificity of cultural goods and services in relation to other goods and services in an international trade agreement, all of these techniques reflect a cultural exception logic, often criticised by states with powerful cultural industries and considered as a defensive approach that runs the risk of not taking sufficient account of market developments, and in particular the unlimited storage capacity offered nowadays to cultural content by the Internet. It has been demonstrated, however, that the unlimited storage space offered by the Internet has not necessarily led to more diversity, in particular due to the lack of visibility (also referred to as the 'discoverability') of diverse cultural content online.[8] In the end, the goal of cultural diversity appears as compelling

[5] (adopted 15 April 1994, entered into force 1 January 1995) 1869 UNTS 183.

[6] eg the Economic Partnership Agreement between the CARIFORUM States, of the one part, and the European Community and its Member States, of the other part (signed 30 October 2008, entered into provisional application 29 December 2008) OJ L 289/I/4 states that 'This Chapter applies to measures by the Parties or by the Signatory CARIFORUM States affecting the cross-border supply of all services with the exception of: (a) audiovisual services' (Art 75(1)). A similar provision may be found in the chapter devoted to commercial presence (Art 66(c)) of the same agreement. Another example appears in the Free Trade Agreement negotiated with Singapore until October 2014, in which audiovisual services are in similar terms excluded from the chapter on services, establishment and electronic commerce (Arts 8.3(a) and 8.9(c)). For further details, see, eg L Richieri Hanania, 'L'action culturelle dans la politique commerciale extérieure de l'UE: assurer la spécificité des biens et services culturels à l'ère du numérique' (2017) 56 (special issue) *Politique européenne* 124.

[7] In the Agreement between the USA, Mexico and Canada in effect since July 2020, for instance, the term 'cultural industry' has been defined as 'a person engaged in the following activities: (a) the publication, distribution, or sale of books, magazines, periodicals, or newspapers in print or machine readable form but not including the sole activity of printing or typesetting any of the foregoing; (b) the production, distribution, sale, or exhibition of film or video recordings; (c) the production, distribution, sale, or exhibition of audio or video music recordings; (d) the publication, distribution, or sale of music in print or machine readable form; or (e) radiocommunications in which the transmissions are intended for direct reception by the general public, and all radio, television and cable broadcasting undertakings and all satellite programming and broadcast network services'. Almost identical definitions have been constant in Canada's trade agreements since the 1994 North-American Free Trade Agreement (NAFTA) (signed 17 December 1992, entered into force 1 January 1994) 32 ILM 296.

[8] See Richieri Hanania, *Diversité culturelle* (n 1); L Richieri Hanania and A-T Norodom (eds), *Diversity of Cultural Expressions in the Digital Era* (Buenos Aires, Teseopress, 2016) www.teseopress.

today as it was before the Internet era, although the means and policies needed to achieve it can (and must) be transformed.

Indeed, the accelerated pace of technological change and its impact on the market of cultural goods and services seem to further justify the need for caution when making trade commitments in these sectors. Similarly, unforeseen situations with an extraordinary impact on the activity and visibility of cultural goods and services, such as the health and economic crisis triggered by the COVID-19 pandemic, also demonstrate the importance of state intervention to ensure the survival of cultural expressions.[9] Therefore, from a position that could at least be close to a precautionary approach, states must strive to maintain the maximum flexibility and policy space with regard to cultural policy, not only to be able to adapt their policies to the new realities of the cultural market, but also to shape these realities in favour of public policy objectives such as cultural diversity.

Techniques of cultural exception in international trade agreements allow states to avoid crystallising trade commitments that may later limit a state's policy space with respect to its cultural sectors. As in other situations where the precautionary approach is relevant, there is no absolute certainty about the magnitude of the risks for the cultures least represented in a given market. Cultural exceptions thus appear to be useful legal techniques for dealing with uncertainty and measurement limitations with respect to the risks to cultural diversity resulting from failures in the market of cultural goods and services,[10] in both analogical and digital contexts. Moreover, the public policy measures adopted also vary from one state to another and may therefore be questionable, particularly if they may be considered to limit or to disadvantage the access of other cultural content to this same market. Such measures will differ, for example, according to the level of protection that each state may find appropriate for each of its cultural sectors, in accordance with the level of development of its cultural industries, as well as its historical, social, political, economic and even administrative circumstances.

This precautionary positioning identified in cultural exception techniques could ideally also be applied when resolving a conflict between cultural and commercial interests before a commercial court. A privileged path could be found in the evolving interpretation of the concept of sustainable development in the context of trade agreements.

com/diversityofculturalexpressionsinthedigitalera/. See notably the following chapters of the latter: M Burri, 'Exposure Diversity as a New Cultural Policy Objective in the Digital Age'; H Ranaivoson, 'The Internet Platforms' Impact on the Diversity of Cultural Expressions: To the Long Tail, and Beyond!'; P Marenghi, M Hernandez Pietro and A Badillo, 'Diversity of the Audiovisual Industry in the Digital Age: The Challenges Entailed in Its Measurement'; M Rioux and K Fontaine-Skronski, 'Transversal Operational Guidelines as a Road towards a Diversified Networked Culture'; O Kulesz, 'Challenges and Opportunities for Cultural Diversity in the Digital Era'. See also O Kulesz, 'Challenges of the Digital Age' in UNESCO, *Re|shaping Cultural Policies: A Decade Promoting the Diversity of Cultural Expressions for Development* (Paris, UNESCO, 2015).

[9] See UNESCO, *Culture in Crisis: Policy Guide for a Resilient Creative Sector* (Paris, UNESCO, 2020) https://unesdoc.unesco.org/ark:/48223/pf0000374631.

[10] On such market failures, see Richieri Hanania, *Diversité culturelle* (n 1) 29–61.

Indeed, an increased recognition of the cultural dimension of sustainable development may be observed in international law, allowing for a better consideration of cultural concerns when interpreting international trade agreements. The CDC is at the heart of such recognition. In effect since 2007 and 152 parties strong,[11] this Convention stresses that cultural diversity is 'a mainspring for sustainable development for communities, peoples and nations' (Preamble) and that 'The protection, promotion and maintenance of cultural diversity are an essential requirement for sustainable development for the benefit of present and future generations' (Article 2.6, Principle of sustainable development). Although a cultural pillar of sustainable development has not (yet) clearly been recognised in international law, the cultural dimension of sustainable development is reflected in the United Nations' Sustainable Development Goals. It can be observed in particular in the Declaration of the United Nations 2030 Agenda for Sustainable Development (§§ 8 and 36) and in Sustainable Development Goals 4.7, 8.9, 11.4 and 12.b.[12]

The strengthening of this cultural dimension of sustainable development could progressively justify taking better account of cultural diversity concerns in international trade law, whether at the level of the WTO or in the implementation and enforcement of bilateral and regional trade agreements. The protection of cultural diversity could then be used not only as a negative defence, based, for example, on the general exceptions under Article XX of the General Agreement on Tariffs and Trade (GATT) 1947 and Article XIV of the GATS (eg via the 'protection of public morals' or, only in the case of the GATT, the notion of 'national treasures of artistic, historic or archaeological value'), but also as a means in itself to promote the objective of sustainable development pursued by the organisation.[13] A precautionary approach in such a context would then be as relevant as it is for the protection of environmental or health interests, especially when the survival of certain cultures or elements of these cultures (eg languages) are identified as potentially endangered.

The CDC indeed affirms the dual nature, economic and cultural, of cultural goods and services, specifying that they 'must therefore not be treated as solely having commercial value' (Preamble). The risks to cultural diversity arising from trade based exclusively on economic considerations have also been highlighted in the 2001 UNESCO Universal Declaration on Cultural Diversity, which emphasises that 'Market forces alone cannot guarantee the preservation and

[11] For the list of parties to the CDC, see UNESCO, 'Diversity of Cultural Expressions – Country Profiles' https://en.unesco.org/creativity/countries?member_parties=1.

[12] United Nations, *Transforming Our World: The 2030 Agenda for Sustainable Development* (2015) A/RES/70/1.

[13] (adopted 30 October 1947, entered into force 1 January 1948) 55 UNTS 194, see F Morosini, 'Taking into Account Environmental, Social and Cultural Concerns through the Objective of Sustainable Development – Perspectives from the WTO Jurisprudence on General Exceptions' in L Richieri Hanania (ed), *Cultural Diversity in International Law: The Effectiveness of the UNESCO Convention on the Protection and Promotion of the Diversity of Cultural Expressions* (Londonk, Routledge, 2014).

promotion of cultural diversity, which is the key to sustainable human development' (Article 11).[14] Both international legal instruments legitimise cultural policies as a means to achieving the objective of cultural diversity. Such policies ultimately address the risks to cultural expressions that are under-represented in the market of cultural goods and services, regardless of the reasons for or origins of such under-representation.

Before a WTO judge or in the framework of a dispute resolution mechanism established under a bilateral or regional trade agreement, such legitimisation of cultural policies and the strengthening of the cultural dimension of sustainable development might support the position of states whose cultural policy measures are challenged on the basis of their potential restrictive effect on trade. As in other areas of WTO law,[15] for the challenged WTO member it would be a matter of demonstrating the necessity and proportionality of the measures adopted in relation to the level of protection pursued, taking into account the importance of the protected object, namely cultural diversity and, ultimately, sustainable development. The seriousness and irreversibility of the potential damage to cultural diversity would be assessed as part of the examination of the level of protection (linked to the acceptability of the risk) established by the state having adopted the measure under consideration. It would thus be conceivable that a first phase of risk assessment by the judge, based on scientific expertise, would be followed by an examination of the adequacy of the measure with respect to the level of protection envisaged, which would involve balancing the cultural and commercial interests at stake.

The progressive implementation of international conventions on culture, including the CDC, may have a role to play in such balancing. Cultural policy measures adopted in accordance with the principles and provisions of these conventions would likely be more easily justified before a trade judge. Presumably, this would be even more the case if such measures were framed within one of the protective mechanisms in favour of vulnerable or threatened cultural expressions envisaged by those international treaties on culture. Such mechanisms are discussed in the following section.

III. The Legitimisation of a Precautionary Approach Based on the International Conventions on Culture

Two recent UNESCO conventions dealing with the protection of culture contain specific provisions applicable to situations of threat: the 2003 Convention for the

[14] (adopted 2 November 2001) UNESCO Doc CLT.2002/WS/9.
[15] See, eg Richieri Hanania, 'Le principe de précaution' (n 4).

Safeguarding of the Intangible Cultural Heritage[16] (hereinafter CSICH) and the CDC.[17] Both have, as their ultimate objective, the promotion of cultural diversity and provide for both national actions and international cooperation. Because of the distinct perspective adopted by each of these two conventions, the cultural policy measures they are intended to cover differ (section IIIA). However, both provide a specific institutional and procedural framework for the protection of threatened cultural expressions, each of which may help to justify the adoption of protective measures, including where they would have a market-restrictive effect. These frameworks allow not only for the recognition of the vulnerability of certain cultural expressions, but also for a certain control and monitoring of the measures adopted to deal with such vulnerability, which may contribute to strengthening the legitimacy of those measures (section IIIB).

A. Measures in Favour of Vulnerable Cultural Expressions

Since the perspectives adopted by the CSICH and the CEDC to deal with cultural diversity are different, the mechanisms they envisage to protect cultural expressions under threat are also distinct. The CDC takes a more economic view of cultural expressions, focusing more directly on the market of cultural goods and services. Although safeguarding the elements of cultural heritage conveyed by these goods and services may also be necessary for their promotion, the cultural expressions targeted by the CDC are those present in visual arts, music, literature, film, television, video games, etc. The CDC aims mostly to protect the 'vitality' of cultures, implying a more dynamic character, in line with the notions of dialogue and interaction between cultures. In its turn, the CSICH emphasises the 'viability', ie the survival, of the expressions, representations, knowledge, know-how, social practices, rituals, traditions and oral expressions that compose the intangible cultural heritage.

At the same time, though, such cultural heritage underlies the cultural goods and services covered by the CDC and constitutes the very foundation of cultural creativity and, consequently, of the production of cultural goods and services. There is therefore an interdependence and complementarity between the two conventions that became evident during the initial discussions on the objectives to be pursued by the CDC, with the CSICH being considered as a 'sound conceptual basis' for the CDC.[18] This complementarity justifies the fact that the protection of

[16] (adopted 7 October 2003, entered into force 20 April 2006) 2368 UNTS 3.

[17] For a comparison between these two conventions with respect to cultural expressions under threat, see L Richieri Hanania, 'Protection Mechanisms for Cultural Expressions under Threat' (2014) 2 *Transnational Dispute Management* www.transnational-dispute-management.com/article.asp?key=2095.

[18] See UNESCO, 'Preliminary Study on the Technical and Legal Aspects Relating to the Desirability of a Standard-Setting Instrument on Cultural Diversity' (2003) 166 EX/28, which states: 'Given the close conceptual links that exist between cultural diversity and intangible cultural heritage, the finalization of

cultural expressions under threat may depend on complementary actions under the legal frameworks of each of these conventions in favour of vulnerable cultural expressions.

The CSICH contains clauses specifically aimed at situations requiring urgent action, including the inscription on a List of Intangible Cultural Heritage in Need of Urgent Safeguarding in accordance with Article 17.1, which reads:

> 1. With a view to taking appropriate safeguarding measures, the Committee shall establish, keep up to date and publish a List of Intangible Cultural Heritage in Need of Urgent Safeguarding, and shall inscribe such heritage on the List at the request of the State Party concerned …[19]

The purpose of inscription on the List is to enable parties to the CSICH to take appropriate safeguarding measures and to benefit from international cooperation and assistance.

Similarly, the CDC contains two provisions, Articles 8 and 17, specifically relating to special situations of risk of extinction, serious threat or urgent need for safeguarding affecting cultural expressions.[20] Article 8 of the CDC (Measures to protect cultural expressions) states that:

> 1. Without prejudice to the provisions of Articles 5 and 6, a Party may determine the existence of special situations where cultural expressions on its territory are at risk of extinction, under serious threat, or otherwise in need of urgent safeguarding.
> 2. Parties may take all appropriate measures to protect and preserve cultural expressions in situations referred to in paragraph 1 in a manner consistent with the provisions of this Convention.
> 3. Parties shall report to the Intergovernmental Committee referred to in Article 23 all measures taken to meet the exigencies of the situation, and the Committee may make appropriate recommendations.[21]

Article 17 CDC, entitled 'International cooperation in situations of serious threat to cultural expressions', stipulates that 'Parties shall cooperate in providing

the convention for the safeguarding of the intangible cultural heritage will provide a sound conceptual basis for a new instrument on cultural diversity' (§ 14).

[19] Such a list is available at UNESCO, 'Intangible Cultural Heritage – Browse the Lists of Intangible Cultural Heritage and the Register of Good Safeguarding Practices' https://ich.unesco.org/en/lists. In Art 17(1), the 'Committee' refers to the 'Intergovernmental Committee for the Safeguarding of the Intangible Cultural Heritage', created under Art 5 of the CSICH and composed of representatives of 24 states parties, elected for a four-year term by the states parties meeting in General Assembly.

[20] For an analysis of such articles, see L Richieri Hanania and H Ruiz Fabri, 'Article 8 – Measures to Protect Cultural Expressions' and 'Article 17 – International Cooperation in Situations of Serious Threat to Cultural Expressions' in S von Schorlemer and P-T Stoll (eds), *The UNESCO Convention on the Protection and Promotion of the Diversity of Cultural Expressions – Explanatory Notes* (Cham, Springer, 2012). See also I Bernier, 'Les expressions culturelles menacées dans la Convention sur la diversité des expressions culturelles de l'UNESCO' (2008) www.unescodec.chaire.ulaval.ca/sites/unescodec.chaire.ulaval.ca/files/2009avril.pdf.

[21] The 'Intergovernmental Committee' refers here to the 'Intergovernmental Committee for the Protection and Promotion of the Diversity of Cultural Expressions', created under Art 23 of the CDC and composed of representatives of 24 parties to the Convention, elected for a term of four years by the Conference of Parties.

assistance to each other, and, in particular to developing countries, in situations referred to under Article 8'.

However, the adoption of measures under Article 8 by a party to the CDC requires the party to ensure that the situation of danger identified cannot benefit from action under other UNESCO conventions, including the CSICH.[22] This is even more significant considering that the binding nature of the two conventions is not the same. The CSICH contains obligations for its parties to act to ensure the safeguarding of intangible cultural heritage,[23] while the CDC limits itself to reaffirming the right of parties to protect and promote the diversity of cultural expressions.

Nonetheless, there are differences between the types of actions and measures envisaged by each of the two conventions due to their specific perspectives, suggesting that inscription on one of the CSICH lists (accompanied by the adoption of measures aiming at the viability of an element of intangible cultural heritage) may not be exclusive of a complementary action under the CDC. It is even likely that such an inscription under the CSICH could help to justify the adoption of measures for the vitality of the same threatened cultural expressions under the CDC.

Indeed, although the two instruments do not provide an exhaustive list of measures that may be adopted, trends can be observed. On the one hand, the CSICH envisages studies, research, inventories, documentation, promoting the visibility of the identified heritage, planning, strengthening institutions working for the protection of intangible cultural heritage and promoting safeguarding programmes, projects and activities.[24] In general, these measures respond less directly to situations of trade imbalance or market failures, which are better targeted by the measures and policies related to the creation, production, dissemination and distribution of cultural goods and services envisaged under the CDC and illustrated by Article 6 of the latter[25] – some of which may justify a party's

[22] UNESCO, 'Operational Guidelines – Measures to Protect Cultural Expressions – Special Situations' (2009) 29–31, § 5.1.

[23] Under Art 11 of the CSICH, 'Each State Party shall: (a) take the necessary measures to ensure the safeguarding of the intangible cultural heritage present in its territory'.

[24] For examples of measures under the CSICH, see UNESCO, 'Intangible Heritage', at https://ich.unesco.org/. See also the projects and programmes aimed at safeguarding intangible cultural heritage implemented in cooperation with UNESCO at UNESCO, 'Projects for the Safeguarding of Intangible Cultural Heritage' https://ich.unesco.org/en/project.

[25] A non-exhaustive list of 'measures aimed at protecting and promoting the diversity of cultural expressions within [the] territory [of each Party]' is provided under Art 6.2 of the CDC, which states that 'Such measures may include the following: (a) regulatory measures aimed at protecting and promoting diversity of cultural expressions; (b) measures that, in an appropriate manner, provide opportunities for domestic cultural activities, goods and services among all those available within the national territory for the creation, production, dissemination, distribution and enjoyment of such domestic cultural activities, goods and services, including provisions relating to the language used for such activities, goods and services; (c) measures aimed at providing domestic independent cultural industries and activities in the informal sector effective access to the means of production, dissemination and distribution of cultural activities, goods and services; (d) measures aimed at providing public financial assistance; (e) measures aimed at encouraging non-profit organizations, as well as public and private institutions and artists and other cultural professionals, to develop and promote the

decision not to liberalise certain cultural sectors when negotiating international trade agreements.

The distinction between measures that follow a viability logic (according to CSICH) and those that target the vitality of cultural expressions (in line with the CDC) may be difficult to identify in practice, as some measures and policies may contribute to both objectives at the same time.[26] The example of endangered indigenous languages may, nevertheless, provide a simplified illustration of the types of measures that may be adopted based on the distinct approaches of these two conventions. Useful measures to ensure the viability of cultural expressions through the protection of language could probably include, inter alia: the study of factors that may lead to the extinction of a given language; the visibility of a threat through awareness-raising; the revitalisation of a language, particularly with regard to social attitudes towards such language; the development of relevant documentation (archives, dictionaries, recording of oral traditions) and access to it; the teaching of these languages to new generations, and the preparation of teaching materials; and also distance-learning in those languages, which has proved to be crucial during the COVID-19 pandemic.[27] The objective of promoting the vitality of cultural expressions reflected in endangered languages, on the other hand, would, for instance, be more observable in measures aimed at ensuring: the financial viability of the book market in these languages; the creation and multiplication of publication opportunities for authors in languages considered rare or under-represented in the market; publication prizes; bilingual publications allowing for the translation of an under-represented language into a language more present and accessible in the market; and access of indigenous populations to media in their own language, not only on traditional radio and television, but also in digital format.

Some of these measures, particularly those prominently based on the CDC, could potentially have the effect of limiting the market access of other cultural expressions not benefiting from such measures. As such, they are potentially challengeable before a trade judge if the state adopting them has assumed obligations of non-discrimination in the corresponding cultural sectors. In such a context, action under the two above-mentioned UNESCO conventions in accordance with their specific provisions on cultural expressions under threat seems particularly

free exchange and circulation of ideas, cultural expressions and cultural activities, goods and services, and to stimulate both the creative and entrepreneurial spirit in their activities; (f) measures aimed at establishing and supporting public institutions, as appropriate; (g) measures aimed at nurturing and supporting artists and others involved in the creation of cultural expressions; (h) measures aimed at enhancing diversity of the media, including through public service broadcasting'.

[26] The wording of the CDC gives the parties a broad latitude as to the measures that may be adopted, allowing states that have not ratified the CSICH but are parties to the CDC (such as Canada) to adopt measures that also ensure the viability of certain cultural expressions as part of their policies and measures to protect endangered cultural expressions under the CDC.

[27] UNESCO, 'COVID-19 Recovery and Indigenous Peoples' (2020) https://en.unesco.org/news/covid-19-recovery-and-indigenous-peoples.

interesting. It may strengthen the recourse to a precautionary approach allowing the legitimisation of certain cultural policy measures, particularly since these mechanisms provide for review and monitoring of the measures adopted by the other parties.

B. Frameworks for Greater Legitimacy

Under the CSICH, the recognition of vulnerability is materialised in the inscription of an element of intangible cultural heritage on the List of Intangible Cultural Heritage in Need of Urgent Safeguarding. This inscription is to be requested by the state directly concerned when certain criteria provided for in the CSICH Operational Directives[28] are present, namely: the element to be inscribed on the List constitutes intangible cultural heritage in accordance with the CSICH;[29] there is a danger to its viability or the element is subject to serious threats; safeguarding measures have been developed for the practice and transmission of the element; participation of the community, group or individuals concerned, who must give their free, prior and informed consent; and the prior inscription of the element in question on a national inventory. In cases of extreme urgency (serious threats to which the intangible cultural heritage element could not survive without immediate safeguarding), the CSICH Intergovernmental Committee may carry out the inscription in consultation with the state party concerned. In such a case, the request may be made not only by the state party in whose territory the element is located, but also by any other state party, by the community concerned or by non-governmental organisations, with the state concerned being informed in due course.

The review and decision regarding inscription on the List are carried out by the Intergovernmental Committee and, once inscription on the List is established, the state in whose territory the listed heritage is present shall report to the Committee every four years. Such report is expected to address, among others, the social and cultural functions of the listed heritage element (and thus the importance of its protection), an assessment of current risks to this element, the effects of the

[28] UNESCO, 'Operational Directives for the Implementation of the Convention for the Safeguarding of the Intangible Heritage' (2008).

[29] Art 2 of the CSICH stipulates that: '1. The "intangible cultural heritage" means the practices, representations, expressions, knowledge, skills – as well as the instruments, objects, artefacts and cultural spaces associated therewith – that communities, groups and, in some cases, individuals recognize as part of their cultural heritage. This intangible cultural heritage, transmitted from generation to generation, is constantly recreated by communities and groups in response to their environment, their interaction with nature and their history, and provides them with a sense of identity and continuity, thus promoting respect for cultural diversity and human creativity. For the purposes of this Convention, consideration will be given solely to such intangible cultural heritage as is compatible with existing international human rights instruments, as well as with the requirements of mutual respect among communities, groups and individuals, and of sustainable development. 2. The "intangible cultural heritage", as defined in paragraph 1 above, is manifested inter alia in the following domains: (a) oral traditions and expressions, including language as a vehicle of the intangible cultural heritage; (b) performing arts; (c) social practices, rituals and festive events; (d) knowledge and practices concerning nature and the universe; (e) traditional craftsmanship.'

safeguarding measures adopted, and the institutional and social context of the safeguarding. The Committee may address specific requests for additional information to the state party in question.[30]

In addition, when a state party or some states parties make a request to the Committee for international assistance, which is to be supplementary to national efforts for safeguarding, the Committee may decide to grant financial and/or technical assistance after considering the safeguarding measures envisaged, the necessary interventions and the anticipated costs.[31] Such a review may be carried out as a matter of priority in cases of emergency. Assistance may, inter alia, take the form of studies concerning various aspects of safeguarding, provision of experts and practitioners, training, development of standard-setting instruments or other measures, the creation and operation of infrastructures, provision of equipment and know-how, and low-interest loans and grants (Article 21 CSICH). To this end, an agreement is established between the Committee and the beneficiary state, which contributes 'within the limits of its resources' to the costs of the safeguarding measures for which international assistance is granted (Article 24 CSICH). A report is also expected from the recipient state on the use of the assistance granted.

It is conceivable that potentially trade-restrictive measures adopted in connection with the safeguarding of an intangible cultural heritage element inscribed on the CSICH Representative List of the Intangible Cultural Heritage of Humanity, and even more so on the List of Intangible Cultural Heritage in Need of Urgent Safeguarding, would enjoy greater legitimacy when debated and justified before the CSICH Intergovernmental Committee under the procedures described above. Their necessity and proportionality would be more easily demonstrated, and the level of protection chosen by the state whose measure is challenged would likely be better justified before a trade judge.

The framework offered by the CDC opens a similar argumentation, which could be particularly useful when it comes to trade-related measures focusing on cultural goods and services operating as a vehicle for cultural expressions under threat. Article 8 of the CDC provides for a first stage of diagnosis by a party of the vulnerability of cultural expressions facing one of the 'special situations' described in the convention (ie a risk of extinction, a serious threat or otherwise a need of urgent safeguarding) on its territory. As mentioned above, the situation should not be subject to action under other UNESCO conventions. It is conceivable that situations of market failure, weakness of cultural industries preventing cultural expressions from reaching or remaining on the market, or threats to their ability to remain profitable on the market, leading to a threat to the viability or survival of the underlying heritage, could configure situations more related to Article 8 of the CDC. For example, the immense economic impact of the health crisis caused

[30] See V.2 'Reports by States Parties on Elements Inscribed on the List of Intangible Cultural Heritage in Need of Urgent Safeguarding' in UNESCO, 'Operational Directives for the Implementation of the Convention for the Safeguarding of the Intangible Heritage'.

[31] See ibid § I.4.12.

by COVID-19 on the various players of the cultural sector (cultural practitioners and professionals, institutions and establishments), as well as the increased vulnerability of certain communities and groups because of this crisis, could likely offer situations that merit attention in light of Article 8 of the CDC. In this exceptional context, where cultural activity has become highly dependent on online consumption, reinforced by lockdown restrictions, digital content calls for increased vigilance, since the discoverability of culturally diverse content on the Internet has become even more important for the survival of cultural expressions.

The conclusion of this first stage of diagnosis of vulnerability and recognition of a special situation confirms the sovereign right of the party concerned to take 'all appropriate measures', which are exemplified in the Operational Guidelines on Articles 8 and 17 as short-term or emergency measures (aimed at immediate effect), the strengthening of policies and measures, new policies and measures, long-term strategies, as well as the call for international cooperation, provided for as an obligation of the parties under Article 17 of the CDC. Because of the perspective adopted in the latter, these measures are intended to particularly target cultural expressions conveyed by cultural goods and services, thus applying to the production, distribution and consumption of these goods and services and having an impact on market conditions.

Once measures are adopted by a CDC party under Article 8, a certain monitoring of the relevance of such measures by other parties and the CDC Intergovernmental Committee takes place, since the party must report to the Committee on the measures taken. Paragraph 5 of the CDC Operational Guidelines on Article 8 indicates which information should appear in the report, including a description of the threat and its potential consequences, the measures adopted, as well as the possibility of a request for international cooperation and assistance.[32] The Committee may then exercise its monitoring function and make recommendations. The Operational Guidelines provide that the Committee's recommendations may relate to remedial measures (§ 9), the dissemination of best practices in similar situations and the suggestion of requests for assistance from the International Fund for Cultural Diversity (§ 10). According to the same Operational Guidelines, the Committee may 'invite' parties to provide mutual assistance (§ 10) and the 'Parties shall cooperate' (§ 12), even in the absence of any request from the party concerned. The Committee could likely encourage more coordinated actions (§ 14) and promote broader and more coherent international assistance programmes.

[32] § 5 of the Operational Guidelines on Article 8 states that 'Whenever a Party reports to the Intergovernmental Committee under Article 8.3, it should be able to: 5.1 determine that the situation cannot be subject to action under other UNESCO Conventions; 5.2 identify the risk or threat to the cultural expression or the urgent safeguarding needed, involving experts, civil society, and including grass root communities as appropriate; 5.3 demonstrate the source of the threat inter alia with factual data; 5.4 determine the vulnerability and importance of the cultural expression at risk; 5.5 determine the nature of the consequences of the risk or threat to the cultural expression, and demonstrate the nature of the cultural consequences; 5.6 explain the measures taken or proposed to remedy the special situation, including short-term and emergency measures, or long-term strategies; 5.7 if necessary, appeal for international cooperation and assistance' (UNESCO, 'Operational Guidelines – Measures to Protect Cultural Expressions', 30).

The discussions within the Committee would be an opportunity for a party to demonstrate to and discuss with other parties the necessity and proportionality of measures adopted, as well as its selected level of protection. Here, again, it can be assumed that the Committee, in its recommendations, would also have a role in legitimising or, on the contrary, not legitimising certain measures adopted. It could support or challenge the need for the specific measures adopted and encourage the adoption of alternative measures based on best practices collected from other countries, possibly with the least restrictive effect on trade in cultural goods and services. Once legitimised within the CDC framework, particularly in a vulnerability situation recognised as 'special' under Article 8, cultural policy measures could more likely be defended before a trade judge. The debates conducted by the Committee within UNESCO could thus have a decisive role to play in balancing the cultural and commercial interests involved.

IV. Conclusion

The characteristics observed in the application of the precautionary approach by the WTO judge in other areas, such as health or the environment, seem transposable to the protection of cultural diversity. When balancing the cultural and commercial interests at stake, it would be a matter of verifying the necessity and proportionality of the challenged trade-restrictive measures in relation to the level of protection pursued by the WTO member concerned, taking into account the importance of the protected value for society, as well as the seriousness and irreversibility of the potential damage, on the basis of risk assessment by expert scientific advice.

The recourse to measures in favour of vulnerable cultural expressions and to the mechanisms provided for in the 2003 and 2005 UNESCO Conventions (CSICH and CDC), so far underutilised, could be encouraged to a greater extent with the awareness of their importance to legitimise action and the level of protection chosen by states. The use of these mechanisms, which provide for the involvement of citizens and in particular the groups and communities affected, would contribute to enhanced cooperation between states, allowing for greater exchanges of information and best practices, in addition to the benefit of access to the expertise of the secretariats and intergovernmental committees of the two conventions.

The precautionary approach or precautionary logic applied to vulnerable cultural expressions could become an additional and effective avenue for greater consideration of the objective of cultural diversity in trade and economic fora. By positively affecting the balancing of commercial and cultural values and strengthening the pursuit of cultural diversity as an objective, such an additional path could offer a particularly impactful new process at the present time, while the health, economic and social impact of the COVID-19 pandemic rekindles the need to cherish and promote culture, creativity and the human values of our societies.

PART III

Cultural Diversity (Still) Beyond the Convention? Communities, Private Actors and Law-Making

7

Moving Online: How Communities have Invested Cultural Spaces in the Domain Name System

LILY MARTINET

I. Introduction

'Linguistic diversity is a fundamental element of cultural diversity.'[1] Language is a vehicle through which identity, cultural expressions and intangible cultural heritage are expressed and transmitted.[2] Language reflects the social and cultural values of its speakers. It can encapsulate a community's worldview and its experience with its environment. For instance, the Sámi people, an indigenous group living in the northern part of Scandinavia, whose subsistence relies on hunting, fishing and reindeer herding, have developed an intricate terminology of about 200 different terms to single out a reindeer in a herd just by describing the shape of its antlers and the aspect of its hide.[3] Culture and language are so tightly intertwined that they share a symbiotic relationship. If a language disappears, then the transmission of the culture associated with it is hampered or halted. Without the underlying language that supports them, cultural expressions, such as songs, stories, legends, traditional knowledge, toponyms and oral traditions, may vanish. Language is the expression of a community's 'whole society and history'.[4] Conversely, measures relating to the use of a language for cultural activities, goods and services may protect and promote cultural diversity.[5]

[1] Recital 14 of the Preamble of the Convention on the Protection and Promotion of the Diversity of Cultural Expressions (adopted 20 October 2005, entered into force 18 March 2007) 2440 UNTS 311 (hereinafter CDC).

[2] Art 2.2 of the Convention for the Safeguarding of the Intangible Cultural Heritage (adopted 7 October 2003, entered into force 20 April 2006) 2368 UNTS 3.

[3] J-C Tamisier (ed), *Dictionnaire des peuples: sociétés d'Afrique, d'Amérique, d'Asie et d'Océanie* (Paris, Larousse, 1998) 281.

[4] D Crystal, *Language Death* (Cambridge, Cambridge University Press, 2002) 48.

[5] Art 6(2)(b) CDC; see also para 5 of the Action Plan for the Implementation of the Universal Declaration on Cultural Diversity (adopted 2 November 2001) UNESCO Doc CLT.2002/WS/9, which had rightly included among its objectives the safeguarding of the linguistic heritage of humanity.

Just like cultural expressions, some languages are seriously threatened or at risk of extinction. Linguists estimate 'that half of the more 6,000 languages currently spoken in the world will become extinct by the end of' the twenty-first century.[6] The ascent and rapid expansion of information and communication technologies have exacerbated pre-existing imbalances between dominant and vulnerable languages. Although the right of a person to 'express themselves and to create and disseminate their work in the language of their choice, and particularly in their mother tongue',[7] is a protected cultural right,[8] in practice, its realisation is moot if the digital environment favours monolingualism and linguistic imperialism. In this respect, the Internet, as a unified communication space, poses the risk of breeding a digital monoculture. The digital environment affects the cultural diversity of cultural goods and services – for instance, streaming services channel contents and values, which become globally ubiquitous. Thus, access to this network and its contents may be feared to erode cultural diversity and to cause homogenisation, triggering calls for the promotion of linguistic diversity in what was previously called 'cyberspace'[9] and is now known as the 'digital environment'.[10]

In its infancy, the Internet was indeed overwhelmingly dominated by English. In the 2000s, English represented almost 50 per cent of the languages used on the Internet.[11] This predominance of English was criticised, notably by a librarian in Abidjan, Bakayoko Bourahima, as a 'second linguistic colonisation', as it imposed on French-speaking Africans a 'proficiency in a second foreign language'.[12] The use of a mother tongue might in this sense be perceived as an obstacle to accessing content on the Internet. The Internet is also riddled with technical biases, as its underlying technologies were designed in an English-speaking environment.[13] The English language infuses the Internet because it is historically linked to the USA. The US government funded the research programmes that paved the way to the development and deployment of the Internet. The infrastructure and governance of the Internet are still managed, among others, by two American non-profit organisations established in the 1990s: the Internet Corporation for Assigned Names and Numbers (ICANN) and the Internet Society.

Cultural diversity only became a concern in the Internet's governance in the late 1990s.[14] The adoption in 2003 of the Recommendation concerning the Promotion

[6] JAR Nafziger, RK Paterson and AD Renteln, *Cultural Law: International, Comparative, and Indigenous* (Cambridge, Cambridge University Press, 2001) 951.

[7] Art 5 of the Universal Declaration on Cultural Diversity.

[8] Committee on Economic, Social and Cultural Rights, 'General Comment No. 21: Right of Everyone to Take Part in Cultural Life (art. 15, para 1 (a), of the International Covenant on Economic, Social and Cultural Rights)' (21 December 2009) para 55.

[9] Para 10 of the Action Plan for the Implementation of Universal Declaration on Cultural Diversity.

[10] UNESCO, 'Operational Guidelines on the Implementation of the Convention on the Protection and Promotion of the Diversity of Cultural Expressions in the Digital Environment' (12 June 2018).

[11] UNESCO, *Cultural Diversity: Common Heritage, Plural Identities* (Paris, UNESCO, 2001) 43.

[12] UNESCO, *Cultural and Linguistic Diversity in the Information Society* (Paris, UNESCO, 2003) 29.

[13] J Paolillo, 'Language Diversity on the Internet' in J Paolillo et al (eds), *Measuring Linguistic Diversity on the Internet* (Paris, UNESCO, 2005) 49.

[14] UNESCO, *Cultural and Linguistic Diversity* (n 12) 25.

and Use of Multilingualism and Universal Access to Cyberspace represented a milestone for the advancement of linguistic diversity in the digital environment.[15] A whole chapter of the Recommendation was devoted to the development of multilingual content and systems, stressing the need to encourage the teaching of languages online and to ensure access to the 'cyberspace in all languages'.[16] The landscape of the Internet has dramatically changed since then, but English still dominates the Internet.[17] The aim of digital multilingualism is not to diminish the presence of English, but rather to grow digital environments that reflect the diversity of the languages of humanity.[18]

Nevertheless, the digital space and the tools the Internet offers are versatile, and may also protect and promote the diversity of cultural expressions. The Internet is a medium relatively free from gatekeepers. There is no need on the Internet for measures like cultural or local content quotas, which exist in the realms of radio or television broadcasting. As a result, the Internet opens up to communities a singular space in which they can express and define themselves anew. In this digital environment, communities are not caught in the dichotomous relationship that opposes them to a state, nor are they trapped in the quagmire of self-determination. The Internet loosens the link between 'geographical location' and identity.[19] Some communities have seized this opportunity to exist online, redesigning themselves by putting forth culture and language at their common core. This emphasis on cultural and linguistic aspects diverts attention away from issues relating to territory, independence and autonomy. One way communities have achieved this digital transformation is by becoming involved in the domain name system. This chapter argues that through this process, communities have, on the one hand, influenced the Internet's normative framework and international law-making, but that, on the other hand, by creating cultural spaces in the infrastructure of the Internet, communities have encouraged online interculturality and linguistic and cultural diversity.

To explain the process of the involvement of communities with the domain name system, this chapter will first explain, in section II, in a concise way, the nuts and bolts of this system, highlighting the different periods of its history and setting out its distinctive features. The third section of the chapter will then draw on the example of the '.cat' domain to explain how a community overcame the hurdles of claiming a digital space online by putting forth its desire to share its

[15] Recommendation concerning the Promotion and Use of Multilingualism and Universal Access to Cyberspace (adopted 15 October 2003) https://en.unesco.org/sites/default/files/eng_-_recommendation_concerning_the_promotion_and_use_of_multilingualism_and_universal_access_to_cyberspace.pdf; see also section 8 of the Declaration of Principles: Building the Information Society: A Global Challenge in the New Millennium (Geneva, 12 December 2003).

[16] Recommendation concerning the Promotion and Use of Multilingualism and Universal Access to Cyberspace, ss 1–5.

[17] 'Internet World Users by Language' (*Internet World Stats*, 31 March 2020) www.Internetworldstats.com/stats7.htm.

[18] UNESCO, *Cultural and Linguistic Diversity* (n 12) 27.

[19] Crystal, *Language Death*, 142.

culture and language and to disseminate its cultural expressions. This section will show how this community reconfigured itself conceptually to fit the domain name system's policies. The last section will analyse how this first foray in the domain name system traced a path for other communities and, by doing so, influenced the adoption of new normative mechanisms enabling community participation, which promote cultural diversity on the Internet.

II. The Organic Growth of a Naming System

On the Internet, data is transmitted through the network by being broken into small packets.[20] Each packet carries a source and a destination address called 'Internet Protocol addresses' (IP addresses).[21] IP addresses are a sequence of numbers, which are convenient for computers but hard to memorise for humans. Consequently, IP addresses are translated into user-friendly, human-readable, meaningful and mnemonic domain names. A domain name is 'a sequence of names separated by periods ordered in a hierarchical way from right to left', forming a tree-like structure.[22] The domain name is the address that an Internet user types in a browser or an e-mail to identify its recipient (eg esil-sedi.eu or lily.martinet@gmail.com).[23] At the top of the hierarchy are the roots of the tree, the top-level domains (TLD), such as .eu. The second-level domains come after TLDs (eg esil-sedi), and these are then followed by third-level domains, and so on. The stability and unity of the Internet require that each IP address is unique and assigned exclusively to a device or a user.[24] The entity responsible for assigning these unique names controls the root of the Internet and the creation of new TLDs.

In the 1970s, when the Internet was still part of a governmental research programme, Jon Postel, a graduate student at the University of California at Los Angeles,[25] was in charge of assigning and recording IP addresses.[26] As the Internet expanded, the management of these addresses evolved from simple tools – a notebook and index cards[27] – into the Domain Name System (DNS). The

[20] F Petillion and J Janssen, *Competing for the Internet: ICANN Gate – An Analysis and Plea for Judicial Review through Arbitration* (Alphen aan den Rijn, Kluwer Law International, 2017) 7.

[21] M Mueller, *Ruling the Root: Internet Governance and the Taming of Cyberspace* (Cambridge, MA, MIT Press, 2004) 32.

[22] L Martinet, 'Accountability Mechanisms: Internet Corporation for Assigned Names and Numbers (ICANN)' in H Ruiz Fabri (ed), *Max Planck Encyclopedia of International Procedural Law* (Oxford, Oxford University Press, 2019) para 1.

[23] T Mahler, *Generic Top-Level Domains: A Study of Transnational Private Regulation* (Cheltenham, Edward Elgar Publishing, 2019) 17.

[24] Mueller, *Ruling the Root* (n 21) 15.

[25] The UCLA was one of the participants of the governmental research programme called 'the Advanced Research Projects Agency Network' (ARPANET).

[26] US Department of Commerce, Statement of Policy: Management of Internet Names and Addresses (10 June 1998b) 63 US Fed Reg 31741, 31741.

[27] BJ Winterfeldt and PV Maran, 'The Internet Assigned Numbers Authority Transition in Hindsight' (2017) 24 *Westlaw Journal Intellectual Property* 1, 1.

primary objective guiding the design of the system was to establish a consistent namespace.[28] English also influenced its design as it relied on the American Standard Code for Information Interchange (ASCII), which is based on the English alphabet and does not support all diacritics (accented letters, used in languages such as French and Spanish).[29] As of 1988, the management of the list of assigned numbers and domain names were known as the 'Internet Assigned Numbers Authority' (IANA).[30] These activities stayed strongly linked to Dr Jon Postel. In 1997, the USA initiated a process to privatise the management of the DNS by issuing a policy statement calling on the 'private sector Internet stakeholders to form a not-for-profit corporation'.[31] Postel answered this call with a letter informing the US Department of Commerce that ICANN, a non-profit structured as a multi-stakeholder-led system, was incorporated in California to 'include the IANA function and in addition take on other coordination and administrative responsibilities necessary for the continued operational stability and growth of the Internet'.[32] Postel's proposal was successful and, in 1998, ICANN and the Department of Commerce signed a memorandum of understanding.[33]

The DNS grew in a somewhat organic way by accumulating stratifications. In 1984, two types of TLDs were defined: country code TLDs (ccTLDs) and general purpose domains, which, as of 1994, are known as generic TLDs (gTLDs) because they are 'created for a general category of organizations', like '.com', which was established for commercial entities, or '.edu', for educational institutions.[34] In 1984, six general purpose domains ('.com', '.edu', '.gov', '.mil', '.org' and '.net') were picked to replace the original domain name, '.arpa'.[35] For ccTLDs, such as '.fr', the decision was made to use the English two-letter codes identifying countries compiled by the ISO 3166 standard for Codes for the Representation of Names of Countries.[36] This standard is aligned with the list established by the United Nations Statistics

[28] Requests for Comment (RFC) are documents that codify Internet protocols, technical developments and standards; P Mockapetris, 'Domain Names – Concepts and Facilities', RFC 1034 (November 1987) https://tools.ietf.org/html/rfc1034.

[29] Paolillo, 'Language Diversity on the Internet' (n 13) 68.

[30] M Mueller, 'ICANN and Internet Governance: Sorting through the Debris of "Self-Regulation"' (1999) 6 *Journal of Policy, Regulation and Strategy for Telecommunications Information and Media* 497, 499.

[31] J Postel, 'Re: Management of Internet Names and Addresses' (2 October 1998) www.ntia.doc.gov/legacy/ntiahome/domainname/proposals/icann/Letter.htm.

[32] ibid.

[33] Memorandum of Understanding between the US Department of Commerce and Internet Corporation for Assigned Names and Numbers (25 November 1998) www.ntia.doc.gov/page/1998/memorandum-understanding-between-us-department-commerce-and-Internet-corporation-assigned-.

[34] J Postel, 'Domain Name System Structure and Delegation', RFC 1591 (March 1994) https://tools.ietf.org/html/rfc1591.

[35] JK Reynolds and J Postel, 'Domain Requirements', RFC 920 (October 1984) https://tools.ietf.org/html/rfc920.

[36] ibid.

Division.[37] The choice of referring to the ISO 3166 standard was underpinned by the desire to neutralise disputes and contentions on the choice of ccTLD.[38]

As the use of the Internet soared in the 1990s and its commercial use grew, flaws were revealed in the DNS system. The number of TLDs was insufficient; this scarcity stifled competition. New gTLDs were needed for the Internet to sustain its growth and to enhance competition. Two rounds were organised for the registration of new gTLDs, in 2000 and in 2003–04. The 2000 round was considered as a proof of concept for introducing new gTLDs.[39] Only seven new gTLDs were activated between 2001 and 2004.[40] In 2008, the Board of ICANN approved a recommendation for implementing new gTLDs to keep up with demand. In 2011, the New gTLD programme was finally launched to open up the root zone to 'an unlimited number of new gTLD[s]'.[41] New subsets of gTLDs were introduced: geographic, community, brands and internationalised domain names (IDN), enabling the use of specific alphabets in the DNS, such as Arabic or Cyrillic (eg '.com' in Arabic is '.كوم').[42] More than a thousand gTLDs were added to the Internet's root with this programme, creating a cornucopia of domain names.[43]

This expansion of the DNS did not go unnoticed. Several communities saw in it the opportunity to claim a space online. In this respect, the emergence of new gTLDs revealed how communities could invest in the DNS. The goals they pursued in this endeavour not only served cultural survival purposes, but also addressed the need to protect the economic interests they have vested in their cultural identity. The policies regulating the DNS had not yet gelled. There were gaps that could be exploited by communities to participate in its development and also some leeway for them to influence its normative framework. In addition, communities used ICANN as a new international forum in which they could affirm their cultural rights. This process has nevertheless elicited tensions, which are especially visible in the case of the '.cat' domain.

III. The Trailblazing Role of the '.cat' Domain Name

The campaign led for the approval of the '.cat' domain shines a light on how ICANN may weigh on linguistic and cultural diversity in the digital environment.

[37] C Manara and V-L Benabou, *Le droit des noms de domaine* (Paris, LexisNexis, 2012) 44.

[38] Mueller, *Ruling the Root* (n 21) 79.

[39] J Weinberg, 'ICANN, "Internet Stability", and New Top Level Domains' in L Cranor and S Greenstein (eds), *Communications Policy and Information Technology: Promises, Problems, Prospects* (Cambridge, MA, MIT Press, 2002).

[40] DM Spencer, 'Much Ado about Nothing: ICANN's New GTLDs' (2014) 29 *Berkeley Technology Law Journal* 866, 870.

[41] M Zalnieriute and T Schneider, *ICANN's Procedures and Policies in the Light of Human Rights, Fundamental Freedoms and Democratic Values* (Council of Europe Publishing, 2004) 15.

[42] For information on IDN, see D Mac Síthigh, 'More than Words: The Introduction of Internationalised Domain Names and the Reform of Generic Top-Level Domains at ICANN' (2010) 3 *International Journal of Law and Information Technology* 274.

[43] Mahler, *Generic Top-Level Domains* (n 23) 22.

Although ICANN's mission 'is to ensure the stable and secure operation of the Internet's unique identifier systems',[44] its functions are not merely technical. In practice, when ICANN manages the expansion of the DNS, it also deals with policymaking. The regulatory frameworks developed by ICANN may have an impact on cultural diversity.[45] Though Postel wrote, in 1994, that 'it is extremely unlikely that any other TLDs will be created',[46] in 1996, following the 'domain name rush of 1994–6',[47] he released a working document entitled 'New Registries and the Delegation of International Top Level Domains', in which he suggested the allocation of additional TLDs.[48] This breach opened up in the DNS was grasped by a Catalan lawyer, Amadeu Abril i Abril.[49] In 1996, a campaign was launched to introduce a TLD for Catalonia under the slogan 'one TLD for our people'.[50] At first, the promoters of this campaign sought the ccTLD '.ct'. The Catalan parliament supported the campaign by adopting a motion, and steps were taken with the International Organization for Standardization (ISO) to secure the two-letter code.[51] Despite these efforts, the request lodged with the ISO was denied, because Catalonia is not an independent state.[52]

The allocation of additional TLDs was put on hold during the transition period of IANA to ICANN.[53] In 1999, Abril i Abril became an ICANN board member. During this period, thanks to his insider knowledge, the strategy was redesigned. The '.ct' option was set aside, and a switch was made pushing forward '.cat', the short code used for Catalan by the standard for the representation of names of language (ISO 639-2). Swapping '.ct' with '.cat' shifted the focus from the Autonomous Community of Catalonia to the Catalan language and culture. In Abril i Abril's words, the solution was 'to change the passport for the dictionary'.[54] This shift broadened the domain name beyond Catalonia to Catalan speakers in other regions and countries: France, Andorra, Sardinia and the diaspora. The application was no longer grounded in a tangible regional territory, but linked to shared intangible cultural references. The transnational nature of the Catalan

[44] Bylaws for Internet Corporation for Assigned Names and Numbers (as amended 28 November 2019), s 1.1.

[45] For the impact of ICANN on human rights, see Zalnieriute and Schneider, *ICANN's Procedures and Policies* (n 41).

[46] Postel, 'Domain Name System Structure and Delegation' (n 34).

[47] Mueller, *Ruling the Root* (n 21) 115.

[48] J Postel, 'New Registries and the Delegation of International Top Level Domains' (June 1996) https://tools.ietf.org/html/draft-postel-iana-itld-admin-01.

[49] P Gerrand, 'Cultural Diversity in Cyberspace: The Catalan Campaign to Win the New .cat Top Level Domain' (2006) 11 *First Monday* 1, https://firstmonday.org/ojs/index.php/fm/article/view/1305/1225.

[50] C Möller, 'New Technology, Minorities and Internet Governance' (2013) 12 *Journal on Ethnopolitics and Minority Issues in Europe* 16, 24.

[51] P Gerrand, 'A Short History of the Catalan Campaign to Win the *.cat* Internet Domain, with Implications for Other Minority Languages' (2006) 8 *Digithum* 1, http://doi.org/10.7238/d.v0i8.528.

[52] D Atkinson, 'Catalan on the Internet and the .ct and .cat Campaigns' (2006) 5 *Journal of Language and Politics* 239, 244.

[53] Gerrand, 'A Short History of the Catalan Campaign' (n 51) 2.

[54] ibid 3.

language also helped to argue, first, that '.cat' should not become a second-level domain placed in Spain's ccTLD '.es', and, second, that it was an initiative free from political claims for independence or self-determination.[55]

A non-profit, Associació puntCAT, was incorporated in 2001 to file the application for the domain name '.cat'. puntCat brought together different types of legal entities involved in the promotion of Catalan language and culture (non-profits, cultural centres and institutes), and excluded from its membership individuals, political parties and administration bodies.[56] The application was submitted during the second round of new generic TLDs (2003–04).[57] During this round, ICANN established a new sub-category of gTLDs: sponsored TLDs (sTLDs).[58] These TLDs are structured around an organisation called a 'sponsor', which acts on behalf of a community. An sTLD addresses 'the needs and interests of a clearly defined community … which can benefit from the establishment of [the] TLD'.[59] The sponsor defines the domain's policy and picks the registry operator responsible for the registration of the domain names inside the TLD.

The application for the '.cat' TLD planned that if the application were successful, Associació puntCAT would be dissolved and replaced by a foundation, Fundació .cat, which would become the sponsoring organisation and manage this 'common asset'.[60] The main organ of the foundation, the Assembly of Trustees, would include representatives from the academic, media, corporate and not-for-profit sectors, and individual holders of .cat domain names. The application highlights that this foundation is designed to be non-partisan and inclusive. The emphasis put on inclusiveness is crucial, as representativeness is a recurrent issue when dealing with communities, minorities and indigenous peoples.

The task accomplished by the '.cat' supporters is particularly impressive, as it required convincing actors at three different levels.[61] First, the local level was needed to prove the existence of the community and grassroots support. Second, at the national level, ICANN requested that the '.cat' application secure formal letters from the government of Spain and Andorra stating that they agreed with an sTLD for the Catalan linguistic and cultural community.[62] The consent of these states was deemed necessary by ICANN as they both recognise Catalan as an official

[55] This issue was discussed in the e-mails received by ICANN during the application process. See, eg J Solà, '.CAT is transnational', e-mail (14 April 2004) https://forum.icann.org/lists/stld-rfp-cat/msg00007.html.

[56] Atkinson, 'Catalan on the Internet' (n 52) 244.

[57] .Cat Application Form, part B (2004) https://archive.icann.org/en/tlds/stld-apps-19mar04/cat.htm.

[58] The selection criteria are exposed in 'New sTLD Application: Part A. Explanatory Notes' (15 December 2003) https://archive.icann.org/en/tlds/new-stld-rfp/new-stld-application-parta-15dec03.htm.

[59] ICANN, 'Request for Proposals (RFP)' (2003) https://archive.icann.org/en/tlds/new-stld-rfp/new-stld-application-parta-15dec03.htm.

[60] J Iparraguirre, 'Elements for a Successful gTLD: Lessons from the .cat Experience for New Community gTLDs' (2013) 63 *Telecommunications Journal of Australia* 3, 3.

[61] M le Béchec, 'Territoire et communication politique sur le "web régional breton"' (Dphil thesis, Université Rennes 2, 2010) 377, https://tel.archives-ouvertes.fr/tel-00551746.

[62] ICANN, 'Status Report on the sTLD Application Process' (2005) https://archive.icann.org/en/tlds/stld-apps-19mar04/PostsTLDStatusRpt.pdf.

language.[63] Third, at the international level, ICANN needed to be convinced that '.cat' would bring value to the Internet namespace. Finally, in 2005, after eight years of campaigning and an investment estimated at €150,000,[64] ICANN approved '.cat' as an sTLD.[65]

The '.cat' application contains several features relevant to linguistic and cultural diversity. First, the application describes the primary value of adding '.cat' to the Internet namespace as enhancing diversity and sending a sign 'to all sort of communities around the world that cultural diversity has its space on the Internet'. Overall, the application reads like a heartfelt plea for opening the DNS to a cultural and linguistic community. Regarding linguistic diversity, the application explains the need to create different linguistic areas in an Internet that at the time was strongly dominated by English:

> If there is a real sense of belonging to a given community within the Internet this is precisely because those belonging to the community are communicating in their own language, no matter which one it is … Even if [linguistic communities] are, most often, completely invisible to the predominant English-based Internet, which many assume to be THE only communications space … English has not one, but many ccTLDs and gTLDs which are predominantly, if not exclusively, devoted to communication spaces where English is the vehicle. Catalan doesn't.

An analogy may be drawn between online communication spaces and what is known as a cultural spaces in the field of intangible cultural heritage. A cultural space is understood as 'a physical or symbolic space in which people meet to enact, share or exchange social practices or ideas'.[66]

Moreover, the application rebuts potential arguments, such as the marginality of the Catalan language or the limited size of the community, notably by citing its rank in terms of online use, and its role in cultural socialisation, by citing famous Catalan figures like Salvador Dali, Joan Miro and Antoni Gaudi. The community associated with '.cat' is defined in reference to culture and language as 'the Catalan Linguistic and Cultural Community'.[67] The criteria chosen to define the community is self-identification, which is one of the key criteria used in international law for indigenous peoples, minorities and communities.[68] The '.cat' Charter further

[63] Gerrand, 'A Short History of the Catalan Campaign' (n 51) 2.

[64] This estimated cost includes notably the '$45,000 non-refundable ICANN fee' cited in Gerrand, 'A Short History of the Catalan Campaign' (n 51) 9.

[65] ICANN, 'Preliminary Report: Special Meeting' (15 September 2005) www.icann.org/resources/board-material/resolutions-2005-09-15-en.

[66] W van Zanten (ed), 'Glossary Intangible Cultural Heritage, International Meeting of Experts at UNESCO' (The Hague, Netherlands National Commission for UNESCO, 2002) https://ich.unesco.org/doc/src/00265.pdf.

[67] ibid.

[68] See, eg the right to self-identify recognised by Art 33 of the Declaration on the Rights of Indigenous Peoples (New York, 13 September 2007), commented on by S Imai and K Gunn, 'Indigenous Belonging: Membership and Identity in the UNDRIP: Articles 9, 33, 35, and 36' in J Hohmann and M Weller (eds), *The UN Declaration on the Rights of Indigenous Peoples: A Commentary* (Oxford, Oxford University Press, 2018) 230–37.

details the community around three aspects: 'The Community includes those wh(1) use the Catalan language for their online communications, (2) and/or promot the different aspects of Catalan culture online, (3) and/or want to specificall address their online communications to that Community.'[69]

Second, the '.cat' Charter cites as examples of potential registrants actors tha are usually identified as promoters of linguistic and cultural diversity, includ ing universities, writers, translators, correctors and journalists publishing work in Catalan, publishing companies and the media.[70] Another interesting featur is a provision in the Charter excluding from registration 'community-assigne domain names' that are 'shared resources for cultural purposes', such as Catala popular culture figures or famous literary works. This provision may be under stood as establishing a form of cultural commons inside the domain name system

The '.cat' TLD experiment proved to be a success.[71] In less than 15 years, mor than 100,000 domain names were registered in '.cat'.[72] By trading the passpor for the dictionary in the '.cat' application, the community of Catalonia redefine itself conceptually in relationship with a digital framework. This new environ ment emancipated the community from its geographical anchorage. Through thi process, language and cultural heritage were pushed forward as shared references which broadened the community's inclusiveness. Under this perspective, the TL became a means of realisation of cultural rights. In addition, the experience of th Catalan Linguistic and Cultural Community started a new path for the attributio of domain names and gave momentum to other projects that were being devel oped at the same time, such as the '.gal' (for the Galician community)[73] and '.bzh'[7 (for the Breton Community).

IV. The Emergence of Community-Based Cultural Spaces Online

The struggle for the attribution of '.cat' had an impact on ICANN's policies. I 2007, the Generic Names Supporting Organisation, one of ICANN's supportin

[69] In the case of sponsored TLDs, a Charter sets out the purpose of the TLD, why it was created an how it is operated.

[70] For the .cat Charter, see www.icann.org/resources/unthemed-pages/cat-appendixs-2006-03-22-e 17 March 2022.

[71] The technical evaluation team had noted the innovativeness of the proposal and highlighted that i was an experiment in 'ICANN, Status Report on the sTLD Application Process' (2005) https://archive icann.org/en/tlds/stld-apps-19mar04/PostsTLDStatusRpt.pdf; see also Iparraguirre, 'Elements for Successful gTLD' (n 60).

[72] See Wikipedia's entry on '.cat', https://en.wikipedia.org/wiki/.cat.

[73] HA Forrest, *The Protection of Geographical Names in International Law and Domain Name Systen* (Alphen aan den Rijn, Kluwer Law International, 2017) 4.

[74] le Béchec, 'Territoire et communication politique' (n 61) 117.

organisations, recommended that communities should be taken into account in the introduction of new gTLDs.[75] Following this recommendation, special status was given to communities in ICANN's 'New gTLD Program' launched in 2011. In 2012, when ICANN opened a new session for receiving applications, communities were taken into account in the application process in two different ways.[76] First, a defensive protection was put into place. An application could be rejected if the community implicitly or explicitly targeted by a gTLD string opposed it. For instance, the Cherokee Nation could object to an application submitted by a car manufacturer for the string '.cherokee'.[77] Second, applications submitted by communities were awarded priority when there was a contention for strings, ie when different applicants apply for a same or similar string.[78] Furthermore, in this round, a new type of gTLD was introduced: the community-based gTLD.

Yet, it is important to stress that the term 'community' is used by ICANN in a very broad sense, including an economic sector, a cultural community or a linguistic one.[79] Community-based TLDs must be 'operated for the benefit of a clearly delineated community'.[80] The applicant must: (i) establish the existence of an ongoing relationship with the community; (ii) prove that the string applied for is strongly and specifically related to it; (iii) propose a framework for the TLD that respects its purpose (registration, use policies, security verification procedures); and (iv) endorse its application by institutions that represent the community.[81] These criteria avoid the application of the first come, first served approach to strings related to a community. However, if a community submits an application for a geoTLD comprising a geographical name, like '.quebec', it must also secure the approval of the government concerned.[82] Governments may also stop an application in its tracks by issuing a 'GAC[83] early warning'.[84]

[75] ICANN Generic Names Supporting Organisation, 'Final Report: Introduction of New Generic Top-Level Domains' (8 August 2007) https://gnso.icann.org/en/issues/new-gtlds/pdp-dec05-fr-parta-08aug07.htm.

[76] For an overview of the gTLD application process, see Mahler, *Generic Top-Level Domains* (n 23) 169.

[77] J Malthouse, 'Interview with Avri Doria on the History of Community gTLDs' (*CircleID*, 5 March 2013) www.circleid.com/posts/20130305_interview_with_avri_doria_on_the_history_of_community_gtlds/.

[78] ICANN Generic Names Supporting Organisation, 'Final Report' (n 75).

[79] ibid.

[80] Module 1, §1.2.3 of ICANN, 'gTLD Applicant Guidebook' (4 June 2012) http://newgtlds.icann.org/en/applicants/agb/guidebook-full-04jun12-en.pdf.

[81] ibid, module 1, §1.2.3.

[82] ibid, module 1, §1.2.3. For an in-depth analysis of the issues raised by geographic names in the new gTLD programme with case studies on the strings '.amazon', '.patagonia', '.spa' and '.africa', see the interview with G Mazzone (ch 9) in this book.

[83] GAC is the acronym for Governmental Advisory Committee, a committee which provides 'advice on the activities of ICANN as they relate to concerns of governments', ICANN's Bylaws, s 12.2(a).

[84] For an example of an application withdrawn following a GAC early warning, see the application for the string '.zulu' No 1-994-74713. For all applications, see https://gtldresult.icann.org/application-result/applicationstatus/viewstatus.

The slippery-slope argument opposed to the granting of the '.cat', professing that it would open the DNS to claims from other cultural and linguistic communities, proved to be not wholly unfounded.[85] Despite steep evaluation fees of $185,000 and an estimated overall cost of $300,000[86] to $500,000,[87] several linguistic and cultural communities followed in the footsteps of '.cat' and submitted an application to ICANN[88] for strings such as:

- '.bzh' for the Breton community;
- '.corsica', for Corsica's population and the Corsican diaspora;
- '.eus', on behalf of the Basque linguistic and cultural community;
- '.gal', on behalf of the Galician linguistic and cultural community;
- '.quebec', on behalf of the Québec community (geoTLD);
- '.scot', for the Scottish community;
- '.tatar', for the Tatars community; and
- '.tirol', for the community of the Tirolers (geoTLD).

Four of these TLDs, '.bzh', '.eus', '.gal' and '.scot', along with '.cat', were part of the European Cultural and Linguistic Internet Domains (ECLID) – a network formed to pool their resources together.[89]

A comparative analysis of the applications reveals similarities in the approaches and discourse adopted by the communities. First, the influence of '.cat' is palpable in all the applications. The delineation of the communities is achieved in a very inclusive way, like in the case of '.cat'. As an example, the Breton community, in the '.bzh' application, is described as 'all the people who feel attached to Brittany, its culture and its languages and who wish to display this attachment by using a specific domain name'.[90] It is worthy of note that Abril i Abril was invited to the

[85] Gerrand, 'A Short History of the Catalan Campaign' (n 51); this argument was also put forward in the e-mails received by ICANN during the '.cat' application process. See, eg in the ICANN Email List Archives, C Ortiz, 'Please Reject .cat!' (7 April 2004) https://forum.icann.org/lists/stld-rfp-cat/msg00004.html: 'If they give a TLD to the Catalan region, where will it stop? Will each of the three linguistic regions of Switzerland be entitled to claim a TLD of their own; will Quebec get its own TLD but none of the other Canadian provinces since they all share the same language and culture, etc'.

[86] $300,000 is the cost evaluated for the '.bzh' application, see M le Béchec, 'L'ICANN et les nouvelles extensions: une ouverture de l'Internet à de nouvelles communautés d'utilisateurs? Communiquer dans un monde de normes', paper presented at 'L'information et la communication dans les enjeux contemporains de la "mondialisation"' (Roubaix, March 2012) 131, https://hal.univ-lille.fr/hal-00825937v3.

[87] 'Some studies even estimate costs could rise up to USD 500,000 depending on the complexity of the application process and/or implementation': PJ Gajardo and JCL Gálvez, 'The Internet Domain Name System and the Right to Culture' (Association for Progressive Communications, 2016) fn 44, www.apc.org/sites/default/files/InternetDomainNameSystemRightToCulture_0.pdf.

[88] An application was also submitted during this round for the string '.cymru' (the name of Wales in Welsh), but it was not earmarked as a community-based TLD. On the constitution of a Welsh online community, see C Honeycutt, 'Welsh without Frontiers? Us of the Community Metaphor in Wale's Sponsored Top-Level Domain Bid' (2018) 24 *The Information Society* 251.

[89] See www.eclid.eu/.

[90] Application for the TLD '.bzh' No 1-989-18963.

first meeting bringing together the members of the '.bzh' project.[91] Moreover, these communities define themselves in a loose way, which espouses the dynamic and evolutive characteristics of culture.[92] With the exception of '.tirol' and '.corsica', which are associated respectively with the Federal State of Tirol and the Regional Government of Corsica, the applications were drafted and submitted by ad hoc legal entities established specially for the TLD, such as the Coordination Center for the Regional Domain for the Republic of Tartarstan or the non-profit organisation Asociación puntoGAL. Thus, the community's perimeter does not coincide with regional or local political entities.

The delineation of the communities may be likened to the fuzzy definitions of some communities in nomination files submitted in connection with the 2003 Convention for the Safeguarding of the Intangible Cultural Heritage. The '.corsica' community is, for example, not limited to the island or the political region of Corsica; rather, it encompasses the community of Corsicans worldwide and 'covers the global community of individuals, institutions and corporate entities that identify themselves with the island of Corsica (Corse), and/or any aspect of its cultural, historical or linguistic heritage'.[93] The linguistic and cultural communities are defined in relation to the Internet and are not bound to a territory or limited by borders. Several applications refer, for instance, to diasporas.[94]

Two purposes transpire from the applications: on the one hand, the desire to express a common and shared cultural identity online;[95] and on the other hand, the need to support economic development. The goal of the TLD is dual in nature: cultural and economic. Communities put forth that the TLD they propose would benefit the Internet and the DNS by increasing cultural diversity. The communities evoke their language, history, culture and cultural heritage. The '.eus' application cites, for instance, dances, music and literature in Basque.[96] The TLD is thought to enhance the visibility and discoverability of the community's cultural expressions it aggregates. The community's access to its culture is also increased, as is its capacity to take part in cultural life. Moreover, a TLD would further the community's reputation and bring to it a form of worthiness and prestige[97] similar to the one that may be sought in the inscription of a site on the World Heritage List or of an element on the Representative List of the Intangible Cultural Heritage of Humanity. Prestige may be an important factor in a language's survival and a way to attract younger speakers, because 'digital communication is universally viewed as more prestigious than communication by traditional means'.[98] Crossing

[91] le Béchec, 'Territoire et communication politique' (n 61) 375.

[92] Applications for the TLDs '.bzh' No 1-989-18963, '.gal' No 1-1278-425, '.eus' No 1-1293-15788, '.scot' No 1-1741-29613 and '.corsica' No 1-937-68428.

[93] Application for the TLD 'corsica' No 1-937-68428.

[94] Applications for the TLDs '.bzh' No 1-989-18963, '.gal' No 1-1278-425, '.eus' No 1-1293-15788, '.corsica' No 1-937-68428 and '.scot' No 1-1741-29613.

[95] See, eg the applications for the following TLDs: '.bzh' No 1-989-18963, '.corsica' No 1-937-68428 and '.quebec' No 1-1663-45909.

[96] Application for the TLD '.eus' No 1-1293-15788.

[97] le Béchec, 'Territoire et communication politique' (n 61) 381.

[98] A Kornai, 'Digital Language Death' (2013) 8 *PLOS One* 10, 2.

the digital divide may be viewed, in this respect, as a form of Darwinian adaptation for survival.

From an economic perspective, linking a cultural identity to a domain name acts as a brand or a label, which facilitates the attribution to a community of the contents, products and services offered online. The domain name acts as an identifier for the community. The image of the community attaches onto the TLD and encourages confidence in the Internet users and consumers. The TLD confers a form of authenticity to the contents, products and services advertised online and differentiates them from the competition. Community-based TLDs are 'subject to registration restrictions'[99] listed in the registry agreement under which the domain is operated. For the '.tirol' domain, eligibility is restricted, for instance, to a 'natural person, legal person, organisation or association of persons' that 'can demonstrate that they have an economic, cultural, touristic, historical, social or any other connection to the Austrian federal state of Tirol'.[100] Restrictions establish trust in the TLD.

The applications also identify different key markets that may benefit from the TLD, such as tourism, the food and agricultural sectors, with products like Corsican wine and ham, cultural industries and, more generally, businesses.[101] In the case of '.bzh', the domain name fits in a broader network bringing together different actions concerning local production and technology. For instance, the PuntuEus Foundation, which manages the '.eus' domain, has set up an observatory to assess the use of the Basque language online.[102] Similarly, 'Produit en Bretagne' (meaning 'produced in Brittany' in English), a non-profit managing a regional collective trademark certifying products manufactured in Brittany and in accordance with ethical, social and environmental standards, is part of the network supporting the '.bzh' domain name.[103] Concerning technology, the non-profit that manages the domain name '.bzh', Association www.bzh, is also responsible more generally for the promotion of the image and the visibility of Brittany in the digital sphere.[104] The association has, for instance, submitted to the Unicode Consortium an emoji request for Brittany's flag that can be used as an ideogram to refer to Brittany in electronic communications.[105] Like ICANN, the Unicode Consortium is a Californian non-profit; it is responsible for the Unicode Standard, which is the

[99] Mahler, *Generic Top-Level Domains* (n 23) 175.

[100] Registry agreement concluded on 24 April 2014 between ICANN and punkt Tirol GmbH, www.icann.org/resources/agreement/tirol-2014-04-24-en.

[101] Applications for the TLDs '.bzh' No 1-989-18963, '.corsica' No 1-937-68428, '.scot' No 1-1741-29613, '.eus' No 1-1293-15788, '.tirol' No 1-1703-3426 and '.quebec' No 1-1663-45909.

[102] For the PuntuEUS Observatory, see www.domeinuak.eus/en/observatory/.

[103] For Produit en Bretagne, see http://pro.produitenbretagne.bzh/produits-services/nos-garanties.

[104] Journal officiel de la République française, annonce No 366, Associations modifications, 151 No 11.

[105] For the campaign for an emoji of Brittany's flag, see www.emoji.bzh.

character coding system that 'governs every character that people read or type on electronic devices'.[106] The Consortium selects from proposals the emojis that it encodes within the Unicode Standard, and that become available inter alia on the keyboards of mobile phones.

However, one may wonder if these community TLDs actually promote cultural and linguistic diversity or if they boil down to regional marketing campaigns. This is especially true in the case of the '.bzh' domain. Breton is used only by about 200,000 speakers, half of which are older than 60 years, and regular speakers of Gallo (a Romance language spoken in the eastern part of Brittany) are estimated to be 28,300.[107] In contrast, the number of Catalan speakers reaches 10 million.[108] A TLD might still constitute a means to revitalise a language. The delegation of the .cat domain is believed to have increased the number of websites in Catalan and the number of web pages published in Catalan by tenfold.[109] Another concern may be that cultural identities are commodified through the development of an identity economy.[110] The economic value of a culture is pushed forward at the expense of its social role. As the digital environment expands continually, a reflection is needed to understand more fully how these efforts to safeguard cultural diversity online may be integrated within wider policies to protect culture in all of its dimensions.

Finally, a community-based TLD fulfils another function, which is to assert the contemporaneity of cultural and linguistic communities. In several applications, to establish their weight, significance, vitality and digital literacy, communities have cited the rank attained by their language on Wikipedia: 'The Galician language has a remarkable amount of publications and translations and has a very dynamic Internet presence. As an example, Galician ranks as the 43rd language in entries on the Wikipedia.'[111] Wikipedia is thought to be a reliable indicator of a language succeeding in its digitalisation.[112] Yet this indicator must be taken with a grain of salt, as some language editions of Wikipedia are closer to a 'hobbyist project' than to 'a true community'.[113]

Corporations may be reluctant to adapt their services and products to languages that are less dominant and represent smaller market segments. Multilinguism may hinder the development of digital technologies as it prevents technical standardisation.[114] A community occupying space online sends a signal of its cultural and

[106] R Scall, 'Emoji as Language and Their Place outside American Copyright Law' (2016) 5 *New York University Journal of Intellectual Property and Entertainment Law* 381, 386.

[107] le Béchec, 'Territoire et communication politique' (n 61) 378; application for the TLD '.bzh' No 1-989-18963.

[108] Iparraguirre, 'Elements for a Successful gTLD' (n 60) 3.

[109] le Béchec, 'Territoire et communication politique' (n 61) 380.

[110] JL Comaroff and J Comaroff, *Ethnicity, Inc* (Chicago, University of Chicago Press, 2010).

[111] Application for the TLD '.gal' No 1-1278-425; see also the applications for '.bzh' No 1-989-18963 and '.eus' No 1-1293-15788.

[112] Kornai, 'Digital Language Death' (n 98) 3.

[113] ibid 10.

[114] Paolillo, 'Language Diversity on the Internet' (n 13) 54.

linguistic liveliness. This online presence forces actors to acknowledge the existence of these communities and to accommodate them. For instance, Google's search engine exists in a Catalan-language version,[115] and Facebook is available in Basque.[116] A TLD helps the matching of language versions with a domain name. The application for the '.cat' domain pointed rightfully to this solution, by stating that 'Google or Yahoo cannot (yet!) use a google.cat or yahoo.cat for their (existing) Catalan-language versions'.[117] Corporations may also decide to customise hardware, such as keyboards, or create software, like virtual keyboards, fonts, spell checkers,or operating systems for the digitalisation of minority languages.[118] Without cooperation from the information and communications technology sector, communities may be forced to use a dominant language online, which may ultimately threaten the existence of their mother tongue and cause the disappearance of their culture.

V. Conclusion

The cultural survival of a community hinges on its capacity to adapt to new technology and media. By disconnecting TLDs from a territory and political entities, the '.cat' domain opened a new venue for cultural and linguistic communities to assert their cultural identity online and exercise their cultural rights. The attribution of TLDs based on a cultural and linguistic community may, in this sense, be construed as a measure to promote the diversity of cultural expressions in the digital environment. The TLD forms not only a space for communities to share a culture and a language, but also a means to protect their cultural activities, goods and services and disseminate cultural expressions. In addition, the cultural spaces formed by these TLDs and the content associated with them facilitate access to culture and the participation of communities in cultural life. By investing in the DNS and identifying ICANN as a new international forum, communities have asserted their cultural rights in an ingenious way. Nevertheless, the application procedure for a gTLD in its current state excludes marginalised and vulnerable communities that lack sufficient financial, legal and technical resources.[119] This is especially true in cases where a community is at odds with governmental authorities.

One of the drawbacks of such TLDs is that they may, in a tense context, put the entity managing the domain name in a delicate position. For instance, although

[115] The Catalan-language version of Google's search engine is available at www.google.cat/.

[116] For the webpage listing all the different versions of Facebook, see https://m.facebook.com/language.php.

[117] .Cat Application Form, part B (2004).

[118] Paolillo, 'Language Diversity on the Internet' (n 13) 66; see also the Google 'Noto: A Typeface for the World' project website for the development of a font family, www.google.com/get/noto/.

[119] Gajardo and Gálvez, 'The Internet Domain Name System' (n 87) 26.

the shift from '.ct' to '.cat' had dissipated fears relating to claims of independence, in September 2017, Spanish judicial authorities requested by judicial order that Fundació puntCAT block access to all domain names that may contain information pertaining to the Catalan Independence Referendum of 1 October 2017.[120] This request created a conundrum for the Fundació puntCAT, which considers itself to be 'the steward of the Catalan speaking community on the Internet' and on which the responsibility for filtering illegal content fell.[121] The CEO of Fundació puntCAT addressed a letter to ICANN raising concern that as a registry operator it was forced to 'censor content and suppress freedom of speech in the .cat domain names'.[122] Without opening the can of worms that is the Catalan Independence Referendum, whose legal complexity is far too intricate to be touched upon in this chapter, this incident shows that even when TLDs are based on a cultural and linguistic premise that steers away from political considerations, they may still be used as instruments of self-determination. The entity managing the domain name is then forced to regulate its content.

Finally, if tensions arise between a community and the authorities, governments may focus their policing efforts on a community-based TLD, for instance, by blocking access to websites registered within the TLD. Solutions must be found to avoid those TLDs that concentrate on specific linguistic and cultural expressions becoming a target in conflicts such that they hamper the practice and transmission of a specific culture and language online.

[120] G Marby, '.Cat Domain Name Judicial Seizure Warrant', letter to ICANN (17 September 2017) www.icann.org/en/system/files/correspondence/lineros-to-marby-17sep17-en.pdf.
[121] ibid.
[122] ibid.

8

Cultural Monopolies: The Cases of International Sports Associations and Internet Platforms

GRISCHKA PETRI[1]

I. Introduction

This chapter highlights the structural affinities between Internet platforms (section II) and international sports associations (section III) with a view to their status as cultural monopolists. It suggests a portability of arguments relating to instruments to control these monopolies (section IV). The potential of the Convention on the Protection and Promotion of the Diversity of Cultural Expressions (hereinafter the UNESCO Convention or the Convention)[2] and the International Covenant on Economic, Social and Cultural Rights[3] to be used as such instruments will be investigated.

II. Internet Platform Providers and their Monopolies

Accounts of big Internet platforms and their abuse of power have become abundant, and it would be impossible to take a survey of even the better-known cases in such a short chapter. This is not to say that it would not be an important task to undertake. As a consequence, the selected examples may seem arbitrarily chosen. The reasons for their inclusion are that they are widely discussed and timely

[1] This chapter reflects part of my research project on cultural monopolies that I was able to conduct as a Fellow of the Käte-Hamburger-Centre for Advanced Studies 'Law as Culture', Bonn, during the summer of 2020. I thank Werner Gephart and his outstanding team at the Centre for their support and hospitality under the challenging circumstances of the COVID-19 pandemic.
[2] (adopted 20 October 2005, entered into force 18 March 2007) 2440 UNTS 311.
[3] (signed 16 December 1966, entered into force 3 January 1976) 993 UNTS 3.

(Trump v Twitter) or that they seem to constitute a paradigm shift for the (potentially un-)democratic handling of digital power (Cambridge Analytica). This kind of democratic deficit is an inherent element of international sports federations, which is why they are offered as a model for comparison.

A. Trump v Twitter

Donald Trump, 45th President of the United States of America between 2017 and 2020, was a prominent user of Twitter, an online platform for shorter communications. At the time of the permanent closure of his account by the company on 8 January 2021,[4] Trump had more than 88 million followers on the platform. Until May 2020, many of his tweets were criticised outside Twitter for being divisive or inaccurate, or both. When Trump claimed on Twitter that postal ballots to be used for the presidential elections later in the year would be fraudulent, his message was marked as inaccurate by the platform.[5] A few days later, under the impression of growing protests after the killing of George Floyd in Minneapolis, Trump announced that he might react by bringing in the armed forces to open fire on protesters. Twitter marked the tweet as glorifying violence, a violation of the platform's terms and conditions.[6] During and after the 2020 US presidential elections, the public got used to tweets by Donald Trump being marked as inaccurate by Twitter, often with a warning that 'this claim about election fraud is disputed'.

These measures received great attention because they seemed to mark a policy change. They deserve our attention because they highlight a particular problem that involves the interaction between private but globally effective norms, such as the terms and conditions of an Internet platform, and legal norms. While Trump criticised Twitter and threatened to introduce legislation against Internet providers, Facebook was criticised (not by Trump, of course) because it did *not* mark postings from Trump and its administration as misleading. Facebook changed its policy after the Capitol riots of 6 January 2021, when it banned Trump for at least the remainder of his term.[7]

In May 2020, Trump quickly signed an executive order 'on preventing online censorship', just days after Twitter had marked his tweet as untrue.[8] The executive

[4] See Twitter, 'Permanent Suspension of @realDonaldTrump' (8 January 2021) blog.twitter.com/en_us/topics/company/2020/suspension.html. Internet sources quoted in this chapter are archived and accessible at archive.org if deleted from their original web space.

[5] twitter.com/realDonaldTrump/status/1265255835124539392?s=20. Donald Trump's tweets are archived at www.thetrumparchive.com/.

[6] twitter.com/realDonaldTrump/status/1266231100780744704.

[7] Facebook post by Mark Zuckerberg, CEO of Facebook (8 January 2021) www.facebook.com/zuck/posts/10112681480907401. The ban runs out on 7 January 2023.

[8] Executive Order on Preventing Online Censorship (28 May 2020) www.whitehouse.gov/presidential-actions/executive-order-preventing-online-censorship/.

order questions a distinction that has been vital for providers of communication platforms in the USA. Similar legislation is in place in other jurisdictions. In the USA, it is to be found in section 230 of the Communications Decency Act from 1996. The provision prevents people from suing providers of an 'interactive computer service' for libel if users post defamatory messages on their platforms. Within the European Union, Article 14 of the Electronic Commerce Directive of 2000 follows a similar model.[9] The law does not treat intermediary website operators as publishers; in this model, the platforms provide an infrastructure but are not responsible for the content. On the other hand, the platforms are free to remove or restrict posts they deem 'obscene, lewd, lascivious, filthy, excessively violent, harassing or otherwise objectionable, whether or not such material is constitutionally protected'. Trump's executive order argues that if a platform acts in bad faith, it should no longer be treated as a provider for other peoples' messages but as a publisher, and be accountable for the published content. It argues that 'When large, powerful social media companies censor opinions with which they disagree, they exercise a dangerous power … Twitter, Facebook, Instagram, and YouTube wield immense … power to shape the interpretation of public events'.

B. Platform Censorship and the Arts

It complicates the analysis that this statement is basically correct – which is unexpected, coming from an administration that was notorious for its fact-bending capacities.[10] Within the art world, Facebook's censorship of nudity has caused an unceasing debate. To mention just two cases, Frédéric Durand, a French teacher, was banned from Facebook because he uploaded a picture of Gustave Courbet's *L'Origine du Monde*. In the end, the case was settled out of court.[11] The photographer Spencer Tunick, who is famous for his mass scenes of ordinary people in the nude which he photographs in public places, joined a group of artists who expressed their criticism of Facebook's censorship. In June 2019, he organised an event with 125 people who posed nude in front of the New York headquarters of Facebook (and Instagram), together with the National Coalition Against Censorship.[12] It is, of course, debatable in itself why artistic freedom has to be

[9] Directive 2000/31/EC of the European Parliament and of the Council of 8 June 2000 on certain legal aspects of information society services, in particular electronic commerce, in the Internal Market [2000] OJ L178/1.

[10] The *Washington Post* has compiled a database of Donald Trump's more than 30,000 false or misleading claims during his presidency, www.washingtonpost.com/graphics/politics/trump-claims-database/?itid=lk_inline_manual_11.

[11] G Harris, 'Long-Running Facebook Battle over Censored Courbet Painting Gets Happy Ending' *The Art Newspaper* (6 August 2019) www.theartnewspaper.com/news/facebook-legal-battle-over-courbet-painting-winds-down.

[12] *The Art Newspaper*, 'Spencer Tunick's Nip Slip' (4 June 2019) www.theartnewspaper.com/blog/spencer-tunick-s-nip-slip.

identified with the public representation of (predominantly female) nudity as in these two cases. To put this traditional, white, male heterosexual aesthetic preference into a more diversified context, artists have formed an alliance to point out Instagram's handling of non-streamlined eroticised content, Artists Against Social Media Censorship. They debate body-shaming, queer and non-binary sexual identities, and in 2020 presented a line of cases in the form of an online exhibition. With a special interest in communities and their definition and normative role in mind, the artists' conclusion is intriguing. They formulate a 'government analogy'. It arises from a structural analysis, in which the platform is compared to a feudalistic state.[13] This analysis denotes a lack of control and an imbalance of powers, as well as a perceived lack of participation in the areas of policy and decision making. From the perspective of the user or citizen, an organisation exercises power. There is, however, a fundamental difference between the norms: governments rely on laws, whereas Internet platforms rely on contracts and the large set of terms and conditions that comes with them. They are sometimes termed 'community standards' (Facebook)[14] or 'Community Guidelines' (Instagram),[15] implying that all the users are part of a single, global community. Such a claim is unconvincing. In his classic treatise, *Community and Civil Society*, originally published in 1887, Ferdinand Tönnies described the emotional component of communities, their 'sense of unity'.[16] Tönnies anchored communities within biological, familial and anthropological frameworks, arguing that they contributed to achieving a degree of mutual protection and help.[17] Besides family ('kinship') and neighbourhood, Tönnies pointed out friendship and comradeship as important kinds of community, based on 'similarity of work or opinion', for example 'artistic sympathy or creative purpose'.[18] This category takes us back to the activities of the 42 Club and other artists' initiatives against the power of Internet platforms. It demonstrates that consumer status alone is not enough to form a community.

C. Collusion of State and Platform and the Case of Cambridge Analytica

Other Internet platforms emphasise their regionality and offer themselves as an alternative for a political or regional community. Parler is a service, modelled on Twitter, that has a large conservative to far-right user base in the USA. In the wake

[13] See the website of the 42 Club, www.midnightsociety.org/ig-government.

[14] Facebook Community Standards, facebook.com/communitystandards.

[15] Instagram Community Guidelines, about.instagram.com/blog/announcements/instagram-community-guidelines-faqs.

[16] F Tönnies, *Community and Civil Society* (J Harris ed, first published 1887, Cambridge, Cambridge University Press, 2001) 22; *cf* ibid 32: 'reciprocal binding sentiment'.

[17] ibid 26.

[18] ibid 29.

of the global COVID-19 crisis, Telegram has become a platform for conspiracy theorists. A prominent example of a regionally successful platform is the 'Russian Facebook', formerly known as V-Kontakte and now concisely branded vk.ru. The design of the website is an explicit echo of Facebook's. These regional alternatives to Facebook can be the leading platforms in their own areas. Another example is WeChat, a Chinese platform that combines the communicative functions of WhatsApp, Facebook and eBay. However, WeChat is tightly controlled by the Chinese government: communications are subject to pervasive content surveillance, and files deemed politically sensitive are used to invisibly train the artificial intelligence of China's political censorship system.[19] As a consequence, not only can a digital platform in itself be powerful because of its monopoly-like position on the global or a regional market, it can also aggregate governmental power depending on the levels of civil rights, freedom and censorship.

While such congruence is plainly visible in the case of WeChat, it is widely expected in Western democracies that fundamental liberties should not be compromised by private platforms, that these platforms should be controlled under the rule of law and that governmental institutions or even political organisations must not make use of the power of digital platforms for uncontrolled, potentially undemocratic purposes. This expectation was thwarted by the Facebook–Cambridge Analytica data scandal, which was disclosed in 2018. Since 2014, personal data of near 87 million Facebook users had been acquired without their consent through apps using Facebook's user data by British consulting firm Cambridge Analytica. While Facebook claimed that this data transfer violated its terms and conditions, it also profited massively from the sales share of the app harvesting the data, called 'thisisyourdigitallife'. The haul included data on user identities, age, users' sexual, religious and political orientation, their interests and job affiliations. The data was aggregated to psychological profiles. These profiles were then used for political advertising servicing the Brexit and Trump campaigns of 2016. Some Facebook ads targeted potential voters for Hilary Clinton and the Remain campaign to demotivate them and discourage them from going to the polls; others camouflaged their partisanship and gave the impression they were an independent news source. The operation involved Steve Bannon, then one of Donald Trump's most important advisers, and the American software company specialising in big data analytics, Palantir.[20] The Cambridge Analytica case demonstrates the dominant position of

[19] See the detailed report by J Knockel et al, 'We Chat, They Watch: How International Users Unwittingly Build up WeChat's Chinese Censorship Apparatus' (*The Citizen Lab*, 7 May 2020) citizenlab.ca/2020/05/we-chat-they-watch/.

[20] For a first sociological assessment of the Cambridge Analytica case, see F Maschewski and A-V Nosthoff, 'Der plattformökonomische Infrastrukturwandel der Öffentlichkeit: Facebook und Cambridge Analytica revisited' in M Seeliger and S Sevignani (eds), *Ein neuer Strukturwandel der Öffentlichkeit?*, Leviathan Sonderband 37 (Baden-Baden, Nomos, 2021) 320–41. In lieu of a comprehensive analysis of the scandal, the relevant Wikipedia entry offers a basic overview and understanding of the events with further references: see en.wikipedia.org/wiki/Facebook%E2%80%93Cambridge_Analytica_data_scandal. *The Guardian* has compiled 'The Cambridge Analytica Files' online, www.theguardian.com/news/series/cambridge-analytica-files.

globally active Internet platforms and the need for their control. This can easily be modelled onto the typical field concept as defined by Pierre Bourdieu.[21] The field of digital cultural communication is deeply informed by the balance (or imbalance) of power. There is a clear deficit of participative options on the side of the users, with corresponding consequences for any social communities that do not fit into the terms and conditions of the digital platforms. The artists against censorship initiative can serve as an example. These structures have an immediate impact on digital communication and creative content.

D. Antitrust Laws, Digital Capitalism and the UNESCO Convention

This analysis is not new in itself, and similar concluding statements have been made in a growing number of publications. From the perspective of the cultural historian, the current platform economy triggers the arsenal of critique from the famous chapter on the cultural industries in Max Horkheimer and Theodor W Adorno's *Dialectic of Enlightenment* and recalls the scathing remarks on mass culture that becomes uniform under a monopoly.[22] More than 20 years ago, a study by Dan Schiller explained how the prevalence of neoliberal thought in the 1980s and 1990s contributed to the uncontrolled expansion of powerful private platforms. He spoke of a 'new neoliberal paramountcy'.[23] The digital capitalism of Schiller's analysis is historically based in Web 1.0, and can be described as the takeover of digital infrastructure for pre-digital ends such as home entertainment, and the corresponding growth of companies investing in and selling this digital infrastructure. In 2015, Michael Betancourt concluded in his *Critique of Digital Capitalism* that platform providers such as Google and Facebook must violate the privacy of their customers in order to function.[24] He tellingly adapted the firms' terminology and used the word 'members' instead of 'customers', thereby involuntarily (?) subscribing to the pretension of a digital community. The common use of a shared infrastructure does not make for a community, which involves a minimal sense of communality. This kind of academic analysis has for a long time entered the area of journalism and become commonplace. John Herrman asked in the *New York Times* what increasingly powerful platform companies actually wanted.[25] Writing for *The Guardian*, Nick Srnicek argued that platforms are too big to serve

[21] For an introduction, see P Bourdieu, *The Field of Cultural Production* (Cambridge, Polity Press, 1993).

[22] M Horkheimer and TW Adorno, *Dialectic of Enlightenment: Philosophical Fragments* (Stanford, Stanford University Press, 2002) 95.

[23] D Schiller, *Digital Capitalism: Networking the Global Market System* (Cambridge, MA, MIT Press, 1999) 203.

[24] M Betancourt, *The Critique of Digital Capitalism* (Brooklyn, NY, Punctum Books, 2015) 76.

[25] J Herrman, 'Platform Companies Are Becoming More Powerful – but What Exactly Do They Want?' *New York Times Sunday Magazine* (26 March 2017) 16.

the public interest and demanded the nationalisation of Amazon, Facebook and Google.[26] Srnicek expanded his critique of digital platforms in a 2017 book that defines them as 'digital infrastructures that enable two or more groups to interact … intermediaries that bring together different users'.[27] In his 2019 study on digital capitalism, Philipp Staab takes a similar analytical perspective.[28] Staab describes the system of a genuinely digital capitalism, which is based on what he defines as 'proprietary markets'. They become operational as digital infrastructures or platforms, which allow groups and individuals to interact, thereby resembling markets.[29] On these 'quasi-markets', information, access, price and power are subject to the control of the platform operators. The corresponding problems become more urgent once the platform rises to a monopolistic position,[30] powered by network effects.[31] Staab concludes that a proprietary market is only perfect when it commands an effective monopoly.[32] Ulrich Dolata distinguishes two main regulatory problems of concern for the global digital platforms: the organisation and regulation of markets for products and services, and the curation of content and communication.[33] This distinction is crucial for the understanding of the antitrust laws' failure to regulate fair communication on digital platforms. They are not designed for the purpose.

Antitrust laws regulate the conduct and organisation of business corporations, generally to promote competition for the benefit of consumers. Their main mechanism, however, is to control companies in their relationships with each other, not in their relationship with consumers. In the antitrust perspective, a monopoly is foremost a problem for the competitors, and the regulative powers are mainly operative on the level of companies and businesses. For example, Facebook is draining away advertising revenue from smaller and often more reliable news sources.[34] In the economic framework of relations between competing companies, antitrust laws protect consumers indirectly by way of focusing on low prices as an outcome of presumptively free competition. However, digital capitalism does not work around a price as an outcome of demand and supply. As a consequence, antitrust authorities have often ignored the digital market, because seemingly free services fell outside

[26] N Srnicek, 'We Need to Nationalise Google, Facebook and Amazon. Here's Why', *The Guardian* (30 August 2017) www.theguardian.com/commentisfree/2017/aug/30/nationalise-google-facebook-amazon-data-monopoly-platform-public-interest.

[27] N Srnicek, *Platform Capitalism* (Cambridge, Polity Press, 2017) 43.

[28] P Staab, *Digitaler Kapitalismus* (Berlin, Suhrkamp, 2019).

[29] Alluding to Jürgen Habermas, Maschewski and Nosthoff ('Der plattformökonomische Infrastrukturwandel' (2021)) speak of an '(Infra-)Strukturwandel der Öffentlichkeit', the (Infra-)structural transformation of the public sphere.

[30] P Staab, *Digitaler Kapitalismus* (Frankfurt/Main, Suhrkamp, 2019) 170–76.

[31] Srnicek, *Platform Capitalism* (2017) 45: more users mean that the platform becomes more valuable.

[32] ibid 178.

[33] U Dolata, 'Plattform-Regulierung. Koordination von Märkten und Kuratierung von Sozialität im Internet' (2019) 29 *Berliner Journal für Soziologie* 179, 184.

[34] S Vaidhyanathan, *Antisocial Media: How Facebook Disconnects Us and Undermines Democracy* (Oxford, Oxford University Press, 2018) 8.

the traditional definition of a market. In contrast, in a digital economy, information values, data and communicative freedoms inform a market effectively regulated by its largest players. At present, several new definitions of markets and monopolies are discussed. A specifically legal perspective is offered by Maximilian Volmar in his analysis of digital market power. He argues for an expanded legal understanding of market power that would encompass the typical platform monopolies, suggesting the application of the instrumental concept of the 'competitive bottleneck'.[35] Volmar also observes a growing number of cases that are considered by the antitrust authorities, more often in Europe than in the USA.[36]

In this context, an interesting approach has emerged under German antitrust law, where § 19 (2) No 2 GWB (Act against Restraints of Competition) defines an abuse case if a dominant undertaking, as a supplier or purchaser of a certain type of goods or commercial services, demands payment or other business terms which differ from those which would very likely arise if effective competition existed. Here, the digital remuneration of personal data can be interpreted as a potential case of abusive business terms; indeed, it plays a crucial role for the applicability of antitrust measures.[37] Consequentially, on 6 February 2019, the German Bundeskartellamt (Federal Cartel Office, FCO) decided that Facebook abused its dominant position on the German market for social networks by imposing unfair terms and conditions with regard to data generated by third-party websites and an ensuing lack of data protection.[38] After the Federal Court of Justice (Bundesgerichtshof) confirmed the FCO's decision in preliminary proceedings,[39] the Higher Regional Court (Oberlandesgericht) of Düsseldorf filed a request for preliminary ruling at the European Court of Justice (ECJ).[40] The FCO had prepared its decision extensively. Under German antitrust law, any legal principle protecting a contract party can be applied to determine whether the terms are exploitative. In the Facebook case, data protection principles provide the relevant test.[41] The

[35] M Volmar, *Digitale Marktmacht* (Baden-Baden, Nomos, 2019) 455; on the competitive bottleneck, *cf* M Armstrong and J Wright, 'Two-Sided Markets, Competitive Bottlenecks and Exclusive Contracts' (2007) 32 *Economic Theory* 353.

[36] Volmar, *Digitale Marktmacht* (2019) 445–48.

[37] J Barth, *Datenschutzrechtsverstöße als kartellrechtlicher Konditionenmissbrauch* (Baden-Baden, Nomos, 2020) 237; *cf* BGH, 24 January 2017, KZR 47/14 (2017) *Neue Zeitschrift für Kartellrecht* 242, where the court had established the possible abuse of a dominant position through unfair terms and conditions; T Körber, 'Die Facebook-Entscheidung des Bundeskartellamtes – Machtmissbrauch durch Verletzung des Datenschutzrechts?' [2019] *Neue Zeitschrift für Kartellrecht* 187, 189.

[38] B6-22/16 bundeskartellamt.de/SharedDocs/Entscheidung/DE/Entscheidungen/Missbrauchsaufsicht/2019/B6-22-16.pdf?__blob=publicationFile&v=8. The FCO had investigated the case since 2016; see also Körber, 'Die Facebook-Entscheidung' (2019) 187–88.

[39] BGH, 23 June 2020, KVR 69/19 (2021) *Gewerblicher Rechtsschutz und Urheberrecht International* 603.

[40] OLG Düsseldorf, 24 March 2021, VI-Kart 2/19 (V) (2021) *Gewerblicher Rechtsschutz und Urheberrecht* 874; Case C-252/21 *Facebook Inc and others v Bundeskartellamt*, [2021] OJ C320/16.

[41] C Carugati, 'The 2017 Facebook Saga: A Competition, Consumer and Data Protection Story' (2018) 2 *European Competition & Regulatory Law Review* 4, 6; WPJ Wils, 'The Obligation for the Competition Authorities of the EU Member States to Apply EU Antitrust Law and the Facebook Decision of the Bundeskartellamt' (2019) *Concurrences* 58, 61.

expected decision by the ECJ will help to disentangle the complex relationships between antitrust law and data protection law. Possibly, further legal areas can in the future be considered within the antitrust framework, and the conclusions of the FCO might inform European antitrust standards.[42]

Does the UNESCO Convention on the Protection and Promotion of the Diversity of Cultural Expressions provide an alternative or additional instrument in the context of platform control? On the one hand, the Convention has often been criticised as a fuzzy piece of soft law that does not command concrete consequences.[43] Kristina Irion and Peggy Valcke have pointed out the EU's awareness of the connection between cultural diversity and broadcasting regulations, but they assess the regulatory impact as marginal.[44] On the other hand, the Convention's scope is extremely broad, as Jan Wouters and Bart De Meester clarify: it is applicable as soon as there is an effect on any aspect of cultural expression if it relates to cultural diversity.[45]

Historically, cultural diversity has been considered an exception to free trade, which, however, has not been integrated in the list provided by Article XX of the General Agreement on Tariffs and Trade 1994.[46] The UNESCO Convention pairs cultural diversity and national sovereignty – the latter is evoked to defend of diversity in a global framework. This is an immediate consequence of the Convention being directed at signatory states but assumes that the nations bound by the Convention act as trustees of their minorities. This is not a trivial precondition, as diversity is not a concept exclusive to national states, and trusteeship of domestic diversity can highlight strong tensions. Catalonia in Spain and Scotland in the UK are prominent Western European examples of such tensions. Furthermore, Beatriz Barreiro Carril points out that the principle of territorial sovereignty, a cornerstone of the Convention, does not apply to the Internet.[47]

While the global scope of Internet platforms goes further than (and in fact challenges) national sovereignty, the dichotomy between trade and cultural

[42] *cf* Barth, *Datenschutzrechtsverstöße* (2020) 245–46; Wils, 'The Obligation' (2019) 63–64; a more critical assessment is voiced by Körber, 'Die Facebook-Entscheidung' (2019) 193–95.

[43] See M Burri, 'The UNESCO Convention on Cultural Diversity: An Appraisal Five Years after Its Entry into Force' (2013) 20 *International Journal of Cultural Property* 357; *cf* J Wouters and B De Meester, 'UNESCO's Convention on Cultural Diversity and WTO Law: Complementary or Contradictory?' in B Demarsin et al (eds), *Art & Law* (Bruges, die Keure, 2008) 342, 348: 'the phrasing … is not very pressing'.

[44] K Irion and P Valcke, 'Cultural Diversity in the Digital Age: EU Competences, Policies and Regulations for Diverse Audiovisual and Online Content' in E Psychogiopoulou (ed), *Cultural Governance and the European Union: Protecting and Promoting Cultural Diversity in Europe* (Basingstoke, Palgrave Macmillan, 2015) 75, 87.

[45] Wouters and De Meester, 'UNESCO's Convention' (2008) 345.

[46] For a historical analysis in the perspective of GATT and the TRIPS agreement, see B Barreiro Carril, *La diversidad cultural en el derecho internacional: la Convención de la UNESCO* (Madrid, Iustel, 2011) 55–95.

[47] B Barreiro Carril, 'How Can China Influence the Transatlantic Governance of Cultural Products in the Digital Age' (2018) 19 *The Journal of World Investment & Trade* 444, 445.

diversity is repeated in the conflicts between platforms and their users. Specifically in this area, the Convention has evolved and deepened its scope with the approval of the 'Guidelines on the Implementation of the Convention in the Digital Environment'.[48] While these guidelines 'primarily address public authorities', they also encourage 'Non-governmental organizations, cultural and creative industries from the public and private sectors, including global digital platforms, Internet service providers (ISP) and other actors in the digital environment … to follow them' (section 7). The guidelines put the principles of the Convention, notably Article 7(I), into more concrete terms. They confirm important values and a continuity of essential freedoms between the physical and digital spheres: 'The distinctive nature of cultural activities, goods and services as vehicles of identity, values and meaning does not change in the digital environment' (section 2). A 'Human Rights-based open Internet' is envisioned (section 3), with a practical call for privacy and freedom of expression (section 8.9). The technological changes, including social networks, 'provide new challenges and opportunities to promote the diversity of cultural expressions' (section 5). This discernment is important, as it takes into account the double position of Internet platforms as enablers and regulators of cultural activities. Related to this double bind is the dual nature of cultural products, which are both economic and cultural, a fact recognised in the Preamble of the Convention and taken up in the Convention's 'Principle of the complementarity of economic and cultural aspects of development'. This concept echoes the classical analysis by Horkheimer and Adorno, who remarked that culture is a paradoxical commodity.[49] However, there is no global consensus on this dual nature, exemplified by the insistence of the USA to refer to 'cultural products' as 'entertainment products'.[50] Indeed, this blurred line has been the concern of the then UN Special Rapporteur in the field of cultural rights, Farida Shaheed, who in 2014 demanded better protection from undue advertising and marketing and the reinforcement of data protection rights.[51] In an article from 2015, Ulrich Dolata is very clear about a connection whose importance can hardly be overestimated: the platform 'ecosystems' are not just technical infrastructures, they are also – and perhaps more importantly so – social spaces.[52]

A preliminary conclusion is permissible here: while the potential of antitrust laws to regulate cultural diversity on Internet platforms needs further evolution, the UNESCO Convention can offer an additional framework for regulatory measures that can specify its principles.[53] An application to the platform constellation,

[48] UNESCO (2017) unesdoc.unesco.org/ark:/48223/pf0000370521.page=92.

[49] Horkheimer and Adorno, *Dialectic of Enlightenment* (2002) 131.

[50] Barreiro Carril, 'How Can China' (2018) 448.

[51] UN General Assembly, 'Report of the Special Rapporteur in the Field of Cultural Rights' (8 August 2014) UN Doc A/69/286, 15, 24.

[52] U Dolata, 'Volatile Monopole. Konzentration, Konkurrenz und Innovationsstrategien der Internetkonzerne' (2015) 24 *Berliner Journal für Soziologie* 505, 511.

[53] *cf* Barreiro Carril, *La diversidad* (2011) 327.

as outlined here, does not fall outside the scope of the Convention. The international bodies are aware of the double nature of cultural activities in digital environments, as these are by default clad in the shape of a service.

III. The Established Monopolies of Sports Associations

This double nature returns in a distinct but related field. It does not come as a surprise that in 2009, the Committee on Economic, Social and Cultural Rights of the United Nations Economic and Social Council (CESCR) included sports in its General Comment No 21, which focuses on the 'Right of everyone to take part in cultural life' (Article 15, paragraph 1(a) ICESCR).[54] The Comment establishes a broad and inclusive definition of 'culture' in Article 13, encompassing

> inter alia, ways of life, language, oral and written literature, music and song, non-verbal communication, religion or belief systems, rites and ceremonies, sport and games, methods of production or technology, natural and man-made environments, food, clothing and shelter and the arts, customs and traditions through which individuals, groups of individuals and communities express their humanity and the meaning they give to their existence, and build their world view representing their encounter with the external forces affecting their lives. Culture shapes and mirrors the values of well-being and the economic, social and political life of individuals, groups of individuals and communities.

Not only does this concept connect sports, the arts and freedom of expression, which is part of the Article's logical basis, it also points out the effect on communities. Today, an outlook is needed that takes the 'social' in 'social media' more seriously and, by extension, the place of the community in digital communicative environments. Evolving from the CESCR's understanding of culture as a multidimensional, transversal concept, it is suggested here that the typical imbalance in communicative freedoms imposed by digital monopolies is not a new phenomenon but reveals a structure that is inherent to a number of established social constellations. As a proof of concept, a focus on the parallel economy of a professional sport, namely football, is offered. There exists a line of scholarship on 'sports capitalism' that comes to conclusions that strongly resemble the interrogations of digital capitalism. This is no coincidence. Sports associations act as a kind of entertainment provider, in many ways similar to Facebook or YouTube. As organisers of their respective global sports events, the International Olympic Committee (IOC)

[54] Committee on Economic, Social and Cultural Rights, 'General Comment No 21: Right of Everyone to Take Part in Cultural Life (art. 15, para. 1 (a), of the International Covenant on Economic, Social and Cultural Rights)' (21 December 2009) UN Doc E/C.12/GC/21. See Barreiro Carril, *La diversidad* (2011) 252–54.

and the Fédération Internationale de Football Association (FIFA) are monopolists, and 'any fundamental change would have to affect the monopoly power that the IOC and FIFA wield'.[55]

Despite its monopolistic power, FIFA remains classified as a non-profit organisation.[56] In fact, sports associations' monopolies are even more solid than those of digital platforms, in that international sports competitions are organised around the principle that every association exclusively represents their discipline. There is only one global football association, only one global athletics organisation, only one global skiing association, etc, which is why the principle can be called the Highlander Principle, after the motto: 'There can be only one!' In sports where such a monopoly is not in place, such as boxing or wrestling, the value of international championships is compromised, because there can be multiple athletes simultaneously holding world titles.

The FIFA World Cup generated $1.6 billion in sponsorship revenue between 2007 and 2010. To maximise these profits, FIFA attempts to influence national legislation to secure its marketing monopoly. It also implements surveillance measures such as 'Commercial Restriction Areas', which limit the marketing opportunities of non-sponsors that could arise from their physical presence at event venues and official sites.[57]

An anecdote serves to highlight the power of FIFA. In the wake of the World Cup of 2014, as is now the rule before such events, the city of Rio de Janeiro underwent an intensive phase of restructuring, demolition and building. Both World Cups and Olympic Games offer attractive financial opportunities for producers of merchandise, for real estate investors and for venture capitalists. The urban environments around the Maracanã stadium in Rio de Janeiro were transformed accordingly, and plans were made to demolish some of the buildings surrounding the stadium to ease access. Then the old building of the Museu do Índio became a potential victim of the redevelopment. Until 1977, the building, erected in 1862, had housed the museum for indigenous cultures; since 2006, it had served as a meeting place for a settlement of about 20 indigenous people. In 2013, the city council acquired the property and announced plans to demolish it to make room for a parking garage.[58] The indigenous inhabitants were removed from the estate by military police.[59] While the local government claimed that FIFA had demanded the demolition of the former museum for the World Cup, FIFA had never explicitly

[55] A Zimbalist, *Circus Maximus: The Economic Gamble behind Hosting the Olympics and the World Cup*, 2nd edn (Washington, DC, Brookings Institution, 2016) 139.

[56] HA Solberg and C Gratton, 'Broadcasting the World Cup' in S Frawley and D Adair (eds), *Managing the Football World Cup* (Basingstoke, Palgrave Macmillan, 2014) 47, 60.

[57] S Chadwick, R Liu and D Thwaites, 'Ambush Marketing and the Football World Cup' in Frawley and Adair, *Managing the Football World Cup* (2014) 63, 71–72.

[58] Zimbalist, *Circus Maximus* (2016) 101.

[59] S Romero and T Barnes, 'Police Storm Squatters at Rio Stadium Site' *New York Times* (22 March 2013) 5.

demanded any such move.[60] It is noteworthy that the authorities could easily operate on the assumption that hardly anybody would question a demand by FIFA for the demolition of the old buildings. The narrative was plausible because of FIFA's position – it could indeed have demanded such a move, but in the course of events FIFA needed to distance itself from the decision. The events contributed to a partial sense of estrangement from the global football party. As Gabriel Kuhn notes, instead of football concealing social contradictions, it was now highlighting them.[61]

FIFA demands a closely controlled, protected commercial environment for its events and for its sponsors. This includes massive infrastructure projects and other measures. Local merchants are forced to close their shops within a designated area near the sports venues or if they do not sell the sponsors' products. Even spectators are affected: they are not allowed to wear t-shirts with political messages and detailed terms and conditions apply to their tickets, which, for example, may not be sold on. FIFA also insisted on the sale of beer in the stadium, something that was at odds with Brazilian laws at the time, which banned alcohol at football matches.[62]

International sports associations act globally, they are in an exceptionally powerful position, they manage a monopoly and they are highly conscious of their position. The architecture of their headquarters does not leave any open questions in this regard. The architecture betrays the common language of corporate power, which was also noted by Horkheimer and Adorno[63] and further elaborated by Fredric Jameson in his study on postmodernism (1991):

> Of all the arts, architecture is the closest constitutively to the economic, with which … it has a virtually unmediated relationship. It will therefore not be surprising to find the extraordinary flowering of the new postmodern architecture grounded in the patronage of multinational business.[64]

Hal Foster notes the sleek surfaces of metal and glass typically offered by the architectural studio of Norman Foster, and how the elegant façades offer media-friendly backdrops for public relations and space for logos. It is a kind of architecture with

[60] I Mello, 'Fifa desmente Cabral e afirma que não pediu demolição do Museu do Índio' *Jornal do Brasil* (18 October 2012) www.jb.com.br/rio/noticias/2012/10/18/fifa-desmente-cabral-e-afirma-que-nao-pediu-demolicao-do-museu-do-indio.html.

[61] G Kuhn, *Soccer vs the State: Tackling Football and Radical Politics*, 2nd edn (Oakland, PM Press, 2016) 250.

[62] 'Brazil World Cup Beer Law Signed by President Rousseff' (*BBC News*, 6 June 2012) www.bbc.com/news/world-latin-america-18348012. Similar policies are implemented by UEFA at European tournaments; for example, for Euro 2008 in Switzerland and Austria, see Kuhn, *Soccer* (2016) 68.

[63] Horkheimer and Adorno, *Dialectic of Enlightenment* (2002) 132 mention 'the imposing buildings of the big companies'.

[64] F Jameson, *Postmodernism, or, the Cultural Logic of Late Capitalism* (Durham, NC, Duke University Press, 1991) 5.

brand-like qualities.[65] A recent study considers the connection between corporate identities and their representation in architectural terms and concludes that

> another period is starting, that of the great twenty-first-century IT corporations, those established powers of neoliberal capitalism, building their own vast corporate campuses for their core creative staff: the 'shining ring' headquarters planned by Apple (designed by [Lord Norman] Foster), the 'futuristic greenhouse' planned by Google (designed by Heatherwick Studio), and Facebook's 'Facebook West' (designed by [Frank O] Gehry) … These new campuses, we might argue, demonstrate a renewed 'dialectic of distinction' between prestigious architects and powerful clients, a desire to project corporate identity, and a need to promote the integration of a corporate community (understood as domination): in this way constituting another reification of social life under capitalism, in which 'everything must change so that everything can remain the same'.[66]

The observation could easily be extended to the headquarters of FIFA (designed by Tilla Theus) and the recently completed Olympic House for IOC (designed by 3XN Architects). In conclusion, the common corporate architecture of global sports associations and platform providers demonstrates their shared understanding of communities as dominated collectives, and a self-understanding as a dominant singularity.

IV. The Role of Communities

The previous two sections of this chapter have offered the insight that Internet platforms and sports associations prove how culture under commercial conditions becomes subject to corporate normativity. For the global digital platform providers, network effects of contractual law, principally only binding partners of a contract, entail collective effects that are much further reaching. For the sports associations, legally non-profit associations or charities, the logic of sports competition evolves into long-lasting and resilient commercial monopolies. It has become a kind of engineered legal butterfly effect, as these providers of communication and culture also provide their own legal frameworks.

The all-permeating commercial logic behind sports events has started to wear off, and the effects have become even more visible during the ongoing COVID-19 pandemic. It has been noted that football has lost some of its unpredictability ('openness of outcome'), which is an essential part of its attraction.[67] This is

[65] H Foster, 'Designing a Second Modernity?' in N Lahiji (ed), *The Political Unconscious of Architecture: Re-Opening Jameson's Narrative* (Farnham, Ashgate, 2011) 97–98.

[66] R Kerr, SK Robinson and C Elliott, 'Modernism, Postmodernism, and Corporate Power: Historicizing the Architectural Typology of the Corporate Campus' (2016) 11 *Management & Organizational History* 123, 140.

[67] E Franck, 'The Other Side of League Organization – Efficiency-Aspects of Basic Organizational Structures in American Pro Team Sports' (2002) Working Paper Series of the Institute for Strategy and Business Economics, University of Zurich, 16: 'openness of outcome increases the economic value of the championship race'.

a side effect of the intense commercialisation of football, which is marketed as a cultural product by the monopolistic associations, for example in the shape of the Champions League. The old German phrase, 'Money does not score goals', commonly credited to Otto Rehhagel, then (1995) manager of Bayern München, has lost much of its truth since broadcasting revenues have become more important than ticket sales for the economy of the football clubs.[68] The confluence of commercial and sporting success has deepened. The (preliminarily stalled) efforts to instate a European Super League in 2021 confirm this development.[69] As a consequence, the successful clubs' dependence on their fan base has weakened, with the side effect of (some) fans turning away from over-commercialised clubs.[70]

The relation between clubs and their supporters was loosened further when, during the early days of the COVID-19 crisis, most football matches were called off. Once the professional leagues resumed their match plan in May and June 2020, no spectators were allowed to be present. In Germany, this format, which is known as 'behind closed doors' in English, is called 'Geisterspiel', a ghost game. In its June issue of 2020, the German magazine for football culture, *11 Freunde*,[71] spoke out in large letters on its cover how much they were missing the fans in the empty stadiums: 'Ihr fehlt!' ('Miss you!'), and the editors added the conclusion: 'Football without fans is just a game.' While this is true for amateur sports, it is not for the professional branch of football. Here, without the fans, it is but an investment. The games in empty stadiums were arranged as a measure to rescue the money from the clubs' television broadcasting rights.

The same issue of the magazine contained an interview with fans of the Gelsenkirchen club Schalke 04, where supporters remembered the good old times and a promotion video that the club had produced after it had won the Euro League in 1997. 'Suddenly I realised what I was missing,' one of the interviewees is quoted, 'The community, the team spirit. Thousand friends standing together.' It is notable that these feelings were prompted by watching a promotion video. Obviously, there was a consensus between club and fans at the time; the emotions at play were

[68] See, eg S Parlasca and S Szymanski, 'When the Whole Is Less than the Sum of the Parts: The Negative Effects of Central Marketing of Football Television Rights on Fans, Media Concentration and Small Clubs' (2002) 4 *Zeitschrift für Betriebswirtschaft, Ergänzungsheft* 83.

[69] D Goldblatt, 'The Greed of the European Super League Has Been Decades in the Making' *The Guardian* (20 April 2021) www.theguardian.com/commentisfree/2021/apr/20/greed-european-super-league-football-billionaires. The original press release of the Super League founders, dated 18 April 2021, is archived at web.archive.org/web/20210419223112/https://thesuperleague.com/press.html. It lists AC Milan, Arsenal FC, Atlético de Madrid, Chelsea FC, FC Barcelona, FC Internazionale Milano, Juventus FC, Liverpool FC, Manchester City, Manchester United, Real Madrid CF and Tottenham Hotspur as founding clubs.

[70] C Sandvoss, *A Game of Two Halves: Football, Television and Globalization* (London, Routledge, 2003) 164: 'As football clubs increasingly embody messages of rationalization and standardization, more and more fans are unable to appropriate these messages within their fandom.'

[71] Literally '11 Friends', after a quote that is commonly (but wrongly) credited to Sepp Herberger, the first (West) German national football team manager after World War II: 'You must be 11 friends!' The motto was in fact engraved on the first German football trophy that was used from 1903.

not over-commercialised but were presented in such a manner that they remained relatively unharmed and authentic. In contrast, the 'ghost games' were perceived as inauthentic, artificial performances. Hans Ulrich Gumbrecht observes an almost metaphysical effect of synchronicity between a football team and its supporters inside the stadium. Historically, he explains, team sports are a modern phenomenon, and the team offers a more natural point of emotional contact for a larger audience. The team effort also extends to the supporters; team and supporters see themselves as united. 'You'll never walk alone.'[72] If the ties between clubs and their supporters are cut by blocking their common ground and meeting place, they might, however, move in different directions.

Football supporters are an example of the kind of communities that can resist the global platform providers. In the end, fan protests contributed significantly to the collapse of the plans to start a European Super League.[73] In fact, it is this power that contributes to the sport's attractiveness to investors. Supporters are an asset, and it is complicated to protect the innocence of fandom in such an environment. In the context of fandom as an asset, it is also significant that Facebook operates with the term 'fans' for those accounts that follow another. The wording reveals the capitalisation of these community forces. Such a move should provoke resistance. Philipp Köster, editor-in-chief of *11 Freunde*, argued in the editorial for the August 2020 issue that supporters should organise themselves after the model of trade unions.[74] Legal instruments of collective labour law are suggested as a real option to empower supporters.

There are international precedents for such a self-empowerment of football supporters' communities, for example, the foundation of the Independent Manchester United Supporters Association (IMUSA) in 1995. The English Wikipedia lists close to 20 different English football supporters' associations.[75] Acts of self-organisation can go even further. In 2005, Manchester United supporters opposed American businessman Malcolm Glazer's takeover of the Premier League club. While the opposition of the IMUSA ultimately failed in stopping this takeover, a series of meetings led to the founding by disaffected supporters of a new club, FC United of Manchester. In his analysis of the events, Adam Brown notes:

> Within these discussions, various references were made to the notion of 'community'. Supporters talked of the need to 'keep the community together' referring to groups of

[72] HU Gumbrecht, *Crowds: The Stadium as a Ritual of Intensity* (Stanford, Stanford University Press, 2021) 104–05.

[73] See T Lewis, 'The Week English Football Fans Bit Back against the Billionaire Owners' *The Observer* (25 April 2021) www.theguardian.com/football/2021/apr/24/the-week-english-football-fans-bit-back-against-super-league-the-billionaire-owners. However, F Röckenhaus, 'Schulden und Schuldige' *Süddeutsche Zeitung* (23 April 2021) 25, points out that strong political interests from Russia and Saudi Arabia also worked against the Super League.

[74] P Köster, 'Organisiert euch!' *11 Freunde* (August issue, 2020) 14.

[75] Wikipedia, 'Category: English Football Supporters' Associations', en.wikipedia.org/wiki/Category:English_football_supporters%27_associations. See S Hamil et al (eds), *The Changing Face of the Football Business: Supporters Direct* (Oxon, Frank Cass Publishers, 2001) for an early academic assessment of football supporters' initiatives.

> fans who had followed the club home and away over the preceding years, essentially match day communities.[76]

The motto printed on t-shirts to help fundraising for the new club, 'Our Club, Our Rules', highlights the normative self-empowerment of the supporters' community, autonomy in its literal sense. FC United of Manchester established itself as a non-profit organisation with a one-member, one-vote governance structure.[77] It is currently the second-largest fan-owned football club in the UK by number of members after Exeter City FC.[78]

The club seems to have been the model for supporters of the Hamburger Sportverein (HSV), who left their club in 2014 to start the Hamburger Fußball-Club Falke. The move was a reaction against the transformation of the professional football division of the HSV into a public limited company. Similar to FC United, HFC Falke offered its members a sense of belonging and established an active community.[79]

Perhaps the most successful example of fans taking over their clubs is AFC Wimbledon. The club was founded in 2002 by (then former) supporters of Wimbledon FC, after the club had made public its plans to relocate to Milton Keynes. Supporters felt that the new club, which soon changed its name to Milton Keynes Dons, no longer represented their local community. Whereas the traditional meaning of the acronym AFC is 'Athletic Football Club', it stands for 'A Fans Club' and the philosophy of the new club, 'By the fans, for the fans'.[80] Starting in the ninth tier of the English league system, the club has been promoted six times (and relegated once) and is currently playing in the fourth tier, or League Two, having previously reached the same league that Milton Keynes Dons are playing in.

These examples demonstrate that communities are not helpless. The decisive step is indeed to organise the community into a potentially legal entity; to turn culture into law. The football clubs in Manchester, Hamburg and Wimbledon have proven the possibility. Communities such as artists against censorship on Instagram are moving in the same direction. Nick Srnicek suggests that 'Rather

[76] A Brown, '"Our Club, Our Rules": Fan Communities at FC United of Manchester' (2008) 9 *Soccer & Society* 346, 347.

[77] ibid 353; D Torchia, 'An Alternative Football Club in a Liquid Modernity: FC United of Manchester' (2016) 22 *Culture and Organization* 203, 209–10.

[78] FC United of Manchester is currently (2021/22) playing in the seventh tier of English professional football, the Northern Premier League.

[79] See C Brandt, '"Eine neue emotionale Heimat": der Hamburger Fußballclub Falke' (2019) 3 *Forum Wohnen und Stadtentwicklung* 141.

[80] D Cook and C Anagnostopoulos, 'MK Dons FC and AFC Wimbledon: Moving the Goalposts and Rising From the Ashes' in S Chadwick, D Arthur and J Beech (eds), *International Cases in the Business of Sport*, 2nd edn (London, Routledge, 2017) 138, 140. For an assessment of the emotional effects of the relocation on supporters groups, see D Potter, 'From Merton to Milton Keynes: Wimbledon Football Club Fans and the Impact of Post Team Relocation Ten Years after the End of the Crazy Gang' in S Dun, M Kalaji and M Stell (eds), *It's How You Play the Game: International Perspectives on the Study of Sport* (Oxford, Inter-Disciplinary Press, 2013).

than just regulating corporate platforms, efforts could be made to create public platforms – platforms owned and controlled by the people'.[81] This is the basic idea behind initiatives such as fan-run clubs. Translated into the environment of digital communication platforms, it might mean accommodating particular communities with tools suited specifically to their needs, to build networks for specific purposes. Indeed, on a technical level, software solutions are already offered to implement such networks. Interestingly, whereas the big global platforms present themselves as communities of fans by using the pertinent terminology, smaller competitors try to reappropriate the term, for example, advertising that users can find their perfect community.

Twenty years ago, Valérie Fournier argued that self-governance and small self-reliant communes are 'the material conditions under which we can start to open up alternative possibilities to neoliberalism and its devastation';[82] indeed, it is a goal shared by artists on Instagram, football supporters and other communities. Virtual communities in a digital environment may be more individualistic than offline communities, but should not be confused with pseudo-individual customisation of consumer demand. Online communities are as capable of sharing common values, ideas and traditions as offline communities, and it would be a mistake to ignore these values. Gerard Delanty argues that we should abandon the distinction between real and imaginary communities.[83]

However, the frameworks of sports and digital communication are only similar, not identical. Fundamental differences between online and offline communities cannot be ignored.[84] The organisational structure of football allows for dissent to a certain degree – communities can split and form new communities. A new club such as FC United or AFC Wimbledon is still part of the same regulatory framework as Manchester United and Milton Keynes Dons. The case is different for digital platforms, which offer communication services that are being used almost universally. The option to terminate the contract and cease using the platform is not always desirable when a platform appears to be the only sensible option for a particular type of communication, or when most or all of your social contacts are based on one particular platform. The exodus from such a platform brings with it the feeling of being expelled. Furthermore, it contributes to the echo chambers of community-driven communication. Virtual communities strengthen existing ones, and rarely create new networks. Deviant communities are marginalised. Delanty sees this as a problem, a missed opportunity to create democratic possibilities to bring together people who are different,[85] an ambition that is part of

[81] Srnicek, *Platform Capitalism* (2017) 128.

[82] V Fournier, 'Utopianism and the Cultivation of Possibilities: Grassroots Movements of Hope' (2002) 50 *The Sociological Review* 189, 206.

[83] G Delanty, *Community*, 2nd edn (London, Routledge, 2010) 137.

[84] M Castells, *The Rise of the Network Society*, 2nd edn (Wiley-Blackwell, Chichester, 2010) 389 struggles with the reality of digital communities, while Delanty, *Community* (2010) 134 emphasises their innovative character.

[85] Delanty, *Community* (2010) 146.

the underlying principles of the UNESCO Convention on the Protection and Promotion of the Diversity of Cultural Expressions, which include interculturality and dialogue among cultures.

Given that these platforms claim a universal status for their services,[86] they must be held accountable according to the Peter Parker Principle, 'With great power comes great responsibility'.[87] In Western democracies, although no longer uniformly accepted, the exercise of power is controlled by several factors, such as a balance of powers, the rule of law, elections and other democratic instruments. The individual is not only subject to authority, but enjoys a number of fundamental freedoms and rights against this authority. Normative limitations of community interactions, implemented by private enterprises, should be legitimised by a balance of mutual respect and consideration, not by the unilateral commercial interests of the platform of communication. There is a growing consensus that there should be some kind of legal control. Platforms that acknowledge the diversity of their users and give them enough space to self-regulate their affairs fit better into democratic requirements than those simply treating their users foremost as customers. Where Reddit allows a multitude of 'boards' according to community interests, Facebook targets individuals as customers. To complicate matters further, diversity on less controlled platforms must have its controlled limits, too – Reddit and 4Chan have been the source, filter bubble and echo chamber of terrorist ideas turned into reality, a script board for actions that threaten societies and many communities alike. The far-right subreddit r/The_Donald, which was closed by Reddit in June 2020, is but one example of boards that should not benefit from a global communication platform. Communities that target other communities and deny their right to exist undermine a prosperous diversity. This is in line with the UNESCO Convention on the Protection and Promotion of the Diversity of Cultural Expressions, which emphasises in Article 1b) that one of its aims is to 'create the conditions for cultures to flourish and to freely interact in a mutually beneficial manner'. Furthermore, in Article 19 of the CESCR's aforementioned General Comment No 21, the need for certain limitations of cultural freedoms is acknowledged. Technically, the place for these limitations is the platform's 'community' regulations. The CESCR stipulates that such limitations must

> be proportionate, meaning that the least restrictive measures must be taken when several types of limitations may be imposed. The Committee also wishes to stress the

[86] On Facebook's idea of 'bringing the world closer together', *cf* S Vaidhyanathan, *Antisocial Media: How Facebook Disconnects Us and Undermines Democracy* (Oxford, Oxford University Press, 2018) 1.

[87] The principle has been popularised by Spider Man comics, where it first appeared in 1962, but expresses a fundamental value that has been articulated before, eg in 1793 at the French National Assembly; see *Collection générale des décrets rendus par la Convention Nationale. Mois de Mai 1793* (Paris, Baudouin, 1793) 72 [entry for 7 May 1793]: 'Les Représentans du peuple … doivent envisager qu'une grande responsabilité est la suite inséparable d'un grand pouvoir'. The principle has also been acknowledged by the US Supreme Court in *Kimble v Marvel Entertainment, LLC* 576 US 446 (2015).

> need to take into consideration existing international human rights standards on limitations that can or cannot be legitimately imposed on rights that are intrinsically linked to the right to take part in cultural life, such as the rights to privacy, to freedom of thought, conscience and religion, to freedom of opinion and expression, to peaceful assembly and to freedom of association.

As a consequence, any cultural platform's rules have to stand the proportionality test. German courts have come to similar conclusions. In its preliminary Facebook decision, the Bundesgerichtshof has pointed out:

> Facebook provides a communication platform that, at least for some consumers, crucially determines their participation in social life and is of major significance for public discourse in political, societal, cultural and economic matters. As a result, the firm has a special legal responsibility under the aspect of informational self-determination when designing the terms of use of the platform.[88]

Significantly, the court here refers to a decision by the German Constitutional Court (Bundesverfassungsgericht) on a nationwide stadium ban issued by a football club in application of the German Football Association's rulebook.[89] The Constitutional Court had established that, under certain conditions, even private associations have to respect fundamental rights, such as the principle of equal treatment.[90] Furthermore, it explicitly referred to Article 15, paragraph 1(a) ICESCR and CESCR General Comment No 21.[91]

V. Conclusions

The comparison between the monopolistic structures of digital platforms and international sports associations has shown that the latter can be interpreted as platforms. Both groups share important characteristics. These non-governmental, global organisations accumulate so much power it requires democratically legitimised, normative control. Such a normative framework is, however, not yet effective. Antitrust laws do not regulate the relationship between monopolistic companies and their customers.

This common structure is not exclusive to digital platform providers and sports associations. The analysis could, for example, be extended to religious organisations, which often follow their own, autonomous legal systems. Recent

[88] BGH, 23 June 2020, KVR 69/19, 2021 *Gewerblicher Rechtsschutz und Urheberrecht International* 603, 614.

[89] *cf* K Wiedemann, 'A Matter of Choice: The German Federal Supreme Court's Interim Decision in the Abuse-of-Dominance Proceedings Bundeskartellamt v Facebook (Case KVR 69/19)' [2020] *International Review of Intellectual Property and Competition Law* 1168, 1179.

[90] BVerfG, 11 April 2018, 1 BvR 3080/09, 148 *BVerfGE* 267, 283.

[91] ibid 284.

developments in biotechnology have led to the emergence of yet another candidate. Writing for the German weekly *Der Spiegel*, Sascha Lobo argues that the mRNA COVID-19 vaccines developed by Moderna and BioNTech are early examples of bio-platforms that are prone to replicating developments from the digital infosphere.[92] To support his analysis, Lobo could have quoted an article from *Nature Reviews*, which presents an overview of mRNA vaccines and 'considers future directions and challenges in advancing this promising vaccine platform'.[93]

Finally, it is proposed that the relation of platform monopolies and the responsibility for diversity be considered a case of socio-legal proportionality: the greater the monopolistic character of a platform, the greater the responsibility to guarantee diversity on the platform. Fundamental democratic principles and the rule of law both legitimise legal control over the monopolistic platforms to enable diverse communities and limit the freedom of diversity. The UNESCO Convention on the Protection and Promotion of the Diversity of Cultural Expressions reaffirms, in Article 1h), 'the sovereign rights of States to maintain, adopt and implement policies and measures that they deem appropriate for the protection and promotion of the diversity of cultural expressions on their territory'. Measures to control global Internet platforms serve this purpose; they are mentioned in Article 6 of the Convention as 'regulatory measures aimed at protecting and promoting diversity of cultural expressions'.

The UNESCO Convention does not provide legal control mechanisms, but it does offer a clear compass for lawmakers,[94] which is further developed into an appeal in section 11 of the Guidelines on the Implementation of the Convention in the Digital Environment (2017):[95] 'Parties are invited to update their legislative and regulatory frameworks.' Manifestly, the Convention operates as a platform itself, a regulatory framework that needs the initiative of governments to start a social and legal transformation of existing monopoly structures: a counter-platform. The first steps in this direction are still exploratory. Adopted by the UN General Assembly on 10 December 2008, the Optional Protocol to the ICESCR[96] introduced complaint and inquiry mechanisms for individuals and groups. Once more states sign and implement the protocol, a much-needed road to stronger guarantees of cultural freedom can be paved. Legal counter-platforms provide an adequate regulatory instrument for monopolistic cultural platforms.

[92] S Lobo, 'Die neue Weltmacht der Bio-Plattformen' (27 January 2021) spiegel.de/netzwelt/netzpolitik/mrna-technologie-die-neue-weltmacht-der-bio-plattformen-a-c87fa211-1897-47cf-8a1b-cd9ded973e6f.

[93] N Pardi et al, 'mRNA Vaccines – A New Era in Vaccinology' (2018) 17 *Nature Reviews* 261.

[94] *cf* Barreiro Carril, *La diversidad* (2011) 250–53.

[95] Guidelines on the Implementation of the Convention in the Digital Environment, Approved by the Conference of Parties at its sixth session (2017) https://unesdoc.unesco.org/ark:/48223/pf0000370521.page=92.

[96] (adopted 10 December 2008, entered into force 5 May 2013) 2922 UNTS 29.

9

Internet Governance and Cultural Diversity: An Intimate but Conflictual Relationship

GIACOMO MAZZONE TALKS TO ANDRZEJ JAKUBOWSKI

Andrzej Jakubowski (AJ): It is not a truism to say that Internet governance is a real challenge and a test for the legal regime established by the 2005 UNESCO Convention on the Protection and Promotion of the Diversity of Cultural Expressions (Convention or CDC).[1] We are very grateful that Giacomo Mazzone, Secretary General of the Association Eurovisioni, a civil society body observer to the Convention since its inception and co-chair of the Policy Network on Meaningful Access (PNMA) group of the Internet Governance Forum (IGF), has agreed to present his views on these matters on the occasion of the Convention's anniversary. Giacomo Mazzone has been one of the experts to the CDC and has followed IGF and World Summit of Information Society (WSIS) processes since their beginning in 2003, representing the media community. In years 2014–16, he was a member of the IGF Multistakeholder Advisory Group (MAG), an advisory group to the Secretary General of the United Nations (UN).

AJ: In the light of your long experience and professional background, I would like to inquire about the origins of the regulatory and institutional history of the interaction between the international agenda for the protection and promotion of cultural diversity and the Internet governance.

Giacomo Mazzone (GM): Thank you very much for the invitation to contribute to this publication and to share with the readers of this book what I have witnessed from the inside in these two processes. Indeed, the path towards to the establishment of the international law regime for the protection and promotion of the diversity of cultural expressions and the global governance of the Internet started quite simultaneously. The Universal Declaration on Cultural Diversity

[1] (adopted 20 October 2005, entered into force 18 March 2007) 2440 UNTS 311.

(UDCD) was adopted by UNESCO General Conference on 2 November 2001,[2] and shortly thereafter, on 21 December 2001, the UN General Assembly approved Resolution 56/183, which set up the WSIS in two phases.[3] The first WSIS took place in Geneva between 10 and 12 December 2003 after a debate among international institutions led by Kofi Annan, the UN Secretary General, that saw as co-leaders: UNESCO, the International Telecommunication Union (ITU) and the UN Conference on Trade and Development (UNCTAD).[4]

Both of the international agendas designed to regulate these two areas – the circulation of cultural products and the development of digital economy – were countered and found their main opponent in the US government, which identified in both processes a crucial risk for the establishment of the dominance of US companies in the new market of the digital economy.

Yet it is important to make a reconstruction of what happened in those days, in order to understand where we are today, and which are the endeavours we are still facing and that we will face in the near future.

Normally, these two processes are not considered as parallel or similar, because the institutions involved are different (the UN, the ITU and the Internet Corporation for Assigned Names and Numbers (ICANN) are the main actors of the Internet governance, UNESCO is the sole body responsible of the CDC and because the negotiating partners are different (ministries of culture on one side, ministries of trade, industry and commerce, and economy on the other). Despite these differentiations, the two processes have followed similar problems and circumstances, and analysing what happens in one arena could help to understand the other. Even if there has not been a direct relation between the two processes, the delimitation of the respective fields of action was very clear in the minds of the governmental negotiators of some of the main countries, which imposed (or tried to impose) their views in both arenas. Finally, both processes are related to the rise in globalisation of the economy and to the reactions that this process provoked in various regions of the world.

All stories have a person behind them, and in this case the man behind both processes was Kofi Annan, UN Secretary-General (SG) from 1997 to 2006. Annan was an unusual kind of SG: he was the first one to come from inside of the UN system (where he has spent all of his career, in various jobs). He was the compromise candidate after the veto of the USA to a second term for Boutros Boutros Ghali, and was finally appointed against the will of France (which had opposed his candidacy until the last round).[5] Annan chose as

[2] UNESCO Doc 31C/Res 25, Annex 1 (2001).

[3] (adopted 31 January 2002) UN Doc A /RES/56/183.

[4] See www.wsis2003geneva.org.

[5] Kofi Annan was a very special UN SG. Not only because he was the first (and the only one to date) to have come from inside the organisation (see his biography: www.un.org/sg/fr/content/kofi-annan), but also because of this background, he knew very well the weaknesses of the UN system and he tried hard to fix those.

counsellor Shashi Taroor,[6] another UN insider, who he appointed as UN Under-Secretary-General for Communications and Public Information in 2001. Both men had a very clear understanding that the global balance of the world (after the end of the Cold War) was dramatically shifting in a direction where multilateral institutions could lose their role. It was the time when Fukuyama's thesis of the 'end of history' looked credible and right. To counter this false narrative, Annan and Taroor tried to give to the UN a new role, tackling the emerging issues, such as the governance of the Internet and the cultural diversity, where the need for global governance was more acute and evident, because both problems transcended national boundaries.[7] For these reasons, profiting from the circumstance that UNESCO and ITU were both led by Japanese officials (Yoshio Utsumi at the ITU, Kōichirō Matsuura at the UNESCO), Annan promoted or supported their initiatives in these areas.[8]

AJ: How would you define Kofi Annan's role in these processes?

GM: He knew very well that both moves could create frictions with the USA, but he expected to have the support of the rest of the world countries, so decided to go ahead anyway, because it was the right thing to be done: to create a new space for the multilateral institutions. In the area of the governance of the Internet, it was becoming more and more evident that the Internet was transforming itself from a US-centric military tool into a global network (still controlled by the USA) of distribution and dissemination of information and contents that could change the world, and would soon circumvent a system of rules that was and still is largely based on national boundaries and regulations. In the area of the circulation of cultural goods and products, it was equally clear that the newly born World Trade Organization (WTO) and the two fundamental treaties supporting its operation – the Agreement on Trade-Related Aspects of Intellectual Property Rights (TRIPS)[9] and the Agreement on Trade-Related

[6] In his own words (as published in *Times of India* the day he left the UN), Shashi Taroor described himself thus: 'I joined the UN in 1978 as an idealistic young man of 22, hoping to serve refugees and discover the world. I did a bit of both. But how much the institution I joined has changed! If I had suggested to my seniors at that time that the UN would one day observe and even run elections in sovereign states, conduct intrusive inspections for weapons of mass destruction, impose comprehensive sanctions on the entire import-export trade of a member state, or set up international criminal tribunals and coerce governments into handing over their citizens to be tried by foreigners under international law, I am sure they would have told me that I did not understand what the UN was all about. Indeed, since those were the late 1970s, they might well have asked me, "Young man, what are you smoking?"' timesofindia.indiatimes.com/home/sunday-times/all-that-matters/shashi-on-sunday-reflections-on-a-changing-united-nations/articleshow/1839956.cms.

[7] This was the thesis of the famous essay by Francis Fukuyama, 'The End of History?', published in 1989 in *The National Interest* No 16, 3–18, just after the collapse of the Berlin wall, in which he forecast the end of multilateralism, because of the definitive victory of the capitalist model of civilisation over the communist model.

[8] Not forgetting that France was very much behind the initiative of cultural diversity, and that supporting the establishment of the Treaty could help to recreate good relations between Annan and the French authorities, who were Annan fiercest opponents during the selection process.

[9] (adopted 15 April 1994, in force 1 January 1995) 1869 UNTS 299.

Investment Measures (TRIMs),[10] were assuring a disproportional and asymmetric power to a few big trade regions (USA, Europe and their allies) over the developing ones and even over some of the old traditional superpowers as defined by the post-World War II arrangements. The WTO (operational from 1 January 1995) and the TRIPS and TRIMs treaties were in fact configuring a capitalism model as the global model for future societies all around the world.[11]

Both these processes formed the basis for what would later be defined as 'globalisation', without introducing any counterbalance or protection for the weaker and the potential losers of this new equilibrium of global powers. This was clear in Annan's vision of the future world, and both ongoing processes – Internet governance and protection and promotion of cultural diversity – were an effort of the UN system to try to introduce some regulations and protections in the forecoming 'digitalisation' and 'globalisation' of the world's economies. This approach was welcomed by the Japanese government and by the governments of some of the Member States of the European Union, which saw in it a way to rebalance powers in the new world that was appearing on the horizon. France especially was very supportive of the UNESCO initiative to adopt an international cultural diversity treaty aimed at establishing some limits to the predominance of the WTO free trade approach, the fiercest enemy of the European concept of the 'cultural exception'. This defensive approach from France and its EU allies (who wanted to use the CDC essentially as a shield to protect their system of subventions to cultural industries against WTO rules) was also the main limit of the exercise, because it pushed them to accept many limitations to the scope of the UNESCO Convention, starting from its famous and controversial Article 20.

AJ: How did these two processes evolve in the post-Cold War reality?

GM: Unfortunately, the efforts of the UN SG did not find among the rest of the world the vast support that he was expecting. On Internet issues, EU countries were not all on the same page. Beyond the EU, Russia was still recovering from the shock of no longer being a superpower, while China had already implemented its plan to create a separate Internet (the 'new Chinese firewall') and so had no interest at all in supporting a battle for the creation of a free Internet space under multilateral control. Under these uncertain premises, Kofi Annan called the first WSIS in Geneva in December 2003 to discuss the future of world Internet governance. After one week of harsh debates, the Geneva talks ended without an agreement,

[10] (adopted 15 April 1994, in force 1 January 1995) 1868 UNTS 186.

[11] The *Encyclopaedia Britannica* explains the reasons leading to the creation of the WTO in 1995: www.britannica.com/topic/World-Trade-Organization. It should be remembered that China was not part of the WTO and joined it only after long negotiations in 2001, while Russia became a member on 22 August 2012. Since then the creation of the WTO was seen as a symbol of capitulation of the communist economic model against capitalism and has been considered the beginning of the globalisation of the economy.

with the USA fiercely opposed to any compromise. The only compromise reached was the promise to postpone any decision to the second summit, two years later in Tunis. Significantly enough, two years later, in the Tunis final compromise document, all references to intellectual property (IP) issues (that is, 'contents'), which were one of goals of the initial Geneva document,[12] had disappeared because the compromise idea was that the WSIS process and its outcomes would not deal with contents, but only with infrastructures and processes.

On the cultural diversity side, there was the same attention to respecting the boundaries and territories of other international treaties and institutions.[13] What was different were the final outcomes. While today the governance of the Internet is still waiting for an international treaty, cultural diversity got its own treaty in only four years. What made the difference between the two tables of negotiations and why did one succeeded and the other not? In Paris, at the UNESCO table, the EU – pushed by France and President Chirac – was unanimously behind the proposal to transform the UDCD into a treaty, and a group of international experts were immediately asked to work on a draft. Thanks to the Canadian government, a group of like-minded countries in favour of a new treaty was created and international alliances were established within the group of 77 countries (which were quite united in supporting this battle) and with the Organisation Internationale de la Francophonie, which was very active in gathering support among developing countries. US representatives participated to the negotiation with the only aim, till the very last day, of delaying the decision or diluting the text of the new treaty. Initially, Australia and even the UK had tried to keep them on board, but at the end – when it was clear that there was no possibility of compromise – they left the USA alone. The process ended on 25 October 2005. In the final vote during

[12] Point 42 of the Geneva Declaration of Principles states: 'Intellectual Property protection is important to encourage innovation and creativity in the Information Society; similarly, the wide dissemination, diffusion, and sharing of knowledge is important to encourage innovation and creativity. Facilitating meaningful participation by all in intellectual property issues and knowledge sharing through full awareness and capacity building is a fundamental part of an inclusive Information Society.' In the Tunis agenda, approved 2 years later at the second WSIS, any reference to IP had disappeared.

[13] A point has been introduced in the text of the Convention to fix the limits of the exercise. The controversial Art 20 states clearly: 'Relationship to other treaties: mutual supportiveness, complementarity and non-subordination Parties recognize that they shall perform in good faith their obligations under this Convention and all other treaties to which they are parties. Accordingly, without subordinating this Convention to any other treaty, a) they shall foster mutual supportiveness between this Convention and the other treaties to which they are parties; and b) when interpreting and applying the other treaties to which they are parties or when entering into other international obligations, Parties shall take into account the relevant provisions of this Convention. Nothing in this Convention shall be interpreted as modifying rights and obligations of the Parties under any other treaties to which they are parties.' An article was inserted at the request of Australia and the UK to try to appease the US opposition, which was judged very negatively by the Cambridge University Press analysis of the 2005 Treaty made five years after its approval. Art 20 was read as an explicit renunciation of the WTO rules on globalisation. See M Burri, 'The UNESCO Convention on Cultural Diversity: An Appraisal Five Years after Its Entry into Force' (2013) 20 *International Journal of Cultural Property* 357.

the UNESCO General Conference, 148 countries voted for and only the USA and Israel voted against it. Australia, Honduras, Liberia and Nicaragua abstained.[14] The CDC was finally adopted. However, the US Bush administration minimised the impact of the new Convention, stating that it could not be applied against the WTO free trade instruments (and this interpretation was supported by Article 20 of the Convention). It also announced that its interpretation excluded any application of the CDC to the rising digital world. According to the USA's restrictive reading of the Convention, a film, a book or a record, when they are dematerialised, become 'digital goods'. As such, they would be subject to the e-commerce agreements of the WTO and cannot be protected under the new UNESCO treaty. Such an interpretation was fiercely rejected by the states parties to the CDC, but it took 12 years before those parties to the Convention could agree on guidelines for cultural goods in the digital world, and even after that there has been no case of direct conflict between the CDC and the WTO.[15] What is true is that some countries and regional blocs (EU, Korea, Canada …) have used the CDC as a shield in bilateral trade agreements to preserve their own internal rules on cultural goods and services, and the USA has substantially accepted or tolerated this defensive approach among peers and refused it to weaker actors.

While, in Paris, efforts to create a Treaty on Cultural Diversity arrived at a positive conclusion against the US will, a few weeks later, in Tunis (on 16–18 November 2005), the second round of the WSIS took place. Efforts to arrive at an agreement on the future of Internet governance failed to achieve any tangible result, but for different reasons.

AJ: Could you explain the nature of the differences of these two processes? Does it mean that some of the failed conversations from the Internet governance space moved to cultural diversity?

GM: Both processes streamlined and concentrated their action, excluding areas that could be on the border of their mandate, such as IP for the WSIS process and the digitalisation process (and e-commerce) from the 2005 Convention. But the main difference between the two processes – and that made a substantial difference in leading to the CDC Treaty in Paris after 4 years but to 20 years of discussions (still ongoing) in Geneva and in New York over Internet governance (IG) – was the fact that the EU family was not united on the matter, in addition to the group of 77 countries. In the IG negotiations, within the European countries, the UK-led position prevailed: it sustained that an Internet controlled by the USA was preferable to an Internet controlled by the UN. Canada, Australia and ultimately

[14] CB Graber, 'The New Unesco Convention on Cultural Diversity: A Counterbalance to the WTO?' (2006) 9 *Journal of International Economic Law* 553.

[15] See UNESCO, 'Guidelines on the Implementation of the Convention in the Digital Environment, Approved by the Conference of Parties at Its Sixth Session' (2017) fr.unesco.org/creativity/sites/creativity/files/digital_guidelines_en_full-3.pdf.

even Japan rallied to this position. China continued to observe the debate from a distance, and so the UN found support only from Russia, part of the group of 77 (led by Brazil and India) and some other countries.

It should be underlined that the compromise that was reached in Tunis was to create two separate tracks for discussion of the future of IG: one for multi-stakeholders, the Internet Governance Forum (IGF), and another for governments only (WSIS follow-up). Both groups were asked to report to the UN General Assembly within five years to propose a definitive solution for the issue of IG. In the years after the Tunis compromise, both tracks of the process registered no visible progress, so UN General Assembly decided twice to extend the IGF's and WSIS's mandates. This delaying attitude corresponded exactly to the will of Kofi Annan's successor UN SG, Ban Ki Moon. He sought to avoid this very thorny dossier and leave it for his successor. In fact, last time, the UN General Assembly in 2013 decided to extend the mandate for other 10 years and this will last now until 2024.[16] In this way, Ban Ki Moon was able to finish his two mandates as UN SG in 2016 without ever having to take a decision on this very explosive topic and left the bomb under the table of his successor.

While discussions on IG at the UN were lagging behind, the pressure worldwide started to mount, ignited by the evidence that the current system of non-intervention in practical terms means applying WTO rules or others contained in bilateral trade agreements (such as the Transatlantic Data Privacy, the EU–US Privacy Shield,[17] and its predecessor Safe Harbour[18]). These agreements are under more and more fire because of the many incidents that have occurred in the last years, starting from the Cambridge Analytica case.

AJ: How did the establishment and reform of the ICANN change the operationalisation of cultural diversity in IG?

GM: The ICANN, established in 1998, is the only world authority that assigns Internet names, and it is not at all impacted by the current debates over IG. Under Obama's administration, the US government, in order to react to the pressure and to the polemics against the US control over the Internet,[19] initiated a reform of the ICANN, trying to enlarge its legitimation. As part of these efforts,

[16] See mail.intgovforum.org/pipermail/igfmaglist_intgovforum.org/2015-December/003954.html.

[17] See Commission Implementing Decision (EU) 2016/1250 of 12 July 2016 pursuant to Directive 95/46/EC of the European Parliament and of the Council on the adequacy of the protection provided by the EU–US Privacy Shield (notified under document C(2016) 4176) (Text with EEA relevance) [2016] OJ L207/1.

[18] 2000/520/EC: Commission Decision of 26 July 2000 pursuant to Directive 95/46/EC of the European Parliament and of the Council on the adequacy of the protection provided by the safe harbour privacy principles and related frequently asked questions issued by the US Department of Commerce (notified under document number C(2000) 2441) (Text with EEA relevance) [2000] OJ L215/7.

[19] Great controversy arose around the decision imposed by US Trade Department on ICANN not to implement the TLD DOT.xxx in 2005: www.icann.org/news/blog/board-discussion-over-xxx.

the US government on 1 October 2016 severed the contract linking the ICANN to the US Commerce Department.[20] Since then, ICANN has formally become a self-regulating body, with legitimacy granted by the presence of 178 governments on its Governmental Advisory Committee (GAC), but it nevertheless remains a private association suject to California's law. In addition, the 2016 appointment of a Swedish citizen (Goran Marby) as the first non-US citizen CEO of ICANN constituted a further step in the direction to internationalise this body. However, the fact that ICANN remains subject to US law and cannot leave the USA (a condition imposed by the US Congress for the approval of the end of the contract with the US government) is interpreted by many as proof that this body is not neutral but is still largely controlled by US interests. According to some experts in the field, the new situation could become even worst then before, because in the past the US government could be questioned about decisions taken by ICANN that affected other countries' interests. As of 1 October 2016, these complaints are easy to decline, because formally the US government no longer has any influence on ICANN's decisions. Hence, while the legitimacy of the CDC to intervene in cultural goods, products and services is still challenged and no new body to regulate global IG will be created any time soon, ICANN is acting, de facto, as the sole and exclusive global Internet regulator.

AJ: Does not the existence of these two parallel orders – ICANN and the CDC – therefore create difficulties for effective global governance of cultural diversity?

GM: Indeed, this brings the world of today into a bizarre and unprecedented situation, where it is a private body (under US law and controlled mainly by US interests) that is the only one that can regulate the Internet, through its most delicate function: the allocation or revocation of the DNS (Domain Name System). A decision taken by ICANN can only by challenged within ICANN internal control processes: the recourse to Californian courts is highly restricted and no appeal to any international body is allowed.

Moreover, the appearance of ICANN in the international regulation world has already had a strong impact on culture and this influence will grow even more in future. Today ICANN can decide effectively on its own on the portrayal of the real world in the Internet world and these last years have shown many examples of how dangerous this undue, unregulated and unchallengeable influence can be for diversity. The recent debate around the possibility of excluding '.ru' (all Russian Internet domains) from the world Internet has proved that this threat exists and is real.[21]

[20] See www.icann.org/news/announcement-2016-10-01-en; www.icann.org/en/announcements/details/stewardship-of-iana-functions-transitions-to-global-Internet-community-as-contract-with-us-government-ends-1-10-2016-en.

[21] www.key4biz.it/democrazia-futura-dalla-cortina-di-ferro-alle-cortine-di-silicio-sara-lInternet-globale-la-principale-vittima-del-conflitto-russo-ucraino/398412.

Examples that occurred in the recent past have proved that ICANN could twist the reality of the physical world, creating a new narrative over the Internet and imposing a unilateral vision of the world that corresponds mostly to the US vision, beliefs and legislation. In 2012, ICANN launched a process called the 'new gTLDs round', aimed at enlarging the number of TLDs (top-level domains), the roots of the Internet. Their numbers exploded from less than 200 existing TLDs – most of them country codes (such as .it, .uk, .de) plus a number of so-called 'generic' codes (such as .com, .net, .int) – up to nearly 2000.[22] This process started the new 'gold rush' and gave space to all sorts of ambitions, in a global competition that started in 2012 and that has led to a huge concentration in the hands of a few US controlled companies. Just some examples of cases that happened in that period could help us better understand the impact of this internal decision of the private body called ICANN on cultural diversity and on the rights of existing communities to obtain and build up their own digital identity.

AJ: The monopoly of such an organisation therefore has a great impact on cultural diversity and the cultural identity of many actors in the world. How does this affect the identity of local communities?

GM: All over the world, the legitimate ownership of the name of a town, a region or a country belongs to their representatives (normally elected), such as the mayor, the governor or the president of the country. This is not the case at ICANN. The current regulation for the assignment of TLDs for geographic names accepts the principle that only state ISO (International Organization for Standardization) country codes are exclusively managed by national governments: so, for example, .ch, the Internet code for Switzerland, cannot be requested by other countries. In contrast, most other geographical names (ie the names of regions, river, mountains, towns) can be assigned to a private company and legitimately used, even against the will of the legal elected representatives of these entities. These interested geographic entities could raise opposition known within a certain amount of time, and even then it might not be enough for it to obtain satisfaction at ICANN.

Despite many efforts made by the GAC (where most of the UN countries are represented and where I sit as an observer), a certain number of conflicts have exploded over geo names, mainly between US companies and developing countries. These conflicts highlight this peculiar situation of a private body, ICANN, that can directly affect culture, languages and the exchange of digital cultural goods and services at the global level and that is accountable to nobody but only to itself.

AJ: How has such a state of cultural diversity governance on the Internet been perceived by international regional organisations?

GM: This worrisome situation within the ICANN-regulated areas attracted the attention of the Council of Europe, which commissioned from a group of

[22] data.iana.org/TLD/tlds-alpha-by-domain.txt. The expected number was higher, but at the end of the selection process, the confirmed applications were significantly fewer than the requests: 1238 out of nearly 2000. 'TLD' means 'Top Level Domain', the first root of internet names (such as .COM).

international experts a paper on the role of ICANN and on its impact on human rights (especially on cultural and social issues).[23] The paper analysed in detail many of the possible violations of human rights principles that could occur in the frame of the ICANN policy of assignment of names and numbers for the use of the Internet.

AJ: What are the biggest challenges in this regard? They would probably concern geographical names and the associated issues of both identity and politics, I would imagine.

GM: That is correct. The most clamorous was the case of the TLD '.amazon'. In 2012, the US company using this name applied for the homonymous TLD. Immediately the six countries of the transnational region sharing the river's borders (Peru, Bolivia, Venezuela, Colombia, Ecuador and Brazil), plus the neighbour Argentina, raised their opposition to the fact that the right to this geographic name over the Internet could be given exclusively to a US company.[24] The opposition was endorsed by the GAC of the ICANN (with the only contrary vote being that of the USA), but it was nevertheless rejected at the end of the long, internal ICANN process. The US Obama administration (until ICANN was linked to the US government by contract in 2016) asked for a suspension of the decision in order to avoid a conflict with the Brazilian government. It was only a small break: once the US government officially exited from ICANN in 2016, the process resumed and finally the ICANN board (the majority of which are private, mainly US interests) decided on 15 May 2019 that there was 'no public policy reason' not to proceed with the '.amazon' application. This decision provoked a huge reaction and a public declaration signed by the presidents of four of the countries concerned[25] (Bolivia, Colombia, Ecuador and Peru), which was not taken into consideration at all.

This was not an isolated incident in the field of geographic names. For instance, there was the case of.patagonia,[26] a name that was requested by the homonymous fashion brand. Differently from the Amazon case, Patagonia's owners – after the Argentinian government had filed an objection against the request (this time with the endorsement of the whole GAC of ICANN) – decided autonomously to withdraw their application.

While the Argentinians won this battle, the same did not happen to the Belgian city of Spa, exclusive use of the name of which was assigned to an Asiatic group called Asia Spa and Wellness Promotion Council Limited.[27] Even worse happened

[23] E Solomon and K Pijl, 'Applications to ICANN for Community-based New Generic Top-Level Domains (gTLDs): Opportunities and Challenges from a Human Rights Perspective', DGI (2016) 17, rm.coe.int/16806b5a14.

[24] icannwiki.org/.amazon.

[25] www.lexology.com/library/detail.aspx?g=ed56ae56-c0ea-47de-8f3a-afaf670cdfcc. The initial five countries became only four after the change of government in Brazil from Roussef to Bolsonaro.

[26] icannwiki.org/index.php/.patagonia.

[27] Asia Spa and Wellness Promotion Council Limited, www.icann.org/en/registry-agreements/details/spa?section=agreement.

to the African Union (AU) with regard to .africa. This TLD was initially given to a South African private group called ZA Central Registry, despite another request submitted by another register, endorsed by the AU. Contrary to ICANN's internal rules, the AU claimed that the use of the name 'Africa' must be attributed to the organisation representing all the states of the continent. Initially, the request from the AU was rejected, until – thanks to a procedural mistake of the first applicant– the initial decision was revoked and the TLD '.africa' was finally assigned to the AU-backed appellant,[28] extracting ICANN from a very embarrassing conflict with the community of African governments.

Geographic names are not the only ones suffering of these extreme US-backed decisions made by ICANN. The US-dominant approach applies also to another area of conflict between the USA on one side and the rest of the world on the other: the area of geographic protections applied to agricultural and food products. This is a still open wound within the WTO, where it was never possible to reach an agreement between the USA (supported by a small group of countries), denying any recognition of 'protection' to products because of their geographic origin, and the rest of the world, accepting the principle of 'international applications of origin', which is currently administered globally by the World Intellectual Property Organization (WIPO).[29] This long debate, which has occupied the WTO and WIPO for dozens of years and is still not resolved, has never been taken into consideration by ICANN, which adopted the US approach by default and so refused to intervene against any measure of protection related to the geographic origins to prevent abuses. A battle arose around the assignation of the TLDs '.wine' and '.vin' between Europeans on one side and the USA on the other. The Europeans fought in vain to obtain the inclusion of provisions in the contract of delegation of the TLDs '.wine' and '.vin' aimed at preventing the sale over the Internet of wines not respecting the 'international application of origins'. The USA vetoed the inclusion of the clause, claiming that there is no unanimously recognised international regulation on this matter. This paved the way to the fact that today a company could promote and sell on the '.wine' TLD 'champagne' produced in China or 'Tocai wine' produced in Zimbabwe.

AJ: What about the so-called 'community-based' TLDs?

GM: In the preparatory discussion leading to the enlargement of the existing TLDs (from 200 to 2000), non-commercial entities participating in the debate obtained

[28] The whole story is reconstructed by the journalists of *The Register*: see www.theregister.com/2018/06/26/dotafrica_icann_trial.

[29] WIPO Handbook on International Applications of Origins, www.wipo.int/edocs/pubdocs/en/geographical/952/wipo_pub_952.pdf; see also Paris Convention for the Protection of Industrial Property (signed 20 March 1883, entered into force 7 July 1884) 828 UNTS 107 (Paris Convention) and Lisbon Agreement for the Protection of Appellations of Origin and their International Registration (adopted 31 October 1958, as revised 14 July 1967, entered into force 25 September 1966) 923 UNTS 205, as revised (Lisbon Agreement).

preferential treatment for their 'community-based' requests.[30] The concept was simple: communities gather around symbols, names and principles, and are not equipped to compete with commercial entities. So the GAC and others within ICANN constituencies identified some areas needing special protection and eased the conditions of access to TLDs referring to them. Among these areas were mentioned the acronyms of IGOs (intergovernmental organisations), such as UNESCO, WTO and WIPO, and communities, such as religious, cultural, social and ethnic groups.

Despite these noble principles being approved by ICANN before the launch of the gTLDs campaign in 2012, the bodies concerned faced significant problems in actually obtaining the TLDs when they made concrete applications. The domain name industries (the few global companies – mainly US – that control two-thirds of the existing TLDs and 90 per cent of the related incomes) were opposed to both groups of names being protected. For IGOs, they agreed to make exceptions only for the Red Cross and the IOC (the Olympic Committee), while they agreed to protect only a fraction of the existing recognised IGOs and only for a limited use. For communities, they formally accepted the rule, but then many episodes of sabotage of concrete applications occurred during the selection process.

This was the case of the TLD .gay, which was requested by a global alliance of national and international organisations linked to the rights of gay communities in many countries of the world. At the end of a long battle through all the degrees of internal recourse within ICANN, DOT.gay was assigned to a private company that was able to withstand the process longer than the others, thanks to its deeper pockets.

AJ: In your view, what are the other implications of ICANN's approach?

GM: Despite these cases, probably the worst consequences of this commercial-only ICANN approach are two: the enormous concentration of new TLD requests in developed countries, and the absolute disproportion between Latin alphabet character TLDs and the presence of TLDs in other characters.[31]

The numbers are quite blunt in describing the hard reality:

> The vast majority of gTLD applicants are from North America (which comprised 911 of the total 1,930 applications filed in the initial round). 611 applicants were from Europe.

[30] Solomon and Pijl, 'Applications to ICANN' (n 23) 34: 'The concept of community priority stems from the GNSO's [Generic Names Supporting Organisation's] policy recommendations on which the implementation of the New gTLD Programme is based. It was expected that community-based TLDs would add value to the namespace in serving the needs of diverse user groups. The benefits of a community-TLD put forward by ICANN are that it creates a rallying point for supporters of your cause, community or culture; it will help strengthen the cultural and social identity of the group and provide an avenue for growth and increased support among its members; it enables the community to control their domain name space by creating their own rules and policies for registration to be able to protect and implement their community's standards and values; it will boost the trust and confidence of its members; the community may be recognized globally; members will be able to register a relevant, shorter and easy to remember domain name; and it will generate income from registration and annual renewal fees of domain names.'

[31] newgtlds.icann.org/en/program-status/statistics.

303 applicants are from the Asia-Pacific region. Latin American applicants comprise 24 of the total applicant pool and there is a total of 17 applicants from Africa.[32]

A study conducted by AM Global consulting in 2016[33] made an in-depth analysis of the reasons for the failure and of the main obstacles for applicants from poorer economies to apply and qualify for TLDs. The high entrance fee (185,000 USD per application, plus ancillary costs estimated to be an equivalent amount) has been identified as one of the main barriers, but not the only one. Language barriers are also very relevant. In 2012, applications could only be submitted in English,[34] and most of the panel of examiners only spoke English. This, of course, made the application process easier for English-speaking companies or professionals and very hard for applicants from the rest of the world. The final results of the selection proved that the risk of discrimination was real.[35]

AJ: This aspect of cultural diversity is indeed extremely important in the global world of communication. What does this look like in the practice of cultural diversity governance in Internet?

GM: Of a total of 1238 new gTLDs introduced in the market between 2012 and 31 August 2020, only 97 (equal to 7.8 per cent) are the so-called IDNs (internationalised domain names), which are TLDs in non-Latin characters (Chinese, Cyrillic, Hebrew, Armenian, etc). Bearing in mind that these languages represent altogether 30 per cent of the world population, it means that nearly one-third of the citizens of the world are not represented in what is the current offering of the global Internet … And this, by far, is the first and the most unjust restriction to diversity provoked by the current system.

AJ: Will the contemporary governance of the Internet be able to protect cultural diversity of marginalised and non-representative communities?

GM: As the already mentioned report of the Council of Europe stated, ICANN would have to has a priority:

> The protection of vulnerable groups or minorities. Community-based TLDs should take appropriate measures to ensure that the right to freedom of expression of their

[32] G Haight, 'The List of gTLD Applicants: A Breakdown' (JD Supra, 15 June 2012) www.jdsupra.com/legalnews/the-list-of-gtld-applicants-a-breakdown-47668.

[33] 'New gTLDs and the Global South Understanding Limited Global South Demand in the Most Recent New gTLD Round and Options Going Forward': community.icann.org/download/attachments/58727397/New%20gTLDs%20and%20global%20South.docx?version=1&modificationDate=1478064796000&api=v2.

[34] As prescribed in Art 5 of the Applicants' Guidebook: 'Language (a) The language of all submissions and proceedings under this Procedure shall be English. (b) Parties may submit supporting evidence in its original language, provided and subject to the authority of the Panel to determine otherwise, that such evidence is accompanied by a certified or otherwise official English translation of all relevant text', newgtlds.icann.org/en/applicants/agb/guidebook-full-04jun12-en.pdf.

[35] See n 30 above.

> community can be effectively enjoyed without discrimination, including with respect to the freedom to receive and impart information on subjects dealing with their community.
>
> They should also take additional measures to ensure that the right to freedom of peaceful assembly can be effectively enjoyed, without discrimination. Such vulnerable groups or minorities include groups of people or interests based on historical, cultural or social components of identity, such as nationality, race or ethnicity, religion, belief, gender, culture or particular social origin or group, political opinion, membership of a national minority, disability, age, and/or a language or linguistic group (non-exhaustive).[36]

Under this profile, the current policy of ICANN is largely unsatisfactory and the fact that this organisation is not accountable to anybody else exposes all its processes to the suspicion that its decisions could be biased and determined by the dominant interest groups, mainly US-based or -controlled.

AJ: Finally, I would like to ask you how you assess the current significance and role of the UN in the global governance of the Internet and the protection and promotion of the diversity of cultural expressions.

GM: Both processes – the creation of a global and shared governance of the Internet and the implementation of the CDC into the area of digital goods and artistic creation – remain largely uncomplete and unsatisfactory. But, at the same time, these developments cannot be avoided. Without both of them being accomplished in a satisfactory manner, globalisation and digitalisation processes will raise more and more negative reactions among citizens and will raise a higher level of conflict among richer and poorer (countries as well as citizens), and among those that are already digitalised and those that are not. Until both these contradictions are solved, a clockwork bomb is placed under the future of the world. The UN SG, António Guterres, who succeeded to Ban Ki Moon in January 2017, is highly aware of the problem and, after two years of hesitations, finally in 2019 decided to tackle the issue of Internet governance. He appointed a high-level panel of experts (chaired by Jack Ma and Melinda Gates) to prepare a report on digital cooperation (a more vague name to avoid the use of 'Internet governance'),[37] under the title 'The Age of Digital Interdependence'.

This report was subsequently adopted by the UN SG, who presented his own plan on 11 June 2020 under the name 'Roadmap for Digital Cooperation', in which a series of concrete measures were announced. The most important of these actions was the appointment of a UN SG special technology envoy: a person that – within the UN SG office – will be in charge of pursuing the objectives of the Roadmap. After a false start on 22 January 2021, when a first Envoy on Technology was

[36] Solomon and Pijl, 'Applications to ICANN' (n 23) 34.

[37] See Report of the UN Secretary-General's High-level Panel on Digital Cooperation, 'The Age of Digital Interdependence' (June 2020) www.un.org/en/pdfs/DigitalCooperation-report-for%20web.pdf; see also 'Digital Cooperation Report' (3 June 2019) digitalcooperation.org/report.

appointed and then suspended,[38] finally on 10 May 2022 a new one – the Indian Amandeep Singh Gill – has been appointed and is now working to set up the 'UN summit of the future' in September 2024.[39] Now there are no more excuses to fix the broken Internet …

AJ: Thank you very much for this critical reconstruction of contemporary Internet governance and the promotion of cultural diversity.

[38] www.un.org/sg/en/content/sg/personnel-appointments/2021-01-22/mr-fabrizio-hochschild-drummond-of-chile-secretary-generals-envoy-technology.

[39] www.un.org/sg/en/content/sg/personnel-appointments/2022-06-10/mr-amandeep-singh-gill-of-india-envoy-technology%C2%A0.

PART IV

Taking the Concept of Cultural Diversity Seriously: The Unavoidable Need of Connecting with Other Sectors of International Law and Other Disciplines

10

The Contribution of the Cultural Diversity Convention to Defining Artistic Freedom as a Cultural Right

LAURENCE CUNY

I. Introduction

Most observers consider the 2013 report of the UN Special Rapporteur in the Field of Cultural Rights (hereinafter the 2013 Special Rapporteur Report) as groundbreaking in relation to artistic freedom.[1] It was indeed the first UN report specifically devoted to the right to freedom of artistic expression and creativity, and 'was to become one of the most important reference points for artists and organisations monitoring artistic freedom'.[2] Before then, the few cases concerning the arts or artists were handled by international organisations and practitioners as falling under the scope of freedom of expression, of which artistic freedom was considered to be a sub-category.[3] Actions were based on Article 19 of the International Covenant on Civil and Political Rights and corresponding articles in constitutions or charters of rights in national or regional laws.[4] This was the

[1] Human Rights Council, 'Report of the Special Rapporteur in the Field of Cultural Rights, Farida Shaheed: The Right to Freedom of Artistic Expression and Creativity' (14 March 2013) UN Doc A/HRC/23/34.

[2] S Wyatt and O Reitov, 'Arts: Protecting and Promoting Artistic Freedom' (Hildesheim, Foundation University of Hildesheim, 2019) 16.

[3] eg Human Rights Council, 'Opinions Adopted by the Working Group on Arbitrary Detention at Its Sixty-First Session: No 32/2011 (Cameroon)' (29 February 2012) UN Doc A/HRC/WGAD/2011/32, para 27.

[4] (signed 16 December 1966, entered into force 23 March 1976) 999 UNTS 171. See also Art 10 of the European Convention for the Protection of Human Rights and Fundamental Freedoms (signed 4 November 1950, entered into force 3 September 1953) 213 UNTS 222; Art 13 of the American Convention on Human Rights (signed 22 November 1969, entered into force 18 July 1978) 1144 UNTS 123. For recent evolutions in the conception of artistic freedom in constitutional and international law, see E Polymenopoulou, 'Freedom of Art' in *The Max Planck Encyclopedia of Comparative Constitutional Law*, online edn (Oxford, Oxford University Press, 2016). For a general overview, see P Kearns, *Freedom of Artistic Expression: Essays on Culture and Legal Censure* (Oxford, Hart Publishing, 2013).

consequence of a lack of international and regional mechanisms to monitor and enforce economic, social and cultural rights.[5] With the adoption of these mechanisms, other paths have progressively (re)opened, as reflected by the UN report. In recalling the international framework, the Special Rapporteur focused on Article 15 of the International Covenant on Economic, Social and Cultural Rights (ICESCR) and 'the freedom indispensable for scientific research and creative activity'.[6] She anchored artistic freedom within the scope of cultural rights and emphasised the contribution of artworks to democratic debate, the right of everyone to enjoy the arts and the right to participate in cultural life.[7] Through this, she brought a more comprehensive vision of artistic freedom. The report was critical to bringing attention to artistic freedom as a matter of both civil and political rights[8] and economic, social and cultural rights.[9] This new focus on artistic freedom appeared in a political context of growing concern for the silencing of artistic voices,[10] which had an impact on the diversity of cultural expressions. It was a matter of protecting artists as well as the right of audiences to access arts works and the world views they presented. The mandate of the Special Rapporteur, established in 2009, made explicit reference[11] to the UNESCO Declaration on Cultural

[5] Most mechanisms on economic, social and cultural rights are recent; see the Optional Protocol to the International Covenant on Economic, Social and Cultural Rights (adopted 10 December 2008, entered into force 5 May 2013) 2922 UNTS 29. At UN level, the mandate of the Special Rapporteur in the field of cultural rights was created in 2009. In the interamerican system, a Rapporteur on Economic, Social, Cultural, and Environmental Rights was established in 2014 and became operational in 2017.

[6] (signed 16 December 1966, entered into force 3 January 1976) 993 UNTS 3.

[7] On the interconnection between these rights, see Committee on Economic, Social and Cultural Rights, 'General Comment No 21: Right of Everyone to Take Part in Cultural Life (Art 15, para 1 (a), of the International Covenant on Economic, Social and Cultural Rights)' (21 December 2009) UN Doc E/C.12/GC/21.

[8] A specific research report on artistic freedom of expression by the UN Special Rapporteur on the promotion and protection of the freedom of opinion and expression was a result of the collaboration between the two mandates. See Human Rights Council, 'Research Report on Artistic Freedom of Expression' (24 July 2020) UN Doc A/HRC/44/49/Add.2.

[9] On previous disequilibrium between those sets of rights, see J Symonides, 'A Neglected Category of Human Rights' (1998) 50(158) *International Social Science Journal* 559. The work of the Fribourg Group to codify cultural rights started in 1993 and involved UNESCO as well as the Council of Europe and the Organisation internationale de la francophonie. The Declaration itself was launched in 2007. See M Bidault, *La protection internationale des droits culturels* (Brussels, Bruylant, 2009); P Meyer-Bisch and M Bidault, *Déclarer les droits culturels: commentaire de la Déclaration de Fribourg* (Geneva, Schulthess/Brussels, Bruylant, 2010); P Meyer-Bisch, *Les droits culturels: une catégorie sous-développée de droits de l'homme* (Fribourg, Éditions universitaires de Fribourg, 1993). Other codification efforts have been made in the context of Wroclaw – European Capital of Culture 2016; see A Mężykowska, 'ECHR Cultural Protocol Debates/CAHMIN' in AJ Wiesand et al (eds), *Culture and Human Rights: The Wroclaw Commentaries* (Berlin, De Gruyter, 2016) 154.

[10] 2013 Special Rapporteur Report, 1.

[11] Human Rights Council, 'Resolution 10/23. Independent Expert in the Field of Cultural Rights' (26 March 2009). The resolution reaffirmed that cultural rights are an integral part of human rights, which are universal, indivisible, interrelated and interdependent. Within its mandate, the Special Rapporteur was to study, among other topics, the relationship between cultural rights and cultural diversity, in close collaboration with states and other relevant actors, including in particular the United Nations Educational, Scientific and Cultural Organisation, with the aim of further promoting cultural rights.

Diversity (UDCD)[12] and the Convention on the Protection and Promotion of the Diversity of Cultural Expressions (CDC, or the Convention).[13] In turn, the Special Rapporteur's work also influenced the priorities of parties to the CDC as, from 2015, violations of artistic freedom entered the agenda as an emerging trend that should be monitored.[14]

The fifteenth anniversary of the CDC provides an excellent opportunity to reflect on how the implementation of the Convention helps to define, monitor and advance artistic freedom at the international level. The work carried out at UNESCO to implement the CDC has been essential in shaping artistic freedom, providing space for discussions and developing the tools and models for parties to implement it. Parties have recognised 'the important steps taken by UNESCO … to enhance global monitoring in areas such as artistic freedom'.[15]

This chapter argues that contribution to the promotion and protection of artistic freedom is a major achievement of the implementation of the Convention. It explores the tools developed in the monitoring of the CDC and their role in the recognition of artistic freedom as a cultural right. In doing so, it confirms the normative role of international organisations and describes the mechanisms that are at play to produce those normative effects and their limitations.

The remainder of the chapter is divided into three sections that examine the contribution of monitoring the CDC in three areas: recognising artistic freedom as an economic, social and cultural right (section II); defining artistic freedom as a cultural right (section III); and informing and advancing the right to artistic freedom (section IV).

II. Contribution to the Recognition of Artistic Freedom as an Economic, Social and Cultural Right: Linking the 1980 Recommendation Concerning the Status of the Artist and the CDC

This section explores the approach on artistic freedom developed since the adoption of the CDC. It examines the preparatory works to highlight the absence of

[12] (adopted 2 November 2001) UNESCO Doc CLT.2002/WS/9.

[13] (adopted 20 October 2005, entered into force 18 March 2007) 2440 UNTS 311.

[14] 9 IGC, 'Item 4 of the Provisional Agenda: Report of the Secretariat on Its Activities' (15 October 2015) UNESCO Doc CE/15/9.IGC/4, Annex IV, 18.

[15] Nordic Council of Minsters for Culture, 'Ministers of Culture on Promoting Diversity of Cultural Expressions and Artistic Freedom in a Digital Age' (2 May 2016) www.norden.org/en/declaration/declaration-nordic-ministers-culture-promoting-diversity-cultural-expressions-and. It should be noted that Nordic States, organisations and experts have been particularly involved in this issue, including in supporting UNESCO's programmes. For instance, a side event was organised by Denmark, Norway and Sweden with the Secretariat of the Convention during the 38th Session of the General Conference at UNESCO on Efforts to Improve the Status of the Artist and Artistic Freedom on 13 November 2015 in the context of the Culture Commission. 9 IGC, 'Item 4' (15 October 2015) 7.

an explicit reference to cultural rights and artistic freedom in the CDC and the progressive recognition of artistic freedom as an area of work. It shows that this has been achieved by linking the monitoring of the Convention to a revitalisation of the 1980 UNESCO Recommendation concerning the Status of the Artist (hereinafter the 1980 Recommendation).[16]

A. The 1980 Recommendation: Economic and Social Rights of Artists and their Free Expression as One Objective

The 1980 Recommendation is considered the first global document to address specifically artistic freedom.[17] It makes references to the freedom of artistic expression and creativity in its preamble as well as in its guiding principles, and encourages governments to 'help create and sustain not only a climate encouraging freedom of artistic expression but also the material conditions facilitating the release of this creative talent'.[18]

The recommendation's approach is thus global, and comprises both freedom of artistic expression and the working conditions of artists.[19] This is a major feature because the connections between these two aspects are rarely covered. In legal practice, labour and intellectual property lawyers and scholars generally write on issues related to the economic and social status of artists (ie author's rights, social protection, tax and income, right to collective bargaining, etc), while human rights scholars take on the aspects of freedom of expression and access to culture. This is also reflected in civil society, where trade unions have taken on the aspects of economic and social rights, while human rights organisations concentrate on censorship of the arts and freedom of expression.[20]

[16] Wyatt and Reitov, 'Arts' (2019) 14.

[17] ibid.

[18] Recommendation concerning the Status of the Artist (adopted 27 October 1980) UNESCO Doc 21 C/Resolutions. Its Preamble reads: 'Recognizing that the arts in their fullest and broadest definition are and should be an integral part of life and that it is necessary and appropriate for governments to help create and sustain not only a climate encouraging freedom of artistic expression but also the material conditions facilitating the release of this creative talent' and 'Considering further that this recognition of their status as persons actively engaged in cultural work should in no way compromise their freedom of creativity, expression and communication but should, on the contrary, confirm their dignity and integrity'.

[19] UNESCO, *Culture & Working Conditions for Artists: Implementing the 1980 Recommendation concerning the Status of the Artist* (Paris, UNESCO Publishing, 2019).

[20] See, eg civil society contributors to the design of the 2014 survey on the 1980 Recommendation: Arterial Network; International Affiliation of Writers Guilds; International Authors Forum; International Federation of Actors (FIA); International Federation of Musicians (FIM); International Music Council (IMC); International Theatre Institute; PEN International; UNI Global Union, MEI Division (Media, Entertainment and Arts).

Despite its non-binding nature,[21] the 1980 Recommendation is used as a reference by states and by international organisations such as the International Labour Organization, and is considered a main standard-setting document.[22] Within UNESCO, it remained dormant for a period of almost 20 years, and was reactivated through the implementation of the CDC, which revitalised it.[23] The first consultation on the Recommendation took place in 1983, a few years after its adoption. The next consultations took place in 2011,[24] 2015[25] and 2019,[26] in connection with the CDC confirming this renewed interest from parties.

Contrary to the Recommendation, artistic freedom does not appear in the texts of the CDC, or in the UDCD that preceded it in 2001. This reflects the fact that the issue was not visible at the time of drafting of the Convention. However, both documents make reference to fundamental freedoms and highlight support for artists as one of the measures that can effectively contribute to the protection and promotion of cultural diversity.[27] Article 5 UDCD is entitled 'Cultural rights as an enabling environment for cultural diversity' and makes direct reference to Article 27 of the Universal Declaration of Human Rights[28] and Articles 13 and 15 ICESCR. It therefore suggests an approach based on cultural rights. This specific reference to cultural rights was lost in the CDC. What happened between the two texts? How did the focus on cultural rights disappear? We find explanations by referring to the preliminary documents.

[21] According to UNESCO, a Recommendation is intended to encourage states to adopt a particular approach or to act in a given manner in a specific cultural sphere. In principle, a Recommendation does not create a legally binding obligation on member states. See UNESCO, 'General Introduction to the Standard-Setting Instruments of UNESCO' portal.unesco.org/en/ev.php-URL_ID=23772&URL_DO=DO_TOPIC&URL_SECTION=201.html.

[22] M Gruber, 'Challenges and Opportunities for Decent Work in the Culture and Media Sectors' (14 January 2019) International Labour Organization Working Paper 324, www.ilo.org/wcmsp5/groups/public/---ed_dialogue/---sector/documents/publication/wcms_661953.pdf.

[23] UNESCO, 'Revitalising the UNESCO Recommendation concerning the Status of the Artist: Survey of Non-Governmental Organizations and Other Civil Society Organizations' (October 2014) igkultur.at/sites/default/files/news/downloads/2017-04-19/ONG_StatusArtist_survey.pdf; UNESCO, 'Implementation of Standard-Setting Instruments: Part I – General Monitoring' (7 August 2015) UNESCO Doc 197 EX/20 Part I, para 25; UNESCO, 'Implementation of Standard-Setting Instruments: Part III – Application of the 1980 Recommendation concerning the Status of the Artist' (4 August 2015) UNESCO Doc 197 EX/20 Part III.

[24] UNESCO, 'Consolidated Report on the Implementation by member states of the 1980 Recommendation concerning the Status of the Artist' (21 October 2011) UNESCO Doc 36 C/57.

[25] The consultations were based on surveys sent out to UNESCO member states on how they implemented the Recommendation. UNESCO, 'Revitalising the UNESCO Recommendation' (October 2014); UNESCO, 'Implementation … Part I' (7 August 2015); and UNESCO, 'Implementation … Part III' (4 August 2015).

[26] See UNESCO, *Culture & Working Conditions* (2019). The study is based on a quadrennial global survey conducted in 2018 on the impact of the 1980 Recommendation concerning the Status of the Artist. Over 90 responses from UNESCO member states and non-governmental organisations were received.

[27] On the importance within the general human rights network of cultural rights for the promotion and preservation of cultural diversity, see Y Donders, 'Do Cultural Diversity and Human Rights Make a Good Match?' (2010) 61(199) *International Social Science Journal* 15, 32.

[28] (adopted 10 December 1948) UN Doc 217 A (III).

B. The Road to the CDC: An Instrument on Cultural Diversity, Not on Cultural Rights

On the road to the CDC, the four options for the elaboration of a new instrument were the following:

- a new comprehensive instrument on cultural rights;
- an instrument on the status of the artist;
- a new Protocol to the Florence Agreement, which would govern the circulation of cultural goods and services; or
- a new instrument on the protection of the diversity of cultural contents and artistic expressions.[29]

The last option was chosen.[30] The Convention was not meant to be a prospective international human rights instrument.[31] Its ambition was to respond rapidly to a political debate between trade and culture, and to recognise the distinctive nature of cultural goods, services and activities as vehicles of identity, values and meaning.[32] Consequently, the CDC is not an instrument establishing individual or collective rights, but is one seeking to guide state action. It contains some obligations, but mostly hortatory of exhortatory language of relative normativity.[33]

The explanation provided for disregarding the Convention as an instrument of cultural rights is the following:

> As regards cultural rights, they are not, any more than is cultural pluralism, the subject of a specific international instrument, and are not so extensively promoted as other

[29] UNESCO, 'Preliminary Study on the Technical and Legal Aspects Relating to the Desirability of a Standard-Setting Instrument on Cultural Diversity' (12 March 2003) UNESCO Doc 166 EX/28.

[30] UNESCO, 'Preliminary Draft Convention on the Protection of the Diversity of Cultural Contents and Artistic Expressions' (July 2004) UNESCO Doc CLT/CPD/2004/CONF.201/1, para 5.

[31] Y Donders, 'Cultural Rights in the Convention on the Diversity of Cultural Expressions: Included or Ignored?' in T Kono and S Van Uytsel (eds), *The UNESCO Convention on the Diversity of Cultural Expressions: A Tale of Fragmentation of International Law?* (Antwerp, Intersentia, 2012); Y Donders, 'Cultural Human Rights and the UNESCO Convention: More than Meets the Eye?' in C De Beukelaera, M Pyykkönen and JP Singh (eds), *Globalization, Culture and Development: The UNESCO Convention on Cultural Diversity* (Basingstoke, Palgrave Macmillan, 2015). On the human rights approach of the Convention, see also G Carbo Ribugent and B Barreiro Carril, 'Addressing the Challenge of Promoting the UNESCO Convention's Notions of Diversity of Cultural Expressions: Educating Young People through the UNESCO Diversity Kit' in V Guèvremont and D Saint-Pierre (eds), *Les 10 ans de la Convention sur la diversité des expressions culturelles (UNESCO 2005–2015): réflexions et témoignages* (Quebec, Teseo Press, 2020) www.teseopress.com/dixansconventionexpressionsculturelles.

[32] C Varin and V Guèvremont, 'La Convention sur la diversité des expressions culturelles quinze ans après: une mise en œuvre effective d'un instrument juridique faiblement contraignant' (2019) 32(2) *Revue Québécoise de droit international* 1; I Bernier, *La Convention sur la diversité des expressions culturelles de l'UNESCO: un instrument culturel au carrefour du droit et de la politique* (Quebec, Ministère de la Culture et des Communications, 2008).

[33] P Weil, 'Towards Relative Normativity in International Law?' (1983) 77 *American Journal of International Law* 413, 414.

> human rights. A fuller acknowledgement of the value of cultural diversity as a factor of human security will permit a more fully developed understanding of these rights, and in particular of their unity and indivisibility. Given the abundance of issues entailed by culture – issues that differ according to the approach adopted, whether anthropological or artistic – international law has yet to reach a clear-cut definition of cultural rights and their content.[34]

Hence, the rationale was that there was not enough advancement on the contents of cultural rights *and* that promoting cultural diversity would be a contribution to defining the contents of these rights. We can argue that the work carried out in implementing the Convention from a cultural rights perspective is thus fulfilling this objective.

C. Revitalising the 1980 Recommendation and Linking it to the Monitoring of the CDC

We have just seen that the CDC was not designed as a human rights instrument. However, Article 2(1) indicates that 'cultural diversity can be protected and promoted only if human rights and fundamental freedoms, such as freedom of expression, information and communication, as well as the ability of individuals to have access to diverse cultural expressions, are guaranteed'. Based on this article and through synergies with the monitoring of the 1980 Recommendation, advancing artistic freedom has gradually emerged as one of the areas of work and monitoring covered by the Convention.

As early as October 2014, the explanatory note to a survey entitled 'Revitalising the UNESCO Recommendation concerning the Status of the Artist' explained that the 'UNESCO Secretariat is pursuing synergies to monitor these two standard setting instruments on common issues related to the status of the artist'.[35] It listed freedom of artistic expression as one of the four contemporary issues that needed further examination.[36]

New resources and financial means were also allocated to develop work on both the status of the artist and artistic freedom. The

> 1980 Recommendation had suffered from the financial constraints (…), the Re-designed Aschberg Programme for Artists and Cultural Professionals provided the Secretariat with valuable means to improve synergies between the two normative instruments,

[34] UNESCO, 'Preliminary Study' (12 March 2003) para 13.

[35] UNESCO, 'Revitalising the UNESCO Recommendation' (October 2014).

[36] 4 CP, 'Diversity of Cultural Expressions, Draft Detailed Summary Record' (9 January 2015) para 211. The delegation of Denmark noted the UN report on the right to freedom of artistic expression and creativity and suggested that issues related to artists become a thematic focus for future periodic reporting exercises.

> both in their monitoring and in the technical assistance provided to member states to translate their provisions into national policies and legal frameworks.[37]

The support provided by the redesigned Aschberg Programme made it possible to highlight cultural policies and measures to protect and promote artistic freedom as a factor for assessing the implementation of the 1980 Recommendation. It has also allowed the adoption of incitative tools for parties, such as training on the status of the artist, which includes elements on artistic freedom and encourages implementation in the areas covered by the Convention.

III. Contribution to the Definition of Artistic Freedom as a Cultural Right

UNESCO was the only UN agency to send a submission for the consultation on the right to artistic freedom called by the UN Special Rapporteur as a first step to drafting her 2013 report. This input reads:

> What is particularly notable from the UNESCO's standpoint is that governments seek support, guidelines and capacity building in order to identify, develop and implement the essential actions that will strengthen their policies and actions. This creates opportunities to inform and advance the right to artistic freedom.[38]

In its submission, UNESCO presents both the 1980 Recommendation and the CDC. It insists 'on the points of convergence with the 1980 Recommendation' and 'generally with the right to artistic freedom', and quotes three articles as relevant to the work on artistic freedom: Article 2(1), Article 6, concerning the right of parties at the national level to take measures aimed at supporting artists, and Article 7, on the measures to promote cultural expressions and recognition of the important contribution of artists and other cultural workers in nurturing the diversity of cultural expressions.[39] Both instruments are examined by the Special Rapporteur in a specific section of her report.[40] In turn, the Special Rapporteur's report and subsequent work on artistic freedom have also contributed to the approach and operational definition of artistic freedom taken by UNESCO.

[37] 13 IGC, 'Item 9 of the Provisional Agenda: Synergies with the 1980 Recommendation concerning the Status of the Artist' (14 January 2020) UNESCO Doc DCE/20/13.IGC/9. Initially dedicated to promoting the training of artists by awarding scholarships for the study of artists-in-residence, the Aschberg Programme, funded through the interests of a building given to UNESCO by Sweden, was redesigned in 2017 to support creative cities as well as the implementation of UNESCO's two normative instruments addressing artistic creativity: the CDC and the 1980 Recommendation.

[38] UNESCO, 'UNESCO's Input to the Consultation on the Right to Artistic Freedom, OHCHR Experts Meeting and Consultation Geneva, 4–6 December 2012', 1, www.ohchr.org/sites/default/files/Documents/Issues/CulturalRights/ConsultationArtistic/UNESCO.pdf.

[39] ibid 3.

[40] 2013 Special Rapporteur Report, paras 17–24.

The UN report on artistic freedom refers to Article 27 of the Universal Declaration on Human rights,[41] Article 15.3 of the International Covenant on Economic, Social and Cultural Rights (ICESC), on the 'indispensable freedom to create', and Article 19 of the International Covenant on Civil and Political Rights (ICCPR), on freedom of expression as the core instruments for the protection of artistic freedom in international law.[42] This framework is of great importance and allows a larger definition of artistic freedom. However, human rights organisations do not necessarily have the connections with the artistic and cultural organisations or the human and financial means to research and follow up cases. The monitoring of the violations of artistic freedom remains low.[43] The Special Rapporteur has made repeated calls to establish a coalition of civil society organisations working on cultural rights as a means to better inform artists, practitioners and organisations of these rights.[44] An important step has been the recognition of artists and cultural workers as cultural rights defenders, an effort to allow them to enjoy the same protection for defending cultural rights that other defenders enjoy for defending civil and political rights.[45]

There are practical implications in recognising artists as cultural rights defenders and artistic freedom as a cultural right, as this opens new avenues for protection and strategic litigation. An organisation that considers artistic freedom in its two dimensions of civil and political rights and economic, social and cultural rights (the right to create, the right to enjoy the arts, the right to participate, etc) will report violations under Article 15 ICESC as well as Article 19 ICCPR. The first

[41] Art 27: '(1) Everyone has the right freely to participate in the cultural life of the community, to enjoy the arts and to share in scientific advancement and its benefits. (2) Everyone has the right to the protection of the moral and material interests resulting from any scientific, literary or artistic production of which he is the author.'

[42] A more recent research report by the Special Rapporteur on the promotion and protection of the freedom of opinion and expression further defines the legal framework for artistic freedom of expression and includes participation in cultural life as one of the components of this right. Human Rights Council, 'Research Report' (24 July 2020) para 5. This illustrates the trend to have a larger definition of artistic freedom of which freedom of expression is an important part. It further explores the dual approach of freedom of expression as the right to seek/receive and impart (see para 8), and puts it in relation with the work of the Special Rapporteur in the field of cultural rights.

[43] L Cuny, *Rights: International, Regional and National Legal Frameworks for the Protection of Artistic Freedom* (Hildesheim, Foundation University of Hildesheim, 2019).

[44] Human Rights Council, 'Cultural Rights: Tenth Anniversary Report, Report of the Special Rapporteur in the Field of Cultural Rights' (17 January 2019) UN Doc A/HRC/40/53, para 45: 'The Special Rapporteur hopes to see the creation of a civil society coalition for cultural rights at the United Nations, modelled on similar coalitions around, inter alia, freedom of religion or belief. Such a coalition could help spread awareness among artists, cultural practitioners, scientists and relevant organisations about how to work within the system. It is time for more actors in the cultural rights sphere to recognize the relevance of the United Nations human rights system for their work and for the United Nations human rights system to pay greater attention to cultural rights'.

[45] Human Rights Council, 'Cultural Rights Defenders: Report of the Special Rapporteur in the Field of Cultural Rights' (20 January 2020) UN Doc A/HRC/43/50; see also L Cuny, 'Cultural Rights Defenders: Strengthening Protections for Artists and Creatives' (5 October 2021) *Georgetown Journal of International Affairs*, gjia.georgetown.edu/2021/10/05/cultural-rights-defenders-strengthening-protections-for-artists-and-creatives.

approach has been predominant to date, and there has been an underreporting of artistic freedom as a cultural right.[46] This situation is changing as justiciability of cultural rights is increasing in particular in the Latin American system. Recent interventions have condemned the harassment of artists, journalists and human rights defenders as a violation of freedom of expression and artistic creation.[47]

In this context, it is important to highlight that the operational definition of artistic freedom as developed in the monitoring tools on the CDC is not limited to freedom of expression. Accordingly, the following rights are protected:

- the right to create without censorship or intimidation
- the right to have artistic work supported, distributed, remunerated
- the right to freedom of movement
- the right to freedom of association
- the right to protection of social and economic rights
- the right to participate in cultural life.[48]

The definition makes reference to cultural rights through the right to participate in cultural life. As has been interpreted by the Committee on Economic, Social and Cultural Rights, this is the right for *everyone* that may be exercised by a person (i) as an individual, ii) in association with others or (iii) within a community or group.[49] The reference to cultural rights that was not included in the Convention appears in the operational definition of artistic freedom. Civil society actors use this definition in their work to promote and protect artistic freedom.[50] It is interesting to note that recent domestic legislation adopted in France to protect artistic

[46] The Committee on Economic, Social and Cultural Rights that monitors implementation of the International Covenant seldom receives information on artistic freedom. However, experience shows that when it does so, it is prompt to adopt recommendations. This therefore appears as a line of action that could be developed by civil society organisations preparing their reports. Committee on Economic, Social and Cultural Rights, 'Concluding Observations on the Second Periodic Report of Lebanon' (24 October 2016) UN Doc E/C.12/LBN/CO/2, paras 66 and 67 on freedom for creative activity.

[47] Inter-American Commission on Human Rights, 'IACHR and Offices of Special Rapporteurs Condemn Harassment of Artists, Journalists, and Activists in Cuba and Call on State to Cease Acts of Persecution Against Those Exercising the Right to Freedom of Expression and Artistic Creation' (13 May 2021) www.oas.org/en/IACHR/jsForm/?File=/en/iachr/media_center/PReleases/2021/119.asp.

[48] UNESCO, 'Artistic Freedom' (Paris, UNESCO, 2019) en.unesco.org/creativity/sites/creativity/files/artistic_freedom_pdf_web.pdf. Artistic freedom is the freedom to imagine, create and distribute diverse cultural expressions free of governmental censorship, political interference or the pressures of non-state actors. It includes the right of all citizens to have access to these works and is essential for the wellbeing of societies.

[49] Committee on Economic, Social and Cultural Rights, 'General Comment No 21' (21 December 2009).

[50] Freemuse, 'Security, Creativity, Tolerance and Their Co-existence: The New European Agenda on Freedom of Artistic Expression' (27 January 2020). Culture Action Europe (CAE), in cooperation with Freemuse, organised the conference 'Listen to the Silenced: The State of Artistic Freedom in Europe' at the European Parliament. A UNESCO representative was invited to give the final talk (4 September 2020).

freedom refers to the Convention.[51] The French legislator interprets the CDC as being a cultural rights instrument. Loi n° 2016-925 is also of particular relevance as it has been highlighted by UNESCO as a model because 'For the first time in international law, it establishes artistic expressions as public goods' and aims to 'ensure greater public access to artistic works'.[52] The law amends the penal code to the effect that those impeding access to an artwork can be prosecuted.[53] This is a very interesting approach because it focuses not only on the individual right of the artist, but also on the right of the audience to access the arts (right to participate in cultural life and right to cultural diversity).[54] That is, the individual has the right to receive an artistic expression without it being censored.[55]

Through its monitoring of the Convention, UNESCO is providing space for discussions on artistic freedom and its new developments, including in the digital environment.[56] This space is most needed as academic research on artistic freedom is still limited.[57] It is only natural that the first commentators and reference books on the Convention did not mention artistic freedom.[58] As we have seen, artistic freedom is not included in the text, nor was it under discussion by the international community at the time of its drafting. The combination of the work of the Special Rapporteur and its consideration as an emerging trend in the monitoring of the Convention have been key in bringing a cultural rights' perspective to the definition of artistic freedom, an outcome that was not to be expected at the time of its adoption and shapes parties' obligations.

[51] Loi n° 2016-925 du 7 juillet 2016 relative à la liberté de la création, à l'architecture et au patrimoine, Journal officiel de la République française n° 0158, 8 July 2016, Art 3: respecting cultural rights as included in the UNESCO Convention on the Protection and Promotion of the Diversity of Cultural Expressions of 20 October 2005 (translation by the author).

[52] UNESCO, 'Artistic Freedom' (2019).

[53] Loi n° 2016-925.

[54] On cultural rights as collective rights, see the important contributions in A Jakubowski (ed), *Cultural Rights as Collective Rights: An International Law Perspective* (Boston, Brill, 2016). The definition given by the Special Rapporteur is the following: 'Cultural rights protect the rights for each person, individually and in community with others as well as groups of people to develop and express their humanity, world vision, means assigned to life and understanding of development', Human Rights Council, 'Report of the Independent Expert in the Field of Cultural Rights, Ms. Farida Shaheed, Submitted Pursuant to Resolution 10/23 of the Human Rights Council' (22 March 2010) UN Doc A/HRC/14/36, para 9.

[55] M Hufner, 'Justice' (Hildesheim, Foundation University of Hildesheim, 2019) 12.

[56] The *Operational Guidelines on the Implementation of the Convention in the Digital Environment* approved by the Conference of Parties in June 2017 include a reference to artistic freedom in para 8.9: 'This includes promoting artistic freedom as a corollary to freedom of expression, the social and economic rights of authors and artists working in the digital environment and the connectivity of all partners with partners of their choice.'

[57] For recent debates on this, see, eg Jornadas 'Libertad, arte y censura', organised by Fundación Gabeiras in 2020; Culture Action Europe, 'Freedom of Artistic Expression in the European Union: An Overview of the Relevant Normative and Jurisprudential Framework' (2021) www.greens-efa.eu/files/assets/docs/cae__freedom_of_artistic_expression_in_the_european_union_en.pdf.

[58] S Von Schorlemer and P-T Stoll (eds), *The UNESCO Convention on the Protection and Promotion of the Diversity of Cultural Expressions: Explanatory Notes* (Cham, Springer, 2012); H Ruiz-Fabri (ed), *La Convention de l'UNESCO sur la protection et la promotion de la diversité des expressions culturelles: premier bilan et défis juridiques* (Paris, Société de législation comparée, 2010).

IV. Contribution to Informing and Advancing the Right to Artistic Freedom

In the last years, attention to artistic freedom has grown, with a multiplication of organisations working in the area.[59] However, monitoring artistic freedom still remains limited. Few organisations document and defend artistic freedom as compared to those defending media and political freedom.[60] An encouraging feature is that increasingly organisations in the arts and cultural sector are developing work in this area.[61]

In this situation of underreporting and lack of visibility, UNESCO has played a major role in maintaining artistic freedom on the agenda. Starting in 2015, its contribution has included education and raising awareness (ie appointing a UNESCO ambassador for artistic freedom, providing spaces for discussions on artistic freedom such as during World Press Freedom Day and Create 2030 debates, releasing the video *What Is Artistic Freedom to You?*, issuing a brochure on artistic freedom and producing a training module for parties), as well as specific monitoring tools (including artistic freedom in the CDC monitoring framework, including a chapter on artistic freedom in the three global monitoring reports,[62] issuing a special report on artistic freedom[63] and developing an online platform for monitoring that includes information on artistic freedom). This, in turn, is shaping the way parties address artistic freedom in all environments.[64]

A. Parties' Obligations to Report under the CDC: The Inclusion of Artistic Freedom as an Area of Reporting

As part of their obligations under the CDC, parties have to submit a Quadrennial Periodic Report on the measures they have taken to implement the Convention.[65]

[59] Originally only a handful of organisations worked on artistic freedom at international level, among them Pen International, Freemuse, Article 19, Index on Censorship and FreeDimensional. In the last years, other organisations have developed work in this area, such as Artists at Risk Connection, Safe Havens Conference, SafeMuse and Siyah Bant.

[60] UNESCO, *Re|shaping Policies for Creativity: Addressing Culture as a Global Public Good* (Paris, UNESCO, 2022) 270 (Global Report 2022).

[61] ibid 274; L Cuny, *Relocating Artists at Risk in Latin America* (Stuttgart, Ifa, 2021) 24.

[62] UNESCO, *Re|shaping Cultural Policies: Global Report* (Paris, UNESCO, 2015) (Global Report 2015); UNESCO, *Re|shaping Cultural Policies: Global Report* (Paris, UNESCO, 2018) (Global Report 2018); Global Report 2022.

[63] L Cuny, *Freedom & Creativity: Defending Art, Defending Diversity*, special edn (Paris, UNESCO, 2020).

[64] UNESCO, 'Artistic Freedom' (2019).

[65] 'Article 9 – Information sharing and transparency. Parties shall: (a) provide appropriate information in their reports to UNESCO every four years on measures taken to protect and promote the diversity of cultural expressions within their territory and at the international level.' In conformity with this article, up to the end of 2020, 248 reports had been submitted, and 20 are expected for 2021.

Figure 10.1 UNESCO Diversity of Cultural Expressions, monitoring framework, https://en.unesco.org/creativity/convention/monitoring-framework

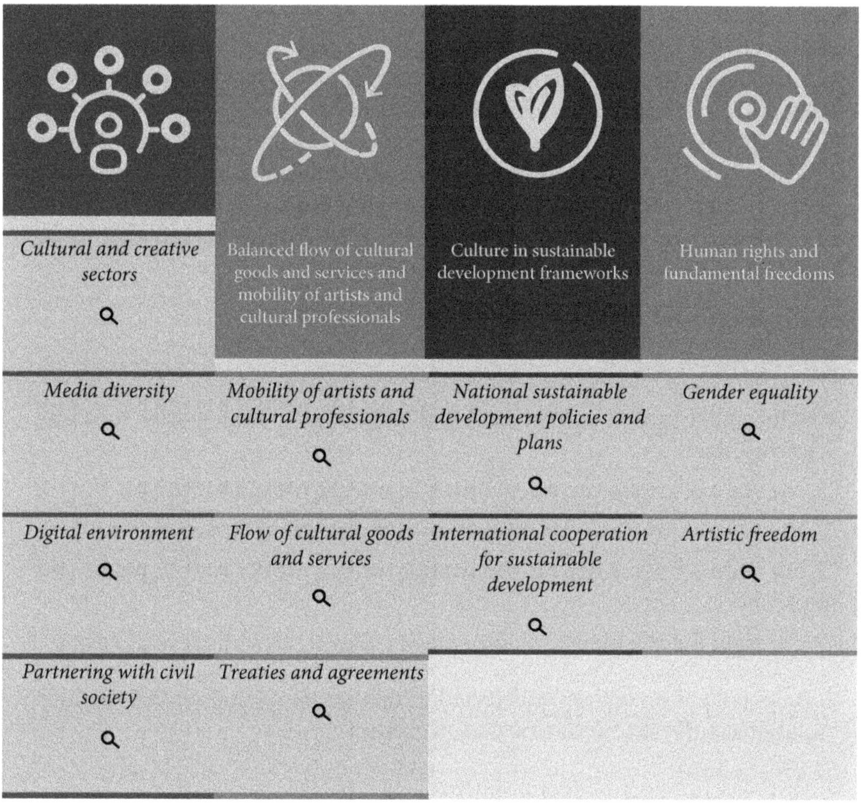

The framework featured in Figure 10.1 has been used since 2015. The inclusion of artistic freedom as a specific area of monitoring represented an important qualitative step. It meant that the Global Report on the Monitoring of the Convention, which is the main publicly available tool to follow progress on the Convention, would include a specific chapter on artistic freedom.[66]

This publication, issued in 2015, 2018 and 2022 in English, French and Spanish, has become a reference for academics and international experts working on artistic freedom. It is based on the information provided by parties in their Quadrennial Periodic Reports as well as other sources, including civil society reports.[67]

[66] HK Anheier, 'Towards a Monitoring Framework' in Global Report 2015, 31; O Reitov, *Challenges of Artistic Freedom* (Paris, UNESCO, 2015) 189.

[67] Global Report 2022, 295. Describes its methodology as based on 96 quadrennial periodic reports submitted by 94 parties to the Convention between July 2017 and November 2020 and enriched by primary and secondary data.

A further major step was taken in June 2019 with the approval by the Conference of Parties to the CDC of a new framework for periodic reporting that is fully aligned with the Convention's monitoring framework.[68] As a consequence, 151 parties to the Convention are now required to report on artistic freedom every four years. Before this turning point, although parties to the Convention may have occasionally reported on policies and measures to promote artistic freedom, they were not required to answer specific questions in this area. This resulted in a loss of information as most countries failed to include information even when they had implemented interesting policies and initiatives.[69] Parties to the Convention now report on legislation and policies adopted on artistic freedom, and they do so to comply with their obligations under the Convention.[70]

KEY QUESTIONS

1. The constitution and/or national regulatory frameworks formally acknowledge:

❒ The right of artists to create without censorship or intimidation

❒ The right of artists to disseminate and/or perform their artistic works

❒ The right for all citizens to freely enjoy artistic works both in public and in private

❒ The right for all citizens to take part in cultural life without restrictions

2. Independent bodies are established to receive complaints and/or monitor violations and restrictions to artistic freedom:

❒ YES ❒ NO

3. Initiatives to protect artists at risk or in exile have been developed or supported by public authorities during the last 4 years (eg providing safe houses, guidance and training):

❒ YES ❒ NO

[68] A comparison between the 2011 Operational Guidelines on Article 9 of the Convention 'Information Sharing and Transparency' approved by the Conference of Parties during its third session and the revised version approved by the Conference of Parties in 2019 at its seventh session will serve to illustrate the evolution. In 2011, there was no reference to human rights or fundamental freedoms.

[69] Global Report 2022, 213. This edition of the Global Report series draws its analysis from 96 quadrennial periodic reports (QPRs) submitted by 94 parties to the CDC between July 2017 and November 2020, ibid 270.

[70] The section on artistic freedom reads as follows: 'Parties shall report on policies and measures adopted and implemented to promote and protect artistic freedom of artists and their audiences. Parties shall thus highlight actions taken to protect and promote: the right to create without censorship or intimidation; the right to have artistic activities supported, distributed and remunerated; the right to freedom of association; the right to the protection of artists' social and economic rights; and the right to participate in cultural life.'

4. Measures and initiatives intended to ensure transparent decision-making on government funding/state grants and awards for artists exist (eg through independent committees):

❑ YES ❑ NO

5. Social protection measures that take the professional status of artists into account have been adopted or revised in the last 4 years (eg health insurance, retirement schemes, unemployment benefits): ❑ YES ❑ NO

6. Economic measures that take the status of artists into account have been adopted or revised in the last 4 years (eg collective agreements, income tax and other regulatory frameworks):

❑ YES ❑ NO

Source: L Cuny, *Freedom & Creativity: Defending Art, Defending Diversity*, special edn (Paris, UNESCO, 2020) 39.

B. The New Reporting Format and its Impact on the Development of Artistic Freedom

From a law-making perspective, it is very interesting to examine how the CDC is generating compliance with a rule, in this case artistic freedom, in various steps: an interpretation of the Convention to include artistic freedom based on Article 2.1; the inclusion of artistic freedom as an area of monitoring with the adoption of the Global Monitoring Framework in 2015 as a new emerging trend (recall that the UN Special Rapporteur's report on artistic freedom was adopted in 2013 and direct reference is made to it); and revised operational guidelines that include a reporting obligation on artistic freedom.

The importance of the reporting form deserves some attention as an element of soft law-making. As indicated above, in the past, even when states had taken measures and policies on artistic freedom, they did not systematically include them in their reporting. This highlights the importance of the format for reporting and its influence in the feeling that states 'should comply' with an obligation.

In the 2015 Global Report, Reitov notes that from 2012 to 2014, 13 parties made specific reference to the freedom of artistic expression in their Quadrennial Periodic Reports.[71] In an article published the same year, Donders analysed 65 reports submitted in 2013 and 2014. She notes that 'most of them follow the reporting format as provided by the Secretariat, some are in different formats and forms'.[72]

[71] Global Report 2015, 195.
[72] Donders, 'Cultural Human Rights' (2015).

She searched the terms 'human right', 'cultural right' and 'freedom', and found that freedom of creative and artistic expression was mentioned in the reports of the Dominican Republic, the European Union, Germany, Montenegro, Peru, Serbia, Sweden and the UK.[73] In the 2018 Global Report, Wyatt notes that only 13 out of the 62 Quadriennal Periodic Reports submitted between 2016 and 2017 made a specific reference to artistic freedom.[74]

An analysis of the 76 reports submitted in the new reporting format adopted in 2019 and available online as of 1 January 2021 shows that only one party did not follow the reporting format.[75] Only three parties following the reporting format do not provide any information under the section on artistic freedom.[76] This demonstrates that, for all other parties, it is acceptable to report under this section. A vast majority of countries, 61 out of 75, indicate that artistic freedom is part of their constitutional framework. However, only a few countries provide detailed information on relevant and applicable laws.

The introduction of the reporting format has greatly increased the data available on artistic freedom. For instance, more than half of the parties (41 out of 75) indicate they have an independent body monitoring artistic freedom. This raw data requires further research to elucidate what parties refer to as an independent body as none of them provide details on these bodies. A definition of such independent bodies would be an interesting contribution as at present there is no indication of UNESCO's expectations.[77] Civil society organisations could provide useful information on these bodies and their functioning.

The Global Report issued in February 2022 confirms these findings. The chapter on artistic freedom is based on data provided between 2018 and 2020 and 'marks the first time that Parties have been asked specific questions on the implementation of measures related to artistic freedom'.[78] Wyatt notes several challenges, 'most notably that the term (artistic freedom) has not yet gained a common understanding among countries, including the 151 Parties to the Convention'.[79]

She further notes that

> [w]hile 20 per cent of the 114 measures reported under artistic freedom relate to the social or economic protection of artists, followed by 14 per cent of measures relating

[73] Global Report 2015, Table 8.1. Overview of references to human rights in state reports, ibid 127.

[74] Global Report 2018, 212.

[75] 'Following the adoption by the 7th Conference of Parties of the CDC in June 2019 of the revised Operational Guidelines on Article 9 "Information Sharing and Transparency", a new online form for periodic reporting has been developed. If your Quadrennial Periodic Report (QPR) is due in 2020 (check your submission deadline here), please note that you need to use the new online form for submission', en.unesco.org/creativity/governance/periodic-reports.

[76] Bangladesh, Comoros and Ethiopia.

[77] eg Albania has provided the answer YES to the question on the existence of an independent body to receive complaints and/or monitor violations and restrictions to artistic freedom, but it does not provide details of this body concerning creation, structure, mandate whether it is a public or private body, etc.

[78] Global Report 2022, 266.

[79] ibid.

to the protection of intellectual property, 25 per cent refer either to programmes that encourage cultural participation of disadvantaged groups or to arts training programmes in early schooling to awaken cultural sensitivity, which do not rightly fit under the notion of artistic freedom.[80]

This finding indicates that the level of appropriation of the vocabulary by the responding parties remains low. Parties seem to have accepted the obligation to report on artistic freedom, but with different understandings of *what* artistic freedom is. This could reflect the evolving status of artistic freedom in international law and a lack of consistency in approaches and terminology.

Another interesting recent evolution that illustrates the impact of the Convention monitoring framework is the document containing the Revised Draft Guidelines on the Use of the Resources of the International Fund for Cultural Diversity.[81] These Guidelines align the terminology of the Fund with the terminology of the monitoring framework to the effect that project descriptions have to be supported by a justification of how the project contributes to achieving one or more of the expected outcomes listed on the Convention's monitoring framework.[82]

C. Advancing Artistic Freedom Through State Compliance

As we have seen, artistic freedom cannot be considered a new rule. It is derived from international human rights instruments, as the UN Special Rapporteur noted in her 2013 report. What is new is the attention it has received in recent years and the subsequent debates on the nature and contents of this right, including its emergence as an autonomous right. For some authors, artistic freedom has acquired a special status within freedom of expression, like the right to information or the right to data protection.[83] Others examine its autonomy in relation to cultural rights[84] and identify a constitutional trend to guarantee artistic freedom with academic freedom separately from freedom of expression. Article 13 of the Charter of Fundamental Rights of the European Union[85] or the debates on the new Chilean Constitution[86] are examples of this. An approach encompassing freedom

[80] ibid.

[81] 15 IGC, 'Item 7 of the Provisional Agenda: Revised Draft Guidelines on the Use of the Resources of the International Fund for Cultural Diversity' (11 January 2022) UNESCO Doc DCE/22/15.IGC/7.

[82] ibid Annex, s 15.3.

[83] L Diez Bueso, *Los límites de la creación artística en Estados Unidos y Europa* (Valencia, Tirant lo Blanch, 2017) 73.

[84] Gabeiras y Asociados, 'Bases para una reflexión sobre la libertad de la expresión artística y sus límites' (1 March 2019) gabeirasyasociados.com/bases-para-una-reflexion-sobre-la-libertad-de-la-expresion-artistica-y-sus-limites.

[85] Charter of Fundamental Rights of the European Union [2007] C 303/1.

[86] Debate 'Y ahora qué? Los derechos culturales en el escenario constituyente' (27–28 October 2021) es.unesco.org/news/unesco-coorganiza-seminario-derechos-culturales-nueva-constitucion-chilena.

of expression *and* economic and social rights seems to be the interpretation that UNESCO's Convention Secretariat has been promoting in the last years.

We have seen how parties to the Convention have accepted artistic freedom as part of their reporting obligations. Through this reporting, compliance with the rule is reinforced.[87] In identifying the factors that can affect compliance, Shelton's analysis can guide us when she explains that:

> soft law can be used to fill the gaps in hard law instruments or supplement a hard law instrument with new norms … Our hypothesis is that soft law adopted pursuant to a widely-accepted hard law agreement will reflect greater commitment and therefore produce better compliance than a new norm in soft law form chosen because there was no agreement on a hard law text.[88]

Shelton's analysis puts the emphasis on capacity as a factor of compliance. 'Capacity may thus be crucial to achieving compliance with positive obligations.'[89] She goes on to say that in the cases where capacity is an issue compliance may be improved by increasing opportunities to engage in the desirable behaviour.

This is exactly the strategy chosen in the implementation of the Convention. As we saw above, the Convention is an instrument that aims at guiding state action. The Secretariat is providing parties with specialised expertise to draft legislation; to collect and analyse data; to engage in inter-ministerial cooperation; and to facilitate public debates on artistic freedom.[90] In doing so, it is increasing the capacities of parties to achieve compliance.

In this context, the Global Reports perfectly illustrate this role of positive social control mechanisms. They are used to praise governments for the policies they have adopted and inspire others through examples of good practice. There is no direct disapproval or 'naming and shaming'. One could argue that the Global Report is exactly the opposite. It refers directly to the statistics on violations developed by Freemuse,[91] but instead of looking at states as perpetrators of violations, it aims at guiding them to be promoters and defenders of artistic freedom. The role of other actors is also highlighted. UNESCO's special edition on artistic freedom contains a graph representing the ecosystem of actors involved in protecting artistic freedom.[92] Among them, judges and lawyers are particularly relevant for

[87] M Hirsch, *Invitation to the Sociology of International Law* (Oxford, Oxford University Press, 2015). The developments on deviance and conformity with international law in ch 6 are particularly relevant for this chapter.

[88] D Shelton (ed), *Commitment and Compliance: The Role of Non-Binding Norms in the International Legal System* (Oxford, Oxford University Press, 2000) 14.

[89] ibid 15.

[90] The countries involved are Algeria, Bangladesh, Burkina Faso, Columbia, Ethiopia, Indonesia, Jamaica, Mali, Mauritius, Mongolia, Palestine, Peru, Senegal, Uganda, Tanzania and Zimbabwe.

[91] This organisation publishes an annual State of Artistic Freedom Report that compiles cases of violation by country and by category and provides analysis. In 2014 it recorded 237 attacks, 430 in 2016 and 711 in 2019, freemuse.org/news/the-state-of-artistic-freedom-2020.

[92] Cuny, *Freedom & Creativity* (2020) 18.

their contribution to case law, which, in turn, can inform strategic litigation on artistic freedom.[93]

To summarise using some of the categories developed by Shelton, we can see how Global Reports help to: 'crystallize a trend towards a particular norm, overriding the views of dissenters and persuading those who have little or no relevant state practice to acquiesce in the development of the norm'; 'precede and help form new customary international law'; and 'consolidate political opinion around the need for action on a new problem, fostering consensus that may lead to treaty negotiations or further soft law'.[94]

V. Conclusion

Since 2015 and the launching of its first Global Report on the monitoring of the CDC, different actors look to UNESCO as a source of information and standard setting on artistic freedom. Currently, its 151 parties are required to include information on artistic freedom in their Quadrennial Periodic Reports. This situation could not have been anticipated at the time of the adoption of the Convention. As we have seen, the CDC is not conceived as a human rights instrument. Artistic freedom is not mentioned in the CDC or in its drafting process. Work on artistic freedom is based on the general principles of the Convention and a revitalisation of the 1980 Recommendation on the Status of the Artist. UNESCO's definition of artistic freedom is in line with the approach developed by the successive UN Special Rapporteurs in the Field of Cultural Rights. It goes beyond the protection of freedom of expression to include economic, cultural and social rights. It is a way to value the contribution that artistic and cultural creators make to the diversity of world views.[95] It is a way to grant protection to cultural defenders when they become at risk, as well as the rights of the audience – all of us – to access artworks and expressions.[96] We have seen how putting artistic freedom on the agenda of UNESCO has contributed to the production of knowledge and a feeling of commitment by states. However, evidence from the analysis of the Quadrennial Periodic Reports shows that although parties comply with the obligation to report on artistic freedom, their understanding of this right seems to vary. There has been an increase in the data collected with the reporting obligation, but this data points to a lack of a common understanding of artistic freedom. It remains to be seen

[93] For an example of lawyers providing pro bono support to teams litigating on artistic freedom, see avantgardelawyers.org/fr/hp_roboto-francais/.

[94] DL Shelton, 'Soft Law' (2008) 7, scholarship.law.gwu.edu/cgi/viewcontent.cgi?article=2048&context=faculty_publications.

[95] Human Rights Council, 'Report of the Special Rapporteur in the Field of Cultural Rights: Promotion and Protection of All Human Rights, Civil, Political, Economic, Social and Cultural Rights, Including the Right to Development' (4 January 2018) UN Doc A/HRC/37/55.

[96] Human Rights Council, 'Cultural Rights Defenders' (20 January 2020).

whether this approach will translate in national laws and courts, ie through the adoption of new legislation or through case law that recognises artistic freedom as an autonomous right or as a cultural right and refers to the Convention.

In this endeavour, all the actors involved have a role to play. The Quadrennial Periodic Reports, with the information on artistic freedom, and the Global Reports analysing them are publicly available material and can be used by scholars, lawyers, governments and civil society organisations. At a time when artistic freedom is under attack in many countries, it can be opportune to adopt a cultural rights approach. In some instances, arguing for cultural rights and the promotion of a diversity of expressions, which is the ultimate objective of the CDC, can be an effective means to protect artistic freedom and complementary to freedom of expression.

11

Cultural Diversity, Intercultural Dialogue and Social Inclusion of Museums. The Case Study of the Interkulturelt Museum in Oslo City, Norway

MÓNICA RIAZA DE LOS MOZOS*

I. Introduction

The migration of human populations is a phenomenon that has occurred throughout history and in all parts of the globe for a variety of reasons. However, in recent decades, globalisation has compressed space and time on an unprecedented scale, and the increase in people's mobility has created radical new cultural juxtapositions, encounters, exchanges and mixes. These characteristics have led to intense cultural diversification and important cross-cultural developments that have evolved into a major concern for established national mechanisms and their cultural policies.[1]

Museums are a clear testimony to the social relations that have taken place throughout history, including the relations and interactions between groups of different origins, which, at a certain moment, coincided in the same space and the same time period. Migrations are reflected in the tangible and intangible heritage of all societies and, consequently, in cultural assets contained within museums.

However, the functions that museums perform today go beyond the obvious tasks of conservation and exhibition. Art is no longer the property of a privileged few, but instead has become part of life for anyone who feels that they are not merely a passive spectator, but a fully active and participating protagonist in their own history. Far from being obsolete points of view that are inadequate in today's

* The author wishes to acknowledge the assistance provided by Andrzej Jakubowski in preparing the final version of this chapter.

[1] K Robins, *The Challenge of Transcultural Diversities* (Strasbourg, Council of Europe, 2006) 19.

globalised and multicultural world, the museums of the twenty-first century orient themselves towards an open, dialogic, interdisciplinary, universalist and inclusive approach. The reason for this position is that the main priority of museums is not the collections but the people who, as the protagonists of their own history and their own culture, are the ones who are called upon to reproduce them and, above all, to reinterpret and transform them.

More and more, museums are positioning themselves as the dynamos of society: open to dialogue with different social movements, and actors of social change and critical awareness. Museums are places of inspiration, education and dialogue, and can become true centres of intercultural reference, as well as playing an essential role in social cohesion and the solidifying of collective references.

This fundamental transformation responds not only to the demands of society, but also to the needs of the museums themselves, since their spaces must maintain relevance and be universally perceived as welcoming places. Museums are committed to their capacity for inclusion, in which there should be no barriers of any kind and where no social, ideological or racial boundaries are imposed on culture.[2] Therefore, museums are called upon to cherish and promote cultural diversity as an essential aspect of society, in which one must take into account such important values as dialogue and acceptance of others on the grounds of pluralism, difference, competition and creativity.

If the main purpose of museums is to serve the people, then they must focus their attention on society. They must be places where new ideas can be explored, where stereotypes can be challenged and where the complexity of cultural diversity can be revealed. Working with immigrants and minority communities to facilitate a more harmonious and just style of integration addresses an issue of great social concern. Achieving interculturality is a process which, with every project and every action, can help to transform not only our societies, but also our museums and the nature of public culture. It is vitally important to serve these new audiences not only as cultural consumers, but also as cultural producers: participants in the process, decision-makers and protagonists in the creation and dissemination of a new kind of museum discourse and practice.[3] Therefore, museums must support projects that directly involve citizens in decision-making in order to create properly open, free and democratic spaces that favour the development of interculturality as part of the process of building a society capable of committing to a common project.[4] Such roles of museums would mean recognising that all people

[2] A Galla, 'El museo inclusivo' (2013–14) 9–10 *Museos.es: Revista de la Subdirección General de Museos Estatales* 40.

[3] C Kreps, 'Foreword' in S Bodo, K Gibbs and M Sani (eds), *Museums as Places for Intercultural Dialogue: Selected Practices from Europe* (Dublin, MAP for ID Group, 2009) 4–5.

[4] See, eg E Manikowska and A Jakubowski, 'On Defining the Participatory Museum: The Case of the Museum of the Second World War in Gdansk' (2021) 9(4) *Muzeológia a kultúrne dedičstvo* 41, 45–53.

have the same dignity and the same rights, that no form of exclusion is acceptable and that all human groups, regardless of their origins, characteristics and possibilities, must be integrated.[5]

Museums have to take on the challenge of establishing a pedagogy of inclusion, in which a sense of belonging is not linked to a particular cultural identity, but is open to the idea that a person might belong to many identities. Museums have the power to deploy narratives and suggest inferences that allow them to act as a platform for reflection on systems of knowledge, beliefs, values and attitudes. The museum's installations, its exhibition spaces and the surrounding urban or natural environment are resources that can be employed to develop new strategies of social dialogue. Museum institutions must respond to new patterns of knowledge production and transmission, as well as to new social configurations within local contexts,[6] where tensions and frictions produced within and across national borders may be evident. Undoubtedly, their spaces can become neutral areas where differences and mutual difficulties of understanding, usually experienced as limitations and sources of conflict, become something valuable.[7] Thus, their work should be geared towards creating museographic expressions and pedagogical programmes that are well suited to contribute to minimising conflicts by means of the discourse of interculturality and the revitalisation of cultural identities. It is therefore important – as the former UNESCO's Assistant Director-General for Culture, Françoise Rivière points out – to recognise, analyse and study cultural diversity and intercultural dialogue as a means of overcoming the differences and tensions that exist in multicultural societies.[8]

Such a broad understanding of museums' new roles and participatory functions also lies in the core of the ongoing debate on the new definition of the museum launched by the International Council of Museums (ICOM) in 2017. This alternative definition was selected by ICOM's executive board and was initially scheduled for a vote on whether to be included in the ICOM Statutes at the 2019

[5] H McGhie, 'Museums and Human Rights: Human Rights as a Basis for Public Service' (UK, Curating Tomorrow, 2020).

[6] Many museums are located in urban areas, and focus their attention on the multicultural character of their respective communities. In this regard, Amareswar Galla, researcher and director of the International Institute for the Inclusive Museum, advised in 1995 that the city museum could 'provide an opportunity to organise critical and intellectual exchanges between all participants representing the various cultural communities of the urban landscape, thus facilitating the exploration of diversity and the vitality of expression and awareness of each other's heritage'. See A Galla, 'Urban Museology: An Ideology for Reconciliation' (1995) 47(3) *Museum International* 40.

[7] E Delgado, 'Museums as Spaces of Negotiation' in Bodo et al, *Museums as Places for Intercultural Dialogue* (2009) 8–9.

[8] UNESCO, *Investing in Cultural Diversity and Intercultural Dialogue: UNESCO World Report* (Paris, UNESCO, 2009) VII.

Extraordinary General Assembly of ICOM in Kyoto.[9] It provides that: 'Museums are democratising, inclusive and polyphonic spaces for critical dialogue about the pasts and the futures.' Moreover, they

> safeguard diverse memories for future generations and guarantee equal rights and equal access to heritage for all people … They are participatory and transparent, and work in active partnership with and for diverse communities to collect, preserve, research, interpret, exhibit, and enhance understandings of the world, aiming to contribute to human dignity and social justice, global equality and planetary wellbeing.

While this proposal has been largely criticised from various grounds and the vote on it was postponed until the ICOM General Assembly in 2022, its scope nevertheless reflects an array of important changes in museum practices worldwide. The definition adopted in August 2022 is:

> A museum is a not-for-profit, permanent institution in the service of society that researches, collects, conserves, interprets and exhibits tangible and intangible heritage. Open to the public, accessible and inclusive, museums foster diversity and sustainability. They operate and communicate ethically, professionally and with the participation of communities, offering varied experiences for education, enjoyment, reflection and knowledge sharing.[10]

In light of the aforementioned developments, this chapter offers an investigation into the role of museums in the face of cultural diversity, interculturality and social inclusion in a globalised context. In particular, it focuses on analysing two standard-setting instruments adopted within UNESCO – the Convention on the Protection and Promotion of the Diversity of Cultural Expressions (CDC, or the Convention)[11] and the Recommendation Concerning the Protection and Promotion of Museums and Collections, their Diversity and their Role in Society (2015 Recommendation)[12] – in order to understand how these international instruments are linked to the profound transformations that the museum sector has witnessed in recent decades. Furthermore, the chapter focuses on the study of the cultural policies of museums in Norway and the case of the Interkulturelt Museum in the city of Oslo as examples of good practices of implementation in the promotion of cultural diversity and mutual understanding between communities in contemporary multicultural societies.

[9] ICOM announces the alternative museum definition that will be subject to a vote, available at icom.museum/en/news/icom-announces-the-alternative-museum-definition-that-will-be-subject-to-a-vote.

[10] ICOM, Museum Definition, https://icom.museum/en/resources/standards-guidelines/museum-definition/.

[11] (adopted 20 October 2005, entered into force 18 March 2007) 2440 UNTS 311.

[12] (adopted 17 November 2015) UNESCO Doc CLT/HER/MHM/2015/PI/H/1.

II. Strengthening Cultural Diversity and Intercultural Dialogue in Museums: The Interplay between the CDC and the 2015 Recommendation

Nowadays, one can observe a trend within the international museum community towards democratising their spaces and making them more accessible to a wider public, as well as being more socially relevant and more responsive to the changing needs and interests of their users. This trend is undoubtedly supported by international organisations. Since the beginning of the twenty-first century, UNESCO's commitment to promoting cultural diversity, intercultural dialogue, culturally sustainable development and also improving the connection – in the broadest sense of the word – between culture, human rights and democracy has been clearly stated in various legal documents. The adoption of the UNESCO's Universal Declaration on Cultural Diversity (2001)[13] represented a real milestone in that it enshrined cultural diversity as a common heritage of mankind. It not only seeks to promote cultural pluralism, reaffirm the universal nature of cultural rights and strengthen the link between cultural diversity and development, but also implicates cultural policy in the protection of diversity and announces the desirability of creating a standard-setting instrument to assist with this issue (Article 12(c)). The adoption of the treaty law instrument in 2005 – the CDC – makes it possible to define new methods and new opportunities for the protection and promotion of cultural diversity. It also gives greater visibility to previously overlooked aspects of cultural development, and makes it possible to focus attention on the profound connections between culture, the economy and social well-being, in addition to clearly demonstrating the importance of culture in all aspects of development and its influence on the general climate of society. The CDC has great potential to mobilise law- and policy-makers in the search for innovative solutions to major social problems related to issues of identity and diversity, and also calls for the establishment of a new system of government which would support the introduction or development of policies and measures that directly affect the creation, production, distribution and access to a range of cultural expressions, including cultural goods, services and activities.

The CDC constitutes the latest addition in a line of previous conventions and other international law instruments, adopted within UNESCO since its creation in 1945, which affect museums despite the fact that they contain hardly any explicit direct references to them.[14] These former instruments were not drafted specifically

[13] (adopted 2 November 2001) UNESCO Doc CLT.2002/WS/9.

[14] The 1954 Convention for the Protection of Cultural Property in the Event of Armed Conflict (Hague Convention) and its two protocols of 1954 and 1999 may be applied universally. The conventions that contain explicit references to museums are as follows: the Convention on the Protection of the Underwater Cultural Heritage (2001) – a brief allusion to museums in Rule 10 (Annex) as contributing institutions in scientific projects related to underwater cultural heritage; the Convention on the

for museums, but rather to respond to specific needs that directly or indirectly impact these institutions, especially needs related to illicit trafficking and heritage preservation. Even so, the CDC has turned out to be a fundamental tool for understanding the role of the museum in contemporary society, since it names the museum as one of the most effective institutions for guaranteeing the protection and promotion of cultural diversity through its collections and, increasingly, the development of society or civilisation, whose role encompasses the study, preservation and enhancement of the diverse aspects of society through its tangible and intangible testimonies.[15] The concept of cultural diversity, which is at the heart of the CDC, encourages the consideration of various aspects of the phenomenon of museums (whether or not they are managed by the state[16]) and their many activities as they develop throughout the world.

The first example that reflects the relationship between the CDC and museums is contained in Article 4 of the CDC. This provision contains definitions for the purposes of the Convention and, consequently, for its scope of application. Over the course of this article's evolution during the treaty-making process, the first draft prepared for the first meeting of intergovernmental experts included two non-exhaustive annexed lists: the first providing examples of goods and services, the second representing cultural policies.[17] The list of goods and services refers to the following list in its cultural heritage category: 'antiquities, collectors' items, museum services, archiving services (documents, recordings of intangible cultural heritages, etc.), conservation services for historic sites and monuments, services related to the safeguarding and transmission of rituals, narratives, folktales, etc.'. A footnote explains that, although certain cultural goods and services on the list are already covered by other UNESCO standard-setting instruments, 'such goods and services may be of interest to this Convention to the extent that derivative products such as films, CD-ROMs, books, catalogs, etc. are put into circulation'. In other words, cultural goods eligible for protection and promotion under other Conventions, such as the World Heritage Convention (1972)[18] and the Convention

Means of Prohibiting and Preventing the Illicit Import, Export and Transfer of Ownership of Cultural Property (1970) – a mention of museums in the considerations section and in Arts 5 and 7, in relation to the role of museums in the prevention of illicit trafficking and the need for them to acquire their collections in compliance with the ethical principles stated by the convention itself. Meanwhile, the Conventions without explicit references to museums are as follows: the CDC; Convention for the Safeguarding of the Intangible Cultural Heritage (2003); Convention Concerning the Protection of World Cultural and Natural Heritage (1972).

[15] F Mairesse, 'Preliminary Study on the Opportunity, Scope, Rationale and Added Value of a Standard-Setting Instrument for the Protection and Promotion of Museums and Collections (Museum Aspects)' (Paris, UNESCO, 2012) 41–42.

[16] The implementation of the Convention can be attributed to the efforts of other actors, as well as states. The text devotes Art 11 to the participation of civil society and Art 15 to methods of collaboration with the private sector and non-profit organisations.

[17] 'Preliminary Draft of a Convention on the Protection of the Diversity of Cultural and Artistic Expressions' (July 2004) UNESCO Doc CLT/CPD/2004/CONF-201/2.

[18] (adopted 14 November 1970, entered into force 24 April 1972) 823 UNTS 231.

for the Safeguarding of Intangible Cultural Heritage (ICH Convention),[19] would fall within the scope of those treaties, while products derived from these goods would fall within the scope of the CDC. On the other hand, in its category on promoting pluralism, cultural and linguistic diversity in and for the information society, the list of cultural policies refers to 'policies to digitise archives, museums and libraries and facilitate access to this content'. Finally, the intergovernmental meetings agreed to delete both annexes from the outset, arguing that keeping both lists would have meant changing the possible interpretation of the scope of application of the Convention, particularly in relation to the practical guidance that would be developed around Articles 7 and 8 (focused on protection and promotion) and 9 (dedicated to information and transparency measures).[20] This was an unfortunate decision, according to researchers Beatriz Barreiro Carril and Honorio Velasco, since the absence of both annexes makes it difficult to delimit the scope of application of the CDC.[21]

When one refers to the terms 'protection' and 'promotion', these are invariably connected to museums. In this respect, the CDC stands out for using these terms in a broader sense in comparison with previous similar instruments: the Convention for the Protection of Cultural Property in the Event of Armed Conflict (1954)[22] essentially covers traditional security measures aimed at preventing damage in the event of armed conflict; the World Heritage Convention generally evokes all the structures that should be implemented to ensure the development of this heritage, but these concepts relate first and foremost to immovable heritage; and the ICH Convention also addresses the actions of protection and promotion; however, the use of the term 'safeguarding' implies a much stronger association with the concept of protection than with that of promotion.[23] In contrast to this, Article 4 of the CDC explicitly includes the term 'protection', stating that it refers to 'the adoption of measures aimed at the preservation, safeguarding and enrichment of the diversity of cultural expressions', while Article 7 expresses the obligation of states to promote cultural diversity in order to give individuals better access to a diverse cultural experience through which they can freely and creatively express their cultural diversity. In other words, the provision focuses its content on those subjects that generate, carry and propagate cultural diversity, and on the different methods and activities through which they creatively express their cultural diversity (taking into account their particular conditions), as well as the role of artists as cultural catalysts and promoters, cultural communities, organisations and all

[19] (adopted 7 October 2003, entered into force 20 April 2006) 2368 UNTS 3.

[20] N Obuljen, 'Article 4. Definitions' in S von Schorlemer and P-T Stoll (eds), *The UNESCO Convention on the Protection and Promotion of the Diversity of Cultural Expressions* (Berlin, Springer, 2012).

[21] B Barreiro and H Velasco, 'Artículo 4. Definiciones' in J Prieto de Pedro and H Velasco (eds), *La diversidad cultural: análisis sistemático e interdisciplinar de la Convención de la UNESCO* (Madrid, Editorial Trotta, 2016).

[22] (adopted 14 May 1954, entered into force 7 August 1956) 249 UNTS 240.

[23] In this respect, see JAR Nafziger, 'Article 1: Purposes of the Convention' in J Blake and L Lixinski (eds), *The 2003 UNESCO Intangible Heritage Convention* (Oxford, Oxford University Press, 2020) 42–43.

other subjects involved in the processes of creation, support and enhancement of cultural diversity. Thus, and based on the content of both articles, researcher Françoise Mairesse considers that the definition of the two terms in relation to museums can be formulated by alluding to the fact that 'protection' represents the adoption of measures aimed at the conservation, safeguarding and enhancement of heritage and museum collections, while 'promotion' represents creation, dissemination and access to museums.[24]

With regard to one of the most important functions of museums – communication (exhibitions, interpretational and educational activities related to mediation and social inclusion, plus publications) – Article 10 of the CDC ratifies the commitment to education and raising public consciousness of the value of diversity of cultural expressions and the importance of their protection and promotion. Researcher Gemma Carbó underscores the relevance of placing the content of this article at the heart of the Convention's text as a whole, thus highlighting the key role of education in such an important treaty and drawing attention to its strategic role in human and sustainable development.[25]

In order to guide the implementation of Article 10, UNESCO notes the need for parties to encourage 'a strengthening of the links between culture and education at the policy, programme and institutional levels'[26] by adopting an integrated approach to educational programmes so that they might foster the promotion of the objectives and principles of the treaty (point 3). It also encourages states to devote resources to developing different types of outreach tools suitable for the variety and characteristics of existing audiences, with the support and collaboration of artists and culture professionals (point 7); and it advises them to 'support the holding of events' that contribute to raising awareness and the wider dissemination of the diversity of cultural expressions, including cultural exhibitions, in partnership and collaboration with public and private actors, organisations and networks of civil society (point 8).

Therefore, the relationship between museums and the content and implementation of Article 10 of the CDC is clear. Although the logic of museums as a communication system is mainly based on economic objectives, nevertheless, and as stated in the introduction of this chapter, in recent decades some institutions have developed a more profuse communicative logic based on the social role of the museum, with educational objectives, interaction with the visitor and a strengthened participatory approach.[27] In this sense, the museum is a vital actor in

[24] Mairesse, 'Preliminary Study' (2012) 10.

[25] G Carbó, 'Artículo 10. Educación y sensibilización del público' in Prieto de Pedro and Velasco, *La diversidad cultural* (2016).

[26] UNESCO, 'Textos fundamentales de la Convención de 2005 sobre la Protección y la Promoción de la Diversidad de las Expresiones Culturales' (Paris, UNESCO, 2015) 52.

[27] See Network of European Museum Organisations (NEMO), *Museums and Social Responsibility: Values Revisited* (Berlin, Deutscher Museumsbund eV, 2020); K Brown and F Mairesse, 'The Definition of the Museum through Its Social Role' (2018) 61 *Curator. The Museum Journal* 525; N Simon, *The Participatory Museum* (Santa Cruz, Museum 2.0, 2010).

education and raising awareness of diversity, and consequently in the development of cultural and artistic skills, as well as social and civic skills.

In the cultural and artistic fields, the work of museums allows us to understand and assess our aesthetic tastes and our expressive capabilities, and consequently allows us to develop creativity, sensitivity, emotion and the ability to enjoy and transmit knowledge and sensations. Similarly, museums make it possible to learn about the aesthetic references, cultural and creative manifestations and practices of others, allowing us to appreciate the heritage of individuals and communities. All people and countries are extremely rich in cultural diversity and creative talent; teaching these skills involves critically assessing different cultural and artistic manifestations. Furthermore, in the social and civic spheres, museums facilitate knowledge about the ways of life and social organisation of other people's realities, and the universal framework of human rights as a guarantee for coexistence within the framework of democratic and global societies. On this basis, it is possible to delve deeper into the importance of understanding and relating the local context with the global in order to feel part of a local, global and interconnected citizenship.

Cultural and artistic skills, together with social and civic skills, are directly linked to intercultural dialogue and peace-building, both essential prerequisites for the protection of the diversity of cultural expressions. Undoubtedly, interculturality (Article 4.8) stimulates dialogue and understanding between cultures with mutual recognition and respect, making way for the possibility of creating shared cultural expressions, a key concept in the Convention to further underpin cooperation in and for development.[28]

All museums, whether newly opened or long-established, public or private, large or small, must deal with two factors that are essential to their operations: the first relates to the human or professional factor, the second to funding. Both factors are increasingly affected by multiple changes at the global level.

Over the years, museum staff have witnessed gradual transformations as a result of the increase in technical exchanges, the development of professional training and various expert meetings. However, this factor shows significant differentiation between countries, manifesting itself unevenly, particularly in the area of recruitment and in the quality of work output, which impacts the overall development of museums. On the other hand, the economic dynamic of globalisation has also generated substantial changes in the financial sphere of museums, where one has seen international public funding, international philanthropy and the attraction of international tourism. The participation of museums in the tourism industry and in the economic development of the region where they are located (including the

[28] Barreiro and Velasco, 'Artículo 4. Definiciones' (2016) 155.

creative economy), with a global focus, stands out as an increasingly relevant and predominant aspect.[29]

With regard to the first factor, Article 16 of the CDC creates an obligation for developed countries to assist developing countries in terms of cultural professionals and agents. The article's text calls for innovative approaches to international cooperation in the professional field, supporting the mobility of cultural professionals from developing countries (I understand that this includes museum professionals) in order to bring about an increase in dynamic and balanced exchanges. In this regard, states parties will create the policies, measures and operational programmes required to strengthen the skills of these professionals by means of training, exchanges and incorporation activities (eg residencies), and thus help them to integrate into professional networks in developed countries.[30]

In relation to the funding aspect, the CDC addresses this issue (without explicit mention of museums) in Article 6 at the national level and in Article 18 at the international level, jointly addressing the need to provide the necessary financial means for the protection and promotion of cultural diversity. Article 6 plays an important role in the overall structure of the entire treaty, giving a solid significance to the sovereign right recognised in the previous provision through the list of actions for the protection and promotion of the diversity of cultural expressions, as well as facilitating the implementation of the provisions included in the two subsequent articles. Among the list of actions contained in Article 6(2)(d) are 'measures aimed at providing public financial assistance'. In this regard, Article 18 of the CDC is devoted to the regulation of the International Fund for Cultural Diversity. The main objective of the fund is to invest in projects that lead to structural changes through the introduction or development of policies and strategies that have a direct impact on the creation, production and distribution of a diverse range of cultural expressions, as well as access to these, including cultural goods, services and activities, while also promoting institutional infrastructures deemed necessary to maintain the viability of cultural industries at the local and regional levels.[31] Clearly, as Beatriz Barreiro Carril argues, the attitude of the states towards the fund is one of the factors that best reveals their real commitment to the CDC, given that lack of resources is one of the main problems facing cultural production in developing countries. This aspect is supported by paragraph 6 of Article 18, which clarifies that those contributions to the fund may not be subject to 'political,

[29] BS Frey and S Meier, 'The Economics of Museums' in VA Ginsburgh and D Throsby (eds), *Handbook of the Economics of Art and Culture*, vol I (Amsterdam, North Holland, 2006); International Council of Museums (ICOM) and Organización para la Cooperación y el Desarrollo Económicos (OCDE), *Cultura y desarrollo local: maximizar el impacto. Una guía para gobiernos locales, comunidades y museos* (Paris, OCDE/ICOM, 2019).

[30] B Barreiro Carril, *La diversidad cultural en el derecho internacional: la Convención de la UNESCO* (Madrid, Iustel Publicaciones, 2011) 277–78; UNESCO, 'Textos fundamentales' (2015) 70–75.

[31] L Albornoz, 'Artículo 18. Fondo Internacional de la Diversidad Cultural' in Prieto de Pedro and Velasco, *La diversidad cultural* (2016).

economic or other conditions that are incompatible with the objectives of this Convention'.[32]

Following the Universal Declaration on Cultural Diversity and the CDC, the Thirty-eighth General Conference of UNESCO approved the 2015 Recommendation, a new standard-setting instrument that triggered a decisive phase in the development and implementation of an innovative and open vision of museums in the twenty-first century. It represents the second instrument to be promulgated by UNESCO that is specifically dedicated to museum management.[33]

This instrument reflects the international community's unwavering commitment to helping museums to fulfil their roles in society, now and in the future, to promote sustainable development and intercultural dialogue, but also the desire to complement and expand the application of international standards and principles relating to the roles and responsibilities of museums worldwide, taking into account that the last instrument dedicated to the subject dates back to 1960.

The preparations for the 2015 Recommendation began in 2011, when Brazil sent a draft resolution related to the protection and promotion of museums and collections to the Thirty-sixth General Conference of UNESCO.[34] As a result, a year later, the city of Rio de Janeiro hosted the first expert meeting to discuss the topic in question, and two reports on the subject were commissioned: one on museums, written by Françoise Mairesse, and one on legal aspects, written by Patrick J O'Keefe. The results of the discussions that took place during the conference, and the information and the conclusions of the reports, favoured a draft recommendation as a new instrument for the protection and promotion of museums because, as O'Keefe explains, this option creates legal obligations for all UNESCO member states and allows them the flexibility to implement the instrument to the extent and in the format that is most appropriate for their specific circumstances, and the content 'can enter into considerably more professional detail; its revision is not subject to the same requirements as in the case of a convention and can thus more easily be updated to reflect new developments if necessary'.[35] In this context,

[32] Barreiro Carril, *La diversidad* (2011) 277.

[33] The first instrument dedicated to the preservation and management of museums was approved by UNESCO in 1960 under the title: Recommendation Concerning the Most Effective Means of Rendering Museums Accessible to Everyone. The document centres on education and public access to museums, with a special focus on students and workers. It calls upon museums to act as intellectual and cultural centres, and suggests several lines of action regarding the physical and intellectual accessibility of museums. In order to promote education in museum institutions, the text advises cooperation with schools and other educational organisations as well as the creation of educational departments within the internal structures. See UNESCO, 'Recommendation Concerning the Most Effective Means of Rendering Museums Accessible to Everyone' (Paris, UNESCO, 1960); A Azor, 'Medio siglo de museos en la UNESCO: las recomendaciones de 1960 y 2015' (2015–16) 11–12 *Museos.es: Revista de la Subdirección de Museos Estatales* 213.

[34] See F Mairesse, 'The UNESCO Recommendation on the Protection and Promotion of Museums and Collections, their Diversity and their Role in Society' in BL Murphy (ed), *Museums, Ethics, and Cultural Heritage* (Abingdon, Routledge, 2016) 95–97.

[35] PJ O'Keefe, 'Preliminary Study on the Advisability of Preparing an International Instrument for the Protection and Promotion of Museums and Collections (Legal and Technical Aspects)' (Paris, UNESCO, 2012) 55.

in 2013, the Thirty-seventh General Conference of UNESCO approved the proposal and the creation of a new standard-setting instrument on the protection and promotion of museums and collections, in the form of a recommendation.[36]

The drafting process of the first version of the document started quickly, thanks to the cooperative work between UNESCO and ICOM. After lengthy discussions to refine the text, the draft Recommendation was ready to be sent to the expert meeting that took place in May 2015. Among the debates that emerged, the most contentious aspects were the terms 'collections' and 'museum' in relation to the title of the Recommendation, as well as the content of the Recommendation itself. It is important to point out that the inclusion of collections in this standard-setting instrument implies special attention to those sets of cultural assets which, although they do not carry out all the functions of museums, are exposed to the public under museum characteristics, and are sometimes unprotected due to the absence of specific legislation. However, Ana Azor argues that the lack of consensus on meaning prevented a greater development of the concept in the document, leaving it up to each state to define the meaning and scope of the term according to their own respective legal systems.[37] For its part, the definition of a museum that was finally included in the text was the one offered by ICOM, as reflected in the Recommendation itself among its notes, which 'brings together, at the international level, the museum phenomenon in all its diversity and its transformations in time and space', as well as including the museum as a public or private non-profit organisation or institution. As a result of its achievements, ICOM's role as the representative of the global museum community was greatly consolidated by the draft Recommendation in three important ways: the organisation was part of the first instrument to be voted on by UNESCO that took a global vision of the role of museums in the world, together with their challenges; the final document accepted the definition of museum[38] as established by the organisation in 2007; and it incorporated the ICOM Code of Ethics into the Recommendation as key source material for good professional practice aimed at protecting and promoting museums.[39]

[36] For a review of the documents from the preparatory phase as well as the decisions and resolutions linked to the recommendation, see UNESCO, 'Recommendation concerning the Protection and Promotion of Museums and Collections' www.unesco.org/new/en/culture/themes/museums/recommendation-on-the-protection-and-promotion-of-museums-and-collections.

[37] Azor, 'Medio siglo' (2015–16) 225.

[38] The definition of a museum was updated in August 2022 at the ICOM Extraordinary General Assembly meeting, after a participatory process with its members involving four rounds of consultations, divided into 11 steps and lasting 18 months. The new definition is: 'A museum is a not-for-profit, permanent institution in the service of society that researches, collects, conserves, interprets and exhibits tangible and intangible heritage. Open to the public, accessible and inclusive, museums foster diversity and sustainability. They operate and communicate ethically, professionally and with the participation of communities, offering varied experiences for education, enjoyment, reflection and knowledge sharing.' see ICOM, 'Museum Definition', icom.museum/en/resources/standards-guidelines/museum-definition/.

[39] F Mairesse, 'Que resuene la voz de los museos: el proyecto de recomendación sobre la protección y la promoción de los museos y colecciones, su diversidad y su papel en la sociedad' (2015) 68(2) *Noticias del ICOM* 6.

Analysing the text of the 2015 Recommendation (Figure 11.1), one can see that it recalls the body of existing international instruments on the role of museums and collections approved by UNESCO (and other institutions)[40] and reaffirms, as did the 1960 Recommendation concerning the Most Effective Means of Rendering Museums Accessible to Everyone, the important role that museums can play in the achievement of UNESCO's aims in terms of emphasising the role of culture and education as key elements in intercultural dialogue, social cohesion and sustainable development (Preamble and Article 2). Its content outlines a framework of reference for museums and collections based on four groups. The first of these defines the concepts of museum, collection and heritage (Articles 4–6). The second confirms the essential functions of museums in the fields of heritage conservation (Articles 7 and 8), research (Article 9) and communication – especially in the field of education (Articles 10–12), highlighting the inventory of collections. The third mentions the challenges faced by museums in society: the influence of globalisation, which allows for greater mobility of collections, professionals, visitors and ideas (Article 13); the relationship between museums and the economy and the quality of life in the cities and regions in which they are located – urban or tourist development (Articles 14 and 15); the social role of museums and their importance for social cohesion, the construction of citizenship and reflection on collective identities (Articles 16–18); and the development of information and communication technologies (ICT), offering important development opportunities to museums as well as their users (Article 19). All of these challenges are linked to sustainable development and intercultural dialogue, and the promotion of the role of museums as creators, generators and communicators of culture and as spaces for reflection for communities. The fourth and last group is focused on the development of the role of states in, on the one hand, adopting measures to guarantee the protection and promotion of museums, assisting these institutions and developing them in accordance with their functions, as well as providing them with the human, physical and financial resources necessary for their proper functioning (Articles 20–23); and on the other hand, adopting functional policies related to museum functions, inventories, protection of non-museum collections, ethics, training, financing, ICT development, public outreach and the role of museums (Articles 24–35).[41]

[40] The list of international instruments directly or indirectly related to museums and collections is listed in detail in the notes of the Recommendation. The list includes eight conventions, including the CDC; the International Covenant on Economic, Social and Cultural Rights (adopted 16 December 1966, entered into force 3 January 1976) 993 UNTS 3); seven recommendations and five declarations, including the UNESCO Universal Declaration on Cultural Diversity (2001).

[41] UNESCO, 'Recomendación relativa a la protección y promoción de los museos y colecciones, su diversidad y su función en la sociedad' (Paris, UNESCO, 2015); Azor, 'Medio siglo' (2015–16) 221–27; F Mairesse, 'Report on the Implementation of the UNESCO 2015 Recommendation on Museums & Collections: Recommendation concerning the Protection and Promotion of Museums and Collections, Their Diversity and Their Role in Society' (Paris, UNESCO, 2019) 9–11.

Figure 11.1 UNESCO Recommendation, 2015

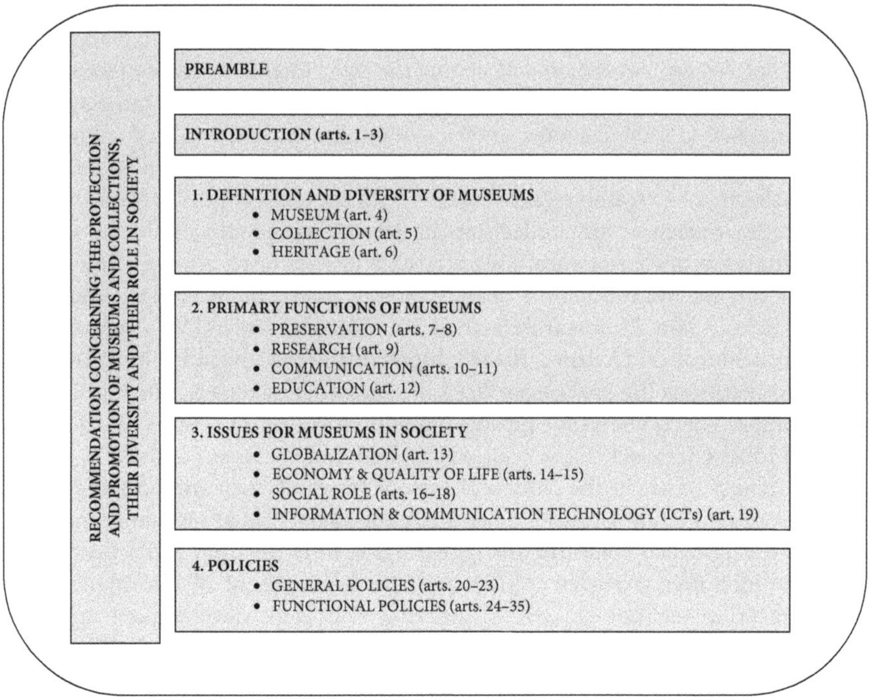

Source: prepared by the author.

Thus, the two most recent instruments developed by UNESCO – the CDC and the 2015 Recommendation – set out this international organisation's response to a new global configuration, with political and economic balances that radically transform the social, economic and cultural landscape. Both have generated important processes of renewal regarding the orientation of museums, promoting new procedures that reaffirm that museums are spaces open to the world and to dialogue. They also confirm how museums have the potential to strengthen the social fabric and act as meeting points and places of dialogue between different cultures.

III. Implementation of the CDC: Museum Policies in Norway and the Case of the Interkulturelt Museum

Information exchange and transparency are at the heart of the CDC. Article 9 of this treaty addresses the need for the adoption and implementation of cultural policies by states parties in order to foster compliance with and the development of the Convention. In other words, it reminds us of the role of the states, whose function does not cease with the ratification of the CDC; indeed, it actually begins from that moment, with the need and obligation to take measures that implement the precepts of the normative document, leaving ample margin for these to be adapted to the local and national contexts.[42] Accordingly, and in accordance with paragraph a) of this article, states must submit 'periodic reports' every four years on the policies and measures adopted and the challenges encountered in the implementation of the CDC. These reports are key for civil society to engage with government officials in assessing the progress made in the protection and promotion of the diversity of expressions and, at the same time, to learn in detail about the experiences and good practices promoted by the parties.[43]

At the time of writing, 150 countries have ratified the CDC and 248 reports have been submitted since 2012, with 2565 measures reported.[44] Although the information provided by each state party contains relevant qualitative and quantitative data, on this occasion and for the purposes of this chapter, I have opted for the data provided by Norway. Specifically, this chapter is based on the 2016 report on the country's museum policy and the measure titled The National Museum Network for Minorities and Cultural Diversity (Nasjonalt museumsnettverk for minoriteter og kulturelt mangfold),[45] which aims to coordinate and strengthen efforts to include minorities and enhance cultural diversity in museum exhibitions, collections, staff and audiences. The measure is both national and institutional, with financial resources allocated by Arts Council Norway (Kulturrådet),[46] the Norwegian Ministry of Culture and the City of Oslo.

Based on this measure, Norwegian museum policy will be analysed as a set of strategies and measures that can provide an important example of good practices that could inspire other countries, identifying priorities within the wide range of possibilities to be adopted in the CDC's context. Next, the case of the Interkulturelt Museum, a museum included in the National Museum Network for Minorities and Cultural Diversity, will be examined. It will shed light on different aspects and factors of museums that are focused on promoting respect and understanding

[42] C Merkel, 'Article 9. Information Sharing and Transparency' in von Schorlemer and Stoll, *The UNESCO Convention on the Protection and Promotion of the Diversity of Cultural Expressions* (2012).

[43] J Baltà, 'Evaluation of UNESCO's Standard-setting Work of the Culture Sector. Part IV – 2005 Convention on the Protection and Promotion of the Diversity of Cultural Expressions. Final Report', IO/EVS/PI/134 REV (Paris, UNESCO, 2014).

[44] See UNESCO, 'Periodic Reports' en.unesco.org/creativity/governance/periodic-reports.

[45] See UNESCO, 'Norway 2016 Report' en.unesco.org/creativity/governance/periodic-reports/2016/norway.

[46] Arts Council Norway is the main governmental actor for the implementation of Norwegian cultural policy, and an advisory body to the central government and the public sector in cultural matters. The institution, established in 1965, is fully funded by the Ministry of Culture. Although it is in charge of a broad spectrum of administrative tasks and activities, in the museum sector it is responsible for ensuring that museums function and develop in accordance with relevant policy, as approved by the Ministry of Culture. Its competencies include standards, sector statistics and industry skills, funding, as well as digital access to collections through open platforms.

of cultural diversity, processes of cultural change and the issues of majorities/minorities of the past and present. A museum is a space for intercultural dialogue involving as wide and diverse a range of people as possible with a remarkably creative and educational approach. Exploring this could be useful to help discover which aspects are most sensitive when imagining and designing future plans and programmes.

Researcher Katherine Goodnow argues that Scandinavian countries offer a special opportunity to investigate the ways in which one can deal with 'several forms of cultural diversity and to ask how they are inter-related: indigenous people, minority groups and recent immigrants'.[47] Scandinavia provides a unique base for exploring how forms of diversity are defined, how they come to have particular implications and how they come to be accepted or negotiated as representations. In this sense, and mainly over the last two decades, Norwegian museum policy has been concerned with these questions and how to consider and interrelate the diversity of cultures that exist within the territory.

The diversity perspective has been a central issue in different reports and studies on Norwegian cultural policy. The first steps were taken in the 1990s, responding to the political agenda for multiculturalism that was becoming established in Europe. Faced with a rapidly growing immigrant population, the government identified the challenge of cultural integration and the need to educate the Norwegian people about cultural diversity. As a result, it was decided to redefine the role of museums in order to create a more tolerant public sphere.[48] The report, titled 'Museum. Diversity, Memory, Meeting Place' ('Museum. Mangfald, minne, møtestad'), assessed Norwegian museums from a general perspective and highlighted their role as social institutions as well as their relationship with the protection of cultural and natural heritage. The text emphasised the need to make multicultural society a priority field of study in Norwegian museums, and to recognise their spaces as places that inspire respect and tolerance for cultural diversity.[49]

Multiculturalism continued to be a priority in the 1999–2000 museum reform. Conceived as a quality reform, its implementation defined the hallmark of the Norwegian museum landscape for the following years, at both the local and the national level, through processes of consolidation. The reform was based on the establishment of two network structures: professional networks on the one hand, and national museum networks on the other. While the latter was comprised of regionally consolidated museums, which strengthened museum administration, management and communication, the professional networks were intended

[47] K Goodnow and H Akman, *Scandinavian Museums and Cultural Diversity* (New York, Berghahn Books, 2008) IX.

[48] L Eilertsen, 'Norwegian Cultural Policy and its Effect on National Museums' in A Bugge and L Eilertsen (eds), *Museum Policies in Europe 1990–2010: Negotiating Professional and Political Utopia* (Linköping, Linköping University Press, 2012).

[49] Norges Offentlige Utredninger, *Museum: mangfald, minne, møtestad* (Oslo, Statens Trykning, 1996).

to stimulate cooperation and better distribute the workload between the museums that were responsible for certain exhibition themes or research disciplines which require specialised expertise, and to support their development as critical and self-critical social institutions. Both networks assumed responsibility for guaranteeing a professional context for museums, a sustainable economic situation and collaboration in the search for new knowledge, investments and common projects.[50] The reform was gradually implemented from 2002 onwards, with the aim of facilitating administrative processes and ensuring proper professional environments. During this process, in 2003, the government established the Norwegian Archives, Libraries and Museums Authority (ABM-utvikling) with the aim of monitoring the work carried out by the reform and facilitating cooperation between the different types of museums.[51] Its responsibilities were focused not only on coordinating the museums and their professional and administrative development, but also on the archives and libraries, thus taking a central role in the implementation of policy in all these sectors.[52]

The beginning of the twenty-first century was characterised by a heightened response to cultural diversity in Norwegian cultural and museum policy. The report 'Museum of the Future: Administration, Research, Dissemination, Renovation' ('Framtidas museums: forvaltning, forskning, formidling, fornying') stressed that the main purpose of museums was to reflect the society that they were part of, and for this reason they should play an active role in said society by demonstrating the diversity of perspectives and realities of national minorities and the country's newer minorities. Facilitating cultural diversity and, consequently, dialogue between cultures was seen as one of the most demanding tasks of the time, with the understanding that this represented the most suitable long-term solution to the challenges facing modern, multicultural society.[53]

In line with these parameters, Norway ratified two very significant UNESCO conventions within the first decade of the new century: the ICH Convention and the CDC. Both established common international platforms for the development and implementation of cultural policy measures, and constituted important reference points in the formulation of Norwegian cultural policy.

The Norwegian Parliament (Stortinget) consented to ratify the CDC based on the consideration that there was a need for a legally binding instrument at the global level, which would provide real opportunities for Member States to adopt and implement a cultural policy that would facilitate the diversity of cultural

[50] *Framtidas museums: forvaltning, forskning, formidling, fornying* (2008–2009 St.meld nr. 49).

[51] In 2010, the development of ABM was discontinued. This meant that the library-related tasks were transferred to the National Library, while the tasks for archives and museums were taken over by the Norwegian Cultural Council. In 2015, there was a further change and the tasks associated with the development of archives were transferred to the National Archives.

[52] *Kulturpolitikk fram mot 2014* (2002–2003 St.meld. nr. 48); Eilertsen, 'Norwegian Cultural Policy' (2012) 45–47; B Brenna, 'Museums and Museologies in Norway' (2018) 1 *Nordic Museology* 111.

[53] *Framtidas museums* (2008–2009 St.meld. nr. 49).

expressions. Moreover, it valued the fundamental vision of the CDC: that diversity, developed within a climate of democracy, tolerance, social justice and mutual respect between peoples, is an absolute necessity for peace and security at the local, national and international levels.[54]

The celebration of the Year of Diversity in 2008 was an expression of the idea that the cultural field was one of the areas that was most important in determining the conditions for full and proper participation in a multicultural society. The experience of this event demonstrated that museums could take up this challenge and were an important faction of the actors involved in the development of strategies and concrete measures. Ninety-four per cent of the museums in the country implemented specific measures related to cultural diversity, with topics focusing on raising awareness internally, skill exchanges, recruitment, getting to know the target audience and partnership building. Alongside these, the museums incorporated diverse perspectives when shaping their programmes – in many cases by means of collaboration with external actors – and led these institutions to reflect on their own profile and how they related to cultural diversity, both internally and externally.[55] As a result of the 1999–2000 reform and the creation of the networks, in 2006 the National Museum Network for Minorities and Cultural Diversity, also known as The Diversity Network (Mangfoldsnettverket), was established with the purpose of promoting work with minorities and cultural diversity within the Norwegian museum landscape, mainly by creating meeting places, exchanging experiences and developing projects. Since its inception, the Network has aimed to be a forum for exchanging knowledge and developing skills, as well as a reference point for inspiring multiculturalism in museums. As a strategy, it opts for the exchange of experiences and new knowledge, as well as expressing an interest and curiosity for the opportunities offered by diversity. This is why the museums that make up the Network broaden local understanding of how to deal with diversity and reflect on the figure of the inclusive museum, while at the same time actively working on issues related to exhibitions, existing collections, data collection and documentation projects, outreach to a wider audience and core museum tasks, among others.

The number of museums involved has varied depending on the location and theme of the active projects, but the Network's activity has not ceased since its creation, thanks above all to the work of its coordinating museum: the Oslo Museum (OM).[56] The OM is a foundation established in 2006 through the merger of three previously independent units: the Oslo City Museum (Bymuseet), the International Museum and Cultural Centre (now the Interkulturelt Museum) and the Theatre Museum (Teatermuseet). Subsequently, the Workers' Museum

[54] *Om samtykke til ratifikasjon av UNESCOs konvensjon av 20. oktober 2005 om å verne og fremme et mangfold av kulturuttrykk* (2005–2006 St.prp. nr. 76).

[55] *Framtidas museums* (2008–2009 St.meld. nr. 49); *2008 som markeringsår for kulturelt mangfold* (2005–2006 St.meld. nr. 17).

[56] *Framtidas museums* (2008–2009 St.meld. nr. 49).

(Arbeidermuseet) joined the group in 2011, and opened its doors to the public in 2013. Paragraph 2 of the OM's Statutes[57] states that its objective is to disseminate knowledge about the history and development of the city of Oslo, the living conditions of its inhabitants through the ages, Norway's multicultural society and immigration patterns, urban culture, the history of theatre and the performing arts. To achieve this purpose, the museum must engage in dialogue with and reflect the community that it is part of, promoting respect and understanding of cultural diversity, processes of cultural change and issues of majorities/minorities in the past and present. The museum is a centre of national competence within its areas, and collaborates with other museums and institutions at home and abroad.

Although the first two years of the Network's existence were focused on developing skills by means of seminars, workshops, debates and exchanges, one of the biggest challenges that it faced in its work on diversity was the recruitment of people with minority backgrounds in the field of culture. Thus, a three-year recruitment project called Diversity in Museums (Mangfold i museene) was initiated in the 2008 Year of Diversity.

The aim of the project was to increase minority participants' knowledge and skills in a range of museum tasks, in order to encourage the recruitment of people with minority backgrounds for professional work in museums. The starting point was the idea that Norwegian museums are strengthened through the participation of minorities, in terms of contact with user groups, and opportunities to see the institution from the outside and to gain skills and understanding in a globalised world. The project was not intended to be a labour policy for minorities, nor did it promise any kind of commitment or employment after the end of the project period, but it did strengthen an already existing interest in the participants and contributed to the mutual understanding of museum diversity work, both for the participating museums and for the individual people involved. The project ended in spring 2012, with 19 recruiters, 11 participating museums, 30 actors and 15 different minority backgrounds represented.[58]

The latest report issued by the government, *The Power of the Culture. Cultural Policy for the Future* (*Kulturens kraft. Kulturpolitik for framtida*), deals with diversity in more detail.[59] The report sets out the general cultural policy direction for arts and culture, establishes a number of priorities, presents new policy objectives for the sector, and includes instruments and measures at the state, county and municipal levels. In reference to the ratification of the two most recent UNESCO conventions – the CDC and the ICH Convention – the main message of the report

[57] See Oslo Museum, 'Årsmeldinger og vedtekter' www.oslomuseum.no/oslo-museum/arsmelding-vedtekter-plan/.

[58] H Einarsen and G Özcan, 'Rekruttering til mangfold i museene' in Kultur og kirkedepartamentet (ed), *Med forbehold om endringer: anbefalinger og rapport fra Mangfoldsåret 2008* (Oslo, Andrimme Forlag, 2009) 148–49; Oslo Museum, *Mangfold i museene: en rapport fra et rekrutteringsprosjekt* (Oslo, Oslo Museum, 2013).

[59] *Kulturens kraft – Kulturpolitikk for framtida* (2018–2019 Meld. St. 8).

is that art and culture are expressions with the power to build society, and that a rich and varied cultural life is a prerequisite for freedom of expression and a well-functioning democracy. It underlines the importance of encouraging participation in cultural activities, as these enable people to familiarise themselves with a range of opinions and different forms of expression. It is in this sense, therefore, that cultural life can promote tolerance and understanding of values, identity and society.

Along these lines, the document identifies museums as key actors in three regards. Museums will be part of the cultural spaces that support or create social cohesion. Their infrastructures will serve as inclusive meeting places that permit diversity and democratic participation. The cultural sector must foster encounters between people, creating the necessary conditions to facilitate experiences that create shared references and build strong communities (objective 5.7). Linked to this, museums will also guide people, foster critical thinking and learning, and strive for quality and knowledge in all cultural information and content. Access to and use of artistic and cultural expressions helps to manage different types of information and perceive contexts, while cultural activities provide education in civic participation which is a prerequisite for a viable democracy (objective 5.3). And museums will undoubtedly continue to be the institutions that enable cultural heritage to be collected and preserved, made available and disseminated. Museums play a particularly important role in documenting and maintaining the living intangible cultural heritage in which Norway's national minorities constitute a priority area (objective 5.4).

Within this framework, chapter 10 of the document ('Relevance and Representativeness in Cultural Life'/'Relevans og representativitet i kulturlivet') sets out Norwegian cultural policy priorities that specifically target intercultural diversity: (i) increasing representation in all areas and ensuring more diverse recruitment for the arts professions; (ii) supporting institutions and actors carrying out specific integration work that need support in implementing initiatives that increase cultural diversity and reach new audiences; (iii) earmarking funds and mobilising volunteers in the arts to stimulate greater cultural participation; and (iv) encouraging grant recipients to develop their own strategies to increase the relevance and representation of their programmes.

Following this brief analysis of Norwegian cultural policy focused on cultural diversity and the role of museums, one finds that the country's inclusive museum practice is under the auspices of The Diversity Network, with contributions coming from museums spread across the whole country. Each of them, together with their professional teams, is particularly valuable in the contribution of knowledge, experiences and reflections related to inclusivity work in museums or in the wider (local) community. Thus, this chapter seeks to contribute with a practical case study, which might serve as a reference to the wide range of potential museum practices and inclusion strategies in this field, with the aim of shedding light on some of its characteristics: that of the Interkulturelt Museum (IKM).

The idea of founding the IKM was formed and developed in the late 1980s by Bente G Møller, at a time when very few Norwegian institutions recognised the fact that the makeup of the country's population was changing. Møller's vision was to create a museum and cultural centre that could cater to Norway's more recent multicultural history and be a stage for art, traditions and other cultural expressions coming into the country through diverse groups of people. The aim, therefore, was to promote respect and understanding of cultural diversity. These objectives took shape and the institution became a reality in the early 1990s as the International Museum and Cultural Centre (Internasjonalt Kultursenter og Museum), dedicated to documenting, researching and disseminating material relating to the history of immigration and cultural change in Norwegian society, by holding exhibitions and conducting activities and seminars covering various perspectives on the history of immigration. From its first years of operation, the cultural diversity of the population was reflected not only in the content of the institution's activity, but also in the staff themselves.

Unlike most museums, the IKM did not start with a collection of objects or materials, but with a collection of ideas. The starting point for these ideas was based on the fact that people arriving in Norway did not bring much material baggage, but instead brought an important set of memories and intangible heritage. In this sense, intangible heritage can be defined as something that creates meaning, a link between the past and the present, and between the individual and the collective. In this way, and understanding that cultural heritage brings people together and plays a vital social role, it is also understood that the immigrant population brings with them a very significant immaterial cultural heritage (music, language, traditions, dance, among others) that participates in the creation of new cultural patterns in Norway.[60]

The IKM is situated in a historic building in the culturally diverse Groenlandia district of Oslo. Built between 1900 and 1902, the building was a police station until 1994, when the IKM moved into the premises. The museum maintained the original layout of the space, including the holding cells, and dedicated several areas to exhibitions related to the recent history of immigration and cultural changes, and in another area, created a contemporary art gallery (the IKM Gallery) reserved for modern artists with a focus on globalisation and multiculturalism.[61]

Now more than 30 years old, the history of the institution has been marked by a number of unique events. Among these, the year 2006 was a decisive period for three reasons, which had a major influence on the subsequent development of the institution. On the one hand, the IKM was named 'Museum of the Year' in

[60] B Møller and H Einarsen, 'As in a Mirror' in K Goodnow and H Akman, *Scandinavian Museums and Cultural Diversity* (New York, Berghahn Books, 2008); Eilertsen, 'Norwegian Cultural Policy' (2012) 51–53.

[61] H Einarsen, 'Fra politistasjon til kulturstasjon: Tøyenbekken 5 gjennom 104 år' (2006) *Fremtid for fortiden* 8–11.

Norway. The jury of the Norwegian Museum Association (Norges museumsforbund) argued that the institution was a shining example of how a museum can become a meeting place between cultures, a place for dialogue and reflection. They highlighted how, through its programme of exhibitions, projects and activities, the museum had made it possible for people from different cultural backgrounds to come together.[62] On the other hand, and as a result of the national museum reform, the Museum and International Cultural Centre merged with two other museums, the Oslo City Museum and the Theatre Museum, to form the Oslo Museum. It was from this point on, and in light of the newly created union, that the institution was renamed the Intercultural Museum (Interkulturelt Museum). Parallel to this change, the Norwegian Archives, Libraries and Museums Authority asked the OM, now the IKM, to be the museum in charge of coordinating The Diversity Network.[63]

Taking into account the vision, objective and general characteristics of the IKM, our analysis of the numerous activities carried out by the institution each year can be divided into three categories: exhibitions and artistic projects; education, activities and communication; and research and study. It is beyond the scope of this chapter to make an exhaustive analysis of all the work carried out within each of these; however, I will discuss them below by considering significant examples that allow one to garner a clear idea of each category.

A. Exhibitions and Artistic Projects

The first exhibitions developed by the IKM dealt with themes of coexistence, cultural diversity and how these related to the daily lives of schoolchildren. The purpose of these exhibitions was to relate art to the opening of new cognitive spaces other than those that can be opened up by theoretical knowledge. Thus, in 1994, the exhibition Similarities in the Difference studied initiation rites with a focus on minority youth in Norway and their rituals of transition from childhood to adulthood.[64] Complementary to this theme was the 2004 exhibition The Beginning of Life. Personal Stories from Multicultural Norway, which dealt with female circumcision, as well as issues of infertility and Pakistani-Norwegian mothers with disabled children. The aim of this work was not only to focus on rituals, but also to highlight the different conditions under which new lives begin in contemporary Norway.[65]

In 2016, the IKM celebrated its twenty-fifth anniversary (a year late) with an ambitious exhibition programme, largely thanks to contributions from artists and

[62] See Norges Museumsforbund, 'Årets Museum' museumsforbundet.no/emne/arets-museum/.
[63] *Framtidas museums* (2008–2009 St.meld. nr. 49).
[64] B Møller, 'Huske, håpe, handle – museumsformidling i et flerkulturelt samfunn' in C Bäckström and A Tyrfelt (eds), *Museer, barn och nordisk identitet* (Köpenhamn, Nordiska ministerrådet, 1997).
[65] Møller and Einarsen, 'As in a Mirror' (2008) 143.

documentary filmmakers, as well as the support of different national and international institutions. The programme for that year included a temporary exhibition that had been very popular in 2014, which dealt with the cultural history and way of life of the Roma national minority in Norway as well as analysing issues related to human rights, the relationship between minority and majority, prejudice, inclusion and exclusion in Norwegian society. The title of the exhibition was: Norwegian Roma-Norwegian Gypsies. One People, Many Voices (Norvegiska romá-norske sigøynere. Ett folk mange stemmer).[66] Alongside this, new exhibitions began to take shape. The exhibition Borders and their Limits, organised in partnership with the National Museum of Migration in Paris and the French Institute in Oslo, consisted of posters that problematised national borders as a political tool of exclusion. Another poster exhibition, in this case with the support of the Arts Council Norway, addressed cross-border cooperation, cultural exchange and the preservation of cultural monuments contributing to diversity, increased tolerance and, in many areas, creating jobs and business development: People and Opportunities (Mennesker og muligheter). Meanwhile, the exhibition Freedom on Hold (Frihet på vent) showed photographs by Ingvild Festervill Melin taken in Lebanese refugee camps, where thousands of stateless Palestinians had lived a large part of their lives, some for more than 60 years. The photos, accompanied by texts by Siri Thorson, reflected people's innermost concerns and dreams for a better future.

Alongside these exhibitions, the IKM Gallery hosted contemporary art exhibitions whose themes focused on globalisation and diversity. Thus, three Romanian artists (Daniel Brici, Vlad Petri and Eugen Raportoru) contributed to the exhibition Bucharest Stories (Bucuresti Stories), thanks to the cooperation of the Metropolis Cultural Association. The installation A Country Road to the End (En landevei mot undergangen) by artist Frithjof Hoel reflected the ideas of racial hygiene in politics. In addition to this, the exhibition The Missing Diamond (Den forsvunne diamant), which dealt with the encounter between Europeans and Africans, hosted works by African artists who were invited by the Norwegian textile artist Vebjørg Hagene.[67]

In 2017, an exhibition opened that has remained part of the museum's programme to this day because of its highly relevant content and the subsequent additions which have enriched it still further: Typically Them (Typisk dem). Initially, the basic idea was to problematise the concept of racism in contemporary society by reflecting on the dichotomy of 'us' and 'the others'. The research process clarified concepts, held theoretical debates, worked with archive material and sought ways to adapt the conclusions reached in order to put together the

[66] A Bettum and G Özcan, 'Dialog om metode – Inkluderingsstrategier ved Interkulturelt Museum 2006–2016' in A Bettum, K Maliniemi and TM Walle (eds), *Et inkluderende museum: kulturelt magfold i praksis* (Trondheim, Museumsforlaget, 2018); IH Rashidi, 'Norvegiska Roma – Norske sigøynere. Oslo Museum (Interkulturelt Museum)' (2015) *Nordisk museologi* 142; G Özcan, *Norvegiska romá – norske sigøynere: ett folk – mange stemmer* (Oslo, Oslo Museum, 2005).

[67] Oslo Museum, *Årsmelding 2016* (Oslo, Oslo Museum, 2017) 23–25.

exhibition design. The result was an exhibition that encourages visitors to share their prejudices through humour, conceptual art and interactivity, and which also boasts a contribution by the French-Danish artist Thierry Geoffroy: his performance The Anatomy of Prejudice.[68]

With a target audience of young people and students, as well as adult education groups in and around Oslo, the exhibition was updated in 2019 with the addition of a new module created in partnership with Collaboration for Inclusive Dialogue (SID). This organisation works to combat young people's social exclusion and their sense of rejection, and prevent recruitment into undesirable groups by creating dialogue and building bridges that give a platform to the voices of young people. In line with these objectives, one of the exhibition rooms featured the voices of young people talking about their experiences of exclusion and inclusion in a visual production entitled Listen to Us, We Also Have a Voice (Lytt till oss, vi har også en stemme).[69]

However, the IKM's programme of exhibitions and art projects has gone beyond the walls of its physical installations, and nowadays it is possible to interact with the exhibitions digitally (online). Those who are interested can now enjoy the exhibition Future of Love, a joint project between Cofutures (an international research group working on contemporary global futurism, science fiction and future thinking with the aim of promoting better connections between local and global imaginaries to address planetary challenges), Oslo National Academy of the Arts (Kungshøgskolen i Oslo, KHIO) and the IKM. Beginning with research into various contemporary practices of love, the exhibition showcases the work of seven KHIO master's students who have speculated on possible future scenarios of how perceptions of these relationships and social situations might evolve for future generations.[70] To this example, the museum has added two further projects. The first of these alludes to an exhibition that collects and promotes the voices of local residents, shopkeepers and people who are connected to the district where the IKM is located, titled People in Grønland (Folk på Grøland). The second project is the exhibition Damn. This Neighbourhood Is Changing – Digitalt, which presents the changes in the neighbourhoods in the east end of Oslo and how the people who live in these areas experience them. This exhibition presents an opportunity to get to know the changed areas of the Grønland and Tønyen neighbourhoods through the eyes of the local people themselves.[71]

[68] Oslo Museum, *Årsmelding 2017* (Oslo, Oslo Museum, 2018) 27; Oslo Museum, *Årsmelding 2018* (Oslo, Oslo Museum, 2019) 26; Oslo Museum, *Årsmelding 2019* (Oslo, Oslo Museum, 2020) 8–9.

[69] AR Bothner-By, 'Lytt til oss, vi har også en stemme! Et samarbeidsprosjekt mellom Samarbeid for inkluderende Dialog og Interkulturelt museum 2018–2019' in Norges Museumsforbund (ed), *Inkluderende Museer: kulturkunnskap og-arbeid som katalysator for god inkludering* (Oslo, Norges museumsforbund, 2019); Oslo Museum, *Årsmelding 2019* (2020) 29.

[70] See Oslo Museum, 'Future of Love' www.oslomuseum.no/aktivitet/future-of-love/.

[71] See Oslo Museum, 'Folk på Grønland' www.oslomuseum.no/aktivitet/folk-pa-gronland/; Oslo Museum, 'Damn. This Neighborhood is Changing – Digitalt' www.oslomuseum.no/aktivitet/this-neighborhood-is-changing-digitalt/.

B. Education, Activities and Communication

As well as the exhibitions, the IKM organises a diverse programme of activities, including different kinds of format and content, both for explicitly educational purposes and for general promulgation. Every year, the IKM educators offer schools a programme including various free educational opportunities for students to become actively involved in the subject area. The planned activities mostly relate to the exhibitions, but also include walks through the city to address issues related to urban change and cultural diversity. The content of the latter activities aims to foster specific skill sets by discussing and showing examples of cultural variations, opportunities and challenges in multicultural societies; reflecting on how people have struggled and are struggling for change in society and, at the same time, how they have been and are still being affected by geographical conditions and historical context; or even identifying and discussing ethical issues related to human rights, sustainability and poverty.[72]

Outside of the school setting, the IKM produces a series of events aimed at families with children (especially families living in the local neighbourhood), children and young people in general, and an adult cultural audience. A large number of these events are developed in partnership with local associations, organisations, institutions or workplaces. Users come to the museum spaces to enjoy activities including narrative theatre performances, film screenings, activities related to international gastronomy, musical performances, debates and conversations about different topics and walks around the city.

Consequently, the IKM works for audience development and every year it tries to expand and vary the programme, with new exhibitions, guided tours, specialised education, conferences, city walks and various family events. The priority target audience includes: children and young people, adult cultural consumers, the elderly and people of international origin. Not all of the annual programme is for everyone, but ultimately the museum tries to offer the public knowledge and experiences at all stages of life, from childhood through to old age.[73] One can find out the number of visitors to the institution by looking at the OM's annual reports and compiling the information across the years (Figure 11.2); in this way, one will discover that the total number of visitors to the IKM has been increasing progressively since 2014, though with a small decrease in 2015, reaching a maximum figure in 2019,[74] with more than 19,400 people.[75]

[72] See Oslo Museum, 'Planlegg skolebesøket' www.oslomuseum.no/interkulturelt-museum/skole/.

[73] Oslo Museum, *Årsmelding 2012* (Oslo, Oslo Museum, 2013) 16–27; Oslo Museum, *Årsmelding 2013* (Oslo, Oslo Museum, 2014) 14–25; Oslo Museum, *Årsmelding 2014* (Oslo, Oslo Museum, 2015) 14–25; Oslo Museum, *Årsmelding 2015* (Oslo, Oslo Museum, 2016) 12–17; Oslo Museum, *Årsmelding 2016* (2017) 23–25; Oslo Museum, *Årsmelding 2017* (2018) 27–29; Oslo Museum, *Årsmelding 2018* (2019) 26–29; Oslo Museum, *Årsmelding 2019* (2020) 31–32.

[74] At the time of writing, the 2020 report has unfortunately not been published, so I have been unable to compare the data for 2020 or study the effect of the COVID-19 pandemic on the public's response to the institution's programme.

[75] Oslo Museum, *Årsmelding 2018* (2019) 16–17; Oslo Museum, *Årsmelding 2019* (2020) 18–19.

Figure 11.2 Interkulturelt Museum. Total visitors, 2014–19

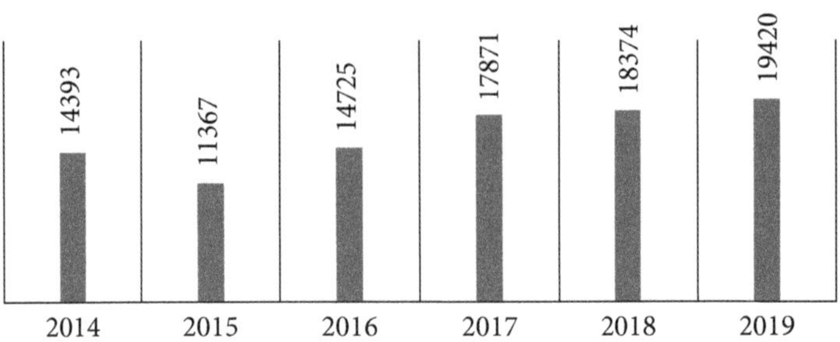

Source: prepared by the author.

This aspect can also be attributed to the significant effort made by the IKM in recent years, together with the other museums that make up the OM unit, towards greater professionalisation and renovation of the communications and marketing department. The goals are to increase the museum's visibility through different channels, increase dialogue with the public, build a museum brand, and disseminate information about the institution's programme according to its vision and strategic plan. In this sense, the institution has prepared media strategies for key launches and presentations; developed a social media strategy; created audience surveys to obtain more knowledge about who comes to the museum and what they want from it; reached agreements with the Tourist Office to promote the museum in the city guides; and drawn up advertising plans for the activities and the online public programme.[76]

C. Research and Study

Research is part of the IKM's social mission. Collecting and cataloguing material for exhibitions and art projects is a fundamental part of the preparatory work at the IKM. The museum has its own experienced scientific staff to carry out these tasks, but occasionally associate professors contribute to the research and development work through additional contracts. On occasion, the museum also asks other museums, educational institutions and research institutions to contribute to its research in order to improve studies and be able to share new knowledge, either through exhibitions or through other cultural or communication channels. Strategic focus areas include knowledge production, especially by minorities, and cultural diversity.[77]

[76] Oslo Museum, *Årsmelding 2019* (2020) 10–11.

[77] Oslo Museum, *Årsmelding 2015* (2016) 29–30; Oslo Museum, *Årsmelding 2016* (2017) 29–31; Oslo Museum, *Årsmelding 2017* (2018) 33; Oslo Museum, *Årsmelding 2018* (2019) 33–37; Oslo Museum, *Årsmelding 2019* (2020) 37–38.

It is clear that what stands out within this great work carried out by the museum is the research associated with The Diversity Network, because of its subsequent implications in the operation of museums for inclusive purposes. As mentioned above, the Network aims to promote work involving minorities and cultural diversity in the Norwegian museum landscape by creating meeting places, exchanging experiences and carrying out projects. In this regard, and with the support of the Arts Council Norway, the Network developed a project called The Disagreement Community (Uenighetsfellesskapet). The aim of this project was to investigate how work on resistance and friction might be used to rethink and develop methods and strategies to support diversity and inclusion work in museums in the CDC's spirit.

The project, coordinated by the OM, was implemented in the museums as part of their daily activity, in order to subsequently develop methods and knowledge based on their own experience and on the reflections gained from professional interactions. The project lasted between 2018 and 2021, based on a three-phase plan: the first phase involved the work programme and the progress plan for the project; the second phase consisted of implementing the project and then sharing the experiences gained in network meetings; and the third and final phase was set aside for the analysis and dissemination of the experiences of the work carried out during the project. The participating museums were: Perspektivet Museum, Varanger Museum, Anno Museum, Kulturhistorisk Museum, Museet Midt, Museene I Akerhus, Oslo Museum, Randsfjordsmuseet, Museene I Sogn og fjordaene, Nasjonalmuseet and Nord-Troms Museum.[78]

IV. Conclusions

This chapter contributes to a greater understanding of the new role that museums are moving into as cultural institutions that listen, discuss and respond to the problems of today's society and are committed to acting as dynamic elements, capable of contributing to social transformation.

In recent decades, concerns about equality, diversity, social justice and human rights have moved from the margins of museum thinking and practice to the core of these institutions. Arguments for engaging diverse audiences, creating conditions for more equitable access to museum resources and opening up opportunities to participate in museum experiences now command a growing consensus, an influence that is reflected in museum programmes, practices, policies and structures.

An analysis of the CDC's provisions and the 2015 Recommendation provides insight into UNESCO's commitment and international normative support for the promotion of cultural diversity, intercultural dialogue, culturally sustainable

[78] See Kulturrådet, 'Uenighetsfellesskapet' www.kulturradet.no/museum/vis-prosjekt/-/prosjekt-museum-uenighetsfellesskapet.

development and the connection, in the broadest sense, between culture, human rights and democracy that has been formulated since the beginning of the twenty-first century. The CDC is an essential instrument for understanding the role of museums in contemporary society – although there are no explicit direct references to them in the CDC's text – while the 2015 Recommendation clearly lays out the roles and responsibilities that museums have in the world, from a contemporary and future perspective. Both instruments represent the fundamental basis for the current social orientation of museums, fostering new procedures that reaffirm these institutions as spaces that are open to the world and also to dialogue, and which have the potential to strengthen the social fabric and act as meeting places.

From a practical point of view, the study of Norwegian cultural policy has made it possible to confirm the commitment and the work of the states around cultural diversity, and the role that museums play in this work, by means of different documents and publications issued since the end of the twentieth century, and with greater profusion since the ratification of the CDC. A review of the periodic reports submitted by the Scandinavian country monitoring the implementation of the CDC allows us to identify the IKM as an example of good practice in promoting respect and understanding of cultural diversity in 2016. Although the institution does not have a collection of objects, by studying its history, strategies and actions it is possible to see how this museum represents an outstanding example of a meeting place between cultures, and an ideal place for dialogue and reflection. The development of an annual programme of exhibitions, artistic projects and activities of different kinds (with a strong educational commitment) makes it possible for people from different cultural backgrounds to meet on a regular basis. At the same time, the IKM represents an example of a museum oriented towards the research and study of minorities and cultural diversity with the aim of, on the one hand, offering a programme that is consistently in line with the institution's objectives, and on the other hand, providing up-to-date training to the professionals who make up the institution's staff.

12

Reflections Around *Despacito* and the Concept of Cultural Diversity: A Defence for an Adequate Interaction between the Cultural Diversity Convention, International Economic Law and International Human Rights

BEATRIZ BARREIRO CARRIL

I. Introduction

At the eleventh ordinary meeting of the UNESCO Intergovernmental Committee for the Protection and Promotion of the Diversity of Cultural Expression, a specialist at the Inter-American Development Bank opened her remarks on the topic of 'Cultural and Creative Industries' by asking who does not know the song *Despacito*.[1] She was trying to make a case for the importance of culture as an important source of economic development. However, the question arises whether this world music hit could be considered as an expression of cultural diversity in line with those deserving protection or promotion under the Convention for the Protection and Promotion of the Diversity of Cultural Expressions (Cultural Diversity Convention, CDC).[2] One must bear in mind that this international treaty has as its main goal the promotion of a more balanced international market of cultural products from a cultural perspective, promoting therefore global cultural

[1] Annex containing the draft detailed summary record of the eleventh session of the Committee (12–15 December 2017), contained in 12 IGC, Item 3 of the Provisional Agenda: Adoption of the Detailed Summary Record of the Eleventh Session of the Committee (12 November 2018) UNESCO Doc DCE/18/12.IGC/3, 47. The source of this specific information is the attendance of the author of this chapter to the meeting of the Committee as an observer.

[2] (adopted 20 October 2005, entered into force 18 March 2007) 2440 UNTS 311.

diversity in a way that cultural minorities' expressions have the opportunity to survive and develop. The CDC would contribute in this sense to create cultural awareness in the context of international commercial relations.

However, a question immediately arises: is *Despacito* a paradigmatic case of what the CDC means by cultural diversity? If one looks closely at the Convention's text, it is unclear whether an affirmative answer can be given: the CDC seeks to promote cultural products because they are channels of identities, values and meanings, putting the focus on the expressions that are at a disadvantage in the global market. Complementarily, it seeks to promote expressions channelled by independent industries. The producer of *Despacito* is the giant Vivendi. Besides, *Despacito* has been posing several problematic issues concerning identities and culture, such as the contribution to cultural stereotypes and other concerns that could fall into the controversial category of 'cultural appropriation'.[3]

Another example of what could be understood as a kind of divorce between the concept of cultural diversity in the text of the CDC and its invocation or application can be found in the concept of cultural diversity used by states in two different situations. Thus, when they invoke rights[4] based on the CDC in the context of interpreting their international obligations in the field of international economic law (IEL), there is a tendency to ignore what could be called the anthropological aspects or components of the concept of cultural diversity (such as meaning, values, identity or creativity). To the contrary, when states use the concept in the context of the international rules and policies of cultural cooperation (to development) established in the CDC,[5] the meaning of cultural diversity reflects all its anthropological content, giving priority to minority expressions and independent cultural companies.

The United Nations' mechanism of the Special Rapporteur on Cultural Rights (SRCR) deserves particular attention in sharpening the definition of cultural diversity and its normative possibilities. It promotes a process of reflection around the meaning of cultural rights recognising all their complexity, something that is in line with the letter of the CDC and its understanding of cultural products as 'vehicles of identity, values and meaning' (Article 1.g). This mechanism is open to consultations with groups of experts (lawyers, anthropologists, sociologists and other experts), as well as with cultural actors and cultural activists, in an interdisciplinary way. The CDC's application would benefit greatly from a similar approach, which is already taking place to some extent thanks in part to the influence of

[3] PR Rivera-Rideau and J Torres-Leschnik, '"The Colors and Flavors of My Puerto Rico": Mapping "Despacito"'s Crossovers' (2019) 31 *Journal of Popular Music Studies* 87 (cited after the authors' version: repository.wellesley.edu/object/ir302).

[4] The case before the Appellate Body of the WTO, *China – Measures Affecting Trading Rights and Distribution Services for Certain Publications and Audiovisual Entertainment Products*, is paradigmatic of this.

[5] This is very clear in the projects founded by the states through the International Found for Cultural Diversity.

civil society and the Expert Facility (an international pool of recognised experts of different disciplines supporting the application of the Convention).[6] An increased interaction between the mechanisms of the CDC and those that seek to advance cultural rights within the UN would ensure better implementation of the CDC in a manner consistent with its concepts, particularly when it is invoked in international trade fora.

This chapter foregrounds the schism in the understanding of the concepts of the CDC. It starts with the presentation of the confusions already existing around the concepts stated from the outset in the CDC. It then moves to the economic international fora in order to show a misunderstanding of the concepts of the CDC within IEL and its consequences. Later, in section IV, this chapter addresses how the implementation of the CDC provisions related to cultural cooperation (to development) is more respectful of the concepts of the CDC. Section V addresses developments in the field of cultural rights within the UN which could, in combination with some developments of the CDC in the field and complementing them, contribute to a better implementation of the CDC from a conceptual perspective. Finally, some conclusions are drawn in order to prevent the implementation of the CDC from reproducing similar dynamics and reinforcing those concepts typical of IEL that the CDC is intended to overcome.

II. Conceptual Confusions from the Beginning of the History of the CDC

From the beginning of the drafting of the CDC, problems around the concept of cultural diversity appeared. The confusion about what would be the meaning of cultural diversity for the purpose of this international treaty was mixed with the decision to choose a narrower scope of application in comparison with the issues covered by the 2001 UNESCO Universal Declaration on Cultural Diversity (UDCD). In this sense, if the latter covered many aspects of cultural diversity (cultural rights, cultural heritage, cultural development, among others), the former was decided to have as the scope of application 'the protection of the diversity of cultural contents and artistic expressions'.[7] By this, the authors of the text were referring to the expressions contained in 'cultural products' commercialised in the international market. The raison d'être of the CDC confirmed this interpretation, since the text was aimed at establishing a counterbalance to the tendency in the 2001 Doha round of negotiations within the World Trade Organization

[6] See en.unesco.org/creativity/partnerships/expert-facility.

[7] UNESCO, 'Preliminary Draft Convention on the Protection of the Diversity of Cultural Contents and Artistic Expressions: Preliminary Report of the Director-General' (2004) UNESCO Doc CLT.2004/CONF.201/CLD.1, 2.

(WTO), dealing with cultural products as if they could be equated with other commercial products, which was the position of the USA.

If one looks into the reports of the meetings of the experts who worked on a draft of the CDC, the confusion between the decision on adopting a narrower or broader concept of cultural diversity and the decision about a narrower or broader scope of application of the CDC, as if one follows the other, is clear. In fact, during one such meeting, 'Several experts expressed the wish that the scope of the convention should be narrower than that suggested by the anthropological conception of culture and narrower than that of the UNESCO Universal Declaration on Cultural Diversity'.[8] It must be noted that the experts who participated in that meeting came from very different disciplines, from international law to economics. Among them were international lawyers Ivan Bernier and Sabine von Schorlemer, the expert in cultural cooperation and legal historian Leila Rezk, the economists David Throsby and Tyler Cowen and the political scientists Bhikhu Parekh and Carlos Moneta. No trained anthropologists could be identified, somewhat surprisingly, since anthropology as a discipline has contributed the most to the development of a technical definition of culture.

In reality, the Convention, like the UDCD, inherited the anthropological conception (known as well as the 'broad conception', in the sense that it goes beyond arts and letters) of culture enshrined in the Mondiacult Conference held in Mexico City in 1982, according to which:

> culture may now be said to be the whole complex of distinctive spiritual, material, intellectual and emotional features that characterize a society or social group. It includes not only the arts and letters, but also modes of life, the fundamental rights of the human being, value systems, traditions and beliefs.[9]

The fact that the Convention has a limited scope of application, as it deals in principle with only one of the many fields covered by the UDCD (that of cultural expressions channelled through cultural products), does not imply it abandons the broad, anthropological conception of culture. Otherwise, it would be difficult for UNESCO to justify its actions on the issue of trade in cultural products, were it not for the fact that it considers them channels for the transmission of meaning and values, which are components of culture understood in the anthropological sense.[10] It must be recalled that the proponents of a CDC at UNESCO needed to work strongly in order that the topic of trade of cultural products could be

[8] UNESCO, 'Deuxième réunion d'experts de catégorie VI concernant l'avant-projet de convention sur la protection de la diversité des contenus culturels et des expressions artistiques' (2004) UNESCO Doc CLT/CPD/2004/602/6 6 (own translation).

[9] UNESCO, 'Mexico City Declaration on Cultural Policies' in *World Conference on Cultural Policies, Mexico City, 26 July–6 August 1982: Final Report* (Paris, UNESCO, 1982) Preamble.

[10] B Barreiro Carril, 'Artículo 3: Ámbito de aplicación' in J Prieto de Pedro and H Velasco Maillo (eds), B Barreiro Carril (coord), *La diversidad cultural: análisis sistemático e interdisciplinar de la Convención de la UNESCO* (Madrid, Trotta, 2017) 130.

removed from the economic fora, and particularly the WTO in order for the topic to enter the forum of cultural nature. Apparently, this confusion seems to have been solved at the second meeting of experts: 'the experts stressed that the convention should propose a necessary and sufficient number of *functional* definitions, to enable its implementation to be made clear in legal terms, without, however, sacrificing the anthropological sense of culture' (original emphasis).[11]

However, during the first meeting of intergovernmental experts, the confusion about the scope of application of the Convention – whether it covered cultural diversity in its broad or narrow conception – was an object of debate. The president of the drafting committee, Kader Asmal, asked for clarification of the negotiating mandate. The UNESCO Assistant Director-General for Culture, Mounir Bouchenake, noted that the subject of the instrument was 'artistic expressions and cultural content'.[12] This subject was later going to take the abridged name of 'cultural expressions', as the final title of the CDC itself reflects. These cultural expressions were generally understood as being the cultural products commercialised in the international market. However, and considering the diversity of actions currently taken under the CDC in very different topics,[13] being reminded that the term 'artistic expression' was in the original scope of application of the Convention may be of some use. In fact, if we examine what the CDC itself says about its scope of application, we find a quite enigmatic term: 'cultural activities'. By itself, this term does not necessarily have a meaning associated to the world of 'cultural industries', from which 'cultural products', which constitute the Convention's field of application par excellence, derive.

If we go to the text of the CDC, we find that under the title 'Scope of application', Article 3 states that 'This Convention shall apply to the policies and measures adopted by the Parties related to the protection and promotion of the diversity of cultural expressions'. Contrary to what the conciseness of this provision suggests, the delimitation in practical terms of the scope of application of the CDC is quite complicated. The apparent clarity of Article 3 contrasts with the confusing definitions of the terms given in the following provision, to which Article 3 itself refers. Article 4 is long and complex, and suggests that not all sorts of effects on the part of the CDC can be ruled out in a number of areas that at the beginning seemed to fall clearly outside of its scope. Despite the fact that the leading states for a CDC expressed to the Director-General of UNESCO concern about the

[11] UNESCO, 'Deuxième réunion' (2004) 12 (own translation).

[12] I Bernier, 'La négociation de la Convention de l'UNESCO sur la protection et la promotion de la diversité des expressions culturelles' (2005) 43 *Canadian Yearbook of International Law* 12, 13.

[13] For these purposes, see ch 10 of this book, by Laurence Cuny. As von Schorlemmer reflected, only the future implementation will say what is the exact scope of the Convention. As she argued, based on Ruiz Fabri, the Convention does not deal with limited matters, so other matters that were impossible to foresee may now be dealt with. See S von Schorlemer, 'Scope of Application' in S von Schorlemer and PT Stoll (eds), *The UNESCO Convention on the Protection and Promotion of the Diversity of Cultural Expressions: Explanatory Notes* (Berlin, Springer, 2012) 129.

cultural imbalance of cultural products in the international market, he prepared a preliminary study in which three other alternative topics were discussed. Thus, an instrument on the topic of 'the protection of the diversity of cultural expression and cultural content'[14] was accompanied by three other possibilities: an instrument on cultural rights; a new instrument on the status of artists; or a new protocol to the Florence Agreement (1950) on the Importation of Educational, Scientific and Cultural Materials.[15] All four options were submitted to the 32nd General Conference of UNESCO (2003), which decided in favour of 'the protection of the diversity of cultural contents and artistic expressions'.[16] However, the CDC is currently dealing with issues typical of cultural rights (artistic freedom) and the status of artists.[17] Going back to the term 'cultural activities', Article 4 establishes in paragraph 1 that 'cultural diversity is … transmitted through the variety of cultural expressions'. Following this chain of conceptual remissions, Article 4, paragraph 4 states that 'cultural activities, goods and services … embody or convey cultural expressions'. This provision ends by saying that a cultural activity 'can be an end in itself, or [can] contribute to the production of cultural goods and services'. The inclusion of the term 'activities', which, unlike the terms 'goods' and 'services', does not in itself have an economic content, and the possibility therefore that cultural activities may themselves fall within the scope of application of CDC confirm that legitimate doubts can arise about whether the CDC addresses other objects beyond cultural products. UNESCO shed some light on this issue through the website dedicated to the Convention, which specifies that the term 'cultural expressions':

> refers to the various ways in which the creativity of individuals and social groups takes shape and manifests itself. These manifestations include expressions transmitted by words (literature, tales …), sound (music …), images (photos, films …) – in any format (printed, audiovisual, digital etc) – or by *activities (dance, theatre …)* or objects (sculptures, paintings …) (emphasis added).[18]

However, whether the activities mentioned (dance, theatre …) are objects of the Convention only when they have an economic value, besides the cultural one, or they are objects of the CDC despite not having an economic value – like in the case of activities developed in non-profit and self-managed cultural centres[19] – is

[14] UNESCO, 'Preliminary Study on the Technical and Legal Aspects Relating to the Desirability of a Standard-Setting Instrument on Cultural Diversity' (12 March 2003) UNESCO Doc 166 EX/28, 8.

[15] ibid 5–7.

[16] ibid 6 and 8.

[17] Again, see ch 10 by Cuny. See also L Cuny, *Freedom & Creativity: Defending Art, Defending Diversity*, special edn (Paris, UNESCO, 2020).

[18] www.unesco.org/new/es/culture/themes/cultural-diversity/diversity-of-cultural-expressions/the-convention/faq/.

[19] See M Lorenzo Moles, 'Nuevas formas de autogestión cultural desde la perspectiva del derecho a participar en la vida cultural' in B Barreiro Carril (ed), *Cultura y humanización del Derecho* (Buenos Aires, Teseo Press, 2017) www.teseopress.com/nuevasmiradasalderechointernacionalylos. Betzler analyses regional cultural centres in Switzerland as privileged places for the application of the principles of the Convention, and in ch 11 of this book, Mónica Riaza deals with a publicly funded

not clear. A literal interpretation of the CDC would suggest that other activities which do not have an economic value could not in principle be excluded. The fact that Article 4 includes a definition of the term 'cultural industries' may lead one to think that the CDC prioritises as its field of action those products deriving from them which have per se economic value. In this regard, Article 4, paragraph 5 states that the term 'cultural industries' refers to 'all those industries that produce and distribute cultural goods or services, as defined in the paragraph 4 above'. The item 'cultural activities' is in fact excluded from those items produced by cultural industries which are mentioned in paragraph 4.[20] Nevertheless, paragraph 4.4, which defines 'cultural industries', is not necessary to understand Article 3, which sets the scope of application of this treaty ('This Convention shall apply to the policies and measures adopted by the Parties related to the protection and promotion of the diversity of cultural expressions'). For their part, 'cultural policies and measures', following Article 4.6, refer to those

> policies and measures relating to culture, whether at the local, national, regional or international level that are either focused on culture as such or are designed to have a direct effect on cultural expressions of individuals, groups or societies, including on the creation, production, dissemination, distribution of and access to cultural activities, goods and services.

All this confirms that the CDC may open the door to focusing on cultural activities which do not have economic aspects.[21] As Betzler states, 'This rather fuzzy, open concept [that of cultural diversity in the CDC] leaves a lot of space for interpretation and allows a great variety of state activism, leading to various kinds of effects and impacts'.[22]

In any case, what it is clear is that cultural products deriving from cultural industries and commercialised in the international market are a priority object of the CDC. It is also clear that this instrument uses a broad (anthropological)

museum referred by Norway in its CDC report. This shows that effects of the CDC beyond products commercialised within international market may, at least in principle, not be excluded. See D Betzler, 'Implementing UNESCO's Convention on Cultural Diversity at the Regional Level: Experiences from Evaluating Cultural Competence Centers' (2020) 27 *International Journal of Cultural Property* 511.

[20] The audiovisual sector has been the paradigmatic example of cultural industries when deciding about the need for a CDC.

[21] However, as will be explained in s III, 'projects related *exclusively* to the production of cultural and artistic works and events' (emphasis added) are not eligible for funding from the International Fund for Cultural Diversity (IFCD) established in Art 18 of the CDC: IFCD, 'Annotated Guide for the Submission of Funding Requests' (Paris, UNESCO, 2022) en.unesco.org/creativity/sites/creativity/files/annotated_guide_13_ifcd_call_2022_en.pdf. They need to contribute to the 'emergence of dynamic cultural sectors in developing countries, by strengthening the means to create, produce, distribute and access diverse cultural goods and services' (ibid 5). It seems that the IFCD asks that projects have an economic value (or an economic intention) that enables them to contribute to a more culturally balanced international market of cultural products. Cultural activities not having such an economic value or intention therefore seem to be excluded from the IFCD.

[22] Betzler, 'Implementing UNESCO's Convention' (2020) 513.

concept of culture that makes them objects for protection under a cultural forum like UNESCO.[23] However, as next section demonstrates, this is not clear within IEL and for some states parties to the Convention.

III. Conceptual Confusions within International Economic Law

When the CDC has been invoked within economic law, this has been done as a possible exception to general commercial rules.[24] The WTO's case 'Measures Affecting Trading Rights and Distribution Services with Respect to Certain Publications and Audiovisual Entertainment Products'[25] is a good example of how a wrong conception of cultural diversity and related concepts is assumed within international economic law. This is highly relevant, since the inadequate understanding of the concepts of the CDC may jeopardise its very purposes. The case was brought before the WTO adjudicatory bodies in 2009. The USA was challenging some of China's measures affecting market access and the distribution services of goods (motion pictures, DVDs, videos, books and other publications). China alleged that the USA disregarded its right to regulate trade in a manner consistent with the General Agreement on Tariffs and Trade[26] (GATT), Article XX(a) of which contains a public morality exception. China invoked the CDC as a supportive tool of such a morality exception.

The final outcome of the case, in which the courts found for the USA because the Chinese measures did not meet the requirement of necessity (since China did not use other measures that were less harmful to the agreement for the purpose pursued), is not so relevant for the purposes of this chapter. What matters most is that neither the WTO adjudicator bodies nor the third parties intervening in the case and which were parties of the CDC at the time – Australia, the European Communities – adequately questioned China's use of the CDC to justify a policy of

[23] This is reinforced by the definitions given by the CDC in Arts 4.2 and 4.3. They refer respectively to 'Cultural content' as the 'symbolic meaning, artistic dimension and cultural values that originate from or express cultural identities' and to 'Cultural expressions' as 'those expressions that result from the creativity of individuals, groups and societies, and that have cultural content'.

[24] It is worth mentioning the very recent judicial Brazilian decision by the Brazilian Supreme Federal Court in *Compulsory Screening of Brazilian Films in Brazilian Cinemas. Screen Quota*, leading case RE 627432 (18 March 2021) stf.jus.br/portal/jurisprudenciaRepercussao/verAndamentoProcesso.asp?incidente=3921612&numeroProcesso=627432&classeProcesso=RE&numeroTema=704. It is a very interesting case because the CDC is also invoked for defending protective measures limiting freedom of market. But the judicial decision presents, contrary to that of the WTO analysed in this section, a better conceptual understanding of the CDC. However, this is a national decision with more limited consequences within international law.

[25] WTO, 'China – Measures Affecting Trading Rights and Distribution Services for Certain Publications and Audiovisual Entertainment Products' (12 August 2009) WTO Doc WT/DS363/R.

[26] (30 October 1947).

protection of public morality, which somehow echoes of censorship.[27] Australia[28] focused on the invocation of Article 20.2 of the CDC[29] in order to make clear that China could not make recourse to the CDC in order to avoid compliance with obligations of the GATT. In this way, it ignores all the potentiality of the CDC in terms of complementary with other international treaties.[30] Regarding conceptual issues, Australia stated that

> It is incumbent upon China to show that there exists a relationship between the cultural value of the items at issue, that is, between reading materials and audiovisual products, including sound recordings, and the standards of right and wrong conduct maintained in China. In Australia's view, China is not able to rely on the cited UNESCO instruments to demonstrate such a relationship.[31]

Australia did not delve deeply into conceptual issues, particularly the problematic aspects of using the CDC in order to justify measures evoking censorship, something which contradicts the concept of cultural diversity used by the UNESCO instrument. Recall that its Article 4 refers to interculturality as 'the presence and equitable interaction of diverse cultures and the possibility of generating shared cultural expressions, acquired through dialogue and an attitude of mutual respect'. Likewise, Article 2 establishes the principles of equitable access and of openness and balance. The first recognises that 'equitable access to a rich and diversified range of cultural expressions from all parts of the world and access of cultures to the means of expression and dissemination are important elements in enhancing cultural diversity and fostering mutual understanding'. The second states that

> when States adopt measures to support the diversity of cultural expressions, they shall endeavour to promote, in an appropriate manner, openness to the other cultures of the world and shall ensure that such measures are directed towards the achievement of the objectives pursued by this Convention.

[27] 'La mesa redonda de la Red de Juristas se interesa en la referencias acerca de la Convención de la UNESCO en las instancias internacionales' (2010) 8 *Coaliciones en movimiento* 1.

[28] The European Communities did not refer to the invocation of the CDC by China in its intervention.

[29] '[n]othing in this Convention shall be interpreted as modifying rights and obligations of the Parties under any other treaties to which they are parties'.

[30] Particularly Art 20.1, which states that 'Parties recognize that they shall perform in good faith their obligations under this Convention and all other treaties to which they are parties. Accordingly, without subordinating this Convention to any other treaty, (a) they shall foster mutual supportiveness between this Convention and the other treaties to which they are parties; and (b) when interpreting and applying the other treaties to which they are parties or when entering into other international obligations, Parties shall take into account the relevant provisions of this Convention.' Also Art 21: 'Parties undertake to promote the objectives and principles of this Convention in other international forums. For this purpose, Parties shall consult each other, as appropriate, bearing in mind these objectives and principles.'

[31] WTO, 'China – Measures' (12 August 2009) 86. One should note, however, the Australian reservation with regard to Art 20(1)(a) and (b), about which Australia states that 'the Convention shall be interpreted and applied in a manner that is consistent with the rights and obligations of Australia under any other treaties to which it is a party, including the Marrakesh Agreement Establishing the World Trade Organization. This Convention shall not prejudice the ability of Australia to freely negotiate rights and obligations in other current or future treaty negotiations.'

This case can therefore be seen as a missed opportunity for alerting against misuses of the CDC in ways that do not fit with its spirit. At the time of writing, Article 25, dealing with the settlement of disputes concerning the interpretation or the application of the CDC, has not yet been activated. More specifically, a conciliation commission for the settlement of disputes foreseen in this article still has not been created. Consequently, there has not yet been an opportunity for the concepts stated in the CDC to be interpreted by a body of cultural nature. It should be recalled, however, that the view of the CDC as a tool for protecting national cultural content from foreign content, without entering into the conditions of the content itself, was a common one at the time the CDC was born, particularly in the context of IEL. Notions present in the CDC, such as the aforementioned one of 'interculturality' or that of 'creativity', seem to have been out of scholarly analyses for a long time. In fact, as has already been pointed out, Article 4.3 refers to 'cultural expressions' as 'those expressions that result from the *creativity* of individuals, groups and societies, and that have cultural content' (emphasis added). Even if the notion of creativity could be difficult to establish, 15 years of existence of the CDC asks this parameter to be taken seriously if the protection and promotion of cultural diversity wants to be something more than a way to assure protection of national content independently of its degree of creativity. As long ago as 2002, Philippe Achilléas, a French public law scholar, warned that some uses of the cultural protection mechanism under European Union law could end up in the Americanisation of European culture. This would have been the case for the French television series *Sous le soleil*, which was very similar in a lot of aspects to the American series *Beverly Hills 90210*, which has been exported to more than 80 countries.[32] In a similar vein, in 2006, the expert Leila Rezk, who contributed to the UNESCO draft of the CDC, pointed to the possibly problematic erroneous invocation of the Convention by some states when she asked herself: 'Does the apparent concern of some countries to preserve global diversity not hide the lack of respect for diversity in their own countries where international instruments fail to provide protection?'[33] This kind of question seems to have gone unnoticed. Such questions are, however, essential if the CDC wants to enjoy a coherent and systematic application. Now, after 15 years of its implementation, reflection on this sort of contradiction is urgent. It would contribute to reducing the fragmentation manifested in the different ways states use this international text. China, which has invoked the CDC in a highly problematic way within the WTO, is one of the states that has contributed most to the International

[32] P Achilléas, 'Le droit international face à la globalisation de la communication: le cas de la télévision' in R Ben Achour and S Laghmani (eds), *Le droit international face aux nouvelles technologies* (Paris, Pédone, 2002) 143.

[33] L Rezk, 'Negotiating Diversity: The Meaning of the Convention for the Arab World' in N Obuljen and J Smiers (eds), *UNESCO's Convention on the Protection and Promotion of the Diversity of Cultural Expressions: Making It Work* (Zagreb, Institute for International Relations, 2006) 261. This has to do also with the need of a systematic application and interpretation of the CDC, eg in relation to human rights instruments.

Fund for Cultural Diversity (IFCD) of the CDC, the organ to which this chapter is going to refer in the next section.[34]

Such a contradiction asks for a more comprehensive approach to the concept of cooperation to (cultural) development within international law, one that passes from an exclusively financial-assistance focus to a behavioural one in which obligations such as those of Articles 20.1.a)[35] and 21[36] of the CDC can be very useful. For example, the reinforcement of cultural diversity in international law would not be determined mainly by states' donations to the CDC's IFCD or other similar funds, but also, and mainly, by positions favouring cultural diversity in the WTO and other commercial forums, where cultural diversity is particularly at stake, especially in the context of the digitalisation of culture.[37] During the drafting process of the CDC, these kinds of 'consistent requirements' were considered, but unfortunately were not reflected in the final text.[38] The fragmented application of the CDC in different contexts – IEL, cultural cooperation (to development) – is directly related to the lack of a serious engagement with a nuanced and precise understanding of its concepts.

IV. The Application of the CDC in the Context of Cultural Cooperation (to Development) Obligations: A Better Understanding of its Concepts

Contrary to what happens within IEL, when states use the CDC in the context of the law and policies of cultural cooperation (to development)[39] – for which the framework are its Articles 12–14 and 18[40] – they do it in a way that is more in consonance with the definitions of cultural diversity and related concepts given in its Article 4. As some of the examples given in states' reports show, actions of

[34] Paradoxically, China has contributed considerably to the IFCD, to a total of 470,000 USD. It was one of the states that stood more solidly with the IFCD at the beginning of the life of the CDC. However, its last contribution dates back to 2016. One could think that the recent lack of any contribution to the IFCD has to do with the fact that the CDC is currently dealing with artistic freedom. Again, for these purposes, see ch 10 by Cuny.

[35] See n 26.

[36] ibid.

[37] See ch 4 of this book, by Véronique Guèvremont and Ivana Otasevic, and ch 5 by Clémence Varin.

[38] The possibility was considered that international cooperation measures, in order to be decided, should take into account as parameters of conduct of the recipient the fact that the latter is committed to cultural diversity. See B Barreiro Carril, *La diversidad cultural en el Derecho Internacional: la Convención de la UNESCO* (Madrid, Iustel, 2011) 179.

[39] A good insight into the conceptual and international legal aspects of cultural cooperation to development can be found in M Maraña, 'Culture and Development. Evaluation and Prospects' (Bilbao, UNESCO Etxea, 2010) UNESCO Etxea Working Papers 1.

[40] Art 12 deals with the promotion of international cooperation, Art 13 with the integration of culture in sustainable development and Art 14 with cooperation for development. The text of the convention is available at en.unesco.org/creativity/sites/creativity/files/convention2005_basictext_en.pdf.

cultural cooperation (to development) that reflect a right understanding of the concepts of the CDC evidence at the same time a consistent approach to other of its current concerns, such as human rights. This is the case, for instance, of the Culture and Development Strategy for Spanish Cooperation.[41] The Strategy's document shows that the Strategy was based on different reports of the UN ('Human Development' – 2004) or UNESCO ('Our Creative Diversity' – 2007), which were highly relevant for the operation and implementation of the CDC, but also on additional research material from sociologists, lawyers, anthropologists and experts in cultural cooperation (to development), as well as on the practice of private foundations and non-governmental organisations (NGOs) working in the field. As a result, it has a full understanding of the concepts of the CDC. Furthermore, and probably precisely because of this, the Strategy connects the challenges and obligations in the field of cooperation with those of human rights in a very accurate way. This is particularly clear where the document refers to the concept of 'cultural freedom',[42] a concept which avoids an understanding of culture as opposed to human rights, which still prevails in some countries,[43] or a direct ignorance of human rights issues (as in the aforementioned case of China's restrictive measures within the WTO).

The archetypal measure of cultural cooperation (to development) of the CDC is the IFCD, established in Article 18, whose 'purpose is to promote sustainable development and poverty reduction in developing countries that are Parties' to the CDC. As the website of the IFCD recognises:

> It does this through support to projects that aim to foster the emergence of a dynamic cultural sector, primarily through activities facilitating the introduction and/or elaboration of policies and strategies that protect and promote the diversity of cultural expressions as well as the reinforcement of institutional infrastructures supporting viable cultural industries.[44]

It must be noted that the IFCD promotes both 'South–South and North–South–South cooperation, while contributing to achieving concrete and sustainable results as well as structural impacts, where appropriate, in the cultural field'. As Luis Albornoz has pointed out, 'The singularity of this multi-donor fund is that

[41] It can be found in the 2012 Spain periodic report to the CDC at en.unesco.org/creativity/governance/periodic-reports/2012/spain-0.

[42] Ministerio de Asuntos Exteriores y de Cooperación, 'Estrategia de Cultura y Desarrollo de la Cooperación Española' (2007) 9, www.aecid.es/galerias/cooperacion/Cultural/descargas/Estrategia_CxD.pdf.

[43] This is the case of many Arab countries, as Leila Rezk seems to suggest: 'The terms of the Convention are in themselves a challenge to Arab countries. How they choose to manage cultural diversity and the expressions thereof, whether traditional or modern, will be a defining factor of what they stand for. The cultural counter argument theory of the Mauritanian Abdoulaye Sow warns against the use of respecting traditional cultures as a pretext to perpetuate harmful traditional practices, for example the religious justification used to maintain the practice of FGMC (female genital mutilation/cutting) in certain Arab countries.' See Rezk, 'Negotiating Diversity' (2006) 254.

[44] en.unesco.org/creativity/ifcd/what-is.

most of its resources are utilized to support the activities of local NGOs that work on cultural policies and industries in developing countries'.[45] Since 2010, the IFCD has provided more than US$ 9.4 million in funding for 129 projects in 65 developing countries.[46] Contrary to other funds, the IFCD allows small NGOs to access funds that in other contexts are reserved for larger NGOs and gives priority to local needs 'without imposing an agenda that inevitably leads to topdown designing/selecting of the programs'.[47]

The nature and aims of the financed projects show a much deeper and more adequate understanding of the different concepts stated in the CDC than those assumed in the context of the invocation of the CDC within IEL. An example would be the project 'Cultural Nests, supporting indigenous cultural start-ups', developed by a Mexican 'non-profit organization committed to supporting vulnerable indigenous communities' that aims to create 'new business models for the cultural and creative industry in Mexico' and to 'develop a more inclusive cultural industry … through the creation of start-up and e-commerce site by indigenous people' which would 'promote the work of indigenous artists'. One of its objectives is to 'promote access to national and international markets for cultural goods and services produced by indigenous peoples'.[48] If it is true that, as Albornoz pointed out, the IFCD's budget and nature makes its contribution to the 'transform[ation of] unequal international and regional flows' – which is one of the main objectives of the Convention – very unlikely,[49] I suggest that discrete cultural actions cannot completely be underestimated in the pursuit of the larger purpose of promoting more equal benefit sharing in cultural industries. Besides, the CDC has other, additional objectives, such as the 'reaffirm[ation of] the importance of the link between culture and development for all countries, particularly for developing countries, and to support actions undertaken nationally and internationally to secure recognition of the true value of this link', and the 'strengthen[ing of] international cooperation and solidarity in a spirit of partnership with a view, in particular, to enhancing the capacities of developing countries in order to protect and promote the diversity of cultural expressions'. These two objectives are established in Article 1.f) and i) respectively.

Projects like 'Cultural Nests' offer a complementary approach to the state-centred project that prevailed when the CDC was born and which focused on correcting the imbalances of cultural flows at the international level by protecting states' cultural content following a state-versus-state approach. From this perspective, typical of IEL, the state's internal cultural diversity was not so relevant. However, the CDC also asks for the promotion of *internal* cultural diversity

[45] LA Albornoz, 'The International Fund for Cultural Diversity: A New Tool for Cooperation in the Audiovisual Field' (2016) 22 *International Journal of Cultural Policy* 553, 567.
[46] en.unesco.org/creativity/ifcd/what-is.
[47] Albornoz, 'The International Fund' (2016) 567. He is quoting a document of the IFCD.
[48] en.unesco.org/creativity/ifcd/projects/cultural-nests-supporting-indigenous-cultural.
[49] Albornoz, 'The International Fund' (2016) 568.

within the state. Projects like 'Cultural Nests' contribute to this not so obvious and initially somewhat neglected objective by, in this case, promoting a space for expressions of indigenous groups within Mexican cultural industries (and within the international market of cultural products, even if this may appear highly difficult to achieve). If, originally, the CDC was presented as a tool for invoking cultural sovereignty among states (based on Article 5.1), now, after 15 years of its application, such an approach needs to be complemented with that of Article 5.2, which states that 'When a Party implements policies and takes measures to protect and promote the diversity of cultural expressions within its territory, its policies and measures shall be consistent with the provisions of this Convention'. Among these provisions, that of Article 7.1.a must be pointed out. It establishes an obligation of states to create

> an environment which encourages individuals and social groups to create, produce, disseminate, distribute and have access to their own cultural expressions, paying due attention to the special circumstances and needs of women as well as various social groups, including persons belonging to minorities and indigenous peoples.

This obligation asks for a good understanding of the concepts established in Article 4 (cultural diversity, interculturality) and does not offer any doubt that an anthropological conception of culture as understood in the Mondialcult Declaration is needed. Projects such as 'Cultural Nests' contribute to reinforcing this conception.

Another interesting project for the purposes of this chapter is 'Strengthening civil society engagement in cultural policy development in Cambodia', undertaken by 'Cambodian Living Arts, a non-profit organization committed to preserving and reviving endangered performing arts'. It 'proposes [among other objectives] to create an independent association to enhance civil society participation in policy making'.[50] This project also focuses on *internal diversity*. Additionally, it may contribute to the practical promotion of human rights, even if the use of this last term is avoided. It should be remembered that participation in cultural policy-making is an essential part of cultural rights, as stated in General Comment (GC) No 15 of the UN Committee on Economic, Social and Cultural Rights (CESCR).[51] It is also in line with the focus on 'creativity' as a condition for cultural expressions to be given protection and promotion under the CDC, as was pointed out in section II of this chapter. This right conceptual understanding of the Convention contrasts with the policies established by the state of Cambodia itself, and specifically with the cultural code of conduct, a legislation that applies to artists 'who behave offensively regarding social morality and national cultural values' and

[50] en.unesco.org/creativity/ifcd/projects/strengthening-civil-society-engagement.

[51] Committee on Economic, Social and Cultural Rights, 'General Comment No 21: Right of Everyone to Take Part in Cultural Life (Art 15, para 1 (a), of the International Covenant on Economic, Social and Cultural Rights)' (21 December 2009) UN Doc E/C.12/GC/21.

which is planned to be extended to the general public.[52] This action contradicts Article 2 of the CDC, paragraph 1 of which establishes the 'Principle of respect for human rights and fundamental freedoms', following which 'Cultural diversity can be protected and promoted only if human rights and fundamental freedoms, such as freedom of expression, information and communication … are guaranteed'.[53] It is clear that projects like 'Strengthening civil society engagement in cultural policy development in Cambodia' act as a counterbalance to government actions, even if one doubts the viability of the project precisely because of these governmental measures. In any case, the project seems to contribute to a better understanding of the concepts and goals of the CDC within Cambodian territory.

Another interesting project offering a very fresh understanding of the concepts of the CDC is 'Entrepreneurs for Diversity (E4D): Strengthening regional creative industries in Mesoamerica'.[54] This aims to create 'capacity building through a blended e-learning platform, mentoring programs and incubators for young cultural entrepreneurs from underprivileged, marginalized and/or underrepresented groups from Guatemala and Mexico'. It shows, therefore, an approach completely in line with the concepts of the CDC, particularly with the definition of 'interculturality' as 'the possibility of generating shared cultural expressions through dialogue and mutual respect', in this case applied to the dialogue within indigenous communities themselves. In fact, the project puts particular emphasis on underrepresented groups within indigenous communities, such as women and people belonging to sexual minorities.[55] This is perfectly in line with the current UN approach to cultural rights, which is dealt with in the next section of this chapter. As the former SRCR Karima Bennoune reflected in her final report:

> Women and cultural dissenters may face the imposition of cultural codes on them that they have no power to determine. The more embattled a group or people is, such as by facing forced assimilation … the more their human rights are threatened, the less space they may have to welcome cultural openness and sharing.[56]

Following this approach, this project looks into *internal diversity* not only within states, by prioritising indigenous expressions over mainstream ones, but also

[52] cambodianess.com/article/a-ministry-of-culture-and-fine-arts-advisor-to-suggest-implementing-a-cultural-code-of-conduct.

[53] The question arises whether the lack of fulfilment of the CDC reporting obligations from 2020 by Cambodia has to do with the inclusion in the report template of artistic freedom (en.unesco.org/creativity/governance/periodic-reports). For these purposes, see ch 10 by Cuny. One must not forget that, as Ivan Bernier and Nathalie Latulippe already noted, the CDC is a treaty that seeks to mediate rather than punish. See I Bernier and N Latulippe, *The International Convention on the Protection and Promotion of the Diversity of Cultural Expressions: Conciliation as a Dispute Resolution Method in the Cultural Sector* (Quebec, Government of Quebec, 2007) www.unescodec.chaire.ulaval.ca/sites/unescodec.chaire.ulaval.ca/files/document_reflexion_eng.pdf.

[54] es.unesco.org/creativity/ifcd/projects/entrepreneurs-diversity-e4d-strengthening.

[55] As the author of this chapter was able to see, being a contributor to the project.

[56] UN General Assembly, 'Report of the Special Rapporteur in the Field of Cultural Rights, Karima Bennoune' (19 July 2021) UN Doc A/76/178, para 39.

within cultural communities, offering a highly rich understanding of the concept of cultural diversity of the CDC. It answers very properly a criticism made by the SRCR when she refers to the concern that

> [g]overnments may only or primarily finance cultural projects carried out by members of some ethnic groups or those that are seen to be ethnically based rather than multi-ethnic or intercultural, or promote certain identities and cultural heritages, or 'ethnicization', through cultural policies and programming.[57]

From the three projects examined above, it is clear that the IFCD reflects an adequate, deep and whole understanding of the concept of cultural diversity and related concepts stated within the CDC, contrary to the inadequate and partial understanding reflected within IEL. After 15 years of its application, the CDC has been shown to be ready to deal with issues that are not directly connected with the concerns that made its birth so urgent – those oriented towards the creation of a more culturally balanced exchange of cultural products in the international market. Together with this objective,[58] actions of cultural cooperation (to development), such as those undertaken thanks to the IFCD, are a privilege field of action of the CDC, and may, even in an extremely humble way,[59] contribute to a more balanced international marking of cultural products in terms of cultural diversity. In this sense, providing possibilities for cultural expressions that are (still) not concretised by cultural products or cultural expressions whose underlying cultural industries are 'languishing'[60] is, in the author's opinion, important, since the CDC covers all the steps of the value chain, from creation to distribution and enjoyment.[61] The 'creat[ion of] the conditions for cultures to flourish' is in fact

[57] ibid para 24.

[58] See ch 4 by Guèvremont and Otasevic and ch 5 by Varin.

[59] The IFCD states that it 'invests in projects that lead to structural change through the reinforcement of human and institutional capacities of public sector and civil society organizations, deemed necessary to support viable local and regional cultural industries and markets in developing countries'. See en.unesco.org/creativity/ifcd/apply.

[60] As is the case for the project financed by the IFCD for revitalising the lambahoany, a cultural expression from Madagascar. The opposite opinion is presented by Albornoz, 'The International Fund' (2016) 567. In fact, Albornoz also analyses the relation between the field of application of the CDC and the inaccurate understanding of its definitions, but in the opposite way to this chapter. He considers that 'the risk lies … in working with inaccurate definitions and, consequently, in extending the FIDC's intervention to support projects that contribute only indirectly to the growth of dynamic cultural sectors' (ibid 567). He very appropriately detected a possible 'tension between a notion of cultural industries – inherited from the Frankfurt School, which is widely extended amongst communication and culture political economy analysts – and the currently fashionable creative industries' (ibid 562). This chapter, as has been shown, also identifies a lack of right understanding of the concepts of the CDC, but, on the other hand, considers it positive that the IFCD extends its founding to expressions that go beyond 'the audiovisual industry' (ibid 562) into sectors such as 'performing arts, painting or artistic design of motifs' (ibid 562) even if they could not have had (and still do not have) an industrial nature at the very beginning of their founding.

[61] See Art 4.1: 'Cultural diversity is made manifest not only through the varied ways in which the cultural heritage of humanity is expressed, augmented and transmitted through the variety of cultural expressions, but also through diverse modes of artistic creation, production, dissemination, distribution and enjoyment, whatever the means and technologies used.'

one of the objectives of the CDC (Article 1.b). It must be noted, however, that for a project to be an object of funding by the CDC it needs to prove its intention and the possibility to be launched on the international market.[62] The three projects looked at above all contribute strongly to the promotion of cultural rights, which is the object of next section. In particular, they contribute to the 'access to cultural participation',[63] an expression mentioned by a document of the IFCD itself – which is curious, since the expression, typical of the organs of cultural rights of the UN, is not found in the text of the CDC. The projects, particularly the third one, have measures to overcome 'gender inequalities in cultural life',[64] another object mentioned in the document of the IFCD.

V. Cultural Rights within the UN Legal System and the CDC: A Necessary Cooperation in Favour of a Right Understanding of the Concepts of the CDC

The connection between cultural rights and the CDC has been made by the UN organs on cultural rights. Cultural rights, as this chapter has shown, was one of the possible scopes of application of the CDC. It was excluded in favour of diversity as cultural expressions. However, as already advanced, practical effects of the CDC in the enjoyment on cultural rights are already a reality.[65] It can be said that the relation between the CDC and cultural rights occurs in two aspects of the latter: artistic freedom and respect for cultural identity. The first aspect is addressed in chapter 11 of this book. This is why this chapter focuses on the second aspect, that of cultural identity. In this sense, GC No 21 of the CESCR, on the right to take part in cultural life, considers in its paragraph 43 that 'States parties should also bear in mind that cultural activities, goods and services have economic and cultural dimensions, conveying identity, values and meanings. They must not be treated as having solely a commercial value'. It also considers that 'States parties should adopt measures to protect and promote the diversity of cultural expressions and enable all cultures to express themselves and make themselves known'. This paragraph of the GC refers both to the CDC and to the UDCD. For its part, Article 7.1 of the CDC states that:

> 1. Parties shall endeavour to create in their territory an environment which encourages individuals and social groups
>
> a) to create, produce, disseminate, distribute and have access to their own cultural expressions, paying due attention to the special circumstances and needs of

[62] See n 19.
[63] IFCD, 'Annotated Guide' (2022) 31.
[64] ibid 5.
[65] See B Barreiro Carril, 'La Convención de Diversidad Cultural y sus retos actuales para los derechos culturales' (2021) 22 *Periférica Internacional. Revista para el análisis de la cultura y el territorio* 56, 59–61.

women as well as various social groups, including persons belonging to minorities and indigenous peoples;

b) to have access to diverse cultural expressions from within their territory as well as from other countries of the world.

Even if the expression 'cultural rights' is not explicitly mentioned in Article 7.2, it is clearly evoked. Besides, the article states that 'Parties shall also endeavour to recognize the important contribution of ... cultural communities, and organizations that support their work, and their central role in nurturing the diversity of cultural expressions'. Consequently, a reading of the CDC in terms of cultural rights ask for focus to be put on the promotion of the cultural expressions of minorities and vulnerable groups. Even though, in the reports' template,[66] this aspect is not mentioned in Goal 4, 'Promote Human Rights and Fundamental Freedoms', which is limited to gender equality and artistic freedom, such concerns appear in other sections of the template, particularly in Goal 3, 'Integrate Culture in Sustainable Development Frameworks'. In this section of the template, 'values and identity, vulnerable and minority groups' are mentioned among the social aspects of sustainable development.[67] The question arises whether excluding these important issues from that part of human rights favouring a sustainable development approach is in their favour, particularly when the 2030 Agenda of Development Goals has a less compulsory nature in legal terms than international cultural rights instruments.[68] The concerns around cultural identities were, however, present in 2009 World UNESCO Report,[69] and the new Secretary-General of the Convention is keen to restore them.[70] After 15 years of application of the CDC, this should be celebrated, particularly as this aspect of cultural rights, contrary to others – such as gender equality or artistic freedom, which has been privileged by the implementation actions of the CDC – was the one at the heart of the concerns giving birth to this international treaty. In fact, the reason why cultural products needed to make the leap from the WTO to UNESCO was that they are channels of identities. Article 1.j) of the CDC considers as one of its objectives giving 'recognition to the distinctive nature of cultural activities, goods and services as vehicles of identity, values and meaning'. However, and just as the former SRCR,

[66] Operational Guidelines of the CDC, Annex – Framework for Quadrennial Periodic Reports on Measures to Protect and Promote the Diversity of Cultural Expressions, https://unesdoc.unesco.org/ark:/48223/pf0000370521.page=28.

[67] See UNESCO, 'Electronic Form for Periodic Reporting to the 2005 Convention on the Protection and Promotion of the Diversity of Cultural Expressions, 2019 edition' (2019) en.unesco.org/creativity/sites/creativity/files/full_qpr_form_2019_en_final_.pdf.

[68] See B Barreiro Carril and K Grecksch, '¿Agenda 2030? Sí, pero sin dejar de prestar atención a la importancia de hacer avanzar el marco internacional en derechos humanos: análisis del vínculo entre derechos culturales y desarrollo sostenible a la luz de la presa de Ilisu' (2020) 21 *Periférica Internacional. Revista para el análisis de la cultura y el territorio* 148, 150–51.

[69] UNESCO, 'Investing in Cultural Diversity and Intercultural Dialogue' (Paris, UNESCO, 2009).

[70] en.unesco.org/creativity/news/extension-call-expression-interest-policy-brief.

Karima Bennoune, reflected in her final report, dealing with the issue of cultural identity is not simple. She particularly warns of the cultural rights consequences of narrowly constructed identity politics.[71] Favouring notions of *créolité*, hybridity or interculturality – which were already objects of reflection in the World UNESCO Report 2009[72] – over that of multiculturalism,[73] she recommends states to 'Ratify and fully implement the 2005 UNESCO Convention on the Protection and Promotion of the Diversity of Cultural Expressions, and ensure reporting under the Convention reflects on cultural mixing and hybridities'.[74] This seems an alarm against misuses of the CDC by states who may favour policies which '[divided] humanity … into separate, internally coherent baskets'[75] and is very relevant for the purpose of this chapter since it can promote a richer and more adequate understanding of the concepts of the CDC by states. It would be very useful for the Secretary of the CDC to consequently take note of this recommendation to proceed when deciding about the content of states' report template. It should be noted that the CDC refers to the concept of 'interculturality' and not to that of 'multiculturalism'.

However, the SRCR was aware of the fact that the exchanges between cultures are not always made in terms of equality. A truly interculturalism, therefore, is very often difficult to achieve: 'Rights-respecting cultural mixing' needs to be constructed 'by overcoming inequalities and challenging those cultural consequences of dominant modes of globalization from above that are negative'.[76] Among these negative consequences, 'Stereotypes and [wrong] representations of cultural diversity'[77] – already addressed in the 2009 World UNESCO Report – could be pointed out. In fact, following the Indian-American anthropologist Arjun Appadurai, who had a very important role in that report,

> [t]here is no question that the media exercise enormous power in shaping our perceptions of, attitudes towards and opinions about 'others'. As the strongest purveyors of globalization, and able to penetrate even the remotest corners of the planet, the media (television, radio, instant messaging, newspapers and magazines, advertising and the Internet) inundate us with representations of how other people look, feel, live, eat, dress and think.[78]

The recent initiative of the Secretary of the CDC, Toussaint Tiendrebeogo, to address these issues is highly welcome. It takes the form of a call launched in

[71] UN General Assembly, 'Report of the Special Rapporteur' (2021) paras 41 and 51. In the same vein, see M Siems, 'The Law and Ethics of "Cultural Appropriation"' (2019) 15 *International Journal of Law in Context* 408, 420.

[72] UNESCO, 'Investing in Cultural Diversity' (2009).

[73] UN General Assembly, 'Report of the Special Rapporteur' (2021) paras 29 and 34.

[74] ibid para 78q.

[75] ibid para 21.

[76] ibid para 38.

[77] UNESCO, 'Investing in Cultural Diversity' (2009) 140.

[78] ibid.

March 2021 to contribute to the 'Policy Briefs' series published by UNESCO's Diversity of Cultural Expressions Entity on the theme 'Diversity and Representation in Audiovisual Content', which seems to point towards giving greater importance to the task of 'empowering individuals and communities' as a way to enable 'diversity and representation' as 'powerful tools to fight systemic discrimination and strengthen fundamental human rights'.[79] The goal is to 'address underrepresentation in audiovisual cultural contents including, but not limited to: television shows, films, theatre plays and video games, of marginalized communities due to factors such as race or ethnicity, gender, disability, migratory status and others'. It starts from the basis that 'Lack of visible representation or stereotypical representation in cultural products, such as TV, film, theatre and music, can play an important role in perpetuating discriminatory dispositions against marginalised groups or identities'.[80] The most recent UNESCO report linked to the CDC includes a chapter on this topic.[81]

In this context, the debate around the song *Despacito* with which this chapter started deserves attention, particularly as the song was mentioned in a debate which took place in the context of the eleventh meeting of the UNESCO Intergovernmental Committee for the Protection and Promotion of the Diversity of Cultural Expression and it may therefore be interpreted as an expression deserving protection under the CDC.[82] *Despacito* is a song interpreted by the Puerto Rican singer, settled in the USA, Luis Fonsi, in collaboration with the reggaeton pioneer Daddy Yankee, another Puerto Rican. It was produced by Universal Music Latin Entertainment, a division within the group Vivendi.[83] The song has been analysed by the experts on cultural politics of race in Latin American and Latina/o communities, Petra R Rivera-Rideau and Jericko Torres-Leschnik. In their view, *Despacito* 'ultimately entrenches racial divisions through its perpetuation of racial stereotypes. The song takes part in a long tradition of the tropicalization of

[79] en.unesco.org/creativity/news/extension-call-expression-interest-policy-brief.

[80] ibid.

[81] L Albornoz, 'Ensuring a Diversity of Voices in the Media' in UNESCO, *Re|shaping Policies for Creativity: Addressing Culture as a Global Public Good* (Paris, UNESCO, 2022). Like that, UNESCO is awakening a link between culture and communication that has been inactive since the political consequences of the McBride report in the 1980s. See B Barreiro Carril, 'La diversidad mediática como garantía de la diversidad cultural: un enfoque desde el Derecho Internacional para la promoción de las identidades' (2016) 21 *CIC. Cuadernos de Información y Comunicación* 27, 29–31. See also ch 9 of this book.

[82] See n 1.

[83] Vivendi is one of the most powerful companies in the musical sector. It was, in fact, included in L Ene, with A Schneeberger, 'Top Players in the European Audiovisual Industry – 2021 Edition' (European Audiovisual Observatory, 2022) rm.coe.int/top-players-in-the-european-av-industry-2021-edition/1680a523e9. Paradoxically, Vivendi partnered the international conference 'Les nouvelles fabriques de la curiosité', or 'Manufacturing Curiosity', which took place in December 2015 at UNESCO's headquarters to mark the 10th anniversary of the CDC. It brought 'together major players from the Internet and media, as well as artists, researchers and representatives of various institutions, for joint reflection on new online methods of shaping individual taste'. See www.vivendi.com/en/news/vivendi-to-partner-on-international-manufacturing-curiosity-conference.

Latina/o music, culture, and bodies, while also marginalizing blackness within both Latin America and the United States'.[84] In particular, *Despacito* would contribute to reinforcing the stereotype of 'African diasporic populations across the Americas as hypersexual'.[85] It would seem, therefore, that cultural expressions of this kind are not those which better fit in the goals and concepts of the CDC. Following these authors, even if *Despacito* could be presented as having 'the capacity to dissolve racial divisions [particularly because of the success of a song in Spanish in the USA,][86] the song actually reinforces them'.[87] In this sense, this song could be presented as a case of inadequate 'commercialization of cultural fusion', a phenomenon about which the SRCR has warned:

> The global market prevents the emergence of the whole-world … One of the challenges, as Senegalese philosopher Souleymane Bachir Diagne has noted, is 'to build a world the market cannot imagine'. To avoid processes of homogenization, commercialization of cultural fusion, corporatizing of cultural borrowing and exploitive models of syncretism, efforts must be made to defend the diversity of cultural expressions in line with international standards …[88]

However, as already stressed, the SRCR warns at the same time against the abuses of the politics of identity and particularly of the concept of cultural appropriation, which does not refer solely to actions already covered by intellectual property law. Actions beyond intellectual property law are included in the concept. In this sense, cultural appropriation could be defined as 'the act by a member of a relatively dominant culture of taking a traditional cultural expression and repurposing it in a different context, without authorization, acknowledgement and/or compensation, in a way that causes harm to the traditional cultural expression holder(s)'.[89] In this sense, *Despacito*, 'like other reggaeton-pop fusions, seems to obscure reggaeton's ties to broader African diasporic aesthetics'.[90] In fact, reggaeton is 'a genre that originally criticized racial discrimination and anti-blackness'.[91] In any case, the concept of cultural appropriation confronts several challenges, such as the difficulty – if not the impossibility – of defining the communities who may

[84] Rivera-Rideau and Torres-Leschnik, '"The Colors and Flavors"' (2019) 27.

[85] ibid 11. International human rights law has been dealing with the issue of stereotypes in recent years. An account of it can be found in E Brems and A Timmer (eds), *Stereotypes and Human Rights Law* (Cambridge, Intersentia, 2016).

[86] This point could be reinforced by the discrimination Fonsi reports having suffered at school because of his accent. F Neira, 'Luis Fonsi: "Con 11 años sufría un 'bullying' terrible por mi acento"' *El País* (10 August 2018) elpais.com/elpais/2018/08/09/icon/1533804573_570421.html.

[87] Rivera-Rideau and Torres-Leschnik, '"The Colors and Flavors"' (2019) 27.

[88] UN General Assembly, 'Report of the Special Rapporteur' (2021) para 40. In the same vein, in an underexplored passage (para 43), the GC No 21 of the Committee of ESCR on the right to take part in cultural life had suggested that states' measures 'may … aim at preventing the signs, symbols and expressions of a particular culture from being taken out of context for the sole purpose of marketing or exploitation by the mass media'.

[89] B Vézina, 'Curbing Cultural Appropriation in the Fashion Industry with Intellectual Property' (2019) 4 *WIPO Magazine*, www.wipo.int/wipo_magazine/en/2019/04/article_0002.html.

[90] Rivera-Rideau and Torres-Leschnik, '"The Colors and Flavors"' (2019) 4.

[91] ibid 28.

suffer a harm from the use of the expression at hand. If these challenges are not adequately addressed, the uses of the concept 'cultural appropriation' could end up as violations of cultural rights, and particularly the violation of the right of artistic freedom.[92] In this vein, the SRCR considers that 'the debate about appropriation should avoid simplistic moralizing or assumptions about cultural ownership in favour of a specific, contextual debate, including about the material consequences and contexts of borrowing and appropriation'.[93] She is particularly concerned about the current use of 'the concept of cultural appropriation … in some contexts to restrict cultural rights, to police claimed cultural borders and to oppose cultural exchange and mixing, without clear contemplation of the human rights consequences of doing so'.[94] Specifically,

> [y]oung people may be told it is inherently offensive to wear the dress of others or to … engage in artistic borrowing and mixing and may be shamed on social media for doing so … There has been a conflation of the material and the cultural in such debates, with less emphasis on resource extraction and land rights than on moralistic claims to the ownership of a static culture.[95]

Mathias Siems, Professor of Private Law and Market Regulation at the European University Institute, proposes some situations which may justify the invocation of the concept of cultural appropriation: 'the deni[al of] the origins of a cultural phenomenon, [the] disrespectful [treatment to a cultural expression] and [the] diminishing [use of the culture at hand] in the source culture'. In any case, 'often a balance between other interests needs to be struck'.[96] Artistic freedom[97] and 'the rights to mix, borrow, traverse and fuse cultures and to engage in syncretic cultural practice [which should be understood as cultural rights themselves]'[98] are highly relevant in that balance. It should also take into account that a case-by-case approach is essential when establishing cases of 'cultural appropriation' in order to avoid uses of culture that 'assume reified identities or lose the pluralistic sense of being'.[99]

The mechanism of the SRCR has in fact already dealt with a case which raised issues linked to the concept of cultural appropriation. The SRCR

> received complaints by minority groups from the Netherlands claiming that the Black Pete [in the Netherlands] celebrations were discriminatory against people of African descent. Proposals in the country to list this tradition as a UNESCO Cultural Heritage were being made at the time.[100]

[92] Siems, 'The Law' (2019) 418.
[93] UN General Assembly, 'Report of the Special Rapporteur' (2021) para 42.
[94] ibid.
[95] ibid.
[96] Siems, 'The Law' (2019) 417.
[97] ibid.
[98] UN General Assembly, 'Report of the Special Rapporteur' (2021) para 14.
[99] For using the words of the SRCR. ibid para 25.
[100] M Bidault and J Bouchard, 'Mylène Bidault and Johanne Bouchard Talk to Beatriz Barreiro Carril. The Meaning of Culture from a Human Rights Approach: The Mandate of the UN Special Rapporteur in the Field of Cultural Rights' (2019) 2(5) *Santander Art and Culture Law Review* 25, 31.

'Black Pete' is a character represented by numerous men and women dressed in costume who accompanied the triumphant entrance of 'Saint Nicholas' in a 'selected city of the Netherlands' in what is 'a popular annual holiday event celebrated from mid-November to December 5'.[101] Nowadays, 'usually a white Dutch person plays Saint Nicholas and white Dutch people in blackface makeup play Black Pete'.[102]

The mandates of the Working Group of Experts on People of African Descent, the Special Rapporteur in the Field of Cultural Rights, the Special Rapporteur on Minority Issues and the Special Rapporteur on Contemporary Forms of Racism, Racial Discrimination, Xenophobia and Related Intolerance reacted to the claims of civil society organisations. They

> raised concerns about allegations that the character and image of Black Pete perpetuates a negative stereotyped representation of African people and people of African descent as second-class citizens, fostering an underlying sense of inferiority within Dutch society and stirring racial differences as well as racism. [They] conveyed how the Black Pete segment of Sinterklaas festival is experienced by African people and people of African descent as a living trace of past slavery and oppression, tracing back to the country's past involvement in the trade of African slaves in the previous centuries.[103]

The government of the Netherlands noted that it 'was aware that Black Pete was considered as offensive by some and that there was no intention to nominate the Sinterklaas festival for inscription on the UNESCO Convention list'.[104] The UN mandates encouraged the Dutch government 'to support and facilitate an open debate in Dutch society, with a view to creating an understanding of how this tradition is perceived by different groups and to identify steps that might respond to the views and concerns of all'.[105] As Mylène Bidault recalls:

> People were shocked that the UN could question a celebration in the Netherlands. But the positive side is that the action taken by special procedures sparked the debate in the country, which I hope is still going on, and raised the awareness of citizens about some problematic aspects of the celebrations. These issues are very complex: I don't think that a practice has to be ignored or disregarded just because it has a discriminatory aspect in cases where it has many other values deserving protection from a cultural rights' perspective. However aspects of a practice that are not in conformity with human rights standards need to be addressed …[106]

[101] Y van der Pijl and K Goulordava, 'Black Pete, "Smug Ignorance," and the Value of the Black Body in Postcolonial Netherlands' (2014) 88 *New West Indian Guide* 262, 263.
[102] ibid.
[103] Office of the High Commissioner for Human Rights, 'Mandates of the Working Group of Experts on People of African Descent; the Special Rapporteur in the Field of Cultural Rights; the Special Rapporteur on Issues; and the Special Rapporteur on Contemporary Forms of Racism, Racial Discrimination, Xenophobia and Related Intolerance' (28 January 2015) OL NLD 1/2015, 1, spcommreports.ohchr.org/TMResultsBase/DownLoadPublicCommunicationFile?gId=20624.
[104] ibid.
[105] ibid.
[106] Bidault and Bouchard, 'Mylène Bidault' (2019) 31.

These developments produced within the UN SRCR mechanism can be very useful for providing an adequate understanding of the CDC when it is confronted with complex issues concerning identities.

VI. Conclusions

Conceptual confusions have been common since the beginning of the drafting of the CDC. In particular, there was a fusion of decisions about the concept of culture (whether the anthropological concept or the narrowed one) to be used and about the scope of the CDC in the drafting meetings of this treaty, such as that choosing cultural products as the scope of application would imply the renouncement of the anthropological concept of culture. Probably, this confusion is at the heart of the lack of a right understanding of the concepts of the CDC by its states parties. This is clear within IEL, as the particular case presented illustrates. The application of the CDC in the field of cultural cooperation (to development) shows a better conceptual understanding of the CDC. It needs to be noted that in this case, and particularly in relation to the projects financed by the IFCD, those who are contributing to such a better understanding are the civil society actors who develop these projects and not the states as such. Civil society is key to the implementation of the CDC, as chapters two and three of this book show. One of the main criticisms of the CDC is that the majority of its obligations are more typical of an instrument of *soft law* than to that of a treaty. In this context, the contribution by the actors of the projects of the IFCD to assuring a better conceptual understanding cannot be neglected. Such an understanding in the field of cultural cooperation (to development) could be progressively consolidated and would eventually irradiate economic fora, where clearly *hard law* affecting the objectives of the CDC is made. The work and guidelines that the CDC Secretariat may elaborate could be important in this sense. If nothing is done to avoid such a *conceptual fragmentation*, the risk exists that the implementation of the CDC within economic fora will reproduce similar dynamics and reinforce the same concepts typical of IEL that the CDC wanted to overcome.

The fragmentation in the application of the CDC in the different contexts – IEL, cultural cooperation (to development) – is directly related to the lack of a correct understanding of its concepts. The link between the CDC and the developments in the field of cultural rights within the UN human rights system can help avoid such a fragmentation. As the reflection around the reference to *Despacito* within Intergovernmental Committee for the Protection and Promotion of the Diversity of Cultural Expressions has shown, there is still a lot of work ahead for a good conceptual understanding of the CDC. A whole and deep understanding of its concepts in connection with the developments on cultural rights would allow the CDC to properly address cultural rights issues such as cultural identity – which has been neglected in comparison with other aspects of cultural rights such as artistic freedom. This would contribute to consolidating a good conceptual understanding of the CDC, which would hopefully extend to economic international fora. It would also avoid abuses of identity politics theories and the concept of cultural appropriation. After 15 years of application of the CDC, the words of the 2009 World UNESCO report are more relevant than ever:

> The challenge posed to the international community is to safeguard the manifestations of cultural diversity while at the same time recognizing the opportunities offered by cultural diversity to further the ability to adapt to different social and political contexts and circumstances.[107]

Together with a blurred conceptual application of the CDC, an extension of the actions of this text to unforeseen areas has been identified. This is the case of the actions in the field of artistic freedom. The assessment of this kind of actions could be qualified as ambivalent. On the one hand, the fact that the CDC is invoked within IEL in a way that evokes censorship while, at the same time, it starts addressing issues of artistic freedom may put its consistency into question, resulting in a loss of reputation and a weakening of its concepts. On the other hand, addressing issues such as artistic freedom can contribute to a more complete understanding of many concepts of the CDC, such as creativity or interculturality. Even if, in a quite disconnected way, the use by civil society of aspects of the CDC – still neglected by many states – can contribute to a progressive change in their cultural policies. This fits with the nature of an instrument that was originally conceived to mediate, rather than punish. In this sense, it could be expected that progressive, albeit it slow, changes in favour of a whole and right conceptual understanding of the CDC within communities and states will take place.

[107] UNESCO, 'Investing in Cultural Diversity' (2009) 23.

INDEX

www.ingramcontent.com/pod-product-compliance
Ingram Content Group UK Ltd.
Pitfield, Milton Keynes, MK11 3LW, UK
UKHW020246290926
15470UKWH00002B/776

9 781509 96144